ALLAN NEVINS
ON HISTORY

ALLAN NEVINS ON HISTORY

Compiled and Introduced by
RAY ALLEN BILLINGTON

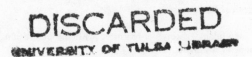
CHARLES SCRIBNER'S SONS, NEW YORK

Copyright © 1975 Columbia University

Library of Congress Cataloging in Publication Data

Nevins, Allan, 1890–1971.
    Allan Nevins on history.

    Includes index.
    1. Historiography—Addresses, essays, lectures.
2. Historians—United States—Biography—Addresses,
essays, lectures. I. Title.
D13.N367   907'.2   75-4870
ISBN 0-684-14320-8

"What's the Matter with History?" "The Newspaperman and the Scholar,"
"The Explosive Excitement of History," "Is History Made by Heroes?" and
"The Limits of Individualism" are reprinted with the permission of *Saturday
Review/World*.

"Not Capulets, Not Montagus" is reprinted with permission from *The
American Historical Review*.

"New Lamps for Old in History" is reprinted with the permission of the
Society of American Archivists.

"Business and the Historian" is reprinted with the permission of the American Petroleum Institute.

"American Journalism and Its Historical Treatment" is reprinted with permission from the *Journalism Quarterly*.

"Recent Progress of American Social History" is reprinted with the permission of the *Business History Review*.

"Advances in the Social Sciences" is reprinted with permission from *The Hofstra Review*.

"Why Public Men Keep Diaries," © 1952 by The New York Times Company, Reprinted by permission.

"History This Side the Horizon" is reprinted with permission from *The Vermont Quarterly*.

"Oral History: How and Why It Was Born," © 1966 by The H. H. Wilson Company. Reprinted by permission.

"James Ford Rhodes as Man and Historian" is reprinted with the permission of the University of Chicago Press.

Contents

CONTENTS

Allan Nevins, Historian:
A Personal Reminiscence

Allan Nevins was a man of strong likes and dislikes. He was excessively fond of navy bean soup, rhubarb pie, and gumdrops (his gastronomic passions), root beer (which he savored with the appreciation of a connoisseur sipping a rare vintage), a succession of terriers, mind-stirring conversation with friends, his two daughters, and above all his adored wife, Mary, who has been aptly described as a good-humored angel. He was openly hostile to self-seekers, time-wasting bores (and even time wasters who were not bores), bigots who had closed their minds to rational argument, and poseurs (he always disliked Josiah Royce because during his freshman year at Illinois he heard that transplanted Californian pronounce *idea* as "idear"). But above all else Allan Nevins loved history, and above all else he despised that mythical character of his own creation, Professor Dryasdust, who clothed historical writing in such pedagogic gobbledygook that it failed to attract average readers.

For Allan Nevins saw the reading of history as man's hope and salvation. Hence history had to be written accurately and objectively, but it also had to be sparked with such explosive excitement that all the world would respond. History in his eyes was the essential ingredient in good citizenship, unrivaled as a medium for transmitting mankind's cultural heritage, and beyond compare as an intellectual exercise. "Again and again," he once wrote, "written history has changed the destiny of nations, and without it there can be neither true liberty nor true patriotism." The study of history was the panacea for the world's ills and could be effective only when deliciously palatable. Nevins's self-conceived function was to write such history himself and to see to it that other historians followed his example.

His baptism into scholarship began in the farmhouse near Camp Point, Illinois, where he was born on May 20, 1890. Because his father, a stern Presbyterian, frowned on earthly pleasures, young Allan cut his intellectual teeth on the five hundred volumes of history, economics, and theology that comprised the family library, rather than on the dime novels and Horatio-Algerish fantasies usually read by the youth of that day. At the University of Illinois, from which he graduated in 1912, he read voraciously, earned a Phi Beta Kappa key, wrote his first book (a biography of the frontiersman Robert Rogers, published in 1914), and began his second, a history of the university that appeared in 1917. The latter, he later confessed, had its shortcomings: "I worked on it when I was an undergraduate." In the meantime he completed work for a master of arts degree. This was to be his last degree—he never bothered to add the usual badge of academia, the Ph.D., to his name. Of Allan it might be said (as George Lyman Kittredge of Harvard's English department allegedly said of himself) that no one knew enough to examine him.

Instead he entered the world of journalism in 1913—a logical choice, for he saw magazines and newspapers as the best media for presenting living history to the people. For a decade he wrote editorials for the New York *Evening Post*, then moved to *The Sun* as literary editor, and from 1925 to 1931 served as editorial writer on the New York *World*. All this time he was squeezing every odd moment from his full schedule to study and record the past; he regularly left his newspaper office after eight hours of writing, dashed to the subway, disappeared into the New York

Public Library, emerged at closing time with an armful of books, and labored over his typewriter at home until he could labor no more. The books appeared in a regular procession: a history of the *Evening Post*; a volume on America as seen by British travelers; his seminal *American States During and After the Revolution* (still regarded as a classic); *The Emergence of Modern America* in the prestigious *History of American Life* series; a laudatory biography of John Charles Frémont, "the West's Greatest Adventurer," that stirred critical acclaim ("it raises biography to the level of literature"); and a stream of articles in magazines and journals. All the while he was slaving at editorial chores rigorous enough to sap the energy of a less dedicated man.

His writings led him naturally into the academic world; for one year he taught at Cornell University, then in 1928 he moved to Columbia as associate in history with two courses to teach and time to continue his editorial writing on the *World*. The next step followed inevitably, for Allan Nevins proved as capable in the classroom as in the editorial chair; in 1931 he was made DeWitt Clinton Professor of History at Columbia, a post that he held until 1958 when he reached the compulsory retirement age of sixty-eight. For Allan, retirement meant only more time for work; he moved that autumn to San Marino, California, accepting a post as senior research associate at the Henry E. Huntington Library. For the next ten years he lived happily in that academic paradise, adding the final touches to the monument that he built for himself: historical writings of quality and quantity unique in the annals of American historiography.

No one knows—perhaps no one will ever know—how many books and articles and reviews Allan Nevins wrote; his bookkeeping habits were as inefficient as his working techniques were efficient. He was the author of well over fifty books, edited at least seventy-five more, and published perhaps a thousand articles, reviews, and essays, many of them in such widely circulated journals as the *Saturday Review* and the *New York Times Magazine*. Many were viewed at the time, and are still viewed, as classics destined to survive the assault of time. Two, his biographies of Grover Cleveland and Hamilton Fish, captured Pulitzer prizes. Two more, his studies of John D. Rockefeller and Henry Ford, altered the views of the profession on writing business history. His monumental *Ordeal of the Union,* surveying the period from 1850 to 1865 and published in eight volumes (two of them after his death in 1971), not only won the $10,000 Scribners Centenary Prize and the prestigious Bancroft Award in History but is generally viewed as a work of such enduring significance that it will be read for generations. These were only the pinnacle of Allan Nevins's towering edifice of publications. His *Gateway to History,* published in 1938 and revised in 1963, indoctrinated thousands in the meaning and excitement of history. His diaries of George Templeton Strong and Philip Hone, meticulously edited, will probably never be displaced. His editorial supervision of the *American Political Leaders Series,* the updated volumes in the *Chronicles of America,* and the still-to-be-completed studies of the impact of the Civil War on aspects of American life has endowed those standard sets with enduring importance. Nor have the dozens of other works from his pen, no matter how trivial the subject (whether a history of the New York Bank and Trust Company or a *Century of Political Cartoons*), failed to break new ground or influence a sizable segment of the reading public.

To concentrate on Allan Nevins's publications, as most people do, is to ignore the fact that most of these appeared while he was teaching an unusually heavy schedule during his three decades on the Columbia University faculty. His lectures in the graduate and undergraduate divisions, and as often as not in the evening extension division as well, were usually written out in full, to be read in his gravelly voice with a minimum of pyrotechnics; history was packed with its own excitement that needed no gilding. But what lectures they were: incisively informative, sparkling with original interpretations, and enlivened by an occasional apt anecdote. Never a spellbinding popularizer, Allan Nevins failed to win a wide following among lazy or indifferent undergraduates; but the graduate students and those undergraduates sufficiently inclined found his instruction a wellhead of information seldom duplicated in American universities.

His teaching interests were threefold, dictated by his own historical specialities. The Civil War, on which he lavished much of his scholarly life, was a perennial subject of discussion in his seminars. His lecture courses mirrored his view that the past is prelude to the present and that yesterday's influence on today is greater than that of the day before yesterday. During his first year at Columbia he documented this belief by lecturing on "Studies in American Political History, 1865–1925," and "American Social History, 1865–1900"—both boldly innovative courses at a time when instruction in the post-1900 era was considered dangerously contemporary. During his remaining teaching years these two courses were reoffered periodically, but usually with a yearly updating to incorporate the latest changes; in 1933, for example, the title of one read "American Political History, 1865–1932." His insistence on carrying his students to the threshold of their present experiences cost him time-consuming reading and hours of preparation as he translated the complexities of the current scene into meaningful terms.

Allan Nevins's third teaching interest was directed toward training disciples who could follow in his own footsteps. To write history students had to be immersed in the methodology of the discipline and had to read carefully the historical masters of the past. Methodology he taught in a "Conference on Historical Method" that he began directing with his permanent appointment in 1931; in this all candidates for the master of arts degree (and they were numerous in those days) studied "methods of historical research and synthesis, with practical suggestions and exercises in the compilation of bibliographies, the taking of notes, and the preparation of essays." Historiography was the theme of History 279, "Literature of American History" (soon retitled "The Great Literature of American History") in which students were expected to make "a careful analysis of the works of all prominent American historians from the colonial period to the present day. . . . Emphasis falls upon ideas and the development of the methods, range, and art of history." Here was a healthy diet indeed for young historians; those who supped came away with a solid knowledge of how and why history had been written in the past, and above all a conviction that they were studying an art as much as a science. Nevins's insistence, repeatedly reiterated, was that a writer with literary talents and transmittable enthusiasm (a Francis Parkman, say, or a James Truslow Adams) reached a wider audience and performed a greater service to civilization than a "scientific" scholar whose labored quest for complete objectivity resulted in leaden prose and few readers.

He also instilled in his listeners something of his own intense love for Columbia University. His passion for the school originated, his close friends came to realize, in his esteem for New York City. To Allan Nevins, New York was the intellectual capital of the United States, the hub of its cultural life, the publishing center whence flowed the books that made the difference between barbarism and civilization. There he could find minds to challenge his own: Walter Lippmann, James Truslow Adams, Henry Seidel Canby, Abraham Flexner, Simeon Strunsky, and a host like them were his friends and companions. Columbia, as New York's foremost university, personified the intellectualism and cosmopolitanism that were his ideals. At Columbia his finger was on the pulse of the nation, and Allan was never so happy as when doctoring society's social or political ills. On Columbia, therefore, he lavished unrestrained affection, working to secure manuscript collections for its library (those of Frances Perkins, Henry Wallace, and James T. Adams among them), blustering his friend Frederic Bancroft into willing it the $2 million needed to subsidize American studies there, and in 1965 giving the university $500,000 to endow a professorship in economic history. This was the supreme tribute, for Columbia had never paid Allan more than $11,500 a year (and usually much less). Yet his frugal living, his well-deserved royalties, and his canny management of investments made his magnificent gift possible. The Allan Nevins Professorship stands as a perpetual reminder of his belief that history is mankind's most essential instrument for progress and that it warrants the attention of all people.

To capsulize Allan Nevins's teaching career, or to recite the bare-bones facts of his scholarly production, is to underline certain traits of his remarkable character. He was, clearly, a man not only of extraordinary ability but of phenomenal energy; only this explains the extent and variety of his accomplishments. Life to him was a continuous race against time, with every second so precious that it must be used for productive purposes. Those who knew him during his years at Columbia recall his frantic dash to or from the subway each day, his arms laden with books and a portable typewriter, his short legs chopping the ground, and like as not a graduate student panting at his side seeking word on a freshly finished chapter of a doctoral dissertation. At the Huntington Library, after he had reached an age that slows most men, Allan slackened not one whit. His entrance each morning was a spectacular event; he came laden with a briefcase bulging with work done the night before, his arms heavy with books and manuscripts. The elevator to the second floor was too slow; his steps pounded up the stairs at breakneck speed; he sprinted down the. hall to his office. Seconds later the steady clack-clack of his typewriter began as his two fingers beat out a relentless rhythm of composition.

Time was Allan Nevins's most precious commodity, for the day held far too few minutes for him to accomplish all that he wanted to accomplish. Luncheon was forgotten unless one of his colleagues extracted him from his chair—not an easy task for always one more thought must be recorded or one more sentence completed. Stopping Allan from work in the evening was so difficult that clocks on the Huntington's second floor were kept five minutes fast to delude him into leaving before the building was locked. I will always treasure a remark that I overheard as he entered one morning. "Mrs. Bean," he said to his secretary, "I've had the best piece of news that I have heard in a long time."

"What was that," asked Mrs. Bean.

"I got up this morning," Allan answered, "thinking it was Thursday. Mary told me it was only Wednesday. I've gained a whole day."

Even the exercise that Allan insisted upon as a needed corollary to a vigorous mind had to be accomplished to secure a maximum return in a minimum time. Walking was a passion with him—not a gentle stroll, but a frantic dash across the countryside, the more rugged the terrain the better. His postluncheon safaris about the 207-acre grounds of the Huntington Library were famed among visiting scholars. They began with Allan circulating among the tables at the little cafeteria where all dined, cajoling reluctant exercisers, recruiting others. Then the rocketlike start, Allan well in front, bent slightly forward as though to urge his feet to greater effort, setting a pace that left the young panting and the old by the wayside, discoursing learnedly the while on the latest historical monograph or the situation in the Near East. No obstacle was too great to be surmounted, whether sprinkler to be braved, thicket to be bested, hill to be climbed, or ditch to be hurdled, whatever the effect on the scholars who straggled in his wake. Occasionally Allan fell victim to his own overenthusiasm, as he did on one unhappy day when he defied the law of gravity by catapulting down a hill at breakneck speed. We picked him up, dusty and bleeding but eager to return to work and impatient with our insistence that he see a doctor. See a doctor he did, to have his wounds treated and his broken nose bandaged. As I walked him home to face Mary's gentle reproofs, he made a remark that was too accurate to be forgotten: "Ray," he said, "my trouble is that I cannot realize that I am not seventeen years old anymore."

Nor could he, even during his last years when the calendar, if not his own vigor, showed him approaching eighty years. Even then any illness was brushed aside as an insignificant bother that would soon cure itself. When a crippling coronary attack placed him in a hospital, he left his bed as soon as the nurse turned her back to push it nearer the window where he could enjoy the view. When a serious stroke impaired his vision and damaged his motor functioning, he still dreamed of books to be written and life to be enjoyed. Now was the time to buy a farm in Oregon where trees and green grass would remind him of his boyhood home in Illinois. "What I shall need," he wrote a friend there, "is a small tract of 10 or 12 acres, with enough woodland to afford good exercise in clearing the land and accumulating firewood by use of an axe, with a few acres also for the development of a vegetable garden where we can grow sweet corn, beans, turnips for eating raw, tomatoes, apples like the old Baldwins, Northern Spies, and Rome Beauties of my boyhood, and perhaps cultivate a few nut trees, pecans and English walnuts." This was Allan Nevins on the threshhold of eighty, permanently incapacitated. The man's spirit was indomitable.

The energy that gave birth to impossible dreams was one ingredient in his success as a historian; another was his insatiable thirst for learning. Books were his passion. From his childhood, when he tried to escape farm chores by burying himself in his father's tomes, he read voluminously, widely, constantly. History was his first love, but he was almost equally at home in literature, economics, politics, science, and even verse. His own collections were remarkable for their extent and catholicity: one sizable library at his office, some fifteen thousand more volumes in his home, another few thousand in a Connecticut farmhouse where he spent occasional summers. More were constantly being added. After every sale of duplicates at the Huntington Library, Allan Nevins staggered home with his arms full of books to be added to the already overcrowded shelves. Once, as we browsed together in a secondhand bookstore, he happened on six volumes of the *Official Records of the War of the Rebellion.* "I have a complete set of the *Official Records* in my office," I heard him mutter to himself, "and a complete set at home. But you can never tell when you are going to need a third set." And he bought them.

The Nevins homes were primarily libraries, every wall lined with books, every nook and cranny filled to overflowing. Their first residence in Pasadena was a three-story house of New England design that appealed largely because the wall space was adequate to sustain countless bookcases. Allan was immensely proud of the number that it held, and he often escorted visitors about, showing case after case with one row in front of another. On one such tour after a dinner party in 1963 he finally led the little group of men who had responded to his invitation to "see his books" into a second-floor bathroom. "I want," he said, "to show you an example of Mrs. Nevins's tyranny." Opening the medicine cabinet, he revealed three shelves, two crammed with books, the other holding a few bottles of medicine. "She will not," said Allan, pointing, "give me that shelf." When his infirmities forced a move to a smaller home nearer the library, the Nevinses chose a pleasant house principally because it had an attached three-car garage—which was promptly converted into bookstacks. Every volume on those shelves was a treasured friend. One of his saddest experiences occurred when the ravages of time forced him to sell his Connecticut farmhouse and divide the several thousand titles housed there, some to be given to neighboring universities, some taken to California. His secretary watched as he fondled each one, struggling with a decision, then announced, "We must keep this one."

Allan Nevins could read those many books and write the number that he did partly because his ability to concentrate was nothing short of phenomenal. Few scholars could cut themselves off so completely from the world around them. To extract Allan from his office at noontime required a patient wait in his doorway, a succession of increasingly noticeable coughs and throat clearings, moving closer in the hope of being noticed, and finally a touch on the shoulder. His jump, and often the "Damn" that he shouted as his chain of thought was broken, attested to the distance that separated him from mundane affairs. His wife testifies that on one occasion, while showing two attractive young ladies about their home, he reached his study, announced, "This is where I work," and started to type, forgetting them entirely. All who knew him can testify that the cocktail hour preceding a Nevins dinner party was presided over by the gentle Mary until the first course was served, just as Allan rushed down the stairs from his study. Once, as we drove together to a party at a friend's home, he suggested, "Ray, let us synchronize our watches, then meet at the door in exactly twenty-five minutes and get back to work." He disapproved of neither strong drink, tobacco, nor cocktail chitchat, but he shunned all three because experience showed him that indulgence slowed his writing. Nothing was allowed to do that.

Such was Allan's intensity of concentration that he personified the absent-minded professor. I have seen him forget his own son-in-law's name, and once he appeared at the Huntington wearing two neckties, one on top of the other, presumably because he forgot that the first had been tied. On one notable occasion a friend arrived at the library, responding to an invitation to lunch. He called Allan from the reception office and was told to wait a few moments while a thought was captured on paper. When those minutes stretched on, and on, and on, the friend gave up hope, made his solitary way to the lunchroom, and was just finishing his modest repast when Allan bustled in. Allan's face lit up; he hurried to the table, hand outstretched. "Why Mr. Blank," said he. "How nice to see you. You must come and have lunch with me some day." Such eccentricities cost Allan Nevins no friendships. All who knew him knew also that work was too important to be sidetracked, even for friends.

They knew also that despite his prodigious work habits and his refusal to squander a single precious moment on frivolity he was always willing to forsake his most essential duties to aid friends—or even chance acquaintances—in their own pursuits. Allan

Nevins was irrationally devoted both to his students and to all historical scholars who captured his attention, no matter how feeble their abilities. Each of the hundred-odd doctoral candidates who earned their degrees at Columbia under his supervision he saw as a personal responsibility, to be welcomed into his book-cluttered sixth-floor office in Fayerweather Hall and to be defended at all costs. Colleagues complained that in the dread oral examinations Allan became a lion at the side of the defendant, arguing his case so vehemently that the other inquisitors were cowed into silence. Even after flying the nest, his students used him mercilessly, asking him to read the manuscripts of their books (I have seen them piled three feet high in the corner of his office), or to write forewords for their publications. All were cheerfully accommodated, even though he complained bitterly that every student he trained was constantly writing books and that he was so busy preparing introductions for theirs that he had no time to write his own.

Allan Nevins served his students well, but his compassion embraced a wider world. He could seldom refuse a request for aid—so long as the supplicant was writing history. His Columbia seminar was regularly interrupted by telephone calls from friends, who were answered with the hurried impatience of a man too gentle to deny any demand but too busy to welcome one: "Yes, yes, I've read your manuscript and want to talk with you about it," or "Yes, yes, a capital piece of work. I'll be glad to review it for you." Even the unworthy were treated with respect. A retired librarian, who had labored overlong at the Huntington Library on an antiquarian study of monumental insignificance had the temerity a few years ago to ask Allan for his criticism. Not only did he read her deadly tome but he prepared a lengthy report, lavishing praise where praise was due and pointing out the need for revisions that would occupy the author's remaining years. For days thereafter she walked with her head in the clouds, proud that the great Allan Nevins had praised her writing and encouraged her to go on. Here was a true measure of his greatness.

Allan Nevins's memory will be kept alive by the students he trained and the scholars he aided, but it will endure even longer in the hundred-odd books and the countless articles that he contributed to the world of scholarship. In these he not only illuminated segments of the past, but also propagandized a belief that vastly influenced the historical profession during his lifetime and will continue to influence scholars for generations to come. History, he preached, was essential to any nation's culture. Hence the duty of the historian was to write history that would be read, not simply by fellow scholars, but by the literate multitudes. This required a palatable style, a stress on the aspects of the past significant to the present, and the use of every tool that could possibly be employed to improve the quality of research. Allan Nevins's emphasis on these points helped give historical studies a new direction of major importance.

Basic to his beliefs was a conviction that history was an art, built on scientific evidence but capable of employing emotional and aesthetic appeals in its quest for a universal audience. History was to be enjoyed, not endured. "Let us," he once wrote, "not undervalue history's ability to give us pleasure; the best historians are admirable storytellers." For him there was no barrier between scholarship and literary grace. The statistician, the quantifier, the demographer, were all essential investigators in the never-ending quest for truth; in some of the essays in this book he pleads for the use of every tool needed to understand the complexity of human behavior, no matter how incomprehensible to the lay public. But to Nevins the truly great historian was the literary giant who translated the findings of the dry-as-dust grubbers and analysts into language that would attract the widest circle of readers. Good history to him was not a battery of statistical tables or a weighty analysis, but a stirring narrative. "The narrative historian," he once told a friend, "will be remembered. What has happened to the scientific school?" In appraising the great historians of the past, as he does in this book, his greatest praise is reserved for the Parkmans, Prescotts, and Motleys whose works have been read and reread for generations. This was the history that he aspired to write.

And did write. Allan Nevins was a superior stylist, drawing on his vast vocabulary for word combinations that would convey excitement as well as exact meaning. This meant repeated rewriting; he usually prepared three or four drafts of each of his chapters or essays, each an improvement over the other, then by hand altered as many as a dozen words on each page before he achieved the literary grace that was his ideal. Some of the books over which he labored most industriously, his biography of Frémont and his *Ordeal of the Union* particularly, sing with the beauty of the language. His, too, was an uncanny ability to convey a sense of drama, even when describing well-known episodes. Today's reader of the battle scenes that he describes with such emotion (he sometimes wept openly as he wrote of those bloody conflicts) finds himself hanging breathlessly on every sentence and wondering who will win. Allan's pen was dipped in magic at such times.

His own writings were deliberately designed to captivate, but, given his faith in history as a palliative for society's ills, this was not enough. Allan Nevins had to convert the historical profession to his belief that history must be written for the many, not the academic few. This was the message that he preached to the brethren in his presidential address before the American Historical Association and in repeated articles in popular and professional journals. This was his purpose when, despairing of converting the staid *American Historical Review* into a magazine that would reach the masses, he was primarily responsible for launching *American Heritage* and cajoling his colleagues into writing readable essays for its columns. Nothing gave him greater satisfaction than watching its circulation climb above the two hundred thousand mark when no professional journal printed more than twenty thousand copies. Allan Nevins, too, was the moving spirit behind the Society of American Historians, dedicated (in his own words) "to the object of making sound historical writing more artistic, and of bringing it more closely home to the American people." Its several awards granted yearly to books and manuscripts in history notable for their superior literary style have done much to further the crusade that he launched so successfully.

He was just as successful in convincing his colleagues that they must take a more tolerant view of the nation's business leaders than that espoused by the Populist-Progressive historians whose "economic determinism" dominated historical writing during the early twentieth century. For a generation these writers had damned the industrialists of the late 1800s as "robber barons," bent on fleecing the government and the people in their greedy quest for wealth and power. Could nothing more be said for these giants of industry? Allan Nevins asked himself. To condemn them as soulless money-grabbers was to indict them for crimes that were not crimes at all in their day. It was also to ignore the fact that they forged an industrialized world power from a weak, agricultural nation "none too soon and none too fast" to allow it to withstand the assaults of Kaiserism and Hitlerism in World Wars I and II. This was the thesis that Nevins argued effectively in his biographies of John D. Rockefeller and Henry Ford. His interpretation was challenged vigorously, both by older scholars who clung to the traditions of progressivism and younger ones who took sadistic pleasure in using big business as a whipping boy; but it was eventually generally accepted and today underlies the extensive investigations into business history currently under way.

Sounder interpretations were a key to readable history; so was documentary evidence in sufficient quantity to allow scholars to approximate the truth about the past. Allan Nevins's awareness of that fact underlay another of his major contributions. The idea of an oral history project was long hatching in his mind. As a newspaperman he had interviewed dozens of prominent persons; each time he did so he was reminded that the invaluable information they supplied him would be unavailable to future scholars. This was particularly alarming at a time when electronic communication and jet travel were relegating letters and memoranda—the prime sources for historical investigations—to the limbo of uselessness, displaced now by telephone conversations and personal conferences ("as ephemeral and irrevocable as breath itself," Nevins characterized them). For a decade he was haunted by a vaguely forming ambition: to "obtain from the lips and papers of living Americans . . . a fuller record of their participation." Every obituary notice that he read stirred his conscience. "What memories that man carries to the grave with him," he wrote.

That dream was realized in 1948 when Allan Nevins persuaded Columbia University to launch the first "Oral History Project" (even the name was his) with prominent New Yorkers the first subjects, Allan the interviewer, and a graduate student taking notes. Tape recorders soon displaced hand recordings, trained interviewers took over the task of probing for information, and a well-stocked office under a full-time director provided for the storage and dissemination of information. This required money, most of it raised by Allan who browbeat wealthy friends and cajoled foundations into providing sufficient funds to assure a permanent project. By the time of his death the Columbia office had recorded more than 340,000 pages of transcripts, while similar projects were operating at more than five hundred universities and institutional centers throughout the land. Allan Nevins found a great deal of satisfaction in these figures; he found even more in the realization that the nation's history would be better recorded and better written as a result of his vision.

To one who found his greatest pleasure in an eighteen-hour day spent in writing history, the end to an active life could only spell tragedy. Allan Nevins suffered a serious stroke in June 1967, with much yet to be done: the last two volumes of his eight-volume *Ordeal of the Union* remained incomplete; a revision of his biography of Frémont was well under way; he had started work on a major revision of his *American States During and After the*

Revolution; work had begun on a biography of Admiral Nimitz. Now his vision was impaired, his motor responses slowed, his mind and memory occasionally clouded. Yet within six weeks he was writing an hour a day—by hand at first, because typing had to be, and was, painfully relearned. A few weeks later when a friend complimented him on his progress, Allan replied: "I'm trying as best I can. I keep writing. Writing is best for me."

Wisely he decided to concentrate his remaining strength on completing his *magnum opus* on the Civil War. The next years demonstrated his indominable will power. Day after day I listened as he dictated to his secretary in her cubbyhole outside my Huntington Library office. Each night he carried home the typed result and found it unsatisfactory; each morning he began again, dictating the same passage over and over again until it reached his standards of perfection. So those two last volumes of the *Ordeal of the Union* inched toward completion, with agonizing slowness. When even more crippling strokes, and eventually death, came in the spring of 1971 they were sufficiently completed to allow his devoted wife and his equally dedicated secretary, Lillian Bean, to oversee their publication. No man could leave a more enduring monument.

His wife, whose life had been spent creating the ideal atmosphere for her husband's uninterrupted labors, was reluctant to let his reputation rest on the many books and articles he had already published, unrivaled though they were. Sorting through his papers after his death she assembled two large cartons of what appeared to be unpublished manuscripts, a few of them complete, more only fragments of work in progress. These she asked me to evaluate with an eye to publication. A week or two of sorting and reading convinced me that most were early drafts of published articles or lectures, but I found that several had not appeared before and that others had been printed in media not ordinarily read by historians or the general public. Those dealing with the Civil War I passed on to scholars competent in that field; those concerned with history and historians I undertook to bring together in this volume.

The result, contained in the pages that follow, provides today's reader with both an insight into Allan Nevins's emergence as a historical giant and some penetrating observations on the nature of history and its authorship. A few of the essays are clearly dated; some are naïve in their assumptions or outmoded in suggesting techniques or fields for investigation that have long since become commonplace. These, the reader should remember, were prepared many years ago and perhaps set in motion the studies that rob them of their timeliness. Far more are as pertinent to today as they were to the yesterday when they were written; American history will be better history, and more readable history, if modern readers accept Allan's advice and follow his example. He would want nothing more than this.

In preparing this book for publication I have studied every available bibliography, searched such of Allan Nevins's own records as were available, and thumbed the pages of a good many magazines to assure myself that certain essays and lectures that I have labeled "unpublished" are actually appearing for the first time. If I have failed and inadvertently included materials already published, I can only apologize and offer as an excuse Allan's woeful inefficiency in recording (or even remembering) all of his publications. In view of their volume, one can understand why.

This book could not have been compiled without the aid of Mary Nevins, who supplied not only the inspiration but all of the manuscripts that are appearing in print for the first time. I am also deeply indebted to Professor Henry S. Commager, Allan Nevins's Columbia colleague and intimate friend, for helpful advice and encouragement, and to Professor Richard B. Morris, another former Nevins colleague, who was good enough to supervise the photoduplication of the sections of the university catalogue that contained information on his teaching career. I have also leaned occasionally on the reminiscences published by some of Allan's close friends: Mort R. Lewis, Louis M. Starr, and Wilbur R. Jacobs. Several of Allan Nevins's former students, particularly Professor William John Niven, Jr., of the Claremont Graduate School, have enlightened me on Allan's teaching methods. To all I am grateful.

Ray Allen Billington
The Huntington Library
San Marino, California

Part One

THE PURPOSE OF HISTORY

To Allan Nevins, knowledge, and particularly knowledge of the past, was mankind's most precious asset. The duty of historians, in his eyes, was not simply to produce monographs detailing minute findings for the benefit of their fellow academicians, but to translate their discoveries into a form and language that would capture the attention of the multitudes. Such a service to humanity would pay handsome dividends— in an educated electorate, a cultured citizenry, and a nation that could build on experience as it progressed into the future. Allan Nevins lived up to his own ideal; his dozens of books, and particularly his monumental *Ordeal of the Union*, bore the stamp of literary excellence as well as of careful research. The four essays in this section plead the cause of popular history—history for the masses that would enlighten but not misinform. In them Nevins sums up much of his own purpose in life and gives some very sound advice to his colleagues.

Another thin and disappointing year in American historical writing, the second in succession, has come to an end. Neither in 1937 nor 1938 was a first-class, blue-ribbon historical work, apart from Charles M. Andrews's continuance of his colonial history (which must be judged as a whole rather than in parts) produced in this country. We had no book comparable to the very best volumes by Beard, James Truslow Adams, or Parrington; comparable to Webb's "The Great Plains," to Bowers's "Jefferson and Hamilton," to Van Wyck Brooks's "Flowering of New England," to the works by Sidney B. Fay and Bernadotte Schmitt on the origins of the World War. That is, we had no volume which could be called distinguished in the highest sense of the word. I do not underrate the solid merit of the books issued by such men as Frederic L. Paxson, Paul Buck, Frank Luther Mott, Everett Dick, James G. Randall, and C. C. Tansill, highly creditable to the authors and to American scholarship. But the merit of these books fell short of brilliancy. Nor did any historical work in these years attain a really wide reading public.

Perhaps thin interludes ought to be taken for granted; perhaps we ought not to expect anything like "The Coming of the World War" or "The Flowering of New England" every second year, or even every third. But with this meek view no real lover of history can agree. The comparatively barren patches in our historical writing are altogether too frequent and too protracted. They point beyond all question to some malady or some crippling disability. It should be considered that we have a population of 130,000,000, equal to that of Great Britain, France, and Italy combined. We have appliances for scholarly and creative work unapproached elsewhere in the world. We have an enormous body of practitioners or would-be practitioners of history. The field open to historians in American materials (to say nothing of the rest of the globe) is remarkably fresh as well as rich. Much of it has been discovered only within the last generation; the history of the Trans-Mississippi West, the history of the South, the history of society, the history of business, all are *new*, and still offer

innumerable opportunities. And yet the le
numerous than the fat years.

Why? Why is it that biographic writir
consistently outruns historical writing? The
ple, yielded two genuinely first-class biogra
"Elihu Root" and Carl Van Doren's "Fran
one, Marquis James's "Jackson." No history
as witty and penetrating as Crane Brinton's '
Why is the record of history so often ba
actually repellent? Beyond doubt the reaso
believe that one reason far outweighs all oth

Vitality, in history as in every other fie
variety. Clio plays on the tender stops of va
one note or in one key. Her domain ha
romantics, precisians, impressionists, Marxist
so on; it needs them all. The more motley the
product. Place can be found for everybody b
insincere, the great pests of history as o
Tolerance for all the varied types of historical
able to the advance of history, and it ope
confusion but to a desirable complexity. The
into history the better, and ideas mean opin
variety of historical materials and the stea
disciplines applicable to these materials (espe
economics) means an ever greater variety of h

But when we turn from views to methods t
simplified. Historical writing, like ancient G
North America, falls into three main sovereig
domain of the pedants at one extreme, of the
other, and in between of the great median
varying degrees of emphasis) tries to unite lit
qualities. This division is well understood
profession itself. It is well recognized by t
which—to use the names of dead writers—h
identifying Herbert Levi Osgood's "American

enteenth Century" as a product of the pedantic school, Henry
ot Lodge's "Story of the Revolution" as a work of populariza-
, and the volumes of James Ford Rhodes or Henry Adams as
onging to the intermediate field. No general reader would
itate for a moment to put Stubbs among the pedants, Guedalla
ong the popularizers, and Macaulay in the central group.
uch terms as these should, to assist discussion, be defined. The
t members of the pedantic school of historians would indig-
tly reject that adjective, and declare that they ought to be
led the scientific school. The best of the popularizers would say
t they constitute the literary school *par excellence*. Let us
erefore attempt a rough statement of signification. By the
dantic school is meant those writers who are so preoccupied
h the scholarly values of historical work—with laborious
oroughness and extreme accuracy—that they totally neglect all
rary values. Most of them are also hostile to ideas as
tinguished from facts. In their conception of history fact is
rything, art nothing. By the school of popularizers is meant
ose who are so preoccupied with the literary values of their
rk—with interest and color—that they are careless or even
ntemptuous of precision and thoroughness. Obviously each
up has many shadings, many subdivisions; obviously the role
ayed by materials in giving one piece of work color and another
dity is great. But the three divisions stand. As they have just
en defined, no one could fail to put Von Holst in one, Cyrus
wnsend Brady in another, and Parkman in the third.
It must be evident to all except the blindest doctrinaires that
e health of history depends upon keeping the median group, the
iters who try to reconcile fact and art, strong at the expense of
e two extremes. This is not to say that the dryasdust monogra-
ers do not sometimes fulfill a useful function, that of fact-
cumulators. It is not to say that the Cyrus Townsend Bradys
d Hilaire Bellocs do not sometimes serve an even more useful
rpose, that of popular entertainers, and even instructors. It is
mply to say that the best history is neither mere pedestrian

1

What's the Matter with History?

Although written in 1939, this essay is as timely today as it
was a third of a century ago. Why, Allan Nevins asks, have so
few recent historical books captured popular attention? He
answers by placing the blame squarely on one of his favorite
antagonists, Professor Dryasdust, whose dull monographs,
parading as "scientific" history, were seemingly deliberately
contrived to repel readers. Guilty of only a slightly lesser
disservice, in Allan Nevins's judgment, is the professional
popularizer who attracted an audience by corrupting the
truth. Of the two he would probably have favored the
popularizer; Nevins was so passionately devoted to usable
history that he could never forgive his fellow academicians for
failing to reach the wide audience that would benefit from
their findings. In this plea for sound, readable history he
anticipates his own major role as a successful purveyor of
accurate facts clothed in readable rhetoric, which he assumed
both in his many widely distributed books and through the
American Heritage magazine that he inspired.

Reprinted with permission from the *Saturday Review of Literature* 19 (February 4, 1939): 3–4, 16.

fact-accumulation on the one side, nor mere pleasant writing on the other, but represents a fusion of facts, ideas, and literary grace in a single whole. This true history is of course not a resultant of two warring forces. It is a development on its own ground, and must hold that ground by hard fighting against the two extremes. History proper can give no quarter, for it will be given none; it must struggle desperately and constantly with both pedant and popularizer, and drive them back to the cobwebs on one side and to pulpwood on the other.

Of the two enemies it is the pedant who is far and away the more dangerous, and who is chiefly responsible for the present crippled gait of history in America. His touch is death. He destroys the public for historical work by convincing it that history is synonymous with heavy, stolid prosing. Indeed, he is responsible for the fact that today a host of intelligent and highly literate Americans will open a book of history only with reluctant dread, and will shun like the plague any volume which contains a footnote. He does his utmost to warp and debilitate the young talent interested in historical writing. He exerts a steady pressure through every possible channel in the direction of his own deadly ponderosity. And in the resulting public neglect of history he finds not regret but delight; for history in his opinion should be the possession of a Germanic-minded few, a little knot of *Gelehrten* squeezing out monographs and counting footnotes.

The pedant is not only the more dangerous enemy, but is far and away the more difficult to dislodge; for he has found means in our university system and our learned societies to fasten himself with an Old Man of the Sea grip upon history. The popularizer has no foundation, no backing, save that which he wins by his own pen. If he writes well enough he may do some good or some harm—but he has only his talents to aid him. Moreover, his work inevitably finds its due level. News that an author is undependable, passed about by critics, newspaper writers, librarians, and college and high school teachers, gradually permeates the literate public. But in the last fifty years, since Parkman and Fiske laid

7

down their pens, the school of pedants has gained control of a formidable arsenal of weapons. Though the touch of this school benumbs and paralyzes all interest in history, it is supported by university chairs, special foundations and funds, research fellowships, and learned bodies. It is against this entrenched pedantry that the war of true history will have to be most determined and implacable.

My initial use of names like Stubbs and Osgood was of course simply to furnish a recognizable label, and carried no suggestion that they were representative of the pedantic school. Compared with these eminent writers, the typical scholiast is Lilliputian. The two men named had remarkable gifts; the hallmark of the ordinary pedant is plodding mediocrity. These two men were highly productive workers, as most distinguished historians have been; the hallmark of the ordinary pedant is sterility. As he infests our colleges and universities (that being his habitat, for nowhere else could he make a living), he conforms to an all-too-familiar type. All honor to the numerous able and productive university men who are genuine historians and who try to reach a broad public! They would all agree upon a composite portrait of the pedant.

He has never written, or at least never published, a real book. Perhaps he was guilty in his so-called youth of printing a doctoral dissertation, but of that he has repented. He regards the man who writes books as self-convicted of superficiality; as not a "true scholar." At long intervals he prints an unreadable paper in some learned periodical. He may once in a decade excrete a slender, highly specialized, and to everybody concerned quite exhausting monograph. Apart from this his literary production is confined to an occasional spiteful review of some real historian. Fellow-pedants then gather in little knots and cackle: "Did you see what a fall Professor Dryasdust took out of Beard's latest book?" or "Did you see how Dryasdust made mincemeat out of Claude G. Bowers?" By this device—for morose jealousy of intellectual superiors is another hallmark of his type—our pedant labors to create the impression that if he were not too scholarly to rush into print, his own books would make Beard and Bowers look small. He adds to this impression by talking, Casaubon-like, of the great *opus* on which he is engaged as the decades drag by; an *opus* never quite finished. By long persistence on these lines a perfectly terrifying reputation for erudition and authority is built up. The cost in effort is almost zero; the return in the esteem of his fellows is enormous.

In other periods and countries pedants of this type did little harm; in America of our generation they have been able to do immeasurable damage to right concepts of historical writing. Some of them hold chairs, even in our oldest and largest universities; and hence they have the training of young men and women who study history and try to write it. They can warp and destroy the talent of these novices, and in numerous instances have done so. They teach ambitious spirits to look for petty monograph subjects, drill them in their own plodding, barren discipline of footnotes and bibliography, and kill the vital spark. They gain control of the research funds that might provide some leisure for really talented men. They try constantly to fasten an autocratic, intolerant grip upon societies founded with broad and generous aims, like the American Historical Association, and to reduce them to strictly academic and narrowly "learned" bodies. They try constantly to fix the same fell grip upon the existing journals of history. The younger periodicals, like the *Mississippi Valley Review*, have kept fairly well out of their clutches; but despite the gallant efforts of several managing editors, including the present incumbent, they have given the *American Historical Review* the imprint of their contracted and esoteric aims. Apart from its reviews, that publication has been not a magazine but a learned work of reference issued in quarterly installments. Its present able head is improving it. But as the most execrable specimens of literary criticism in print can be found in the *Journal of the Modern Language Association*, so the worst examples of how history should never be written can be discovered in past files of the *American Historical Review*.

9

The result of all this is evident if we but look about us. By whom is the real history being written today?—by whom has most of it been written in recent years? To an overwhelming extent, by the men and women farthest removed from the deadly touch of the academic glossologists. A younger generation of university men, I am happy to say, is springing up and manifesting a healthy impatience with pedantry. They are being encouraged in not a few colleges and universities by older men who are finished literary craftsmen, and who believe that history is defeated and worthless if it does not gain a popular following. But by far the larger number of our best historical writers are still to be found outside academic lines. Nearly all of those with a genuine public, with a following at all comparable to that achieved by Prescott, Parkman, and Fiske, are outside. Charles A. Beard, trained as a political scientist and not a historian, has not taught since World War days and was always far more a publicist than a university scholar. Claude G. Bowers, James Truslow Adams, Marquis James, Van Wyck Brooks—they have kept as far from the droning voice and envious pen of the mere scholiastics as did Beveridge or Captain Mahan or Henry Carey Lea.

With all due respect to the great body of excellent work that over any extended period is produced by academic historians; with all due respect to the men of broad views and high talents in academic seats, from Samuel Eliot Morison on the Atlantic to Herbert E. Bolton on the Pacific, we must admit that our colleges and universities are not setting the pace. It is being set by another group. Ask the well-read American, possessed of some real critical faculty, to name our best living writers of history and historical biography. He will suggest a few university scholars, of course. But he will name far more of the outsiders. In addition to the figures I have just listed, he will think without great effort of such writers as Tyler Dennett, Walter Millis, M. A. De Wolfe Howe, Douglas Freeman, Ray Stannard Baker, Burton J. Hendrick, Constance Rourke, Bernard DeVoto, Constance Lindsay Skinner, William Allen White, Ida Tarbell, Roger Burlingame, Frederick L. Allen,

Miriam Beard, Mark Sullivan, Henry Pringle, John Chamberlain, Herbert Agar, Philip Ainsworth Means, Charles Warren—but why go on? The list simply cannot be matched in the academic world. And yet this world offers the leisure, the facilities, the special knowledge that theoretically should make it the pulsing heart of our historical work.

Still another consideration is to be noted. History proper is constantly importing new talent from the field of the popularizers. Young workers with native gifts often begin amateurishly and train themselves (for they have nobody to mistrain them) into good historical writers. A promising book like Hugh Russell Fraser's "Democracy in the Making" this year may, despite all blemishes, presage a new figure of importance. But once a Pangloss, always a Pangloss. History proper recruits nothing from that bleak quarter. Who enters *that* road, and has not the foresight to turn back at its first milestone, is lost forever.

Since the school of pedants is the principal enemy, and since they are so well entrenched, what is to be done? It is not enough to say that time will take care of the problem. It has not done so in the past. This pedantic area of the historical field is well organized, while the great main body of historians is not. The best writers are essentially individualistic. They are busy with their own imaginations and ideas; they have no time to think of societies, reviews, funds, and the other appliances of scholarship. They are often scornful of them—the more so because the pedants have gained so much control over them. Most of the writers listed above have never once attended a session of the American Historical Association. They spend no time thinking of rights, privileges, and petty possessions; the pedants have nothing else to think about. And thus the pedantic school maintains and even extends a grip that has been disastrous to history in the past and will continue to be disastrous in the future.

The unescapable fact is that organization must be fought with some degree of organization. Some body should be created to unite the best of the university writers of history—those really interested in its presentation in attractive literary form—with the best of the outside writers. Such a body is needed. At present most non-academic authors have no touch with any historical organization. They do not want any; and yet they would profit by it. A new society such as I have described, literary rather than scholarly in intention, might coöperate with and strengthen the American Historical Association. It could encourage those members who strive to hold the pedants within bounds; who wish to make the Association a propagator of historical information along broad lines, not a petty learned society intent on footnote erudition. But the new organization could have important aims of its own. It might do much to promote the ideal of sound history in attractive garb, to encourage and protect those who believe in this ideal as opposed to pedantry or excessive popularization. It might help to create a broader reading public for history.

But above all, an organ is needed for those who believe in history as literature. Nothing would do so much in this country for the right kind of historical writing as a general monthly magazine devoted to it; a magazine offering a wide variety of accurate historical material, written with enough grace, color, and verve to be interesting to the lawyer, the doctor, the college student, the high-school teacher, the intelligent layman everywhere. In a nation so huge as ours, it is deplorable that practically no market now exists for even the best-written of historical articles. Most monthly magazines have a rule, formal or informal, which excludes historical matter from their contents. For this rule we must partly blame the pedants, who have filled the public with such a terror of history; we must partly blame the political and sociological preoccupations of our generation. But a distinct place exists for a popular historical magazine. It would do much to educate Americans in the dignity and fascination of their own past, and in the historical backgrounds of many a world problem of today. It would do equally good service for a union of scholarship and literature in the historical field. Such a magazine is certain to come in time, and if well edited, is certain of a resounding success.

2

Not Capulets, Not Montagus

Few professional historians have shown less interest in the numerous historical societies that provide academia with associational activities and guidance than did Allan Nevins; on the few occasions when he attended a national convention, he usually disappeared into the nearest library to continue his own research. The American Historical Association, however, believed that his contributions to scholarship, if not to its own welfare, deserved its highest honor: its presidency. When this was conferred upon him in Chicago on December 29, 1959, Nevins used his presidential address to belabor the pedants in his audience who sacrificed literary excellence for "scientific" exactness and to urge the writing of narratives that would elevate public knowledge, train informed voters, and provide the reading public with such palatable intellectual fare as William Hickling Prescott, John Lothrop Motley, and Francis Parkman had provided earlier generations—such fare, in other words, as he was to produce in his stirring *Ordeal of the Union.*

Reprinted with permission from the *American Historical Review* 65 (January 1960): 253–70.

A century ago, as the older studies of American letters remind us, a famous school of literary historians, insouciantly romantic, was flourishing in this country. Prescott's masterpiece, *The Conquest of Mexico*, was but a dozen years old, and the third volume of his Philip II was fresh from the press; his admirers looked forward to the fourth, which he never wrote, for we mark this year the centenary of his death. Motley, after long grubbing in the coalpits of black-letter folios and European archives, had recently published his *Rise of the Dutch Republic*, and was toiling on the vivid pages of *The United Netherlands*. The magniloquent George Bancroft was in full career. Parkman, retarded by nervous disease, had already gained some reputation from *The Conspiracy of Pontiac*, and his *Pioneers of France in the New World* lay only a few years ahead. In Great Britain, Hallam, Macaulay, Napier, and Carlyle were world famous, read everywhere, and Froude had begun to achieve his more narrowly Anglo-American reputation. This school ruled history with a golden scepter of self-confident mastery. Macaulay, who went to his grave in the Abbey a century ago, had said that he expected to be read in the year 2,000, and dared add: "I sometimes think of the year 3,000."

But at that very time, a century since, historical writing was entering upon a colder and more austere era. Principles termed "scientific" were storming the fortresses of historical learning in Europe, and echoes of their conquests were reaching the United States. If we paused for definitions, we would tread upon dangerous ground. But with some sense of quaintness we may recall how leaders like Buckle discarded the religious interpretation of events and the Hegelian framework of thesis and antithesis; how they scorned the anthropomorphic doctrine that nations mature, decay, and die much as individuals grow, age, and die; and how they rejected Carlyle's belief that history is a tissue of the acts and ideas of great men. From the natural sciences they borrowed a mechanistic vocabulary, asserting that history is governed by forces or pressures. If the terminology thus first employed was primarily Newtonian, their ideology soon owed more to Darwinian thought. But they remained insistent on scientific methods, and set scholars to investigating the ecology of Greek culture, the structure of the Tory party, or the climate of Jacksonian thought, as if these were precise concepts.

That with the demise of the romantic, unscientific, and eloquent school of writers, our history ceased to be literature, is a fact so well accepted that recent works on American letters omit history altogether. It is less often noted that the rise of scientific history sharply limited the influence of the subject upon democracy. Historical study became compartmented into many specialities, economic, constitutional, social, political, and intellectual; it was approached with a more and more intricate elaboration of method; and much of it was completely dehumanized. Especially as written in our universities it lost the large public authority it once possessed. Its ideas counted, for nothing can stay an idea, but its texts made scant appeal to the general citizenship. When Macaulay sold 26,500 copies of his third and fourth volumes in Great Britain within ten weeks, and heard from Edward Everett that they out-distanced in America any book but the Bible and a few school manuals, he felt he was achieving his cardinal aim: he was affecting the ideas and action of the whole people. A workingmen's meeting sent him a vote of thanks for writing a book that they found as interesting as it was profitable. As scientific history rose, those ample days vanished; populations swelled, libraries became universal, but the acceptance of historical works seemed to contract.

All the arts and the sciences, in contributing what they can to the instruction of democracy, face an increasingly difficult problem in communication.

The predicament of some branches of science is particularly painful, for their new-found power shapes the destiny of a citizenship which they can no longer reach. The mathematical physicists and nuclear specialists cannot hold effective intercourse even with the biologist, chemist, and astronomer, much less the lawyer, doctor, or merchant. For one reason, part of their

15

THE PURPOSE OF HISTORY

knowledge is so esoteric that it can be explained only to a few highly proficient men; for another, national security forbids them to divulge more than a safe fraction of what is communicable. Nor is the scientist in these sensitive areas always sure of his knowledge. When Enrico Fermi reached the critical stage of his labor on the Manhattan project, he was not at all positive that the next step might not be catastrophic. He took every precaution, he had a cadmium solution ready to flood the atomic pile, but he could not give General Leslie R. Groves a firm guarantee of the result; it might be harmless or it might be stupendously disastrous. Science today originates weapons and strategic plans that shape not military decisions alone, but the most vital national policies. Yet the scientist is to a great extent insulated from the electorate which has hitherto believed that all major decisions rest with it or its chosen leaders. If anybody supposes that this fact does not give our scientific experts the profoundest uneasiness, he knows little about their recent discussions.

Meanwhile, such arts as music, painting, sculpture, and poetry face a quite different set of impediments in communicating with the public. In these august domains, innovation constantly wrestles with conservatism; and in recent years the gulf between the new music and traditional music, between modern painting and classic painting, between the sculpture of St. Gaudens and the sculpture of Henry Moore, has widened. The observer must straddle the gap between a small and growing body of enthusiasts on one side, and a determinedly skeptical body of Olympians on the other. In poetry the schism has become especially formidable, for not only does much recent poetry seem deliberately obscure, but as C. S. Lewis tells us, its obscurity is of a new type. In painting, the struggle, if of less general interest, is even more bitter. The enthusiasts believe they are conducting a happy revolution; the conservatives try to hold the line against what they regard as anarchy; and the public watches. All these arts should be democratic possessions, but which school is a democracy to accept? In its heart the public prefers the familiar and recogniz-

16

NOT CAPULETS, NOT MONTAGUS

able, but in its mind it knows that new wine is always bursting old bottles. It realizes that when Mahonri Young commented acridly on Henry Moore that he liked sacred art but not holey art, he might be taking the same stand that Jeffrey took when he exclaimed of Wordsworth: "This will never do." The public cultivates tolerance, but meanwhile it feels confused. The arts, in short, are in such a state of internecine warfare that they find it hard to communicate.

History, in its efforts to reach the broadest public that it can profit, faces no such difficulties as science, for it is not impossibly esoteric in its discoveries. It faces no such difficulties as painting or music, for it remains firmly traditional in form; our most radical historians gladly cast their work in the same molds as Prescott and Parkman. History, apparently, should be able to keep its ancient rapport with the intelligent public without any severe perplexities. Why, then, the loss of its old status?

For the proud pretensions which historians once made to the instruction of a whole nation have long been abandoned. George Bancroft spoke of himself as holding his lamp to the feet of all good Americans, "the intelligence of the common mind," in accordance with his dictum: "The measure of the progress of civilization is the progress of the people." Richard Hildreth expressed a confident belief that America, and especially Americans of the younger generation, would read him with sympathetic appreciation. James Schouler in his first two volumes asserted that it was his intention "to interest and instruct my countrymen in a period . . . whose lessons are most salutary even at this day." Nicolay and Hay as late as 1886 could address the entire republic: "We commend the result of so many years of research and diligence to all our countrymen, North and South. . . ." While these assertions were not immodest, for their authors coupled with them an admission that they might fail, they are refreshing as the statement of an exalted ambition. They did honor to the historians and to the country. But nobody today would venture to speak to our 175,000,000 people in such terms.

17

Is this because Americans have lost their large degree of homogeneity? No such decline has taken place; our people use the same goods, live by the same basic assumptions, and show an even excessive standardization of· taste. Is it because the educational level has fallen? Obviously it has risen. Is it because nationalism or patriotism has loosened its hold? The idea is absurd. Is it because changes in social habits, recreational impulses, and cultural pursuits have narrowed the ranks of serious readers? Not if the statistics of publishers and libraries are accurate. Why, then, do historians no longer speak of instructing the nation, and why do so few aspire to a general democratic public?

The full answer is complex, rooted in the increasing complexity of our civilization. But the central explanation of the change is connected with the sweeping transfer of history into scientific channels, and the effect of this transfer in widening the gap between history that is broadly acceptable and history that is academically acceptable. In proportion as history took a scientific coloration, employed mechanistic or evolutionary terms, and abandoned its old preoccupation with individual act and motive, it lost much of its serviceability to democratic needs. In proportion as it turned from Prescott and Parkman, Macaulay and Froude, to the new approaches represented by Buckle, Renan, and Burckhardt (I still speak of changes a century ago), its significance to the ordinary citizen paled. For it tended to place men and communities in a position where they were controlled by inexorable, impersonal pressures; where the citizen lost power to decide or move. The new history was soon given a special position in the United States by the rise of graduate instruction, emphasizing abstract ideas and detailed research. It became more original, but more confusing; more expert, but grayer and grimmer. The democratic public turned away from it. It turned to its own preference, the popular writers who remained faithful to a human, romantic, and stylistically appealing type of presentation; for it was this which Demos found usable.

At this point history lost much of its authority. Well-read men

18

and women, even the college trained, began to feel that history must be either authoritative and dull or interesting and untrustworthy. Our academic historians did little, in general, to abate this suspicion; rather, they confirmed it by writing dull books and abusing bright ones. The democratic public, faced with this choice, never hesitated; it took the book which emphasized human motive and action almost every time.

But what, I may be asked at this point, is meant by the phrase "democratic public"?—and here we do clearly need a definition. Whenever I think of the relationships of history to democracy, I revert to an evening scene in a house just outside Dayton, Ohio. More accurately, it was a great stone and brick mansion of Georgian architecture, set in a grove of fine oaks, elms, and hickories overlooking a verdurous countryside. Its owner called it "Trailsend." Every evening he and I would return from some joint labor we were pursuing in town, where he owned the two principal dailies. While we ate dinner he would talk of his farm boyhood, his rise to wealth and power as editor-publisher, and of the reason why he housed his newspaper in a marble building resembling a bank—for the banks had once refused him some credit he desperately needed, and he took his amiable revenge in demonstrating that a great newspaper could occupy a building finer than any banking house. He would talk of his friendships with Newton D. Baker and Tom L. Johnson, his skirmishes with Warren G. Harding and Boss George Cox of the opposite party, and his devotion to Woodrow Wilson.

Then, nightly, my host would settle me for further work in a sitting room upstairs, and down the vista of a long hallway I would see him in his library, in a pool of golden light from his lamp, reading. Two hours would pass, and he was still absorbed in his book. He read chiefly history and biography, for his name was James M. Cox, and he had made history himself. He had been governor of Ohio in a critical time, a counselor of great men, and a candidate for the presidency who, as everyone will now grant, should have won. At breakfast next morning we would talk

19

sometimes of the news, but more often of the history he had read the previous night. Since the ten days at "Trailsend," I have thought of history for democracy as the kind of history preferred by my distinguished host. He had been too poor to continue schooling beyond the age of sixteen, and later too busy to educate himself systematically; but he had a keen appreciation of good historical writing, a lively mind, and a muscular grasp of problems past and present. His feeling for history was much that of another practical man of affairs with whom I often talked and corresponded, William Allen White—a journalist, a man unversed in scholarly lore, but a devourer of books and an acute judge of their merit. Their criteria of history were amateur criteria, but from every important standpoint but the expert's they were incisive and informed criteria.

These men, in a superior way because they were superior persons, typified the best democratic audience a historian can find. They expected the books they read to meet certain fundamental requirements, which, in an ascending order of importance, I would enumerate as four.

One is that history shall be offered in God's plenty, so that it shall be available for every need, taste, and mood. A broad catholicity should open it to the rich in knowledge and to those as ill-schooled as Macaulay's workingmen, to lovers of bare fact and votaries of interpretation, to the imaginative and the prosaic. Neither the pendant's nor the poet's contribution should be undervalued—and as Hazlitt says, pedant and poet are in some respects brothers. The second basic prescription is that a considerable part of history should be written with gusto, for those who will read with gusto; written with a delight that communicates itself to style. Who is the historian of gusto, of vivid delight? "He will make us see as living men the hardfaced arches of Agincourt, and the war-worn spearmen who followed Alexander down beyond the rim of the known world. . . . We shall hear grate on the coasts of Britain the keels of the Low Dutch sea-thieves whose children's children were to inherit unknown continents." So wrote a president of the American Historical Association who was also, in his time, President of the United States. A third requirement is that a great part of the history shall be assimilable to current needs. The donnish mind retreats too easily into an antiquarian past, losing itself in Hannibal's strategy or Charlemagne's politics or Lollard pamphleteering as if they were detached entities. But the democratic public lives in the present and future, and except in moods of escapism wants history at least as directly apposite to its concerns as Gibbon's study of the Antonines was apposite to eighteenth-century England—which was very directly indeed.

The fourth and cardinal requirement is that the history offered a broad democratic public should not be dehumanized; that instead of dissecting impersonal forces, or presenting those misty wraiths the economic man or sociological man, the historian should narrate the past in terms of living men and women seen as individuals, groups, or communities; and that he should give due emphasis to personal motivation and initiative. John Richard Green said that English historical work had one special superiority, the sense of its writers "that government and outer facts are but the outcome of individual men, and men what body, mind, and spirit make them." Nor will the historian fail to allot due place to the accidental and irrational; those elements which, as Graham Wallas thought, make up a great part of current politics, and which have offered so much of the drama of this great motley, colorful, unpredictable world. Human choice and irrational fortuity are compounded in the kind of history that democracy recognizes.

The democratic audience which makes these requirements is not, I repeat, an audience merely of middlebrows and devotees of waist-high culture. It contains innumerable people who approach the competence of James M. Cox and William Allen White. It numbers many an austere intellectual. No less a thinker than Arthur O. Lovejoy, author of The Great Chain of Being, told me during the Second World War that he had gone into a shop to buy a book on disloyalty. He was shown two recent books on Civil

War Copperheads, one of solid thoroughness by a university historian, with a full analysis of forces, and one by a newspaper editor which emphasized human elements. "I quickly saw which was the book for *me*," said Lovejoy; and with true democratic instinct, he took the human treatment. But those are poor Americans who make much of the lines which seem to separate lowbrow, middlebrow, and highbrow. In the last analysis we have but one democratic public—the public to which Emerson and Lincoln spoke; and the rule of the historian in approaching it should be the hoary maxim of the newspaper offices, "Never overestimate the information of the public, but above all never underestimate its intelligence."

The gap between popular history and academic history which, as I have said, the rise of scientific ideas long ago widened, would have been less serious but for a certain animosity on both sides. A phrase I have just used, the donnish (or professorial) mind, sums up the prejudice of the lay writer. On the other side, scholastic folk who speak with respect of a popular movement or popular faith will refer to popular history with scorn. This attitude is akin to the belief of some literary critics that since Longfellow and Walt Whitman are popular poets they must be bad poets. It also springs, more legitimately, from the belief that history is a discipline, and that the amateur or lay practitioner stands outside the fold. The gap is on many counts unfortunate, and should be narrowed by better understanding, better taste, and better civility on both sides. Any inquiry into the mode of effecting this result must begin with a scrutiny of the causes of distrust.

The suspicion which we historians of the academic guild feel for our lay brethren outside has something to support it in this just-mentioned assumption that history at its best is an arduous discipline. In every field, the conscientiously trained expert reprobates shortcuts to mastership. The professional musician who devotes years of toil to mastery of the piano knows that an advertisement offering proficiency in ten easy lessons is just a cruel hoax. The true economist knows that nobody is more dangerous

22

than the politician who merely *thinks* he knows the principles of economics. The professional student of literature, trained in prosody, philology, and criticism, is contemptuous of the man who supposes that an easy chair and a five-foot shelf will produce a literary scholar. In all learning, the promise of a shortcut is the will-o'-the-wisp glimmering over a perilous bog. The dullest monograph writer, meticulous in stating facts and conclusions, at any rate helps to build a granite foundation, while the random popularizer destroys true knowledge.

The new mass media have heightened the spirit of apprehensive caution within our guild by increasing the danger that careless popularizations of history will mean their vulgarization. Motion pictures, radio, and television are guilty of some horrible distortions of truth. Perhaps the direct harm they do is seldom great. As Francis Bacon said, "It is not the lie that passeth through the mind, but the lie that sinketh in and settleth, that doeth the hurt"; and the worst inflictions of the mass media seldom sink in far. Nevertheless, they destroy a taste for what is veracious and fine in the same way that meretricious books destroy a taste for literature. In looking at popularizations in any form, moreover, the experienced guild historian feels a certain despair over their inevitable simplifications. He knows how intricate are the complexities of great events, how deeply submerged are the subtler elements, how delicate are the shadings to be put into an interpretive painting. Truth, writes Renan, lies in the nuances— and how seldom does popularized history have any nuances. Some of its productions possess a flash and glitter that momentarily delight us, but when the moment passes, we wryly comment: "C'est magnifique, mais ce n'est pas l'histoire."

We professional historians have other hesitancies and objections. One of the most important arises from our feeling that the work done by general writers is, taken as a whole, spasmodic and unplanned, and that the profit motive is too exclusively the stimulus. By contrast, we say, our well-marshaled ranks try to cover the past in systematic fashion. Our careful division of areas of interest assists us in this. Some leading scholar will point out a gap; instantly a half dozen younger men leap to fill it. Or another scholar propounds what seems a fruitful thesis; at once disciples arise to apply it to this or that segment of the past. It is we who have toiled most continuously to build specialized libraries and fill teeming archives; we who have organized research projects, and trained the workers; we whose criticism is the best touchstone separating good books from poor ones. We, in short, have given history its firmest foundations.

The guild historian also takes a just pride in his carefully developed equipment: in his knowledge of the rules of historical evidence, in his techniques ranging from medieval calligraphy to present-day diplomatic usages, in the tough-minded skepticism and flashes of insight gained by long study. By such expertness alone he avoids pitfalls like Carlyle's use of the Tompkins forgeries in his life of Cromwell. He knows that the footnotes to which amateurs take exception not only guide other searchers, but serve the writer by compelling him to restrict himself to validated materials. On all this he does well to insist. But if he plants himself too arrogantly on such advantages, and if he tries to limit the popular function in historical writing, he will have to reckon with the court of last resort, the democratic public.

For the general writer of history, appealing to the general reader, has a basis for equally trenchant suspicions of the academic approach. These suspicions are not to be taken lightly, if only because he has with him the weight of numbers and influence. The engineer, the physician, the chemist would feel deeply disturbed by a suggestion that he was losing rapport with the public he serves. The professional historian cannot afford to be less sensitive. He affects democratic action in three principal ways, by giving occasional guidance to leaders, by affording instruction to the general citizenship, and by helping create a climate of opinion. He will do well to listen respectfully to criticism from workers outside the guild. In most fields, in this country with its long tradition of the versatile amateur, a well-led revolt against excessive professional claims is always assured of wide support. From the days of Winfield Scott to those of Tasker H. Bliss and George Marshall, our people have rejected the idea that only West Point graduates should command our armies. The aphorism of Clemenceau about war and military experts has been applied in our time to experts in pedagogy who asserted a complete right to control our schools: "Education is too important to be left to the educationists." Were we less modest, it could be applied to us: "History is far too important to be left to the professional historians."

The principal reproach that writers outside the guild bring against us is rooted in a different sense of values from ours, which we may well pause to examine.

In striving to present the truth about the past, any historian must rely upon the fullest possible research, upon strict care to avoid factual error, upon his best powers of insight and judgment, and upon due use of the imagination. Of these four parts of his panoply two are easily measured. It is not difficult to demonstrate the adequacy of research in Channing, and inadequacy in much of Schouler; the infrequency of factual error in Gardiner, and frequency in Froude. The failure to use insight to reach a deeper truth, however, is not so easily detected. As for imagination, its absence will never be noted by many pedestrian students, some of whom will even omit it from the list of historical essentials. Yet its supreme importance is stated with characteristic force by Parkman in the preface to *La Salle and the Great West*. "Faithfulness to the truth of history," he writes, "involves far more than a research, however scrupulous, into special facts. Such facts may be detailed with the most minute exactness, and yet the narrative, taken as a whole, may be unmeaning or untrue. The narrator must seem to imbue himself with the life and spirit of the time. He must study events in their bearings near and remote; in the character, habits, and manners of those who took part in them. He must be, as it were, a sharer or spectator of the action he describes."

The principal criticism which general readers and writers level

25

against our guild is this, that of the four parts of our equipment—fullness of research, accuracy, insight, and imagination—we overvalue the first and second, and undervalue the last two. The democratic audience which yearns for a usable image of the past knows that any history falls short of complete truth. Knowing this, they set less store on absolute precision of detail than we professional historians do. Every historical work of any scope contains inaccuracies; the scrupulously careful Douglas Freeman once told me with pardonable pride that he had found only about fifty slips in his four-volume *Lee*. General readers brush minor errata aside. When a historian gives a picture of the Armada's defeat in the compelling form in which Froude and Motley give it, they will feel no sense of outrage if the number of guns in Drake's command is slightly misstated. Their complaint against the academic historian is that his sense of values is often faulty. For most academic historians, alas, will insist that the number of guns be stated with documented precision, but leave the narrative of the Armada so opaque that no reader catches his breath as that great sinister cloud of canvas creeps up over the Channel horizon.

That a piece of historical writing may be accurate in every detail and yet misleading, while another narrative may be flawed with inaccuracies and yet luminous with truth, is a fact which James M. Cox knew without benefit of high school. The intelligent reader knows also that an author of insight may make more from a few artifacts than the most laborious investigator sometimes makes from a rich archive. He knows, too, that the historian's imagination, used aright, need go only half way to inspire the reader to use his own imagination for the rest of the road. For the best reader of history, as of poetry and fiction, wishes to build something by his own vision; to assist the author in what Michelet said Thierry achieved, a resurrection. Human life without some form of poetry is mere animal existence, and the lay or democratic reader of history is often quicker to value its poetic elements than is the academic student. He lifts a book with the hope that it will kindle his imagination.

26

How does imagination speak to imagination in history? Why, just precisely as in poetry. Milton created in *Paradise Lost* a heaven, a hell, and a Garden of Eden—a cosmogony which dominated the imagination of the English-reading world so effectively that it came to be accepted as verity. Churchmen complained that Milton's Seventh Book supplanted the Biblical account of the same matters. Scientists complained that the Miltonian image took a firmer hold on men's minds than the Copernican reality; Huxley, for example, in the middle of the nineteenth century said that it seemed impossible to overthrow that epic cosmogony. How did Milton accomplish his feat? By the imaginative use of materials already in men's possession. He did not have to create his celestial, infernal, and mundane personages, for they already existed. Everybody was familiar with the Father and Son, with Satan and Beelzebub, with Adam, Eve, and the archangels; everybody, when Milton wrote, believed intensely in them. By quickening and brightening the familiar data in his own alembic, Milton kindled the public imagination to the point where it accepted a whole new universe.

Similarly, the democratic reader opens a book with hope that the historian will use men and events already vaguely familiar to him, kindle his imagination, and thus help him create a rounded world. Such readers know a good deal about Washington, Adams, and Jefferson, about George III, Lord North, and Lafayette, about Mount Vernon, Windsor, and Versailles; they are ready to have these images enclosed in a radiant new sphere even more real than the everyday world about them. They know a great deal about Elizabeth and Mary of Scotland, Burleigh and Essex, Raleigh and Bacon; they hope the historian will not merely provide new facts and fresh insights, but weave an incantation about these personages that will give the Tudor era as much immediacy as the Eisenhower era. The inert reader, like the unimaginative historian, never penetrates deeply into the past; but many readers are passionately anxious to make themselves spiritually, almost corporeally, at home there. Perhaps one error we guild historians too often make is to suppose that all readers are inert vessels; perhaps a complementary mistake is to suppose we must conduct readers every step of the way, spelling out each detail. How the cry of Xenophon's men as they reached the Trebizond shore, "Thalatta! Thalatta!" has echoed down twenty-four centuries; yet how few lines Xenophon gave that dramatic moment in his *Anabasis*—so few that when blind Joseph Pulitzer heard his secretary read the famous passage, he could not restrain his disappointment. Xenophon had left something to the imagination.

Not only do nonacademic writers of history question our sense of values in putting too much emphasis on research and accuracy at the expense of insight and imagination. They question our sense of values again with respect to the comparative worth of the closet approach to history, and the approach through the practical world. They ask us if the political historian who has never testified before a congressional committee, or written a speech for a governor or mayor, or haunted the city hall for a year, is not handicapped as compared with the man who has; whether Claude G. Bowers' secretaryship with Senator John W. Kern of Indiana was not worth more to him than a graduate school. It is important to study the world of books, but it is equally important to study the book of the world.

And though it is true that in the recent wars most of us heard the bursting of bombs and bore our shield and buckler, the danger of a retreat into the sequestered tower remains. Perhaps the conviction of Gibbon—less than five feet tall, with a mincing carriage and humiliating ailments—that he wrote better history because he had been a militia officer and a member of Parliament was partly vanity. But Macaulay's emphatic endorsement of the statement is still worth our recollection. "We have not the smallest doubt," wrote Macaulay, "that his campaigns, though he never saw an enemy, and his parliamentary attendance, though he never made a speech, were of far more use to him than years of study and retirement would have been. If the time he spent on

NOT CAPULETS, NOT MONTAGUS

parade and at mess in Hampshire, or on the treasury bench and at Brooks's, during the storms which overthrew Lord North and Lord Shelburne, had been passed in the Bodleian library, he might have avoided some inaccuracies; he might have enriched his notes with a greater number of references; but he could never have produced so lively a picture of the court, the camp, and the senate house." There spoke the historian whose *Criminal Code* was the law of India for decades. What would Macaulay have made of Sir Winston Churchill's training as historian?

We of the academic fold must admit that here the outsiders have their point. Lord Acton probably never saw Thomas Hart Benton's boast in his *Thirty Years' View* that he possessed one qualification for writing history in his *inside* knowledge of how it was made. But Acton would have approved it. For Acton, as Bryce once remarked, believed that the best explanation of what occurred in the light was to be found in what had occurred in the dark. "He was always hunting for the key to secret chambers, preferring to believe that the grand staircase is only for show, and meant to impose upon the multitude, while the real action goes on in the hidden passages behind. . . . One was sometimes disposed to wonder whether he did not think too much about the backstairs. But he had seen a great deal of history in the making." If Acton's view is valid that seven-eighths of history, like the iceberg, lies submerged, then the hidden mass will be less readily divined by a closet-scholar measuring from the tip than by a George Bancroft who knew the secrets of Polk's cabinet. How valuable James Breck Perkins must have found his long service in the House, culminating in the chairmanship of the Foreign Affairs Committee, for analyzing the policies of Richelieu and Mazarin; how useful Albert J. Beveridge must have found his familiarity with Indiana politics and the Senate chamber in assessing the actions of Lincoln, Douglas, and Trumbull.

Finally, if we guild historians complain that most general writers produce their books in random, unplanned fashion, the lay historians can say in reply that our academic pressures distort historical writing in two antithetical ways. First, we demand of immature scholars that they publish, or pay the penalty in years of unpromoted purgatory, and second, we simultaneously paralyze some mature and gifted men by making them feel they must run the gauntlet of critics who require perfection. The first distortion is not important, for immature books that answer questions nobody ever asked, or ever will ask, soon find oblivion. The second distortion is real and disastrous. Rarely outside academic circles do we meet the historian who achieves a massive reputation by the book he is always about to publish, but never publishes. There we too often meet him. Reports circulate of the coming masterwork, scholars refer to it in awed tones, and at the end we find a repetition of Balzac's story of *Le Chef d'Oeuvre Inconnu*. Such a scholar is always telling us when he will finish his book, but he never tells us when he will begin it. The writer may be numbed by a variety of circumstances, but too often it is by fear of his critics.

For a long generation our historical guild very properly reverenced no name more than that of J. Franklin Jameson. He embodied an ideal spirit of intense, dedicated scholarship. His active career spanned the period between the last books of Bancroft and Parkman and the first books of many men writing today. So broad was his knowledge, so disciplined his mind, so refined his taste, that to converse with him was to feel a bracing northwest wind. He used to say to friends, as he once said to me, "I have never written a book"; and though this was not literally true, it was true in the sense he intended. His services to history would have been richly memorable had he never penned a line. Then, in 1925, the aging Dr. Jameson, contrary to his rule, consented to deliver a series of lectures. He picked up again the lectures he had originally prepared for delivery at Barnard in 1895. The result of this invitation from the Vanuxem Foundation of Princeton was a book he had never really intended to publish, *The American Revolution Considered as a Social Movement*. For him this was a great concession, the more remarkable in that it was really a book of popular history—for any scholar who accepts such a lectureship contracts to be interesting to a wide audience. These four lectures might have been printed as magazine articles. When they were finished Dr. Jameson was a little astonished at himself, as his friends were astonished. The brief volume, now a classic, sharpens our feeling of regret that this great scholar was not so circumstanced, or so self-impelled, that he wrote more books. Perhaps he too feared the critics—above all, his self-criticism.

The nonacademic historian will never admit that overproduction can be as bad as denial of production, for time winnows it. Theodore Roosevelt in reviewing several new historical books once stated the lay attitude. After noting that Gilbert Murray's *The Rise of the Greek Epic*, Henry Osborn Taylor's *The Medieval Mind*, and T. R. Lounsbury's *Fenimore Cooper* were actually disliked by some scholars because they were beautifully written and divorced from aridity, he expressed his views on productive effort with characteristic emphasis. "What counts in a man or nation," he wrote, "is not what the man or nation can do, but what he or it actually does. Scholarship that consists in mere learning, but finds no expression in production, may be of interest or value to the individual, just as ability to shoot well at clay pigeons may be of interest and value to him, but it ranks no higher unless it finds expression in achievement. From the standpoint of the nation, and from the broader standpoint of mankind, scholarship is of chief worth when it is productive, when the scholar not merely receives or acquires, but gives." Of all the parables, declares the lay writer, the academic world should most ponder that of the talent laid away in a napkin.

And if we academic historians can say, as assuredly we can, that our zeal has done most to build the specialized libraries and fill the teeming archives, that we have organized the great research projects and trained the workers, that our criticism goes furthest to separate the grain from the chaff, that in short we have laid the firmest foundations, the nonacademic historian has his counterclaim. It is we, he says, who have done most to keep the interest of the masses in history alive; it is we who have created and nourished a large popular market for historical and biographical books; and it is we who keep the breezes of concern with the human and dramatic aspects of history whipping into your stuffy classrooms.

History, writes Ludwig Dehio in his recent book on Germany and world politics, has lost influence in continental Europe. This is not the fact in Britain or America, where its spontaneity and exuberance have never been greater. In this country countless newspapers and magazines carry historical material, our hundreds of radio stations are glad to use historical lectures and dramatizations, and history is a frequent visitor on television. It blossoms forth in novels, in collections of pictures, and in the book-magazine *American Heritage* with its circulation of 330,000. Our great industries publish historical brochures that are often conscientiously written and illustrated. The spate sweeps into the best-seller lists a steady line of books ranging in theme from Katharine of Aragon to William McKinley, from the tragedy of Wolsey to the tragedy of Wilson. The academic world and the lay world should be sharers in the inspiration and opportunities of this torrential demand.

The annals of the republic have no more remarkable illustration of the force with which popular interest in history may burst aloft, like a released fountain, than in the passion with which our democratic public has taken up the Civil War. This impulse long anticipated the centenary of the conflict. Purely spontaneous, it can be traced to no book or event, though *Gone with the Wind*, *John Brown's Body*, and Sandburg's *Lincoln* doubtless helped to ignite the interest. With astonishing suddenness, as the last survivors died, books on the war multiplied, enthusiastic study circles bloomed in towns and cities all over the map, a quarterly review sprang into life, and men young and old became greater experts in Stonewall Jackson's strategy than in Babe Ruth's exploits on the diamond. Nor did this passionate rediscovery of our most epic years have merely superficial effects. It has produced several books which may be called literature, it has found a wide market for works of the most robust scholarship, it has encouraged university presses as well as commercial publishers to revive standard historical works, and it has altered the whole popular perspective on the past.

Such an ebullition suggests that the appetite of 175,000,000 Americans for history—Americans more and more largely educated through high school if not college—will not be satisfied in the future without a distinct broadening of effort, and in particular a greater attention to a humanized and attractive presentation of the past. It suggests that in this broadened effort the mutual suspicions of the guild historians and the popular historians will be increasingly out of place; that they should join hands, not Capulets, not Montagus, but partners. Indeed, a rapprochement has already taken place. The guild has become more humanistic and literary, and the best nonacademic writers have grown more scholarly; the H. L. Mencken jibe at the professoriat, and the pundit's sneer at the unlearned, both have a hollow note. Certainly when the academic historian pauses to look at the diplomatist who has written the history of Soviet-American relations just after the First World War, the airline executive who has penned a masterly biographical volume on Theodore Roosevelt, the free-lance woman writer who has reburnished the fame of Lord Coke, the musician · who has so eloquently explored the four-century chronicle of the Rio Grande, and the newspaperman who has told how silence fell at Appomattox, he will not feel the partnership unequal. In increasing degree, we are all amateurs, we are all professionals.

If history is to regain its place as instructor of the whole democracy, if it is to communicate with intelligent men as freely as in the year when Prescott and Macaulay died, the academic scholar will have to teach the layman something about precision and depth, while the lay writer will have to teach us a good deal about human warmth and literary form. We can be severe on both sides without animosity or arrogance. We are both servants of Truth, with about an equal amount of selfishness and

unselfishness, conscientiousness and carelessness. Cardinal New-
man remarked in *The Idea of a University* that mutual education
is one of the great incessant occupations of human society,
"carried on partly with set purpose, and partly not." In what is
taught without set purpose, by examples, we of the guild will have
most to learn. But in that part of mutual instruction which is
undertaken of set purpose, we professional historians should make
the largest advances, for we have the greater duty.

Ours is the greater duty because we are organized, and the lay
writers of history and biography are not. Along with our academic
and professional organizations, we have a wealth of apparatus—
the libraries and manuscripts, the grants, the favorable arrange-
ments as to work and leisure, the basic security—which most
outside historians lack. Moreover, the guild historian occupies a
position to which (though it may be hard for him to believe) the
extra-academic writer usually defers. No one who has not been
outside the guild, as I long was, can appreciate how keenly the lay
historian, often all self-taught, all unguided, feels his exclusion
from what he deems the advantages of the professional sphere.
Most well-established university teachers have often been embar-
rassed, I dare say, by the diffidence with which important authors
outside Academe have come to them, as if they had access to
some arcanum of knowledge and skill which few could hope to
share. And as a final reason why we have a greater duty in effecting
harmonious relations, in establishing some sense of partnership,
nearly all of us are attached to what we may loosely call a
public-service institution. We should see that public service means
something.

Greater cordiality toward writers of history and biography who
are not teachers, and a stronger effort to draw them into our
councils, would befit a body theoretically so catholic as the
American Historical Association. The work of these men and
women is by no means ignored, for it is far too important to be
ignored. But how much are they made to feel at home with us? A
list of authors, for example, of standard lives of American

Presidents includes nearly a score of living or recently living writers of nonacademic positions: Douglas Freeman for Washington; Claude G. Bowers and Marie Goebel for Jefferson; Catherine Drinker Bowen for John Adams; Irving Brant for Madison; Marquis James for Jackson; Holmes Alexander for Van Buren; Freeman Cleaves for Harrison; Sandburg and Ben Thomas for Lincoln; George Fort Milton for Andrew Johnson; myself in newspaper days for Cleveland; Margaret Pulitzer for McKinley; Carleton Putnam for Roosevelt; Henry Pringle for Taft; and William Allen White for Coolidge. How many of these were earnestly and frequently urged to write papers, or sit on committees, or hold offices in this Association? Of all the persons I have listed, only one ever became president of this Association, and he, I fear, only because he rose (or sank) from a position in the fourth estate to a chair in Columbia University. Yet Douglas Freeman, like Claude G. Bowers, like, I may add, James Truslow Adams, like other outside historians, would greatly have valued the distinction; and the active participation of one or most of them in our affairs would by no means have detracted from the Association's vitality of action or breadth of view.

We are all amateurs, we are all professionals. Perhaps what we all most need is a dual sense of humility; humility because we know that however hard we search for Truth we shall not quite find it, humility because we are in the last analysis servants of the democratic public. That public has just come through a terrible period of confusion, effort, and disaster, and lives on in a period of intense strain. It needs all the sense of pattern, all the moral fortitude, all the faith in the power of liberty and morality to survive the assaults of tyranny and wrong, that historians of every school can give it. This is a time not for arrogance, disdain, or rivalry, but for union in a common and exalted effort.

3

The Newspaperman
and the Scholar

When Allan Nevins retired from his professorship at Columbia University in the spring of 1958, a number of his friends,
drawn largely from his own two fields of specialization—journalism and teaching—honored him with a testimonial dinner
that marked one of the high points of his career. As usual on
such ceremonial occasions he was called upon to speak. He
responded by speculating on the relationship between his two
professional interests and what they had to offer each other.
His remarks, printed shortly afterward in the *Saturday
Review*, reveal amusing incidents in his own career, as well as
helpful hints on what the newspaperman can teach the
historian. These, inevitably, have to do with the popularization of good history, for Allan Nevins could never rest until
the entire world shared his intimate knowledge of the past.

Some of us look back over the tumultuous decades with a
sense that if history can make us wise, we should be wise indeed.

Reprinted with permission from the *Saturday Review* 41 (June 21, 1958): 11–13.

We look back over two world wars; over the birthpangs of twenty new nations; over revolutionary shifts in the balance of continents; over the acceptance of the Welfare State at home and the first strong world organization abroad; over the advent of the nuclear age. We look back to the misty peaceful pre-war period, which Winston Churchill among others has described, when a uniformed man in the streets was a rarity, when people traveled everywhere without passports, when the airplane, the wireless, and the income tax were innocuous toys, when nearly all American wealth was devoted to peaceable pursuits; when a happier optimism, a more innocent wonder, filled the world than now seems possible.

Fortunate are those who in this period have known one guiding tradition. As I have known two, the journalistic tradition and the academic tradition, it seems fitting to venture a few observations on their special characteristics, and the lessons one may teach the other. Especially I would emphasize the lessons that Academe may learn from the great tradition of the press as it comes down to us from the days of Defoe and Addison.

At first glance the traditions of journalism and scholarship seem completely unlike: journalism so bustling, feverish, and content with daily oblivion; the academic world so sheltered, deliberate, and hopeful of enduring products. It is true that both are concerned with the ascertainment and diffusion of truth. In journalism, however, the emphasis falls on a rapid diffusion of fact and idea; in academic work it falls on a prolonged, laborious ascertainment.

When I left *The New York World* in 1931 to come to Columbia University, the contrast struck me with a shock. "We always have to write from a half-knowledge of the facts," Rollo Ogden (editor first of the *New York Evening Post*, then of *The New York Times*) had once lamented to me. Suddenly I was transplanted to a field where we were expected to gain a full knowledge of the facts. The journalist works to an exigent deadline in headlong haste. "We can't wait until we get everything exactly right just before the day of judgment," Samuel Bowles says in one of his letters. The academic world disdains deadlines. It does this so completely that many a scholar has gained fame by the great work he planned to write but never wrote, like Lord Acton with his history of liberty.

So great is the contrast that each tradition appeals to a special temperament. Many a newspaperman, like Frederick Jackson Turner, has gone to the academic world with a sense of relief; many a university man, like Carl Van Doren, has moved into the world of journalism with elation. Lord Bacon pointed out this temperamental difference three centuries ago. "Some minds," he wrote, "are proportioned to that which may be dispatched at once or within a short return of time; others to that which begins far off, and is to be won with length of pursuit." A few temperaments bridge the gap: Douglas Freeman, for example, journalist half the day, a scholar immersed in sustained tasks the other half. In general, however, they are alien to each other.

The journalistic tradition which I shared for fifteen years had been molded in America by powerful men of diverse endowments. The humblest newspaperman was aware that James Gordon Bennett had instilled into journalism a spirit of enterprise that made news-gathering a passion; that threw into a thousand dark corners the lantern rays of a driving, indefatigable, critical search for facts. Every newspaperman knew that Horace Greeley had made his *Tribune* a tremendous engine of democracy: the spokesman of the laborer and farmer, the foe of privilege, the tireless antagonist of slavery, the popular teacher in all the arts. Newspapermen knew that Henry J. Raymond, founder of *The New York Times*, had shaped his paper in Burke's belief that national unity and sound government depend on moderation and compromise. He used it to reduce antagonisms and promote workable agreements. Still more mightily did Adolph S. Ochs, who inherited the paper, use it to create an enlightened moderation. Newspapermen well recalled what eloquence William Cullen

Bryant of the *New York Evening Post* had shown in vital causes; how effectively E. L. Godkin had thrust his lance into whatever was shoddy, vulgar, or corrupt; and what tempestuous crusades Joseph Pulitzer had headed.

The private in the ranks knew the fame of these generals. One private had the rewards, if also the toils, of carrying a musket under officers whose renown should extend far into the future: Rollo Ogden, Fabian Franklin, and Simeon Strunsky of the old *Evening Post*; Paul Elmer More and Oswald Garrison Villard of the *Nation*; Frank I. Cobb and Walter Lippmann of the *World*. He can testify to the dedication of these men to high public objects. He can testify also to their warm respect for the best learning in the academic world, and for the expertness of the university specialist. Of these men, Fabian Franklin had himself occupied a chair at Johns Hopkins at a time when a professorship there held a unique distinction. Simeon Strunsky was one of the most brilliant of Columbia's many brilliant sons.

The journalistic world is hungry, to a degree which university men hardly comprehend, for the solidity, exactness, and special expertness of the best scholars. It constantly strives to import into its columns as much of these qualities as it can get in proper form—for the form has to be suited to general consumption. It bids for academic contributors energetically but blindly, and receives all too feeble a response. A more intelligent collaboration is needed. The university might well undertake to bring the mass media—press, magazines, radio, television—into close relations with a large body of academic experts. The mass media want specialized knowledge, attractively presented; the specialists would gladly sell such knowledge, attractively presented, but know not how to reach the market.

When I went into university teaching it was with a dire fear of the specialists. I was afraid that I would meet Dr. Blank, the world's greatest master of Icelandic literature, and Dr. Dash, the preeminent authority on the price mechanism in Hanseatic commerce, and they would put the upstart down. Instead, I met

Carl Becker, as broadly humane a scholar as the country ever produced. He had begun teaching in Emporia College. "I taught eighteen hours a week," he once told me. When I expressed amazement at the burden, he added: "It was easy. I didn't know anything then." At this I took heart; I didn't know anything either, but I might learn. And, studying Carl Becker, I began to understand what the academic tradition at its best, so far removed from stuffiness or pedantry, might mean. Like the journalistic tradition, it is largely expressed in the names of the remarkable men who have nurtured it.

A poor world we should have without the best type of scholar, whose mind is given exactness by study and depth by long thought, but whose view is broad and whose spirit is mellow. Journalism has a special vitality of its own, in which alertness and quickness count most. Academic life has rather a vitality of underlying ideas and fertile discoveries. President McCosh used to ask about a new appointee: "But, mon, is he alive?" Think of asking that about Professor Bliss Perry or Professor Woodrow Wilson! Some years ago my friend Charles Warren published an essay, "A Plea for Personality in Professors," in which he lamented that the day of men like Francis J. Child, Nathaniel Shafer, and Charles Eliot Norton had passed away. Of course, such men are unusual. President Butler in his annual report for 1919 wrote that a fair supply of good teachers could always be had. "Of great teachers," he went on, "there are not many in a generation, and nothing is more certain than that such are born and not made. Once in a long while there appears a Huxley, or a Du Bois-Reymond or a William Graham Sumner." But such men are perhaps less rare than Warren or Butler supposed.

Certainly anyone at the University of Illinois in my day could find at least three examples of what a wise, ripe, exact scholar could be: Evarts B. Greene, later at Columbia, so austerely yet genially a guardian of truth as a sacred flame; Clarence W. Alvord, the spiritual father of the Mississippi Valley Historical Association and its *Review*; and Stuart P. Sherman, on one side a learnedly conservative critic of literature, and on the other a rebel exhorting students to follow the advice of Emerson's Aunt Mary Moody: "Do whatever you're afraid of." Anyone attending Columbia when as a young newspaperman I roomed on Morningside Heights could find other great scholars and humanists: William P. Trent in literature, Wesley Clair Mitchell in economics, and Charles A. Beard in government. Once later an almost fabulous figure took sudden physical shape in the Faculty Club, and then disappeared into the grave: nobody present will forget the electrifying experience of hearing John W. Burgess tell with marvelous eloquence, how, standing guard on the battlefield of Murfreesboro, with the dead and dying all about him, he conceived the idea that bloomed into the Faculty of Political Science.

Vitality and breadth the best university men do not need to learn. But as the world of journalism would gladly take gifts of expertness and exactness from academic sources, so the universities can learn something from the journalistic tradition. One lesson it might well learn is the importance of presenting facts and ideas in attractive garb. Sometimes a new discovery, a fresh hypothesis, is so abstruse that it defies popularization; sometimes it is injured by an expression that does not insist on dry analytic precision. But too often the academic tribe simply does not take the trouble to make its work decently alluring. Lincoln Steffens once wrote a brilliant fable which seems to me to be entirely wrong in its implications. He relates that he was walking down Fifth Avenue one fine day with Satan. Debonair, handsomely dressed, darkly compelling, Satan was in gay mood. Suddenly across the street appeared a man bearing a jagged fragment of Truth. Sharp-edged, it flashed and glittered in the sun. "Look, Satan," said Steffens, "that man has hold of some Truth. He could kill you with that if he tried!" But Satan was unperturbed. "No danger," he replied. "He will take that fragment home, chisel it, rub it, dull it, until it has no power whatever."

The fable is arresting, but all wrong. Truth, like the South

41

African diamond, is a dull, cloudy pebble when first discovered. Long labor and the nicest art have to be applied to cut it into those well-polished facets which give it scintillating power. That labor and art the academician too often shuns.

The other lesson to be learned from the tradition of journalism is more important: it is a lesson in devotion to the public interest. Nobody ever worked on a newspaper of the finer type, from *The New York Times* to the *St. Louis Post-Dispatch*, from the *Raleigh News and Observer* to the *Arkansas Gazette*, without feeling that its responsible servants were continuously interested in the betterment of politics, the vindication of social justice, and the elevation of community life. From the day when an editor and a cartoonist smashed the Tweed ring, conscientious journalists have been conspicuous in most of the reformative and constructive movements in public affairs. They have risked the libel suit, the enmity of influential groups, even, like Harry Ashmore, the mob. Think what so quiet and cultivated a man as George William Curtis did for the improvement of our civil service. Why? In part, because the tradition of journalism required it. No comparable tradition exists in our universities. But universities should be more than citadels of science, philosophy, literature, and the arts; they should be citadels with sally-ports for attack. And sometimes we university men, I fear, think too much of our note-padded cells, too little of the breastworks to be manned and armed.

4

Reading in a
Book-Crowded Age

This address, delivered before a responsive audience at the Santa Ana Public Library on April 20, 1967, in commemoration of National Library Week, typifies Allan Nevins's passionate devotion to books and learning. His own concern was the production and popularization of accurate history, but his tastes were so catholic and he read so widely—in literature, the arts, economics, public affairs, and even science—that he felt both disdain and pity for those lacking the inclination to spend most of their leisure hours between the covers of a book. In his eyes librarians were mankind's most essential servants, for they presided over—and distributed—civilization's greatest treasures. In this address he glorifies their devotion to duty and elevates them to hero status. "Dr. Nevins," reported the scribe for the occasion, "emphasized that the responsibility for survival of classical literature and preservation of our cultural past falls on libraries and librarians." So he did, in a message that summed up his own faith in the power and glory of the printed word.

This address, the manuscript of which was found among Allan Nevins's papers after his death, was delivered under the title of "Reading in the New Areas of Learning," although he had given it the title used here. I am indebted for this information and for other facts about the presentation at the Santa Ana Public Library to Josephine Cook, reference librarian in that excellent institution.

All older people, and some younger, will remember Mr. Nicodemus Boffin in the novel by Charles Dickens called *Our Mutual Friend*. Mr. Boffin makes the acquaintance of Mr. Silas Wegg, a man with one leg, whom he sees buying some old ballads. At once Mr. Boffin sets Wegg down as a literary man. He himself cannot read, poor fellow, for his education has been neglected. But he admires Mr. Wegg immensely, for as he puts it, he is "a literary man—with a wooden leg—and all Print is open to him." In fact, he looks upon Wegg with admiration amounting to awe, or "had-miration amounting to haw," because all Print is open to him. And Wegg admits with modesty: "Why, truly, sir, I don't believe you could show me a piece of English print I wouldn't be equal to collaring and throwing." On the spot, too! The upshot of their conversation is that Boffin engages Wegg to read to him a great six-volume work called *Decline and Fall of the Rooshan Empire*, at a crown a week.

This is a piece of Dickens's wonderful humor, but it is something more. It is streaked with compassion for the illiterates, to whom all Print was a closed world. England had plenty of them in Dickens's time, and America had more. In addition, it intimates a fact of which we should be more conscious: the fact that to have all Print open to us is a privilege of the first magnitude, which we should regard with high appreciation and use not only with energy but with enthusiasm. All librarians, and all supporters of public libraries and school libraries, in particular, should feel a touch of enthusiasm over this gift which Mr. Boffin regarded with positive awe. If libraries do not inculcate enthusiasm for reading they might as well be locked up except for a few hours a week.

The duty of a librarian is not only to know books and to hand them out over a counter but to buy them enthusiastically, read them enthusiastically, and insofar as the books deserve it, talk about them enthusiastically. By enthusiasm I mean gusto, to use the word of which William Hazlitt was so fond—gusto for one quality or one content if not for all. It is said of Dr. Johnson that, staying at the house of Bishop Percy, he took Percy's little girl on his knee and remarked to her: "Now tell me, my dear, what you think of the story of *Pilgrim's Progress.*" "I have no ideas about *Pilgrim's Progress,*" said the little maid. "Then I have nothing to do with you," said Dr. Johnson, pushing her off his knee. No doubt he did this playfully; but his reply would have commended itself to Theodore Roosevelt, who found in *Pilgrim's Progress* one of his most effective political images: the Man with the Muckrake. Both Dr. Johnson and President Roosevelt regarded reading with enthusiasm, for it fed their active minds with much of what they most desired.

In my younger days I knew two men who never read a carefully selected book without enthusiasm and never failed to talk about it enthusiastically. Very different men, they had this in common; one was Carl Van Doren, the other was Claude G. Bowers. Neither could be called excessively bookish, for they led very active lives. To hear Carl Van Doren talk of a rather obscure classic, such as Samuel Butler's *Erewhon* or *Erewhon Revisited,* was to be filled with a determination to go home and read all of Samuel Butler at once. To hear him talk of a shining discovery of his, such as *The Education of Henry Adams* when it first became current, was to feel that a door to a brilliant new world lay just in front and must be pushed open at once. Claude G. Bowers's impulse was different. He was not a litterateur like Van Doren; he was a devotee of politics, who loved its drama and never tired of its dramatic personages. Upon all the good books that touched Jeffersonian days, or Jacksonian days, or the days of Theodore Roosevelt, he would descant with effervescent enthusiasm. His emotions were particularly touched by any book which had a background in his native Indiana; and he was as thrilled as Van Doren by a new discovery. How well I remember the positive delight with which he would talk of Lew Wallace, his *Ben Hur* and his autobiography. Nor did he confine himself to America and politics. The story of the Brontës, so poignantly sad, was one of his passions; in his ambassadorial days he had taken his wife and daughter to the Brontë country; and as he told how he positively panted with excitement in ascending the hill in Haworth to the humble parsonage of the Reverend Mr. Patrick Brontë, all the immortal books, *Jane Eyre* and *Wuthering Heights* and Mrs. Gaskell's *Life of Charlotte Brontë*, took on new life.

We all rove about in Mr. Boffin's world of Print; we all read books with some enthusiasm; but how many of us have the kindling impulse to talk about them enthusiastically? If we did so we could make the world more interesting to ourselves and our friends; we could do something to accelerate the pace of letters and culture. Books are powers when people read and talk about them with enthusiastic interest. For proof of this we need only cite two current examples. One is Mr. Ralph Nader's recent book on safety in automobiles. That book affected market demand for cars throughout the country, ruined one particularly vulnerable automobile model, and provoked important legislation by Congress. Another example is the recent book by Norman F. Dacey called *How to Avoid Probate*. Highly controversial, it has stung the legal profession into angry rejoinders, caused professional organizations of lawyers to examine the need for reform in their practices, and led the legislatures in state after state to debate laws for better management of the disposal of inheritance. "It must have touched a nerve." Mr. Nader and Mr. Dacey have shown that a book can move a whole nation.

Their books have little literary dignity, but literature also, when men read it and talk about it with feeling, can be powerfully influential; as influential as Tom Paine's *The Crisis*, or *Uncle Tom's Cabin*, or *The Grapes of Wrath*. A single poem can kindle a nation, or a group of nations.

Men read in accordance with their tastes, needs, and opportunities. The early examples I have given, the books by Samuel Butler and Henry Adams and the Brontës, accord with a taste for *discursive* reading among books of high literary and stylistic quality, but some *restricted* forms of reading may be as elevating, as disciplinary, and as profitable. Lincoln, who holds a secure place among American writers as among American moral preceptors and statesmen, was not a man of wide and discursive reading. Although he showed his innate taste in his high regard for four fundamental classics—the Bible, Plutarch, Shakespeare, and Robert Burns—he was not devoted to belles-lettres. He knew the value of a few books well mastered. "Anybody who gives me a book is my best friend," he said, and his instinct for the books that were useful in maturing his powers was unerring. He trained himself to think by Abel Flint's *System of Geometry and Trigonometry*, by "nearly" mastering six books of Euclid's *Geometry*, and, I think, most of all by studying Blackstone's *Commentaries* upon English law. He nourished his imagination by *The Pilgrim's Progress*, *Robinson Crusoe*, and Aesop's *Fables*, three volumes owned by his stepmother. He corrected his English by Kirkham's *English Grammar*, for which his teacher, Mentor Graham, said he walked eight miles—the very copy is in the Library of Congress. In his busiest years, in the White House during the Civil War, he kept on reading the Bible and Shakespeare, and their cadences ring in his best public utterances. He knew the writings of the fathers of the nation and the main authors and exponents of our Constitution as few men did.

The important facts about Lincoln's reading are that although he used comparatively few books, he read them with intellectual enthusiasm and made them entirely his own. He did not read to amass a great body of information and ideas, as Thomas Jefferson and Theodore Roosevelt did. He read to assist himself to reflect and to express his well-pondered conclusions with precision. He had a deliberate but retentive mind; like a piece of steel, as he put it—"very hard to scratch anything on it, and almost impossible after you get it there to rub it out." According to a Connecticut clergyman who rode on a train with him just after his Cooper Union address, he remarked: "I am never easy now, when I am handling a thought, until I have bounded it north and bounded it south and bounded it east and bounded it west." He was not a

47

copious reader like Jefferson, Roosevelt, and Churchill; he was a precise reader; but he shared their enthusiasm for reading as an intellectual process.

The whole basis and character of reading has changed with the last few decades. It has changed because we have so many more books; in our language alone the United States in 1965 published 28,595 titles and Great Britain published 26,358, while Canada, Australia, South Africa, and India swelled the total. These books fall into many more categories than a half-century ago, so that even a small library like that of Bowdoin College lists its new volumes in twenty-two different categories. The specialization of books goes far beyond previous limits. The student of art finds himself staring, perhaps a little bewildered, at a title like *Art Forms and Civic Life in the Late Roman Empire*; the student of education at a study of *Mental Health and Achievement*; the man interested in literature at a book on *Existentialism and Alienation as Concepts in Criticism*; the worker in government at a treatise on *The Politics of Modernization*; and the psychologist at an enquiry into *The Memory System of the Brain*—to mention only a few recent books of comparative simplicity and obvious importance. Reading grows more and more imperative in our complex society. But reading with enthusiasm amid our flood of books becomes more and more difficult.

How can the problem implicit in these facts be solved? Is it really possible to be a well-read man today, as Macaulay and James Russell Lowell were well-read men a century and a half ago? If it is possible today, is it really desirable? Should one man load his brain with enough knowledge and ideas to make even a pretense of being acquainted with science, with economics, with history, with literature, with religion, and with sociology? The answer to this question is obviously "No." But if he confines himself to a few well-related fields, such as philosophy, religion, and ethics, can he nowadays try to be well read even in this lesser territory? Can he at the same time know a decent smattering of other fields of knowledge? What path should he choose?

It seems to me that every man should know the main literary classics of his own tongue. Our English and American classics are an indispensable foundation of culture, of thought, and of character. If educated members of our society master them, the classics will knit that society together as nothing else can. Beyond this, the specialist should know the cardinal works of his own field well. The educator should know the fundamental texts and the best recent writings in pedagogy since, say, John Dewey; the economist, the standard economic texts from Adam Smith to Keynes and the best recent writings even to econometrics; the biologist, the same mixture of his standard works and the ablest recent advances into the unknown.

All this I may illustrate briefly by reference to my own field of history. Reading in history has undergone the same sweeping revolution that has reshaped other areas of study. The historian today is expected to know all about what is termed the conceptualization of history; that is, the application to historical study of the ideas, tools, and discoveries of all the other social studies—of economics, psychology, geography, anthropology, sociology, social psychology, and so on.

Ideally, the historian today should know as many facts about social structure as Sidney and Beatrice Webb mastered in England or John R. Commons on this side of the Atlantic. He should know as much about psychology in relation to historical change as William James or Josiah Royce knew, so that he could interpret the mind of the South in 1850 and the mind of the South in 1870. He should try to learn as much as R. H. Tawney learned about the way in which political doctrines, religious beliefs, and economic interests are knit together by a thousand threads and should try to display his knowledge as lucidly as Tawney did in *Religion and the Rise of Capitalism*. Perhaps in addition he ought to be able to apply some knowledge of computors to a numerical analysis of his historical data. All this means an enormous amount of reading and thought; but at least some of it can be done, and done with enthusiasm.

I know that students of history ten years ago read with enthusiasm the very effective book of Ruth Benedict applying to history her own form of conceptualization. She was a social anthropologist. Her book was called *The Chrysanthemum and the Sword*. It was written just after the last great war at the request of our government and was a study of the Japanese national character in historical terms. General MacArthur in his postwar administration of Japan found it of the greatest value, and so did many other military and civil officials. What Miss Benedict did in *The Chrysanthemum and the Sword* was to try to analyze and explain the contradictions in Japanese psychology. These were the contradictions, as she wrote, between "their aesthetic sensibility and unimaginative ruthlessness, [their] loyalty and treachery, [their] passionate interest in the new and fervent attachment to the old, [their] discipline and insubordination, [their] stoicism and sentimental self-pity."

This was of great value to the military administration in Japan. It was also of great value, this contribution of the social anthropologist, to the historian of Japan. In fact, the ablest modern historian of Japan, Sir George Sansom, has paid an unusual tribute to it. Sansom tells us that he had often felt impatient and confused because of his failure to grasp the Japanese national character; that he had almost concluded that only the creative artist could do the job—the novelist, perhaps. But when he read *The Chrysanthemum and the Sword* he took heart. "It is a valuable book," he writes, "for not only does it give in very clear language an accurate picture of certain dominant features of Japanese life, but it also encourages us to believe that, in skilled hands, the technique of the social anthropologist may presently be applied with success to the study of other great societies."

If I might give another brief example of the kind of wide reading that benefits the present-day historian, it would be not an anthropologist but a sociologist. Everybody knows that the life span of man has lengthened. When the Roman Empire was in its prime the average citizen could expect to live twenty years. An American citizen born in 1870 had a life expectancy of forty years. A person born in America in 1950 might expect seventy-three years of life. This lengthening of the life span has had a profound effect upon the whole psychology and outlook of man as well as upon his economic position. The first able scholar to show in detail the impact of this new psychology and new economic and social position upon history is, I think, Mr. Peter Laslett of Cambridge, England. He shows that the whole thought and temper of a society in which the average life span was thirty years, as in Elizabethan England, was unescapably quite different from the thought and temper of England today where the average life span is seventy-five years. And of course the whole structure of society has changed; the modern youth allot more time to education. Here again we see that wide reading, to be done with enthusiasm, is essential today in the preparation of the specialist in any field.

Yet at the same time knowledge of our classics remains indispensable; and here it is that the library and the librarian have an invaluable function to perform. They are guardians of our fundamental culture and the disseminators of our classic books. They should be prepared today to perform a duty which we can no longer, alas, count upon our schools to perform. They can see that the truly great books of our civilization are kept available, are called constantly to the attention of the public and especially the youth of the land, and are talked about with enthusiasm. Our school systems once saw to it that the great poets from Shakespeare, Milton, and Tennyson to Longfellow and Walt Whitman, the great novelists from Scott, Dickens, and Hardy to William Dean Howells and Henry James, the great essayists and travel writers, were read with attention and affection. The schools seem guardians of the sacred flame no longer. But into their place can step the librarian, armed with his or her own classic reading, and his or her own vibrant enthusiasm.

51

Part Two

BROADENING
HISTORICAL HORIZONS

Although Allan Nevins placed his faith in narrative history as a means of reaching the wide audience that would benefit from a knowledge of the past, he recognized that the nature of historical studies must constantly change to mirror shifting national attitudes and interests. This meant not only new techniques, but also new subjects for investigation and revised interpretations of older viewpoints as popular tastes altered with the times. One group of his writings, typified in the next five essays, developed this theme. In them Nevins examines the forces underlying shifts in historical interests and urges his fellow practitioners to reexamine the history of business enterprise, newspapers, society, and the local scene if they are to approximate an accurate knowledge of the American past.

5

New Lamps for Old in History

In this essay, delivered originally as an address before the
Society of American Archivists meeting in Dearborn, Michigan, during the autumn of 1953, Allan Nevins examines the
pressures that require the repeated rewriting of history—the
demand of a constantly changing intellectual environment
for fresh interpretations, the opening of new vistas as new
tools are brought into use, the discovery of unused sources—
and illustrates his point by examining the manner in which
recent scholarship has altered our understanding of the past.
The result is a compelling argument for the writing of "new"
history by each generation, as well as a searching appraisal of
the works of scholars who have contributed most to the
reinterpretation of the nation's understanding of its past.
Nevins also suggests that historians should take a fresh look at
the industrial titans of the past—the Rockefellers and
Carnegies and Fords—not as "robber-barons," but as "builders of a strength which civilization found indispensable." His
judgment stirred a flurry of newspaper comment and helped
launch a reappraisal of the role of business in the history of
the United States.

Reprinted by permission of the Society of American Archivists from the *American
Archivist* 17 (January 1954): 3–12. The essay also appeared, with only a few changes,
in the *Saturday Review* 37 (February 4, 1954) as "Should American History Be
Rewritten?"

One curious thing about history, as Guedalla said, is that it really happened. Another curious fact about history is that while it was happening, nobody really understood its meaning.

John Fiske, pausing one day in his young manhood before the window of Little, Brown in Boston, saw a volume within entitled "Pioneers of France in the New World" and noted that its author was identified as the man who had written "The Conspiracy of Pontiac." He remembered that when that earlier volume appeared, he had wondered whether Pontiac was a barbarous chieftain of medieval Europe. He recalled also that some teacher at Harvard had once expressed the view that the French and Indian War was a dull squabble of no real significance to students of history. Passing on, Fiske wondered why anyone should write about French pioneers in America. He lived to pen an essay on Francis Parkman which not only placed that author at the head of American historians (where he yet stands) but recognized that the epic significance of the struggle of Britain and France for the mastery of North America—a significance which Parkman had first expounded—could hardly be overstated. An interpretation of our continental history which nowadays we assume no child could miss had been beyond the grasp of the brilliant young John Fiske in the 1860's.

This idea that history can ever be so well written that it does not need rewriting can be held only by those foolish people who think that history can ever ascertain exact truth. It cannot. We can go further than the assertion of that truism: we can say, "Fortunate for history that it cannot ascertain exact truth!" If history were a photograph of the past it would be flat and uninspiring. Happily, it is a painting; and like all works of art, it fails of the highest truth unless imagination and ideas are mixed with the paints. A hundred photographs of London Bridge look just alike and convey altogether a very slight percentage of the truth, but Turner's Thames and Whistler's Thames, though utterly different, both convey the river with a deeper truth.

All parts of our history are always being rewritten; no segment of it, from 1492 to 1952, is not now in need of vigorous rewriting. Whenever an expert applies himself to the scrutiny of a special area, he at once sounds a lusty call for more searching exploration of the terrain. Douglas Freeman, carrying Washington through the Revolution, agreed with Bernard Knollenberg, writing a history of that war, that every part of the Revolutionary struggle needs the most searching re-examination and the boldest reinterpretation. Merrill Jensen states in the preface to his study of the Confederation that the entire period 1783–89 demands a study that will embrace every State and every act of Congress. There are men who believe that the historical study of the Civil War period has but just begun—and they are right. Margaret Leech, just completing a study of the McKinley administration, is convinced that a hundred research workers should be set to exploration of the dark nooks and secret crannies of the time.

"In vain the sage, with retrospective eye," writes Pope, "would from the apparent what conclude the why." The three main reasons why history constantly needs reinterpretation include something more than the impossibility of ever learning all the truth about all the motives and actions of the past.

The chief of the three reasons is the need of every generation for a reinterpretation to suit its own preconceptions, ideas, and outlook. Every era has its own climate of opinion. It thinks it knows more than the preceding era; it thinks it takes a wider view of the universe. Every era, too, is affected by cataclysmic events which shift its point of view: the French Revolution, the Metternichian reaction, the movement for national unification in Italy, the United States, and Germany, the apogee of Manchester liberalism, and so on down to the multiple crises of our atomic age. We see the past through a prism which glows and sparkles as new lights catch its facets. Much of the rewriting of history is a readjustment to this prism. George Bancroft's spectrum was outmoded a few years after his laborious "last revision"; Charles A. Beard's begins to be outworn today, for we possess what Beard would have called a new frame of reference.

As a second reason, new tools of superior penetrative power are from time to time installed in the toolshed of even our rather unprogressive race of historians. Our council for research in the social sciences (it should be studies) justly emphasizes the value of overlapping disciplines. Much could be said for the contention that the best historians nowadays are prepared in some other field than that of history. Thus Wesley Clair Mitchell, the historian of the greenbacks, of business cycles, and of the ebb and flow of economic activity, whose National Bureau of Economic Research inspired so much fruitful historical writing, was trained as an economist. (He also was trained by John Dewey, who gave courses under all sorts of titles, but "every one of them dealt with the same subject—how we think.") Beard was trained as a political scientist. Parrington was trained as a student of literature. Carl Becker was trained in European history but wrote in the American field. James Henry Breasted was first trained in theology, a fact which stood him in good stead when this pioneer of Egyptology in America began to trace the development of conscience and religion in the ancient East. Not one historian in fifty knows as much as he should of the tool called statistics, or of psychology, or of economic geography, or of ecology. The kinship between Halford J. Mackinder, the geographer, and Frederick J. Turner, the historian, in loosing seminal ideas showed what the geographer could learn from history and the historian from geography.

But the third great reason why history is rewritten is simply because the constant discovery of new materials necessitates a recasting of our view of the past. We might think that this would one day cease, but it never does. Everyone who has laboriously mapped any historical subject knows how steadily the dust of new facts falls upon that map, blurring some lines and defining new ones. Happy are those who live to rewrite their books, as even Parkman rewrote one of his—"LaSalle and the Great West." One would have said that all the materials for a history of the Revolution had been assembled in print by the innumerable agencies, local, State, and national, devoted to that effort, but

Freeman assures us that the great depositories like the Massachusetts Historical Society, the American Philosophical Society, and
the main State libraries, bulge with unstudied documents. One
would have said that all the material for the history of the
Confederate War Office had been studied and restudied; but,
behold: the diary of the third officer of that department, Kean, is
suddenly deposited in the University of Virginia, and we find a
complete reassessment of the Southern military administration
possible.

Thus the idea that history is photography is set at naught. It is
art; it constantly requires a new mixture of pigments, new points
of view, new manipulation of light and shade; and as an art it
presents an endless challenge to the writer who perceives that the
highest truth of history will always transcend a statement of fact;
that indeed, historical fact is but a foundation for the truth won
by imagination and intellectual power.

The best history is always interpretive, but this does not mean
that the best history is consciously or ostentatiously interpretive.
The work of the historical masters, from Thucydides to Trevelyan,
illustrates the fact that interpretation is most effective when
implicit rather than explicit. The true historical attitude is a
search for truth about a situation, force, or event—the War of
1812, the abolitionist impulse, Pearl Harbor—which slowly,
painfully, accurately, dredges up an unforeseen interpretation.
That is, history properly operates by the inductive, not the
deductive, method. The merit of an Olympian historian like
Parkman is that he says, in effect: "Let us collect and collate all
the relevant facts, and find what conclusions emerge from their
impartial analysis." The cardinal weakness of a controversial
historian like Beard is that he repeatedly gave the impression—
perhaps falsely—of having said to himself: "Let us take this
provocative theory of the fact, and see how impressive an array of
facts we can collect in its support." Ideas in history, that is, should
be applied in subordination to the ascertainment of all the facts,
and not in control of the ascertainment of one picked body of

facts. Hence it is that nothing could be more absurd than to try to predict in advance the interpretations to be applied to our history by future writers—who will certainly go their own way. But we may legitimately make some guesses as to the general drift of some of the new interpretations lying ahead of us.

As American history lengthens and the past falls into longer perspective, we tend not so much to discard major interpretations entirely as to place new ones beside them; not so much to substitute one simple synthesis for another as to embrace old monistic views in a new and complex synthesis. Let us take a sweeping view of the first century of our national history, 1775–1875. In that tremendously variegated and baffling sea of events, forces, personalities, tendencies, and fortuities, let us assume that three great dominant developments lift themselves above all others.

These three—let us assume—are the establishment of American independence, political, economic, and finally cultural, from Europe; the westward movement for the conquest and development of the continent; and the abolition of slavery and a Southern way of life in a civil war which vindicated national unity. Some students, to be sure, would select other elements in our historical fabric, but three special students out of five and nine lay readers out of ten would, I believe, choose these. Now it is evident to a cursory view that each of the three lent itself at first to a simple monistic interpretation, expounded in the work even of subtle historians, and that within one or two generations this simple view of the past was replaced by a dual or multiple interpretation. What had been a flat telescopic image was given depth and reality by a stereopticon lens.

The Revolution seemed to our primitive historians, down to and including George Bancroft, simply a political upheaval; richly interesting as it was, it was the epic story of the establishment of political liberty in a new nation in a new world, as a guiding torch to all mankind. Before long, however, historians doubled the lens. They showed that the Revolution was a social no less than a political convulsion; that the internal transformation of America was quite as significant as the external; that a broad sequence of changes was set in motion, or rather accelerated, which rolled inexorably on through the Jeffersonian and Jacksonian eras. Some of this truth was visible to that early historian Richard Hildreth, who was as realistic as he was conservative; more of it to Moses Coit Tyler and John Bach McMaster; and all of it to a later school headed by J. Franklin Jameson, Parrington, and others.

The westward movement and the taming of the continent were first treated in terms of the transforming impact of man on nature; the expulsion of the Indian and wild beast, the hewing out of pioneer farms, the building of roads, and the ultimate planting of school and factory where the fur trader had trod. Then arose the eminent historian who perceived an equally rich meaning in the impact of nature, the wilderness, upon man; who explained how the frontier converted the European into an American, how it transformed men of caste-ridden minds into belligerently democratic individualists, how it manufactured nationalists out of separatists, and how, in short, it altered the whole pattern of thought, emotion, and conduct. This binocular view of the westward march was infinitely more interesting and arresting than the old monocular view. Parkman, Justin Winsor, Reuben Gold Thwaites, Edward Eggleston, Theodore Roosevelt, H. H. Bancroft, had been roughly accurate in their delineation of the westward thrust, but their interpretation had lacked depth and distinctness. When Turner substituted his perceptive and penetrating image of the frontier for this flat photograph, it flashed into life, color, and meaning; and behind Turner came a new body of writers who saw with his eyes.

To Hermann Von Holst the abolition of slavery seemed to mark the climax of 70 years of national life. America, to this German of Lithuanian birth, this hater of Russian and Prussian tyrannies, was the home of freedom and democracy; and the development and exemplification of these two inestimable gifts had been its principal mission in the world. But Liberty in

61

America had suffered from a cancerous social institution—slavery —which sadly impaired her usefulness in the sisterhood of nations and threatened her very life. This interpretation possessed more validity than some recent writers have been willing to allow; indeed, within limits it was entirely valid. But it was too obvious, and it left too many historical phenomena of the period unexplained. The antagonism of North and South by 1860 transcended slavery, even though the conflict over slavery was certainly its central element. The simple monistic view of our great upheaval in the middle of the nineteenth century had to be amplified.

Hence arose the interpretation of that upheaval as one which included conflicts of economic interest, of philosophies of life, and of ingrained prejudice; a conflict between the eighteenth-century and the nineteenth-century mind; a conflict between the nascent industrialism of the North and the entrenched agrarianism of the South. Such an interpretation had been adumbrated by Southern politicians and publicists like Yancey during the war; it was stated with emphasis by a Southern historian, Percy A. Greg, soon after Appomattox. It had the merit of both widening and deepening the canvas. It demonstrated the links which joined Thaddeus Stevens, the antislavery covenanter, with Thad Stevens, the ironmaster, and Thad Stevens, the high-tariff legislator. If used as a constructive interpretation and not as a cloak for our political shortcomings and errors or as a means of glozing over the hideous blot of slavery, it had immeasurable value.

So much for three great developments in American history: the severance from Europe, the conquest and settling of the continent, and the elimination of slavery and the State rights doctrine as retarding agencies in our national growth. The character of a fourth great development, accomplished and sealed in the last 50 years of our national life, can hardly be missed. On that new phase of our history, too, general agreement will perhaps be found. We have become first a great world power, and then the great world power. We have moved first into the open arena of world affairs, and then into the very center of that arena. We now view our national past from the vantage point of this new turn and with the changed perspective which it gives us.

Just as John Fiske saw our history from 1607 to 1789 as an evolutionary preparation for the gift to the world of practical democracy and the Anglo-American principle of self-government in the shape of our Constitution and Federal system, just as Von Holst saw the whole period from 1776 to 1861 as a preparation for the vindication of human liberty and national unity, so now we have historians who view our whole national life as an unconscious preparation for the time when we should become Protector of the Faith for all democratic peoples; when, having turned away from Western European affairs until we gained first place among the nations, we returned to them as the pivot and support of Western European civilization. These writers regard American history not in terms of the Western continent but in terms of an Atlantic community. We find, indeed, that we never left that community; that the Seven Years War was our first world war, the Revolution our second; that we have but awakened to our consciousness of a global role. And when these historians write of our national future, they speak not of short-term objects, but of what Lincoln called "man's vast future."

This tremendous change of the past 40 or 50 years—this emergence of America to the leadership of the Western World—will undoubtedly affect our children's children, and the long generations to come, in the most sweeping way. It will loom up, in time to come, as tremendously as the great changes which preceded it—as the Revolution, internal and external, the American conquest of the frontier and the frontier's conquest of the American, the death of slavery, and the birth of machine industry. But the full significance of this development will not become evident until it, too, is given the dual or multiple interpretation that historians gave these older developments. We shall not understand its essential character until all the accompanying phenomena, social, economic, and intellectual, have been analyzed, and some mind as electric as Parrington's and as penetrating as Turner's has pierced nearer its heart. What then will be its significance? That is a question we cannot answer; it is for the oncoming generation of historians.

My own guess is that this great development by which America has been projected into world leadership, with all the exhilarations and perils, the opportunities and costs of that position, will in some fashion be connected, by future interpreters, with the advent of an age of mass action, mass production, and mass psychology in American life. From being one of the most unorganized, the most invertebrate of nations, in 1860, we have grown into the most powerfully and efficiently organized people on the globe. Our population of 155,000,000 disposes of its resources through such mass combinations, political, social, and economic, as mankind never saw before. Our thinking in 1865 was still individual thinking; today it is largely mass thinking, shaped and colored by mass media of unparalleled and sometimes dismaying potency—press, radio, television, cinema. No one can go to what were recently primitive frontier communities in America—say Texas and California—without being struck, and a little appalled, by the complexity and efficiency with which they have organized their life. It was our mass production which won the two last world wars; it is our genius for making big organizations work which has built the means for saving Western democracy since the latest world war. Our national outlook, once that of the individualistic pioneer, has become a social outlook. Without this pervasive internal change, our new position in the world would have been impossible.

The striking shift in our character and our world position in the last half century of course has some direct results, already visible, in our interpretation of history. We are evincing a greater militancy in asserting the virtues of our political and social system. The apologetic attitude of the years of the Great Depression is gone. We can henceforth be more confident and more energetic in asserting that our way of life, called decadent by our enemies, has proved itself historically to be freer, more flexible, and more humane than any other in history. We can be as emphatic and frank as ever in describing our past weaknesses, from slavery to slums, but we shall insist more rigorously on the fundamental healthiness of our system and on its proved ability to mend its defects and give us a constantly self-regenerating society.

We shall also evince, I think, a tendency to insist more emphatically on the fundamental unity of the United States with Western Europe and the various other nations sprung from Western Europe. All kinds of Western institutions and virtues now find their principal stronghold in the United States. The literature written in the English tongue increasingly has its main center of vitality in America, a fact well recognized by the London *Times* Literary Supplement. The Roman Catholic Church, like the Protestant churches, finds its chief springs of wealth and power in the United States. The Atlantic Community, as many publicists term it, has taken the place of the former division between Europe and the Americas. Oldtime quarrels between America and Western Europe have lost a great part of the significance which was once attached to them. What does the War of 1812 count for, compared with the maintenance and growth of the political, social, and cultural ties that have made the English-speaking nations so nearly a unity? The nationalistic view of our history will increasingly be replaced by the international view, treating America as part of a great historic civilization with the Atlantic its center, as the Mediterranean was the center of the ancient world; with the tides of population, power, and influence first moving from Europe to America, and then beginning to flow in the opposite direction.

We may look forward also to a more appreciative attitude toward our material strength and to a more scientific treatment of the factors which have created this material power. In the past our historians were apologetic about our love of the dollar, our race to wealth, our interest in material objects; they deprecated our worship of size and deplored our boastfulness about steel tonnage, grain production, and output of machinery. Clio, with her tradition of devotion to moral values, was scornful of any others. Our writers in general—for the historians but followed the poets, the novelists, and the dramatists—intimated that America had grown too fast, too coarsely, too muscularly; they exalted the rural virtues as against industrial might, the rarefied air of the study as against the smoky atmosphere of the mill.

Without denying that many accompaniments of our swift industrialization were unhappy, we can now assert that this historical attitude was erroneous. The nation grew none too fast. We can see today that all its wealth, all its strength, were needed to meet a succession of world crises—and we still dwell in a crisis era. Had we applied restrictions to keep our economy small, tame, and timid, we would have lost the First World War. Had the United States not possessed the mightiest oil industry, the greatest steel industry, the largest automotive factories, the most efficient machine-tool industry, the best technological schools, and the most ingenious working force in the world, we would indubitably have lost the Second World War. Were we significantly weaker today in technical skills, in great mills and factories, and the scientific knowledge which gave us priority with the atomic bomb and hydrogen bomb, all Western Europe would be cowering—we ourselves would perhaps be cowering—before the knout held by the Kremlin. The architects of our material growth—the men like Whitney, McCormick, Westinghouse, Rockefeller, Carnegie, Hill, and Ford—will yet stand forth in their true stature as builders of a strength which civilization found indispensable. As that realization spreads, industrial archives like that created in Dearborn by the vision of the Ford Motor Company will take their place as equal in importance to the political and cultural archives so long indispensable to students of our past.

It will yet be realized that the industrial revolution in the United States came none too soon and none too fast; and that the ensuing mass-production revolution, as yet so little understood by Americans, was not born a day too early. That is a fact which may well be stated in this birthplace of mass production—Detroit. It is

66

a fact well appreciated in Manchester and London, in Paris and Berlin, and in Moscow. We shall also come to realize that the turmoil and human suffering which inescapably accompanied the industrial revolution and the mass-production revolution were not after all a tremendous price to pay for their benefits. The price was smaller in the United States than in foreign lands. The industrial revolution cost less in human travail here than it did in England, where it first came to birth; less than in Germany or Japan; far less than it is costing in Russia. Here is a wide field for the rewriting of American history and for the re-education of the American people, a field in which all archivists may contribute their due share.

Our material might, to be sure, is valuable only as it supports and carries to victory great moral ideas, only as it buttresses a civilization in which spiritual forces are predominant. But the fundamental difference between the democratic world and the totalitarian world lies precisely in the superior position which we give to moral and spiritual values. It is we, not our enemies, who have the right to talk about what Lincoln called man's vast future, for we really value men as individual souls. Behind our dreams of man's vast future, we mobilize an unconquerable strength. In time, when future historians look back on this period, which to us is so full of struggle, sacrifice, and anxious uncertainty, they will perhaps give it an interpretation of exalted character. They may say: "The era in which the United States, summoning all its strength, led democracy in winning the First World War, the Second World War, and the ensuing struggle against the Communist tyranny, was one of the great eras of history. It stands invested with all the radiance of the Periclean era, the Elizabethan era, and the era of Pitt and the long struggle against Napoleon."

6

Business and the Historian

If a future biographer of Allan Nevins seeks to isolate his two greatest enthusiasms, he might well single out his eagerness to convert the past into a molding force for the present and his determination to win for the nation's business leaders a fair trial at the bar of historical judgment. This does not mean that Nevins was a tub thumper for trusts and corporations; he bowed to no one in condemning abuses of corporate power in the late nineteenth century. But he was among the first to recognize that for every Jay Gould or Jim Fisk there was also an Anson G. Phelps or a Peter Cooper who aided the nation's growth by their enlightened business policies. When he addressed the annual dinner meeting of the American Petroleum Institute's Division of Refining in New York in 1953, he chose the revision of business history as his theme, isolating the reasons why scholars had misunderstood and misrepresented past industrialists and urging present-day corporations to open their records as a first step toward a more equitable treatment. The biographies of John D. Rockefeller and Henry Ford that he later produced show how well he followed his own guidelines.

Reproduced with permission from the *American Petroleum Institute Proceedings* 33, no. 1 (1953):85–89.

How many Americans—how many New Yorkers, even—
have ever heard of the "cotton triangle"? Probably very few. Yet
the "cotton triangle" made the city of New York great, and
shaped a large segment of American history. Everyone knows,
presumably, that the Erie Canal made an important contribution
to the growth of this metropolis, for it enabled New York to take
the lion's share of western trade. But the "cotton triangle" was
almost equally influential.

This was a system of trade by which New York ships carried
cotton from the southern ports of Charleston, Savannah, Mobile,
or New Orleans, to Europe—most of all to Liverpool and Havre.
They then brought back to New York a cargo of general freight
and immigrants. Selling the cargo in New York, they took on
more freight to carry down to the southern ports.

Between 1830 and 1860 this triangular trade contributed
enormously to the wealth of our city. During this period the
cotton bale was the most important single item in American
commerce. New York shipping was hungry for commodities to be
carried overseas. Vessels could have made an empty run to
England and France to bring back merchandise; but it was about
three times as profitable to carry cotton eastward and transport
mixed freight on the two other legs of the triangle.

Had it not been for this "cotton triangle," the whole course of
American history might have been different. It was within the
power of the South to create its own great ports and shipping
businesses in Charleston, Mobile, and New Orleans. It could have
shipped out its own cotton and brought back its own mixed
freight—English textiles, cutlery, farm implements, china, and the
rest.

New York would have lost much of the impetus toward its
growth. The 800,000 tons of American shipping engaged in
carrying raw cotton to Europe in 1852, and the 40,000 and more
American seamen manning these vessels, would have been largely
southern. Charleston, Mobile, and New Orleans would have
accumulated capital and begun to take up manufacturing. When

the Civil War began, the South would have had a merchant navy convertible to war uses. It would have had trained sailors; it would have had workshops, a stronger railroad system, and an imposing array of business talent. Actually Charleston, Savannah, and Mobile, taken together, in 1860 had only 91,000 people and almost no factories. The economic strength of the North overwhelmed the South.

And why did the North press so far ahead while the South missed its opportunity? Primarily because of the superior enterprise of New York men of business. New York not only had famous merchant princes, like John Jacob Astor, Archibald Gracie, and Robert Lenox, but a host of more obscure entrepreneurs like Jeremiah Thompson, who did most to found the Black Ball Packet Line and to block out the "cotton triangle."

It had builders of marine engines like James P. Allaire; bankers ready to invest money in trade, like Moses Taylor, the head of the City Bank; it had courageous importers and traders like William E. Dodge, Seth Low, William H. Aspinwall, and Moses H. Grinnell.

In the South the planters regarded manufacturing and trade with disdain. The landed gentry left business to clerks and bookkeepers while they devoted themselves to agriculture and politics. But New York, with a chamber of commerce which dated back to 1768, had a different tradition. It was the New Yorker Robert Fulton who gave the world its first successful river steamboat; another New Yorker, Nicholas Roosevelt, who put the first steamboat on the Ohio and Mississippi; still another New Yorker, Moses Rogers, who took from an East River yard the first steamship, the *Savannah*, to cross the Atlantic. The New Yorkers who put on the ocean the Black Ball Line, the Red Star Line, the Collins Line, and the innumerable packets saw to it that the metropolis by 1860 handled two-thirds of all the nation's imports and one-third of its exports.

Now American historians have until lately been very much like the southern planters of rice, cotton, and sugar; they have regarded trade and manufacturing with disdain. They have been intensely concerned with political history—the history of the State.

Our first great historian, Bancroft, was trained by a German economic historian, Heeren; but he turned his back on economic history, and dealt entirely with political forces and statecraft.

Our historians have shown an unfailing interest in exploitation and the conquest of the West. Parkman wrote an immortal account of the tremendous struggle of the French and English for the mastery of the American continent. Theodore Roosevelt dealt with the "Winning of the West"—the Ohio Valley. Others, like Mr. De Voto, are still concerned with the theme. Still another school of historians, led by John Bach McMaster, has tried to recreate the history of the plain people, the masses. A vigorous school under Vernon Parrington, a great name, has delineated the history of ideas and thought. We have had a line of able military historians—among them, Douglas Freeman.

But American historical writers in general, like James Hammond and Alexander H. Stephens and Jefferson Davis, have turned an indifferent shoulder to business history. Like the southern planters, they have lost a great deal more than they supposed by this chilly disdain.

The neglect of business history was not merely capricious or accidental. We can identify perfectly clear historical reasons at its root:

1. A certain social prejudice entered into it. The Old World notion that the warrior, the churchman, and the statesman were the important figures in society, and that the tradesman stood on an inferior, less dignified level, took firm root in early America.

The historian William Hickling Prescott spoke contemptuously of the staple American occupation of "making money." The historian Parkman was scornful of what he called our "weak-kneed industrial civilization."

2. Many historians thought business dull. To them war seemed vividly interesting . . . as it is; the struggles of political parties and

the rivalries of Hamilton and Jefferson, Clay and Jackson, Lincoln and Douglas, seemed full of color and suspense . . . as they are; the clash and sparkle of ideas, from William Penn to Henry George, seemed fraught with vital significance . . . as they are. They never realized that business has its wars, its group and party struggles, and its clashing ideas—also replete with interest. They only dimly comprehended that economic forces, which have to be studied first in single businesses, shape the conflicts of parties, States, and ideological interests. Business is bookkeeping, they said, and bookkeeping is dull; they did not understand that business is life, and the very foundation stuff of life. But historians had more creditable reasons for avoiding business.

3. Business and industry are sordid, they said. They are shot full of greed and anti-social impulses. They are on a low ethical plane.

In the generation or two after the Civil War this was true. The United States had industrialists of the highest ideals—men like Peter Cooper and Abram S. Hewitt, whose lives I wrote; like Anson G. Phelps and William E. Dodge, whose careers have just been traced by Robert G. Cleland; like the Roeblings, father and son, and the Studebaker brothers.

It also had men of a vulgar, dishonest, debased character, whose careers drew an ugly smirch across American history—the Jim Fisks, the Jay Goulds, and the Collis P. Huntingtons, the men who made Amalgamated Copper infamous.

It was natural that journalists and the historians should fasten their attention on the darker pages in the record—not only natural, but within limits healthful.

Henry Adams and Charles Francis Adams—scions of a great family, men of unimpeachable veracity, and good historians—brought out their famous book, *Chapters of Erie*, in 1871. It did much to set a pattern for others to follow.

A sheaf of books on railroad abuses followed the Hepburn investigation. Henry Demarest Lloyd, an emotionally unbalanced and intellectually dishonest crusader, began his attack on Standard Oil in 1881, and brought it to a climax in 1894 with his book,

Wealth Against Commonwealth. A few years later the muck-rakers—Ida M. Tarbell, Lincoln Steffens, David Graham Phillips, George Kibbe Turner—were in full cry.

Beyond question the indictment had great truth. Business was sordid, and in part anti-social. It was natural that the attitude of the critics and muckrakers, especially as it was backed by reformers from Theodore Roosevelt and Woodrow Wilson onward, should be transferred to the minds of teachers and the pages of standard texts. The uglier passages in business history were emphasized, the brighter chapters forgotten. The fact that business morals, like political morals, were in a state of evolution upward was ignored.

A fourth reason for the injustice done by historians to business lay in the influence of Marxian thought. Socialist writers, and after them the communists, were eager to show that private enterprise means private rapacity; that capitalism is identical with corruption; and that the business leader is the business pirate.

No extreme leftist ever gained a real standing as a historian. But such books as Gustavus Meyer's *History of the Great American Fortunes,* Matthew Josephson's *The Robber Barons,* and Lewis Corey's *Life of J. P. Morgan*—all written by avowed socialists—nevertheless did a good deal to color the attitudes of more careful writers and teachers of history.

They stated the case against capitalism with vigor, eloquence, and an apparent buttress of documented thought—and they were not answered!

Gustavus Meyer, for example, whose book picked out all the more lurid and discreditable episodes in the careers of John Jacob Astor, Commodore Vanderbilt, Jay Gould, Jay Cooke, E. H. Harriman, and other magnates—rigidly suppressing whatever was creditable—boasted until the end of his long life that not a single statement in his work had ever been disproved.

Everybody who reads Josephson's or Corey's books carefully perceives that they are tendentious, one-sided, and meant to serve the Marxian cause. But they are entertaining; they have an air of verisimilitude; they are placed on history-reading shelves in colleges and universities; they affect the thought of young men and women. They did something to give even sober, conservative historians a prejudiced attitude toward business.

Nobody has written a comprehensive history of the great American fortunes representing such hard, devoted labor as Meyer put into his pamphleteering work; nobody has written an impartial account of the business era after the Civil War as swift-paced, colorful, and entertaining as Josephson's book. Frederick Lewis Allen has indeed published an effective life of J. P. Morgan, but it is short—and not based on Morgan's papers, which are still withheld. The vigor of the Marxian onslaught, although it obviously produced bad history, did something to distort the vision of scholars.

And this mention of the lock-and-key treatment of J. P. Morgan's papers suggests the final and most important reason for the historian's failure to deal adequately with business; i.e., the sources have largely been closed. The House of Morgan explains that its relations with clients were those of a confidential agent, and that to open its papers would be a breach of faith. This may be true. No such reason can be offered to justify the refusal of railroads, large manufacturing concerns, and mercantile houses to open their records.

Down until 1900 the business historian had almost no materials upon which to work; down even to 1925 he had very few. Until the rise of the various university schools of business, or business administration, it was difficult to give would-be business historians a specialized training; and even then they long had no proper facilities. A brilliant young writer who wanted to deal with the history of politics in Grover Cleveland's era found the libraries stuffed with manuscript collections. A brilliant young historian who wished to deal with business development in the Cleveland era found no business data. He could write an entertaining little history of how Bell invented the telephone, but he could not even begin to write a history of the Bell Telephone Company.

For these half-dozen reasons, then—the old social prejudice in favor of the warrior, cleric, and statesman; the belief that business is dull; the conviction, long half true, that it is sordid; the influence of the Marxians; and the want of a proper body of source material—the historian fell short of his duty.

Meanwhile, what of business? The lack of materials was in a double sense its own fault. In too many instances business failed to collect, keep, and assort its records. After 5 years, or 10 years, all but the most precious documents went into the furnace. And, even when the records were all kept, the corporation regarded them as private property to be held for strictly private uses. A railroad system, a meat-packing house, a steel company would say: "They're nobody's business but our own." Even when the president of a corporation was ready to give the historian access, some director would raise an angry objection: "What good would it do to invite the historian in?" he would ask. "How can we be sure that he is not a wolf in sheep's clothing?—that he is not another Gustavus Meyer masquerading as a Francis Parkman? And what untold possibilities of harm lie in his entry? Why, he may find out about those frauds on the government back in the 1890's—about that treasurer who was dismissed for embezzlement, although it was all hushed up—about those shady advertising practices! No! Be discreet! Let's keep the dirt to ourselves."

My impression is that the desire for secrecy in the past arose from two main reasons: one minor, the other major. The minor reason was a fear that public relations would be injured by disclosure of the full truth—the bad as well as the good pages of the record.

A dozen years ago I wrote the history of Standard Oil under John D. Rockefeller, a book re-issued this spring in new form with much new material. Rockefeller throughout his long presidency of the Standard Oil Company set his face firmly against any historical searching of the record, any exposure of the past.

Now the Standard Oil story was in the main highly constructive, tremendously creative, and in most lights creditable. The personal record of Rockefeller was that of a wise, farsighted, broadminded organizing genius, who in business built far more than he destroyed. Rockefeller and the Standard Oil were blamed for much which, had the full truth been known, would not have been laid at their door. The public somehow got the impression that they invented railroad rebating and profited exclusively by it. The fact was that railroad rebates long antedated the establishment of Standard Oil; were almost universal from 1860 to 1906; and benefited the Standard's competitors as much as itself. But for a brief period at the close of the 1870's and beginnings of the 1880's the Standard did exact a rebate not only on its own shipments, but those of competitors.

The public also got the impression that the Standard's marketing methods were extremely brutal; that, as Miss Tarbell put it, the company "cut to kill." But the truth is that Standard Oil was not a unitary company; that there were units of the federation, viz., Chess, Carley, and Waters Pierce, which could not be controlled by the central offices; and that they committed indefensible acts, which Rockefeller and his associates condemned. It was true also that one manufacturing unit, in Rochester, did some rough work in trampling down a very rough competitor. That was about all.

But Rockefeller knew he could not defend what was defensible without admitting what was indefensible; he could not vindicate the home office without placing heavy blame on Daniel O'Day; on Chess, Carley, and Waters Pierce, and the Everests in Rochester. He could not prove that most of the Standard's record on rebates was decent without confessing that some patches of it were indecent. And so he was against explanations, publicity, or history.

The major reason for the old-fashioned emphasis of business on secrecy is somewhat more admissible: Business feared that its relations with the government would be injured by the full truth. For a long half-century Americans strove to work out a reasonable system of governmental oversight and control. This was done by a halting, irregular, stumbling succession of steps—with much trial and error, much fumbling and embarrassment on both sides.

Laws were passed which did not, and could not, work—which were really against the public interest. The old state laws forbidding companies under state charter to own property in other states, or stock in other companies, for example, were narrow, parochial, and by 1880 quite anachronistic. It is an open question whether the Sherman anti-trust act was not a mistake. While the law remained uncertain, and while prosecuting officers and courts were attacking business on grounds which business often considered unreasonable, a state of great uneasiness prevailed. Railroad pools, for example, were regarded by many of the ablest and most statesmanlike Americans as just and healthy; the interstate commerce act of 1887 made them illegal—but pooling did not die. The whole province of business-government relations was enveloped in a haze which is even yet not entirely dispelled. This being so, companies were loath to open their records to the public gaze. "I'll never sign a letter," one corporation executive told me in the 1930's, "without feeling that Thurman Arnold is looking over my shoulder at its text." Until a fair stability in the legal position of business was attained, secrecy seemed to many businessmen desirable, and to some indispensable.

Today we have in most areas a fair stability. Railroads at least are no longer uncertain of their status under the law. The law respecting combinations has been clarified. Most corporations occupy an unassailable position. A few concerns may still be a bit uneasy; most of them enjoy a sense of confidence. They can throw open their records without qualm.

More of them would unquestionably do this if they had complete confidence in the historian, just as more good historians would be drawn into this special field if they had complete confidence in business. And why is it that this mutual confidence is not what it ought to be?

Some of the reasons are implicit in what I have just said. Many businessmen fear that scholars are tainted with Marxianism, or radicalism, or an irresponsible attitude toward great corporations.

Many scholars fear that businessmen are a bit sordid and grasping. The main reason, however, lies a little deeper.

A fundamental difference exists between the psychology of the historian and the psychology of the business leader. It is complex and hard to define, but it exists. The professional historian, like scholars and writers in general, tends to take a liberal attitude toward the purposes and instrumentalities of government. He believes that the State was made for man, not man for the State; that the government is to be used by the people for their general betterment; that an expansion of the functions and powers of government is often a very healthy thing.

He believes, too, that the common man—and particularly the common American—needs only to be given due opportunities to be capable of constant progress; that he is a person, in Thomas Jefferson's phrase, of "indefinite perfectibility." This common man ought to have the help of his fellows, of business, and of his fate in his march toward perfectibility. The scholar and writer also looks at recent events and current problems in a way peculiar to himself. He thinks of them a little bit *sub specie aeternitate*. The historian, in particular, sees them as fitting into a long pattern of past, present, and future. He, therefore, constantly analyzes present and future.

Now the businessman's psychology, if I may venture an analysis, is somewhat different on all these heads. The businessman takes a dubious, grudging, half-hostile attitude toward the purposes and instrumentalities of the State. He is suspicious of government. He believes that it is constantly encroaching on his own domain; that, when glib leaders use government, as they say, for the betterment of the people in general, they often hurt business directly and the people indirectly.

The ordinary industrialist, again, has a more limited faith in the potentialities of the common American than Thomas Jefferson or Charles A. Beard had. Especially if he is an employer of the run-of-the-mill labor, he is likely to be hardboiled about human capacity. Henry Ford in 1915 had unbounded faith in ordinary human beings. His factory superintendents, like Charles Sorensen, had very little faith in their hands unless they were driven. It was one of the tragedies of Ford's career that the Sorensen idea triumphed over his own ideal. Most industrial leaders believe more in perspiration to develop human capacities, and less in inspiration, than most writers.

Finally, the businessman thinks very little of the long past and the longer future. He is of necessity earnestly intent on the present, and on the emerging problems of tomorrow and next week. He finds safety in short views, and danger in guesses at future patterns.

These differences in psychology make for a certain gulf between businessman and historian. They augment the mutual suspicions and misunderstandings of the past. But it is fortunately not an unbridgeable gulf, and piers are being thrown out on both sides.

We are making progress. I could greatly expand this speech by listing some of the hopeful partnerships effected in recent years between business and the historian. The Standard of New Jersey, by a remarkably generous grant to the Business History Foundation, organized by Professor Gras and other Harvard scholars, has made possible a multi-volume history which is expected to reach a high standard of scholarliness and literary quality.

The Standard of Indiana has similarly made possible, by a grant to Allegheny College, an impartial history by Paul H. Giddens.

The Bigelow-Sanford Carpet Company has opened all its source materials to Harvard University, two scholars from which are writing a complete history of that concern.

The American Life Convention, the trade association of American and Canadian life insurance companies, has given full access to its records to Professor R. C. Buley of Indiana University for the writing of a comprehensive history of life insurance in the United States and the Dominion of Canada.

The Detroit Edison Company, by a grant to Wayne University, supplemented by technical assistance, has provided for a candid independent history of its development. Numerous corporations are either putting their archives in order for historians, like General Motors, or have deposited them in public archives, like the Burlington and the Illinois Central Railroad records—which have gone to the Newberry Library.

This list could be lengthened. It is encouraging. But more encouraging still is the fact that a general pattern for sound work in business history is being perfected. No longer is it possible for a corporation to indulge the idea that it can get a sound history, commanding public confidence, written by a hand-picked writer who is given a fee, told to take such records as are doled out to him, and required to submit the result to the officers of the company for approval.

The result is usually mortification for the author, and frustration for the company. Independence is essential. The abler the historian, the more insistent he is on independence—absolute and unfettered. He does not want a large fee—he is used to poverty. He does not want fame—he is used to obscurity. He does want self-respect and an opportunity to do absolutely sterling work.

Now a modest grant of funds for a university, which then takes absolute responsibility for the product, protects company and author alike. It makes possible the focusing on the project of a variety of talents; for experts in engineering, finance, labor, law, and other subjects can all contribute to the analysis.

That is the course which the Standard of New Jersey and the Standard of Indiana, in very enlightened spirit, have followed.

It is the course, too, of the Ford Motor Company, which in some respects has now taken a position of leadership in this area. The Ford company has created at Dearborn what is universally admitted to be the model business archives of the United States; and it has made an arrangement with Columbia University which will result in a business history written under the freest possible conditions.

The university simply informed the company that it was interested in business history. The Ford company replied that it was pleased to learn the fact, and was making a modest grant for the promotion of such work. And the university then chose a small body of men—paid only their usual university salaries—to make a beginning in business history. By a strange accident, they chose the history of the Ford company as a place to begin.

It is impossible to write the history of America without doing full justice to the development of our great business institutions. Nay, it is impossible to write the history of the period since 1865 in the United States—of what is now nearly the whole past century—without giving business history a fundamental position; for it is more important to the development of the republic, and to an understanding of our civilization, than our political history or intellectual history. Rightly understood, it is full of the most alluring adventure and romance. And I predict that the generation which follows our own will deem it the most exciting chapter in the whole course of American history.

7

American Journalism
and Its Historical Treatment

Delivered originally as an address before the Committee on
History of the Association for Education in Journalism at its
annual convention in the summer of 1959, this analysis of the
history and historians of American newspapers is broader
than its title suggests. In his indictment of nearly all authors
who have prepared such histories in the past, Allan Nevins
reveals his disapproval of any scholar who does not adhere to
the canons of thoroughness, objectivity, and complete honesty, as he himself did in his excellent *The Evening Post: A
Century of Journalism* (1922). As usual when lecturing his
fellow craftsmen, Nevins concludes with positive suggestions
for improvement, first by detailing the faults of earlier writers,
then by listing steps to better the products of authors of
newspaper histories in the future.

Everyone will agree that since the days of Benjamin
Franklin the American press has made a more interesting,

Reprinted with permission from the *Journalism Quarterly* 36 (Fall 1959): 411–22,
519.

variegated and important record than that of any other nation. But how should that record be written? As a chapter in our culture? As a striking part of American business enterprise? Or in relation to the workings of democratic government? The answer is, of course, in all three lights; but there can be no question that the third is the most significant.

Early this year the International Press Institute in Zurich published a study of *The Press in Authoritarian Countries* which every journalist and historian should read. It showed how much of the world's press, from Russia to the Dominican Republic and Indonesia, is in chains. It demonstrated how fatal to healthy journalism are authoritarian controls; in Santo Domingo, for example, the total circulation of all newspapers is below 75,000. It brought out clear evidence that in all totalitarian lands educated people feel a deep thirst for a press which can freely tell the truth. In short, the report made it plain that a vigorous democracy and a vigorous free journalism have the closest interrelationships, so that one cannot exist without the other. This interdependence is the central theme in the history of the press in any free country.

During the last century a series of memorable phrases were invented to characterize the role of the press in good government. A regent of sovereigns, a tutor of nations, said Napoleon I. Edmund Burke's remark that journalism is the Fourth Estate was given popular currency by Carlyle's *French Revolution*. Carlyle himself said that journalists had become the true kings and clergy, and that newspaper dynasties had replaced the Tudors and the Hapsburgs. Norman Angell termed newspapers the chief witnesses upon whose evidence the daily judgments of men on public affairs are based.

One of the most emphatic statements of the social and governmental importance of the press can be found in the defense which Italian Fascism made of its laws for controlling the press. The state manages the public schools, said the Fascists, so that they may always teach patriotism. Newspapers are "schools for

character, lecture rooms for daily teaching, pulpits for preaching";
hence they also must be tightly controlled. But the Fascists forgot
the truth reiterated by the International Press Institute, that a
tightly controlled press is a dead press.

Journalism can be the best single instrument of democratic
self-government, informing the mind, enlightening the conscience
and freeing the spirit of intelligent citizens. It can also be a mortal
foe of modern democracy, and that sometimes in subtle ways.
Only history can place the achievements and shortcomings of the
newspapers of any land in full and fair perspective. Sound
historical works on the press and its leaders are as important to the
United States as sound works on presidents and cabinet officers,
generals and admirals, inventors and industrialists. This branch of
history should be expert, incisive and candid—as sternly critical
for recent periods, especially as our histories of Second World
War campaigns, written by Bradley, Montgomery and Alan-
brooke, as unflinching as the assessments of Munich and Pearl
Harbor, as outspoken as the best estimates of Stanley Baldwin and
Herbert Hoover. Of such history we have as yet the barest
beginning.

We cannot take much comfort from the fact that poor as our
journalistic history is, it is better than that of any other nation. No
history of German journalism in the last generation, for reasons
which need no statement, has yet been written. For reasons quite
different, no respectable history of modern French journalism has
ever been published. The greater newspapers of Paris—*Le Temps,
Le Moniteur, Le Matin, Figaro,* and so on—are each so closely
identified with specific economic or political groups, or with some
compelling individual, that any historian who approached them
would find himself dealing with the ruling regime, the group or a
prominent leader. A history of the mid-19th century *Moniteur* is
only a history of Napoleon III, and a history of *l'Homme Libre,*
later *l'Homme Enchainé,* is but a history of Clemenceau.

Even the history of British journalism has been less ably covered
than ours. It is in some respects the most distinguished press

record, running from Daniel Defoe to Sir William Haley, in the world. One unmatched mountain-peak of historical achievement, the five-volume study of the London *Times* by Stanley Morison and others, fittingly commemorates the work of the most powerful single newspaper. But beyond this the historians have done little, particularly for the last century. It is unfortunate that so illustrious a journal as the Manchester *Guardian* is represented in our libraries by nothing but a slight 200-page sketch, and so important a paper as the London *Telegraph and Morning Post* by nothing at all.

But the deficiencies of other lands cannot be made an excuse for our own, for we have greater advantages and larger responsibilities than European countries. Our democracy is preeminently a newspaper-reading public. Since Jacksonian days every foreign visitor has noted our devotion to daily and weekly publications. Nor is our journalism dominated, as in Britain and France, by a few great centers, for it is spread from the Penobscot to the Pacific. Local and regional pride is enlisted behind many of our newspapers to an extent impossible in Western Europe. Far more money is invested in and spent by our press than in and by that of any other land. Journalism in America is more highly professionalized than in any but a few other countries.

Why, then, do we have so little good history that the number of volumes which can be termed excellent can be counted on the fingers of two hands? Assuming that the history of the press is better worth writing here than elsewhere, for we have more of it and have it more powerfully; assuming also that it must be expert and objective, or it is not worth writing at all, what can we do to improve its scope and quality? Paul Lazarsfeld wrote in *Journalism Quarterly* in 1948: "If there is one institutional disease to which the media of mass communication seem particularly subject, it is a nervous reaction to criticism." The best cure for this sensitivity is more good history of slashing honesty.

The thinness and unevenness of work in this field is largely explained by one simple fact: the fact that, as Thackeray said in

Pendennis, "All the world is in the newspaper." The files are replete with entertaining detail on a thousand topics, from wars to women, from music to murders. How easy, the amateur says, to fill a volume with amusement and instruction. Actually, the super-abundance of jumbled, disparate and mainly trivial details in the files place on the writer a burden of assortment and synthesis under which most men break down.

Compare the task of the biographer of a newspaper with that of the biographer of such a public figure as William Jennings Bryan. The author of a life of Bryan has to relate him to the history of his times—and ours; but only to the history of politics, for apart from a few unhappy episodes like his enlistment in the battle of fundamentalism against evolution, Bryan was merely a political animal; and even in politics only a restricted number of issues, of which currency and imperialism were the chief, need be considered. But the man who writes the history of a great newspaper for the same period has to take cognizance of a thousand subjects from the poetry corner to corners in wheat. If he does not fix on the right principles of selection and synthesis he might as well throw himself into the nearest vat of printer's ink.

When we add that most histories of individual newspapers are prepared with an eye to pious commemoration, or profitable promotion; that the veteran reporter who, if well trained, would today make the best historian, usually lacks any training whatever; and that the writer is subject to covert pressures, ranging from loss of his job to threats of libel suits, and too often yields to them by evasion if not mendacity, then we can understand why such histories are in general poor.

The tasks of selection and synthesis, and the even greater task of finding matter of real historical novelty, are complicated by the universal failure of American newspapers to preserve any data on two subjects of cardinal importance: the method of getting news, and the facts behind the news. Practically no effort is made in our editorial offices to get and keep such material.

86

The unapproached distinction of Stanley Morison's five volumes on the London *Times* lies in two facts. The first is that for much more than a century the *Times* has been an integral and important part of the political structure of Great Britain. Its news and its editorial comment have in general been carefully coordinated, and have at most times been handled with an earnest sense of responsibility. While the paper has admitted some trivia to its columns, its whole emphasis has been on important public affairs treated with an eye to the best interests of Britain. To guide this treatment, the editors have for long periods been in close touch with 10 Downing Street. Thus when Morison came to write his history, he found the task of selecting the material already largely accomplished.

The *Times* itself had selected what was most important, had lifted it to a proper plane, and had given it the right emphasis. To give one example out of many, the Berlin Conference of 1878, from which Disraeli brought back peace with honor, was covered for the *Times* by the fabulously expert Paris correspondent M. De Blowitz; he kept in close touch with the editor Thomas Chenery, who had just succeeded Delane, and with the chief owner, John Walter III; they in turn maintained close relations with the foreign office. Morison could feel sure that what the *Times* had reported, and what Chenery had said in his leaders, was history of a specially significant type.

The second reason for the distinction of Morison's volumes is that the *Times* kept an unrivaled archive of the news behind the news. De Blowitz, writing to Walter and Chenery, gave the secret history of many episodes and conversations which it was impossible to print, and they told much that now adds color and life to the narrative. Not infrequently the editors, governed by a cautious sense of high responsibility, suppressed perfectly truthful dispatches that it seemed indiscreet to print, and they went into the archives. So did significant letters from a great number of men in public and private life. The *Times*, we may recall, scooped all other newspapers on the text of the Treaty of Berlin, which De

Blowitz's assistant, Donald Mackenzie Wallace, carried from Berlin to Brussels sewed in the lining of his coat, and thence telegraphed to London. But the *Times* was quite capable of suppressing a scoop if Disraeli or Gladstone or Salisbury wished it; and then it lay undiscovered until Morison levied upon it for his history.

Most American newspapers have some intimacy with the stream of events, even though it is on a small scale. They deal with affairs for their city or state as the London *Times* dealt with affairs on the national and international level. The difficulty is that they do not bring to them, in most instances, any high sense of responsibility; and this handicaps the historian. They could keep an archive, if they were not too careless or indolent. Any newspaper could ask its best reporters to write memoranda on significant bits of what Thomas Hart Benton in his *Thirty Years' View* called inside history—more important, he said, than external history. Any editor who spent 15 minutes a week dictating his own confidential memorandum or diary would soon have a record priceless to the future historian. An office diary identifying the author of all unsigned articles of note should be an essential part of the machinery of every daily—and comment could be added.

Why are archives not kept? Hurry, lack of space, preoccupation with crowding daily tasks, are excuses that seldom have much validity. What is needed is a sense that the newspaper is history beyond the day. My own special activities once led me to search carefully the offices of the New York *Evening Post,* New York *Herald* (before its merger with the *Tribune*) and New York *World* for archival material. They were practically bare. Readers of my life of Grover Cleveland will see that I did discover in the *World* morgue one paper of importance. After the dramatic battle in 1893 over the repeal of the Sherman Silver Purchase Act, which opened an irreparable breach between the President and the party majority in Congress, the Washington correspondent of the *World* wrote a confidential history of the struggle as he had seen it from the lobbies of the capital and the offices of members. This was all.

Lunching with Arthur Sulzberger and some of the editors of the New York *Times* three years ago, I called their attention to the value of an archive preserving confidential materials. Mr. Sulzberger then and there gave instructions to have such an archive formed; but whether these directions were ever carried out I do not know.

In an effort to escape the difficulties of selection and synthesis from the hodgepodge material in the ordinary newspaper file, writers have resorted to two expedients which on a casual view appear legitimate, but which too often lead to an abdication of their proper function. The first expedient is the adoption of a biographical approach, so that the record is treated in terms of a few prominent men. The New York *Sun* becomes personified in Dana, the Springfield *Republican* in Samuel Bowles, the Chicago *Tribune* in Joseph Medill. This is proper for that part of our journalistic history dominated by great editors, but for that part alone. It is this particular segment of our journalistic annals that has thus far been most efficiently treated. The biographies of Horace Greeley by James Parton, Glyndon Van Deusen, William H. Hale and others, of Samuel Bowles by George S. Merriam, of Dana by James Grant Wilson, of Henry J. Raymond by Francis Brown, of Bryant by Parke Godwin, of Henry Watterson by Joseph Wall and of George William Curtis by Gordon Milne, taken together, provide an adequate impression of the work of the editorial thunderers. Large gaps yet exist. Greeley deserves a really thorough two-volume biography; Joseph Pulitzer merits a much better-informed and less superficial life than Don C. Seitz gave him; and Edwin L. Godkin should long ago have been rescued from the incredibly ill-organized, helterskelter chronicle written by Rollo Ogden. Nevertheless, by and large, our great editorial personalities have been amply displayed. We can readily discover how the most powerful captains of the press applied their talents to the problems of the day, where their judgment erred, and what they accomplished. This is the simplest element in newspaper history, the most dignified and impressive, and with a proper use of quotation, the most pungent. A dehumanized page on the treatment the New York press gave the great Hungarian patriot, Kossuth, is now but pallidly interesting. But a page on the banquet to Kossuth in 1850 at which Bryant presided, Henry J. Raymond was the principal speaker and Greeley was an enthusiastic participant, cannot but be fascinating.

The other expedient used in simplifying the vast melange of material in a newspaper file is the related device of emphasizing opinion at the expense of reporting, views at the expense of news. This, too, is legitimate for the period when opinion was the chief staple of a great newspaper, as it assuredly was for a long generation in the middle of the 19th century. But it becomes a painful distortion when we reach the modern era in which news reigns paramount over opinion. Contrast the *Tribune* of Greeley's day with the New York *Times* as Adolph S. Ochs developed it after 1896. Greeley's chief concern was with the shaping of public policy by a daily page of informed, positive and sometimes eloquent editorials, and he marshaled his news, his special articles and even the letters to the editor to support his page. To Ochs, news—full, honest, objective, clean news—was the heart and soul of the *Times*; he would have dispensed with the editorial page with a relatively minor pang, and always kept it to a minor role.

It is ironic that at the very time the far-reaching revolution which minimized opinion and exalted the news was taking place, historians of journalism busied themselves with the views of the great editor and neglected the news-gatherers. American reporting has become the most enterprising, the frankest and most courageous and the most humanly appealing, though not the best written, in the world. It is much more tough-minded and skeptical than British reporting, much more objective than French. Yet where can we find a narrative which tells just when and why the change took place? In general terms, it is well treated in the admirable histories of journalism by Frank Luther Mott, and by Edwin Emery and Henry Ladd Smith, but they have no space for explanatory detail and telling examples. It is in relation to this change that we most need a thorough analytical biography of Ochs. The task of writing one was first entrusted to Claude G. Bowers, who, working in faroff Chile, failed so completely that the family never used his book; it was then undertaken by Gerald W. Johnson, whose readable volume is deficient in research—especially that kind of research which drains the memories of all surviving associates. It is chiefly with reference to influence on news-gathering that we need a better biography of Pulitzer than that of Don C. Seitz, whose main interest lay in the counting-room. No one can run through the sheafs of telegrams and memoranda in Pulitzer's papers at Columbia without discerning that he was a true genius both in ferreting out news, and in creating it.

If historians must use the biographical approach, it is effective managing editors rather than brilliant editorial writers who since 1900 most deserve their attention. Lord Bryce in *Modern Democracy* remarks that civic opinion is better instructed in America than in Continental Europe because of better news: "the publicity given by the newspapers to all that passes in the political field." Walter Lippmann has said that the greatest successes of present-day journalism lie in "the objective, orderly, and comprehensive presentation of the news." But I know of only one incisive study of an eminent managing editor, James W. Markham's *Bovard of the Post-Dispatch.* This paints a living portrait of an arrogant man who made his newspaper a force for the betterment of St. Louis and Missouri; who taught his best reporters, including Raymond P. Brandt, Paul Y. Anderson and Marquis Childs, to get not only the facts but the truth behind the facts.

We lack an adequate book about an even more distinguished managing editor, Carr Van Anda. More than Bovard, Van Anda saw how complex the truth is, and realized that to discover it a great newspaper must have not simply a slick skill in reporting surface news, but a patient, scientific-minded exploration, by well educated specialists, of intricate situations. An event is a force momentarily made visible. The good news specialist must look for the force behind the event, as something to be explored, measured and analyzed.

It is through the news pages, special features and the exploratory work of labor specialists, educational specialists, sports specialists, economic specialists and others that the best newspapers today exercise leadership. But where is the historical record of this change? A reader may go through a long shelfful of books searching for light on news-gathering and news-analysis, and end in despair. Sam Acheson's history of the Dallas *News*, for example, entitled *35,000 Days in Texas*, is primarily concerned with editorial positions on local, national and international issues since 1842. We learn of the newspaper's attitudes toward Texas banking laws and Ma Ferguson, the Grover Cleveland and Woodrow Wilson campaigns, and the Spanish War; but we find no discussion of news-gathering in connection with these or other subjects. Archer Shaw's *The Plain Dealer* offers two 10-page sections on news, one of which sketches wartime reporting, but the record of the *Plain Dealer's* valiant fight for Tom L. Johnson's crusades, which earned Johnson's special thanks, is written in editorial terms. Joseph E. Chamberlain's *The Boston Transcript: A History of Its First Hundred Years*, is similarly disappointing. He tells well such stories as that of the skinflint manager William Durant, the most picturesque of the *Transcript's* heads, who consistently opposed raising the wages of employees on the ground that more money would demoralize them. The one memorable item on news policy in the *Transcript* history records that in the excited days of Jackson and Nullification, the editors invited the public to visit the office and read the news they had not printed. Thomas E. Dabney's book on the New Orleans *Times-Picayune, One Hundred Great Years*, is a waterless Sahara so far as the treatment of news-gathering goes.

It is refreshing to list a few shining exceptions to this category of failure. The general histories by Mott, and by Emery and Smith, give excellent running accounts of progress in news-gathering, and such books as Leo Rosten's *The Washington Correspondents* and Douglass Cater's recent *The Fourth Branch of Government*, while not history, contain many historical perceptions and episodes. The best of all our newspaper chronicles, Meyer Berger's volume on the New York *Times*, is the work of a skilled reporter. It deals thoroughly and expertly with the method, development and outstanding achievements of news-gathering, especially during the last half-century. With an important story to tell, Berger relates it so brilliantly, in fact, that we hesitate to add one critical reservation: his book is written in pure journalese, undiluted by a touch of stylistic elegance. It had an able preceding volume to surpass, Elmer Davis's; but that, while in better English, is more largely concerned with the editorial conduct of the *Times*. Erwin D. Canham's history of the *Christian Science Monitor, Commitment to Freedom*, has the balance that we would anticipate from its author. John P. Young's *Journalism in California*, a volume concerned generally with San Francisco and specifically with the *Chronicle*, is spasmodically strong in its analysis of reporting, and in relating the *Chronicle* to the social milieu. Young analyzes the news in its historical and social context, discusses such topics as the effect of high telegraph charges on conciseness, and investigates the truth of the *Morning Call*'s statement that San Francisco reporting in the early decades was "beneath contempt," concluding that this was because newspapermen were untrained in observation.

The sparkling volume by Gerald Johnson, H. L. Mencken and others on the *Sunpapers of Baltimore* does partial justice to news, almost equating it with opinion. Across the continent Dana Marshall's *Newspaper Story: Fifty Years of the Oregon Journal*, the work of a reporter and special writer who became head of the editorial page, carefully relates the development of news to the growth of Portland. Here the paper and community appear inseparably wedded, serving each other, and all the crusades in which the *Journal* played a part, from campaigns for better mayors to campaigns for better milk, can be found in some detail. We may find material of value on news-gathering in such dissimilar books as James Weber Linn's life of James Keeley, the greatest of Chicago managing editors, who found zest in a hundred exploits, from his personal chase of a murderer through the swamps of Arkansas to his chase of Senator William Lorimer through the swamps of Chicago politics; Ralph E. Dyar's *News for an Empire*, revolving about the Spokane *Spokesman-Review*; and J. Cutler Andrews's study of the Pittsburgh *Post-Gazette*, which discusses reporters and illustrators along with editors and circulation managers.

Of course it can be said that the greatest reporters tell their own stories most entertainingly, as they have done from the time George Wilkins Kendall of the New Orleans *Picayune* penned his narrative of the *Texas Santa Fe Expedition* in 1844 to Herbert L. Matthews's *Education of a Correspondent* more than a century later. What newspaperman cannot learn a hundred lessons from the second book of Lincoln Steffens's *Autobiography*, with two hundred pages on a newspaper reporter's work in the days of Boss Croker, Jacob Riis and Police Commissioner Roosevelt?

But systematic history holds a larger usefulness. The reporting of the Civil War by American correspondents has at last been comprehensively analyzed by trained historians, Louis Starr of Columbia University, Bernard A. Weisberger of Antioch College, Emmet Crozier, and J. Cutler Andrews of the Pennsylvania College for Women. Mr. Andrews is a product of Arthur M. Schlesinger's Harvard seminar. So is J. Eugene Smith, whose *One Hundred Years of the Hartford Courant* is the most skillfully planned of all newspaper histories. Similarly, Harry Baehr's capable book on *The New York Tribune since the Civil War*, with a sound account of the way in which the line was held against sensational news in yellow-press days, Candace Stone's treatment of *Dana and the Sun* and Joseph Wall's life of Watterson, three exceptionally good books, were products of a Columbia graduate seminar.

If newspaper history is marred by thinness and spottiness, and overemphasis on editorial personalities and opinion as distinguished from reporters and news, it has one still more glaring fault. Taken as a whole, it is deplorably uncritical and some of it is dishonest. With too few exceptions, the authors wrote like kept hacks. In their silences they imitate some present-day attitudes of the press itself. Newspapers have long been accused by such observers as Oswald Garrison Villard and Walter Lippmann of refusing to criticize themselves, or each other, or journalism in general. An excessive regard for press comity estops each journal from speaking ill of others, or from noting even egregious blunders and offenses. Many newspapers are unwilling to print intelligence about libel suits against their contemporaries. Most offices have sacred cows stabled somewhere, but the greatest sacred cow is journalism itself. Yet bad as newspaper practice is, some press historians go further; they gloss over blunders, defend misinterpretations and injustices, and sweep glaring omissions and lost opportunities under the bed.

Why? Theoretically, the veteran newspaperman is a hardboiled, tough-minded writer, ready in pursuit of truth to cut his own mother's throat. Actually, in historical vein, he often writes like a mawkish sentimentalist, or a party wheelhorse at convention time recalling the greatness of James G. Blaine. We have mentioned one reason, the promotional origin of many histories. Another reason is that employees fall in love with their paper; they awaken every morning saying to themselves (to paraphrase H. J. Massingham), "I wonder how the dear old slut is this morning? Damn the hussy! I must do something for her." Knowing her sins, they love her too much to expose them. A third reason is that all ephemeral media, like the stage, the ballet, the motion pictures or the circus,

95

become invested with a romantic aura and encrusted with legends. As a result, the typical newspaper historian is a *laudator tempus acti*, who hangs nothing but spotless linen on the line.

This is easy, because the newspaper reflects light from so many facets; it so often gets on both sides of important issues—and if a third side existed, would get on that; and it can so easily be quoted out of context. The America-Firster attitudes of the Chicago *Tribune* just before Pearl Harbor, and the defense of Joseph McCarthy by the Hearst press, were foolish and immoral, but any agile newspaper historian could find quotations to prove that they embodied a profound patriotism. Of course most historical dishonesties are on a minor scale, and can be labelled simply special pleading; still, they are dishonesties. It was dishonest of me in the *Evening Post* history to suppress the bitter quarrel between the owner, Villard, and the editor, Rollo Ogden, both then living and both hypersensitive. It was dishonest of Elmer Davis to treat Charles R. Miller's *Times* editorial of September 16, 1918, urging unconditional acceptance of the Austro-Hungarian proposal for a non-binding discussion of peace terms, as shrewd and judicious, though Woodrow Wilson's wiser treatment of the proposal showed that Miller was guilty of a deplorable *gaffe*. We can read Frank M. O'Brien's book on the New York *Sun* without the slightest realization of the harm wrought by Dana's cynical defense of Tammany, hatred of civil service reform, spasms of jingoism and constant demands for the annexation of Cuba and Canada. Henry Adams tells us that he could have found a place on Dana's staff, but he knew that he could never please himself and Dana too, for "with the best intentions he must always fail as a blackguard, and a strong dash of blackguardism was life to the *Sun*." To grasp the blackguardism, a reader must drop O'Brien and read Candace Stone's book.

The history of the London *Times* by Morison and others is in general unflinchingly honest. It tells everything, for example, about the libelous *Times* accusations against Charles Stewart Parnell, based on forged letters, and about the ruinous penalty;

for the ensuing suit cost the *Times* almost £200,000. But even this admirable history has been accused by no less a person than Lord Beaverbrook of flinching at the full truth when it deals with the abdication of Edward VIII. This story is told in an appendix to the final volume.

Morison makes it plain that the *Times* was one of the principal agents in compelling the abdication. Indeed, its editor, Geoffrey Dawson, a man of formidable intellectual and personal force, stood next to Prime Minister Stanley Baldwin in the unseating of Edward VIII. Dawson was one of the first men in Britain to learn of the king's love affair. Horrified, he set out on what Beaverbrook calls a "propaganda canvass" of public men. The king offered Baldwin a plan for a morganatic marriage, by which he would take a wife but not a queen. The prime minister notified Geoffrey Dawson of this before he consulted the Cabinet, or the heads of the great dominions, and the puritanical editor was again horrified. He at once began a tremendous campaign in the *Times* upon the importance of keeping the Crown completely free from any taint of personal scandal; and according to Beaverbrook, he published one article which was innocent on its surface, but which carried "wounding and malicious innuendo." At the outset public opinion in Britain had been heavily on the side of the king and his proposal. Dawson and the *Times* swayed it in the opposite direction, until on a foggy December night the Duke of Windsor boarded the destroyer *Fury* for a French port. No reader of Morison's pages can doubt that he has told the story with general accuracy, making plain the vital part played by the *Times*. But according to Lord Beaverbrook, he did not make it plain that Dawson had used unfair weapons.

Our newspaper historians have not told the truth about the external pressures which have so often colored news and opinion. Murat Halstead remarked to the Wisconsin Press Association in 1889 that he saw no objection if readers should "find out that the advertiser occasionally dictates the editorials." "No objection at all to that," rejoined E. L. Godkin; "the objection is when they don't find it out." Direct advertiser-dictation has largely disappeared; but the treatment of news is still prostituted, all over the map, to the acquisition of larger and more vulgar bodies of readers, so that circulation managers may go to advertisers and boast of the clientele which their paper reaches. Historians have failed to emphasize properly the stupid conservatism of most of the press, its blind attachment to the status quo, and especially the economic status quo. Franklin D. Roosevelt in 1938 remarked on this reactionary hostility to change, saying of the papers using the Associated Press or United Press services that he estimated "85 percent of them have been inculcating fear in this country during the past year." He was quite right; the newspapers, themselves business enterprises, have repeatedly been too responsive to business in opposition to needed change.

Press historians rightly make much of Paul Y. Anderson's part in remorselessly following the oil scandals under Harding to the doors of the Republican National Committee, but they say little of the general inertia and complacency of newspapers in Harding's day. They say even less about the callous indifference of most metropolitan newspapers to depressed economic groups, such as the farmers, miners and textile workers, during the boom of the 1920s. Mr. Dyar in *News for an Empire* quotes the statement which President Truman made in Spokane in 1948 about the *Spokesman-Review*: "This paper and the Chicago *Tribune* are the worst in the United States." But he does not explain the sins of omission and commission which led to this outburst.

Long ago Dr. Johnson spoke of the debasing effects of great conflicts upon press ethics: "In wartime a people only want to hear two things—good of themselves, and evil of the enemy. And I know not what is more to be feared after a war, streets full of soldiers who have learned to rob, or garrets full of scribblers who have learned to lie." But we still lack a full *exposé* of the effects of the First and Second World Wars on the hysterical and irresponsible parts of the American press.

We have numerous accounts of the more blatant indecencies of yellow journalism, with special attention to such episodes as the Spanish War. As Matthew Arnold said long ago, sensational papers offer "the best means to efface and kill in a whole nation the discipline of respect, the feeling for what is elevated." The blatant indecencies, however, often do less harm than those of a subtle, insidious kind. A recent book by Judge Irwin D. Davidson and Richard Gehman, entitled *The Jury Is Still Out*, explores at length the murder of a crippled New York boy, Michael Farmer, by a street gang. Not the least important part of the book analyzes the contribution to social disorder steadily made by the gutter press. Honest depiction of the immense but hidden harm long done by sensational journalism is much needed in every section of the country. The extent to which lurid reporting under slanted headlines has interfered with the administration of justice in the courts offers another problem which the historian could profitably explore.

Much could also be said of various requirements, as yet badly met, in the history of newspapers as business institutions, for their financial record bears on their stability and their independence. Most newspaper histories neglect even a partial account of circulation revenue, advertising revenue, profits and losses, because records are wanting, or secrecy is desired, or such matters seem dull. It is curious, for example, that after Ochs's original purchase, the financial history of the New York *Times* is almost entirely omitted from Meyer Berger's otherwise complete narrative. When I wrote the history of the *Evening Post* I found no financial records anterior to 1900, and few later; the Villard family had some, which were not open to me.

Far more important than this, however, is a proper treatment of the public service function of newspapers. It is of the first importance, now that so many cities have but one newspaper, that historians study the question whether a correlation can be traced between a good newspaper and a well-governed community, a bad paper and a badly managed community. Was the Boston of James

99

Curley what it was partly because Boston newspapers (the *Monitor* excluded) were so wretched? Was Louisville a specially healthy city because of the public spirit of the *Courier-Journal*? Mayors come and go, but a newspaper is a continuing institution.

No subject is of more importance than this to the political scientist, the sociologist, the general historian—and the aspiring young newspaperman. The best young men and women enter the profession because they hope to make not only better newspapers, but better towns and cities. Many evidences point to the fact disclosed by Columbia University's examination of the young people who attend its Scholastic Press Convention each year. They state that they know that journalism seems less attractive than law, medicine, engineering, science or even university teaching; as a profession it is low in pay, low in amenities, low in social prestige. But they believe they can play a more direct and fruitful part in community improvement through newspaper work than through any other calling. Their first task, of course, is to improve the newspapers, and it is discouraging to see how little our fast-multiplying schools of journalism have thus far done for such betterment. The theory of Dean Luxon of North Carolina that 50 years is too short a time to measure their effect is rather cold comfort. But ambitious young entrants have their eyes fixed on the greater goal of service to town, or city, or state; and every history which can tell a story of such service will give them inspiration.

What, then, are the principal requirements to be satisfied if we are to have the adequate histories of journalistic effort that we now lack? They are implied in what I have already said, and may be summarized under a few headings.

First, it is of cardinal importance that the newspaper have a history worth honest research and honest writing. That, alas, cannot be said of most dailies in the United States. Mere size and power are not proper criteria. We can say of a number of prominent dailies that they should not have histories because a really veracious record would be impossible, and even a counter-feit record would be repellent or painful. But every good journal is worth a history, which will benefit the paper, the community and the nation.

Second, every newspaper which deems its record worthy of commemoration should keep an archive. This means that some member of its staff should learn the rudiments of archival method; that an elementary office diary should be kept; that editors and reporters should be encouraged to make memoranda, save significant in-letters, and keep carbons of important out-letters; and that in general, some record be made both of the methods of news-gathering, and of the untold truth behind the news. The problem of room for an archive can sometimes be solved by the cooperation of the nearest historical society or library.

In the third place, the choice of a writer should not be left to chance or impulse. It will of course depend on circumstances. A history written as promotion is better than no history at all, but the promotional motive should be secondary. A writer selected within the office, and particularly in the newsroom, will be more expert than an outsider; an outsider will be more objective. Any writer should make the fullest use of oral reminiscences. The advice of a good college or university department of history can be obtained more readily than most newspapermen suppose, and will be more valuable than they generally believe. University teachers write badly, but they have a sense of organization, and they will see aspects of the subject that newspapermen may miss.

In the fourth place, this association, it seems to me, could make one important contribution to the systematic cultivation of press history in the United States. It might do something to improve current newspaper practice, and a great deal to guide future historians, if every five years it published a critical review, by regions, of the attitudes and activities of the principal newspapers. One committee in each region—that is, in say 10 areas of the country—could be made responsible for the critical evaluations. The members of this association, holding close relations with the principal newspapermen of their states, regularly reading the important journals, and possessing a keen critical sense of what is good and bad in journalism, could provide this review more easily and expertly than anyone else. Such a quinquennial volume, written with verve and penetration, would be accepted by any publisher, and would be sure of a large sale. Money needed to support the research and pay the essayists could readily be obtained from one of several foundations. As these volumes grew across the shelf, their impact on journalism, and their value to historians, sociologists, economists and students of government would grow too.

Finally, the historian should hang over his desk an amended version of the motto with which Joseph Pulitzer adorned his newsrooms: Honesty, Accuracy, Honesty.

8

Recent Progress of American Social History

Two years after publishing his first major work in American social history, the *Emergence of Modern America, 1865–1878*, Allan Nevins was still sufficiently excited by the importance of that new and novel approach to the study of the past to urge its use on his fellow historians in this essay, which first appeared in a scholarly economics journal in 1929. In it he exalts the significance of social history; examines its use by such writers as Macaulay, Henry Adams, and John Richard Green; describes its revival during the 1920s; and shows the extent to which knowledge of the past had been altered by its use. The essay is a "period" piece, long since outmoded by scholars in their increasingly sophisticated employment of social data in analyzing past societies. Yet it is well worth reading, partly because it admirably describes the dovetailing of social history into the mainstream of historical thought, partly because it mirrors the excitement of the young scholars who first developed the techniques that have since become commonplace. It demonstrates, too, that Allan Nevins, although a self-proclaimed narrative historian, was

Reprinted with permission from the *Journal of Economic and Business History* 1 (May 1929): 365–83.

always alert to new methods and subjects that stressed analysis rather than storytelling, and that he was willing to pioneer in their adoption if the result was better history, more widely read.

History, like nearly every other literary form, has been subjected to an increasing variety of influences, all operating simultaneously. But in the last half century two main tendencies have asserted themselves in American historical writing. The first has been the tendency toward a more scientific treatment; a tendency foreign in origin, and bearing some relation to the nineteenth-century revolution in the natural sciences. The German leaders, Von Ranke and his pupils Von Sybel, Giesebrecht, and Waitz, found disciples throughout Europe, like Duruy in France and Seeley and Stubbs in England; but they had no followers more enthusiastic than the university men, notably Charles K. Adams and Herbert B. Adams, who first brought their method to America. The scientific historians have insisted upon precision, exhaustive research, and a dispassionate, critical spirit bent to the one object of setting before the reader the fact as it occurred. At almost the same time there appeared in America the other great tendency, which was undoubtedly also stimulated by the development of natural and social sciences and especially of evolutionary thought; the tendency toward a steady broadening of both the materials and methods of history. The historical field became so enlarged that, one after another, new phases of human activity slipped under the lens; the political historians who once held the stage almost alone have had to make way for historians dealing primarily with intellectual movements, like Henry Osborn Taylor and James Harvey Robinson; with geographic and climatic factors, like Ellsworth Huntington; with economic factors, like Charles A. Beard; with sociological elements, like William Graham Sumner; and with psychological and other factors.

Both these movements represent a stronger rationalism in history. The broadening of history, with which I am here chiefly concerned, represents a great deal more than the simple annexation of new topics; it represents more than a desire on the part of the historian to write about literature or business where once he wrote about politics and war. The real difference lies in a broader interpretation of causes and results. The old-time history regarded the Revolutionary events of 1775–76 as caused by a series of political acts beginning about 1763. The new view is that the political revolution was not merely connected with, but was chiefly the outgrowth of, a profound social and economic revolution; that this latter revolution could not occur rapidly in a slow-moving agricultural society of fairly uniform prosperity; and that its roots go back to the first English settlement on American soil, and to the psychological changes of the very first months that men spent on the rim of our savage continent. A new synthesis of materials is required. Even the historian who would chronicle the military events of the Civil War can no longer dip his pen in the simple spirit of the older writers, but must take account of industrial changes, social phases, mass psychology, and many other elements.

Social history is the history of the permutations and growth of a whole society in a definite period and place; not the political society, not the industrial society, not Society with the big S, but the entire community, great and small, rich and poor, intellectuals and hod-carriers. The emergence of a distinct genre of social history is a natural consequence of the broadening process just mentioned. Its practitioners would not give it too hard and fast a definition. They realize that its boundaries must be rather vague, just as the boundaries of older types of history have been blurred. Political historians have, ever since the time of Thucydides, included many facts about population, industries, education, and public opinion; the limits of economic history have necessarily been equally nebulous. But the social historian does believe that, in his treatment of complex and interacting forces, he has a firmer hold upon the essential stuff of history, a clearer appreciation of its true aims, than any narrower school of historical writing can have. He treats the life of the whole, and tries to get at its permanent and compelling forces; they treat but a part, and are often content with surface currents and eddies when the master-tides lie beneath. Those who are trying to promote social history believe also that it has been unduly and unjustly neglected; and they feel that there is no question as to the principal reason for this neglect—its difficulty.

The idea of difficulty in social history is surprising to most people; they think of it as entertaining, superficial, and pictur-esque. The author gathers a few books of travel, some files of yellowed newspapers, some memoirs and old letters, and patches up a brightly amusing account of how people dressed, what they ate, the topics they talked about, how they travelled, what theatres they attended, and what books they read. It can be made cleverly allusive and of delicious sprightliness. A sly irony can light up the quaint ways of old times. But this is not social history; it is mere "fireworks," to use Stubbs's phrase. It is of about as much value to real students of history as Meissonier's bright and spirited painting of Friedland is to a strategist studying that battle. Social history, like any other history, is found by anyone who gets fairly below the surface to be full of problems. The material for resolving these problems is innumerable in its sources, dismayingly scattered and fragmentary, and often baffling to those who would interpret it. Moreover, society has so many facets that once the problems begin to be solved and part of the material to arrange itself in orderly fashion, the task of synthesis becomes profoundly difficult. It is easy to find illustrations in contemporary life of the difficulties the social historian must face. Everyone knows that many years must pass before the political historian will be able to deal adequately with such a topic as, say, the present issue of naval limitation between England and America. Not even Sir Austen Chamberlain or Mr. Kellogg knows a great deal about it at present. The future historian will have to study their papers; the secret views of Senators and members of Parliament, as revealed in letters and diaries; their public views, as revealed in debate; the role of Japanese and French armaments; the pressure of shipping and steel interests; the attitude of the Dominions as revealed in the Ottawa and Canberra archives; public opinion; and so on endlessly. But this will be child's play compared with the task of the future social historian who has to deal with the effect of the automobile upon American society between 1900 and 1917. We all have a confused impression that it has almost remade our society, altering it in a thousand ways; we all realize that to explore a fraction of these ways would be a gigantic task, and that our present-day perspective would probably be all wrong anyway. Yet the time will come when this crushing task will have to be shouldered.

It is not strange that as yet very little social history has been written. It is natural that much of what has been published is biased, hesitating, and tentative. We are just beginning to obtain a history which really studies social problems, and maps the intricate network of social factors. It is just beginning to replace the panoramic writing, entertaining and mildly stimulating but quite lacking in analytic quality, which used to be called social history.

Of this panoramic and rudimentary social history there are two conspicuous instances, both justly renowned for their fine literary quality: Macaulay's famous third chapter in his *History of England* (1848), and the first six chapters of Henry Adams's *History of the United States* (1889). They have much the same character. Macaulay offers a vigorous and strikingly colored sketch of the English population in 1685, the army, the navy, agriculture, the clergy, the mercantile towns, the watering-places, the London police, coffee-houses, and literary circles, the roads, the stage-coaches, the highwaymen, the newspapers, child-labor in industry, and the number of paupers; all this deriving a great part of its interest from the glaring contrasts between 1685 and 1845. No particular attention is paid to cause and effect, and there is no

107

philosophical comment more penetrating than the mild concluding observations on "the delusion which leads men to overrate the happiness of preceding generations." Henry Adams's account of American society in 1800 is equally preoccupied with mere description and equally devoid of analysis. But it grants a more generous attention to economic facts and intellectual characteristics, dealing with the cotton gin, modes of agriculture, diet, amusements, subscription libraries, the postal system, the newspapers, the influence of the clergy, the state of history, science, and pure literature, the character of the schools and colleges, and the manners and minds of people in the coastal cities. Once more a good deal of the effect of the treatment rises from the contrast pointed between the conditions of Jefferson's time and those of Grover Cleveland's. Both of these studies were written with a wealth of lore derived from travels and antiquarian works, and with a sense for the composition, the lights and shades, which any good picture must have; but both are pictures only.

Decidedly more important, because they possess a broader scope and are kinetic and not static in effect, are the numerous chapters on social history scattered through John Bach McMaster's rather uneven *History of the People of the United States* (1883–1927). McMaster modelled his style upon Macaulay, and his emphasis upon the life of the masses as distinguished from the governing groups or classes owed much to the example set by John Richard Green's *History of the English People* (1877–80). But he went into greater detail than Green, who presented his materials in a swift, almost kaleidoscopic, succession of brief, bright pictures. Indeed, the thoroughness of each of his scattered segments of social description is remarkable; he depends upon the effect of a mass of circumstantial fact for his effects. Moreover, he is genuinely interested in tracing surface changes throughout the periods he discusses. To distinguish between American society in 1783 and in 1795, or between our society in 1820 and 1840, is a far more difficult matter than to do what Macaulay and Henry Adams did. An excellent example of both the aim and the methods of Dr. McMaster may be found in his fourth volume. He pauses in his narrative of the War of 1812 to draw for us an admirably vivid picture of the streaming westward spate of population in the years which witnessed the introduction of steamboats upon the Ohio and Mississippi, the commencement of the Erie Canal, the admission of Indiana and Illinois, the rise of St. Louis above its old status of fur-post, and the first heavy movement of immigrants from Europe then deep in the trough of post-Napoleonic depression. It is done with animation and zest. We fairly see the seaboard merchants staring at their depopulated streets, the legislatures quarreling over internal improvements, and the Western speculators platting their new towns. There is much that is like this in McMaster's nine volumes. But he also belongs to the panoramic school. His work, in which the detail too often blurs the main lines, is descriptive or narrative, and offers little of real analysis.

McMaster has a direct successor in Ellis P. Oberholtzer, whose *History of the United States Since the Civil War* (1917–) is a spirited work using the familiar descriptive and narrative methods. The first volume offers a panoramic picture of post bellum society in precisely McMaster's vein, drawn with the same wealth of detail from newspapers, memoirs, travels, and similar sources. The two succeeding volumes, however, are devoted almost entirely to politics. A much fresher and clearer note is struck by Mark Sullivan in the two volumes, the first of four, which he calls *Our Times*; the subtitle of one being *The Turn of the Century, 1900–1904* (1926), and of the other, *America Finding Herself* (1927). In these two large books we have a series of topical essays, somewhat journalistic in style, which blaze a variety of trails through the jungle of recent social and political history. They constitute materials for the future historian rather than history itself; they sometimes seem to begin anywhere and end nowhere. But Mr. Sullivan has a keen realization of the profound changes which have remade American life in the last generation, of the gulf which separates the urbanized society of today from the still largely rural society of 1890, and of the significant alterations in schooling, ideas, and ideals as well as in industry, organization, and modes of living. Much of his material is refreshingly original, for he has gone to contemporary witnesses whose testimony might have been lost but for his zeal. His record deals principally with surface events and movements, but it is provocative of thought and of unflagging interest.

The best of the newer writers strive in scientific spirit to emphasize the analytic. When Macaulay wrote, the study which Herbert Spencer later named sociology was quite unknown; when Henry Adams and McMaster published their first volumes, it was in its infancy. Today we look at society with more scientific eyes. We send out workers trained in anthropological methods to survey our cities and towns and produce such books as *Middletown* to classify scientific data for the future social historian. Society has ceased to be a panorama and has become a structure, to be analyzed as the biologist analyzes his special world of animal or plant life. But, to make this scientific examination possible, we first require the combined labors of a great variety of research workers. The materials for the analytic historian have to be collected for him by specialists in the different elements of the social structure. Before extensive work in modern social history can be prosecuted it is necessary to possess a large number of monographs dealing with economic factors, with immigration, with labor, with education, with humanitarian advances, and so on. Of this specialized work much remains to be done, and some of the gaps are glaring.

Still, the social historian looks back over the past twenty years with gratitude for the progress in what from his point of view are special studies. Take, for example, literature. Since 1917 we have had the first full history of American letters given us by a co-operative band of scholars under the leadership of W. P. Trent and others, the *Cambridge History of American Literature*, of which the first volume appeared in the year named. Moreover, this work distinctly reacted against the aesthetic or belletristic position, and took a stand allied to that of the social historian. Once only "pure" literature was studied; now literature is viewed as an expression of American social life. As Stuart P. Sherman said in his introduction, "To write the intellectual history of America from the modern aesthetic standpoint is to miss precisely what makes it significant among modern literatures, namely, that for two centuries the main energy of Americans went into exploration, settlement, labor for subsistence, religion, and statecraft. . . . There is something absurd in a critical sifting process which preserves a Restoration comedy and rejects Bradford's *History of Plymouth;* which prizes a didactic poem in the heroic couplets and despises the work of Jonathan Edwards." In accordance with these wise principles, we find long chapters given to travellers and observers, to the great American political writers, and to newspapers and magazines, while a poet like Fitz-Greene Halleck is dropped with a few paragraphs. We find, again, that William Bartram's fascinating *Travels,* which are a mine of information for the social historian, receive more space than the lyrics of Philip Freneau, and that Fenimore Cooper's caustic account of *Home as Found* is accorded as full a treatment as his *Last of the Mohicans.* Since the publication of this four-volume history, the same impulse has given us several good treatments of literature as a reflection of sectional society. One is Maurice G. Fulton's *Southern Life in Southern Literature* (1917); a second is Ralph M. Rusk's rather too formal *Literature of the Middle Western Frontier* (1925); and a third is Dorothy A. Dondore's *The Prairie and the Making of Middle America* (1927). All of these books are chilly toward "pure" literature as compared with the literature which presents social history.[1]

[1] Studies of the American mind tend too frequently to the doctrinaire. Lewis Mumford's brilliant *The Golden Day* (1926) has much of value to the social historian, though many of its generalizations are debatable. The social historian will find much also in such penetrating biographical estimates as Constance M. Rourke's *Trumpets of Jubilee* (1927), written with the social background constantly in mind; and in Gilbert Seldes's *The Stammering Century* (1928), the first consecutive and careful account of American cults and manias.

But the most striking example of the social interpretation of literature is afforded by Vernon L. Parrington's *Main Currents in American Thought*, the first two volumes of which have but recently appeared (1928). Discarding aesthetic judgments, Parrington has tried to trace the stream of American ideals and ideas; and he understands perfectly that both are largely an outgrowth of the social and economic background. For example, in giving a searching chapter to Calhoun, William Grayson, and Thomas Dew, with their "Dream of a Greek Democracy," he points out how this militant attitude of the slaveholding class was an inevitable concomitant of the westward thrust of the cotton belt and the apparent necessity for an expansion of slavery to support the supremacy of cotton. His treatment of Bryant is equally interesting; he dismisses the poet curtly, and places in the foreground the militant editor, an exponent of the urban wing of Jacksonian democracy and of the radical revolt against *laissez-faire* capitalism. Equally good is his treatment of the "plantation mind" in the writings of William Wirt and Beverly Tucker and, in contrast with it, of the "frontier mind" of David Crockett and Augustus Baldwin Longstreet. Literature in these volumes appears as the resultant of agrarian change, industrial change, new forces in education, sectional loyalties and antagonisms—in brief, precisely the same factors which shape social history.

The social aspects and implications of economic history have not yet been so radically and thoroughly explored. It is lamentable that so little has been done for the history of American business, a subject whose romantic and almost epic possibilities have been merely indicated in a few books. There is a great deal of material for the social historian in Ida M. Tarbell's *History of the Standard Oil Company* (1904) presenting in its two volumes the story of the hectic exploitation of the Pennsylvania fields, of the rise of the first great trust, and of the transformation wrought by oil in illumination and transportation; but almost no other work on this model has appeared. The most impressive study of a similar nature is Edward Hungerford's *History of the Baltimore and Ohio*

Railroad, also in two volumes (1929). On a much smaller scale we have H. N. Casson's readable *History of the Telephone* (1910) and Joseph Husband's *Story of the Pullman Car* (1917). The rather slender book of F. J. Allen on the history of *The Shoe Industry* (1916) ignores many of the social aspects of the subject; but fortunately R. A. Clemen, in his voluminous and engrossing treatise on *The American Livestock and Meat Industry* (1923), is alive to every side of his theme—the rise of the cattle ranges, the marvelous growth of the Chicago packing-houses, and the changes effected in American diet. Other titles might be named. In particular, the two sketches contributed by John Moody to the Yale Chronicles, his *Masters of Capital* (1919) and *The Railroad Builders* (1919), appeal to the imagination by throwing light on the main outlines of stories which are not merely of basic importance in modern American history, but are packed with adventure and color. But how many aspects of economic and business history have been completely ignored! When shall we have a comprehensive history of American railways? When shall we have more than just a beginning made upon the vast and varicolored history of our agricultural development?[2]

It is true that the social historian has the benefit of some excellent studies of agrarian discontent, written with an eye chiefly

[2] Recent books in this general field include such diverse titles as Arthur H. Cole's *The American Wool Manufacture*, in two volumes (1926), which is written almost entirely from the economist's standpoint; Samuel E. Morison's *Maritime History of Massachusetts, 1783–1860* (1921), a fascinating study of the role of commerce and fisheries in shaping New England life; E. P. Hohman's more specialized essay in the same field, *The American Whaleman* (1928); Waldemar Kaempffert's *A Popular History of American Invention* (2 vols., 1924), with essays of uneven merit from various hands; three volumes in the Pageant of America Series, Malcolm Keir's *The Epic of Industry* (1926) and his *The March of Commerce* (1927), and Ralph H. Gabriel's *Toilers of Land and Sea* (1926). A picturesque record, exceedingly sketchy, is Seymour Dunbar's four-volume *History of Travel in America* (1915); while C. E. MacGill's *History of Transportation in the United States before 1860* (1917), and Victor S. Clark's *History of Manufactures in the United States 1607–1860* (1916) and the second volume for *1860–1914* (1928), are compendiums of facts from which the social historian has to extract what he can. P. W. Bidwell and J. I. Falconer have written a *History of Agriculture in the Northern United States, 1620–1860* (1925). Ulrich B. Phillips's *American Negro Slavery* (1918) is excellent from both the economic and the social point of view.

upon its dramatic and far-reaching political consequences. Solon
J. Buck's *The Granger Movement* (1913) was followed by his
more popular but also broader *Agrarian Crusade* (1919). Here we
see the embattled Western farmer, whose sad social estate from
1870 to 1900 is ably sketched, compelling the great corporations
to bow to government control and espousing various sound
political reforms as well as certain economic heresies. The
socialization of politics is the theme also of two volumes by Fred
E. Haynes, *Third Party Movements Since the Civil War* (1916),
and *Social Politics in the United States* (1924). Both are
essentially studies in the interrelation of social and economic
history on the one side, and political history on the other; and
both deal with farm organizations, labor organizations, the fight of
frontier individualism against corporate monopoly, and the profound influence of social depression upon government.

The social historian has had the benefit, again, of a massive
History of Labour in the United States, by John R. Commons and
various associates (1918). Its two volumes are exceedingly dry and
the co-operative authorship is responsible for a good deal of
repetition, but they are a storehouse of facts, and the social
significance of these facts is frequently well defined. Labor
movements thrive in a time of industrial prosperity, when
competition for workers is keen; they lose strength in times of
depression, when a multitude of hungry job-hunters makes strikes
impossible. Labor tendencies are thus a virtual barometer of
economic and social well-being. The forms which labor organizations take are also directly dependent upon the underlying social
structure. A rudimentary industrial fabric, with few skilled workers, is favorable only to the "one big union"; a fabric comprising a
large body of highly trained workers is favorable to crafts unions,
which may easily be federated. We thus have the first great
American labor organization take the shape of the Knights of
Labor, a huge pool of employees of all types and degrees of skill;
we later see it supplanted by the American Federation of Labor,

an organization of skilled craftsmen. Their exploration of different sides of labor history constantly carried Commons and his associates into the social field. In one subject after another of which they treat—the Chinese question, the eight-hour movement, co-operative factories, the Greenback-Labor upheaval, the American reception of anarchistic and socialistic ideas—they give the social historian both new materials and new avenues of approach.

To turn to a very different field of specialized study, recent years have provided us with an increasing number of what may be called histories of American manners. Unquestionably the most solid individual contribution in this field was made long ago by a woman, Alice Morse Earle, in a sheaf of volumes on everyday life in colonial and post-colonial times. Her *Home Life in Colonial Days, Child Life in Colonial Days, Stage Coach and Tavern Days*, and their companions, most of them dating from the late 'nineties, are in the antiquarian vein; a mass of detail, gathered from old books, gazettes, and letters, and arranged somewhat mechanically. Still, they combine a variety of most useful information with entertainment, and if anyone wishes to learn precisely what a Conestoga wagon was like, the development of the sampler, the permutations of lights from the phoebe-lamp to Count Rumford's lamp, and how the macadamized road originated in America and not England, he must go to these volumes. One similar work has appeared in recent years, Richardson Wright's *Walkers and Hawkers in Colonial America* (1927). But most writers on manners have preferred the easy task of lighting up the picturesque, the quaint, or the lurid aspects of some past age by an exposition based upon obvious sources. It is the quaint which is emphasized in Meade Minnegerode's account of *The Fabulous Forties* (1923), with its account of the log-cabin campaign, Fanny Ellsler, the Macready riots, and the rise of Barnum; it is the lurid which appears in Don C. Seitz's *The Dreadful Decade* (1927), with its record of the Credit Mobilier

115

scandal, the Erie War, and the disputed election of 1876. These books are pleasant entertainment; but of solid historical worth they have little.

Fortunately a distinctive value attaches to one book of similar motive but genuine originality and careful workmanship, Thomas Beer's ironic account of the 'nineties in *The Mauve Decade* (1926). Its mannered and sometimes elaborately precious style, and its sardonic point of view, should not blind any reader to its underlying merits. It deals in surfaces, painting manners with very little attention to causes or effects; but to reproduce a surface so authentically is a difficult achievement. There was a good deal of surface in American life by the 'nineties, and Mr. Beer's allusive method covers a careful personal investigation among the survivors of that epoch. One may learn how a thousand clergymen regarded Oscar Wilde; how disgustedly William Graham Sumner responded to the current abuse of Mark Hanna; how after the World's Fair the suffrage movement awoke with a roar; the ample and incredible record of American prudery under the provocation offered by "Trilby" and "McTeague"; the contrast between Ward McAllister and John P. Altgeld, between Jesse James and E. L. Godkin, between Matt Quay and Ambrose Bierce, each typical of one facet of the American scene. The chapter on our depravities, which Americans then took so seriously that a lady stalked up to Lawrence Barrett in the Fifth Avenue Hotel and ordered him to have the wine cups removed from his current play, is as good as the chapter on our literary revival in the years of *The Red Badge of Courage*, *The Damnation of Theron Ware*, and *Vandover and the Brute*. In all the tangled scene offered by Populism, free silver, the Spanish War, the A. P. A., the Dalton gang, and what not, Mr. Beer is interested in one unifying fact: the reaction of the American mind to these phenomena. There was an American mind, and it is not drawn in flattering strokes.[3]

[3] Recent years have witnessed a marked production of books dealing with the history of Western society and manners. The one good general treatise on the westward advance is Frederic L. Paxson's *History of the American Frontier* (1924),

But what of efforts to synthesize these and other scattered contributions?—for synthesis and interpretation are the main tasks of the social historian. For a generation the chief prophet of the creed that the great controlling forces of our history are social and economic was Frederick J. Turner. Not himself widely known as a writer of history, though his *Rise of the New West* (1906) is an able political history made distinguished by its chapters of social analysis, he has been of almost unequalled influence as a teacher of historians. His essay on "The Significance of the Frontier in American History" (1893) possessed a seminal power of the profoundest kind. Here he propounded the doctrine that American social development has been shaped by the continual renewal, the "beginning over again," on our westward-moving frontier; he showed how this fluidity, the individualism which it bred, the egalitarian spirit and democratic radicalism which sprang from it, the speculative temper which gave a tendency toward inflation and wildcat banking, the nationalistic loyalties fostered by dependence on the Federal government, permeated the whole structure of American society and determined the course of our history. His thesis made social history our real history. He declared that "behind institutions, behind constitutional forms and modifications, lie the vital forces that call these organizations into life and shape them to meet changing conditions." From time to time he published essays elaborating his ideas. Thus in 1910 his thoughtful paper on "Social Forces in American History," appearing in the *American Historical Review*, carried his challenge to the older kind of historiography still further. We need only look at the contemporary political agitations and reform movements, he said, to see that what the old-style historian thought to be side eddies have not seldom proved to be the concealed entrances to the main current, while what had once appeared the

---

which promises to hold the position of a standard work. There are too few such books as Philip A. Rollins's *The Cowboy* (1922), a minute and scientific treatment of one of the most typically American figures. There are rather too many such books as W. N. Burns's *Saga of Billy the Kid* (1926), emphasizing the sensational.

central stream led only to blind channels and stagnant bayous. In Turner's ideas we find the first firm basis laid for a social synthesis.

Hard on the heels of Turner's essay of 1910 appeared two incisive studies by Dr. Charles A. Beard which revealed an almost ruthless application of Turner's principles. As his titles *An Economic Interpretation of the Constitution of the United States* (1913) and *Economic Origins of Jeffersonian Democracy* (1915) indicate, he emphasized economic considerations. But he by no means neglected the broad social factors and influences allied with them; for indeed, economic and social forces must always be inextricably combined. Beard spoke of his books as a considered attempt to ascertain "what classes and social groups" had done for the drafting and adoption of our Constitution, and for the formation of our first parties. Though his studies were with some justice attacked as placing an exaggerated emphasis on pocket motives, they gave us an entirely new view of many parts of American history between 1776 and 1805. They were wholesome, if rather drastic, correctives to the conventional type of political history. But these volumes, important in themselves, now appear also in the light of preliminary studies for the most successful attempt at a synthesis of our whole social history as yet made: *The Rise of American Civilization*, in two volumes by Charles and Mary Beard (1927).

The very dividing line between these two volumes indicates the authors' insistence upon social and economic movements as the real creative forces in our American record. The first volume is devoted to "The Agricultural Era" and the second to "The Industrial Era." From beginning to end American history is subjected to a radical survey in which a great part of the conventional interpretations from the old political standpoint disappear. For example, the authors vigorously reject the easy theory of Macaulay to explain the rise of such rival parties as the Federalists and Republicans—the theory that in every nation there is a conservative party of order and a progressive party of experiment. This is not sufficiently penetrating, says Beard; it was no social accident that the leader of the party which despised the masses was a New York attorney, and the leader of the party which exalted the people was a Virginia planter of frontier birth. Mr. Madison's war is no longer treated as an affair of heady "war hawks" and of national pride outraged by impressment and blockade. Instead, it becomes a war of "agricultural imperialism", of farmers eager to acquire the Floridas and Canada, and still further increase their supremacy over the seaboard commercial groups. The authors give Benjamin Rush, William Maclure, and other early educational reformers more space than all the generals of this war. The economics, manners, ideas, and social pattern of the new Western States are carefully analyzed, while the squabbles of Clay, Crawford, Adams, and Jackson for the presidency are rapidly passed over. The Mexican War is regarded as simply the inevitable result of the heedless westward thrust of our land-hungry people. The Beards are at no pains to make it seem moral, as Justin H. Smith did, or immoral, as James Schouler did; to them it is merely unmoral, like the floods, the frosts, the tides, and the other phenomena of nature.

In similar fashion the Civil War ceases to be the product of a political contest over slavery and state rights, and becomes in great degree a collision of vast interests of class and property. It marks also, to these authors, a culmination of the rivalry between the agrarian forces dominant in the Jacksonian era, and the new industrial organization which had already largely transformed the North. It brought to a sudden upheaval the deep-running forces which effected a permanent shift in the center of gravity of American society. The day of Jefferson, Jackson, and Harrison ended in sunset; the effulgence of the new day of Blaine, Aldrich, and Mark Hanna—effulgent at least for certain economic interests—lit up the East. Beard believes that students of our history between 1845 and 1860 have kept their eyes fixed too closely on the Wilmot Proviso, the Kansas struggle, and the Dred Scott decision; they have not paid sufficient attention to the rise of inventors like Howe, McCormick, and Lyman Blake; the develop-

119

ment of the factory system; the emergence of great industrial organizers—the Lawrences, Abbotts, Vanderbilts, and Brookses; the growth of an astonishing network of railways. Lincoln's election was a great political landmark; but this history points also to the landmark offered by the census of 1860, which showed the value of factories, transportation systems, and city property as for the first time greater than the value of all farms and plantations. Thus Beard pursues his story. As the social historian must, he heavily weights the recent decades. The multiform growth of the last 60 years receives as much space as the events of the entire 370 years between Christopher Columbus and the election of Grant.

Even the friendliest reader will wish to take many exeptions to Beard's sweeping strokes. His view of the Civil War and its causes, for example, is plainly open to doubts and reservations. He himself would admit that his survey of the crowded epoch since 1890 will undoubtedly, to historians a generation hence, seem lacking in perspective and in a right weighing of action and reaction. Much of his history, in brief, is hypothesis, and will have to be tested part by part as we assemble fuller data through the work of monographic writers. But his bold use of hypothesis, this arching of the flood of years by a great bridge of novel design and structure, is of lasting value even if many spans of the bridge are defective.

While Beard was carrying through his ambitious work, Arthur M. Schlesinger and Dixon Ryan Fox were planning a co-operative history which should cover the whole period of American social development in much greater detail and with more precision. Their plan, involving the assignment of each volume to a separate writer, was a decided improvement upon that used by H. D. Traill in editing his *Social England*. As yet this new *History of American Life* is but one-third published, with another volume now in press. The four volumes which appeared in 1927 were T. J. Wertenbaker's *The First Americans, 1607–1690;* James Truslow Adams's *Provincial Society, 1690–1763;* Carl Russell Fish's *The Rise of the Common Man, 1830–1850;* and Allan Nevins's *The Emergence of*

Modern America, 1865–1878. These volumes differ in arrangement, style, and to some extent in method. But they are alike in
general content, analyzing the life of the whole people and all the
elements—economic, sectional, cultural—which affected it; compressing into a few hundred pages the data of an immense number
of monographs and articles; and each showing laborious original
research. The completed series will give us more than 4,000
pages—perhaps 5,000—devoted entirely to our social development from 1492 to the present day.

Some conclusions regarding this admirably planned series are
already possible. We can say at once that even to well-read
students it will be a revelation of the variety, richness, and color
which American life has exhibited during the past three centuries.
It will bring home to readers as never before the fact that ours is
really an old society, with a spacious past; that the continental
domain upon which it has expanded, its sectional, geographical,
and racial variety, the rapidity of its changes and growth, its
remarkable energy, especially in industrial fields, its exuberant
optimism, the novelty of many of its institutions, ideals, customs,
and even religious phenomena, and its distinctive psychology, give
the story an extraordinary interest. Again, the complete series will
inevitably call attention to a good many gaps in the treatment of
important elements of national growth. It will also dispel many
misconceptions. Wertenbaker, for example, corrects the old
impression that the upper South in colonial times had a distinctly
Cavalier society, when actually it was as plebian as New England's;
Adams makes it plain that Puritanism was by no means always
pure, and shows that the lot of the poor settler grew worse, not
better, during the eighteenth century; and Fish exhibits in the life
of the 'thirties a broad impulse toward social reform and state
interference which, if the slavery question had not shut down
upon it, might shortly have made America the most progressive of
democracies. It is likely also that the series, when completed, may
be uneven. The volumes may not quite dovetail in material or
harmonize in outlook. And, as with Dr. Beard's book, much in

121

even this thorough co-operative history is bound to be hypothesis, and when fuller investigation is made, will be superseded. Perhaps in time there will appear a historian who, with his single hand, will write our social history on as broad a scale as the largest political chronicles—Bancroft's, McMaster's, Channing's—and will give his record the advantage of a uniform philosophy and point of view.

Undoubtedly the outlook for this branch of historiography is bright; the spirit of the times favors it. But great as its future will be in other countries, it should be particularly great in ours. Dr. J. Franklin Jameson noted nearly forty years ago in his volume on *Historical Writing in America* that, as compared with English or French practice, a great proportion of our historical work was already going into the history of institutions, economics, and manners. This is a natural and healthy tendency. We have here a prosperous democracy, partly exempt from the constant wars and more jarring political conflicts which engross the Old World historian, its people showing the greatest variety of race, cultural origins, and traditions in the world, and developing a land with an equally great variety of scenery, climate, resources, and occupations. The whole is one of the richest fields imaginable for a study of the forces which interact in the upbuilding and transformation of society. Because of its very richness, it may be long before we are in a position to survey it adequately; but it is a challenge to our best energies.

9

The Universal and the Local

In this brief paper, hitherto unpublished and probably
originating as a lecture, Allan Nevins explores still another
form of historical exposition. Local history, he argues, if
properly written, serves as a medium for the expression of
universal values no less than does national or international
history. To prove his point he examines two forms of
historical writing popular a generation ago: the antiquarian
chronicles prepared by jobless spinsters and retired parsons
that have traditionally recorded the local scene, and the
impressionistic regional studies then in vogue as volumes in
the *Rivers* and *Lakes* series that studded the best-seller lists.
The former he judges too narrow in scope to be of value, the
latter too lacking in substance to be enduring. Between the
two, Nevins maintains, lies a field for properly trained local
historians that could illuminate much of the past. He
concludes by laying down four rules for the proper preparation of such history.

This essay was found among Allan Nevins's literary remains, with no indication of
its origin. All efforts to locate a published version have failed.

George Santayana tells us that Charles Eliot Norton once commented on the growth of John Fiske: "He began with the history of the Universe; he went on to the history of the United States; and he may yet advance to the history of Cambridge." Norton's comment held much common sense. Fiske's *Cosmic Theology* is outlived by his picture of Jamestown. Let no one despise local history, for it often proves the most universal kind of history.

Indeed, local history is a contradiction of terms; for if any piece of writing is true history, it is bound to transcend the local. Can a history of Athens, or Florence, or Oxford, be local?—for it must deal with forces that made the wide world wider. Is a history of one year in the life of Thoreau's Walden or Thomas Hardy's Dorchester, as these men saw it, local? Is Marcotte Chute's *Shakespeare of London* (nine-tenths London and one-tenth Shakespeare) or Mrs. Pulitzer's *Reveille in Washington* local? The greatest book yet written in New Zealand, Herbert Guthrie-Smith's *Tutira: The Story of a New Zealand Sheep Station* (1921), and one of the greatest books of its kind in the world, is the history of a single sheep station; a book so full of social, economic, geological, biological, and intellectual meat that it can be read with fascination by anyone from Scandinavia to Argentina—for it speaks to universal experience, experience with land, climate, beast, bird, markets, labor, and the general human lot.

It is evident to observers of recent literary trends that a striking change has passed over what used to be called local history. It was once the proudest field of the amateur. In America, as in Britain, any industrious minister, newspaperman, town clerk, or jobless spinster could turn to local history. The production was tremendous; the array of poor books was staggering; the emergence of a good one was distressingly rare. Anyone who looks at the shelves creaking under old-style county histories, books on *The Prominent Men of Northern Ohio*, tomes on *Selma and Her Leading Citizens*, and six-volume state histories issued by the State History

124

THE UNIVERSAL AND THE LOCAL

Commercial Publishing Company, finds his limbs trembling and his feet leading elsewhere.

Here and there, in these juiceless wastes, gushes a fount of living water like H. G. Graham's immortal book on Edinburgh in its golden age of Scott, Adam Smith, Jeffrey, Hume, and Rawburn; like Reginald Hine's richly sympathetic story of Hinchin in England; or like James Truslow Adams's history of Bridgehampton, almost a model of what such a book should be. These three writers were trained scholars. Now and then an amateur drove his shaft down to open a sparkling wellspring. A memorable example is Andrew D. Mellick's classic record of Somerset in New Jersey, first published more than sixty years ago as *The Story of an Old Farm* and later reissued as *Lesser Crossroads*—the work of an almost lifelong cripple with a passion for antiquarian detail, a quick eye for the humanly appealing, and a natural sense of style.

Now the human mind does not intimately grasp the history of a hundred millions or a hundred and fifty millions; it respects and admires rather than loves the epic of our national past; it needs something smaller to dwell upon with fond affection. Men have a genuine hunger for good history enshrining the tutelary gods of their own community. They have a hunger, too, for the radiance which imagination can cast over familiar scenes: the radiance of Carl Sandburg describing Chicago—"Here is a tall, bold slugger set vividly against the little soft cities"; of Henry James describing New York City—"its instinctive refusal to be brought to book, its boundless liability to contagion and boundless incapacity for attention, its ingenuous blankness today over the appetites and clamors of yesterday, its chronic state of besprinklement with the sawdust of its ripped-up dolls." It was certain that the passion for setting human nature in intimate local detail which gave us local-color fiction—the fiction of Page, Cable, Miss Murfree, Miss Wilkins, Bret Harte, John Fox—would in time seek historical channels. Against the general gloom of stodgy amateur mass production sparkled a few omens of a better day: books like Grace

King's *New Orleans*, Mrs. St. Julien Ravelel's *Charleston*, and, on a very different plane, Josiah Royce's vivid, factual, searching *California*.

Then came the full charge of the new cohorts. The field of the plodding amateur has been overswept by an army of professional and semiprofessional writers; the old formality has been broken up by a delight in arresting new patterns. Nothing better symbolizes this change than the success of Constance Lindsay Skinner's *Rivers of America Series*. A city, a county, or a state is a formal unit. But the very idea of a river defies formality. A river has none of the systematic quality which marks a road, a canal, a highway, or a boundary line. It wanders at its own errant will; it sends off branches into every upland; it mirrors every cloud, bird, or tossing tree limb above it; it is haphazard, unpredictable, rich in a multiplicity of interests, and poetically alluring. Hence it was that the volumes on our rivers became a venture in impressionistic history. The best of them, like Tristram Coffin's *The Kennebec*, Henry S. Canby's *The Brandywine*, Hodding Carter's *Lower Mississippi*, and Donald Davidson's *The Tennessee*, ably combined truth with art. Pleasantly vagrant, shimmeringly allusive, here swift in narrative and there placidly reflective, they did not so much survey an area or period as drain its higher points, encircle its headlands, and furnish a path through its most picturesque valleys. After the *Rivers* series came the *Lakes* series. It is seldom, as Rupert B. Vance makes clear, that a river or lake is the center of a true region, and so offers a really scientific opening into history; for the region tends to have its own economy, its own social phenomena, and its own culture. But the planners and projectors of this new local history were not thinking about science; they were thinking of events, human beings, social scenes, and literary effectiveness. And writers upon the more conventional local units, such as Margaret Snyder in her fascinating biography of a pioneer Minnesota town, entitled *The Chosen Valley*, and Gerald M. Capers in his incisive study of Memphis, emphasized the literary note.

This impressionistic and literary approach has given life to what once looked like the prophet Ezekiel's valley of dry bones; it has brought local history into a million American homes to be read, not cobwebbed. It has shaken a vast amount of the American past into fresh and gleaming patterns. But it has had its distinctive shortcomings, which need to be assessed.

Set any product of the new approach beside such a magnificent example of the old formal history as Lindsay Fleming's *History of Pagham* in Sussex, which by virtue of two or three volumes of close research is probably the most thorough account yet written of an English parish, and perhaps of any community anywhere, and it seems by contrast weak and thin. Set it beside such a book, even, as Bayrd Still's thorough and conscientious *Milwaukee: The History of a City*, and its superficialities become evident. The anecdotal and the picturesque have their place in local history, but they are easily overdone; their due place is not wide unless they are new, they are typical, and they are related, like Lincoln's stories, to a larger truth. Too much of the impressionistic history consists of a *rechauffée* of long-known episodes and events, a new presentation of striking personages, even if not significant, and a repetition of amusing but often quite untypical details of social life. Emphasis falls upon those early areas where printed sources are abundant; save in rare instances, the narrative stops with a jerk about 1880 or 1900, leaving the rich contemporaneous materials lying all about the historian slighted because library work is so much easier than legwork.

In short, the impressionistic and literary approach often gains its goal of readability at the expense of the deeper historical values. This is quite unnecessary, for local history has one great central vein of interest which other types of history lack—the same vein that the novelist exploits in dealing with commingled characters and environment. The special opportunity offered by local history is that it brings us closer to the plain human being than grand-scale history can do. It gives the writer a channel to show Bill Tompkins letting his red-hot horseshoe cool on the anvil

127

as he discusses Squire Bailey's attitude toward horse racing at the county fair. It makes possible a discussion of Catholic-Protestant relations in terms of the outlook of Terence Mulvaneu on one side of the railroad tracks and Bradford Winthrop on the other side. The writer, like Mellick in *Lesser Crossroads*, can describe the life of slaves, paupers, and indentured servants, or the eighteenth-century farmhouse lore of witches and ghosts. He can, as in Margaret Snyder's *Chosen Valley*, relate when the first sewing machine came to the village and what it meant. He can explain, as Mrs. Constance Green does in her delightful history of Naugatuck, why the town discussion club found it fruitful to deal with the question: "Is the possession of a bad life a greater evil than the loss of a good one?" All human nature as related to changing environment lies open to the local historian as to no other; and it is here that the chief literary opportunity lies.

All in all, we are justified in stating (not too dogmatically) that a few fundamental rules may be laid down respecting local history as a branch of historiography in general. At any rate, we may name three or four:

First, that local history written for a local audience is bad history; local history written for a national or international audience is good history.

Second, that local history should come down to the present day. A wagonload of secondhand, rethreshed straw relating to colonial and early national history is worth less than a peck of real grain drawn from the history of the last fifty or twenty-five years. And in this connection the possibilities of the tape recorder should not be neglected.

Third, that in good local history, it is the typical that counts. The writer should bear in mind what Mrs. Green wrote in the preface to her history of Naugatuck: "In writing this chronicle I have attempted constantly to present against the background of the universal the distinctive features that made Naugatuck."

Fourth, that the special advantage of the local historian is that

128

he can come closer to the individual man, woman, and child than the large-scale historian; and if he makes the most of this opportunity, he can at once perform the greatest service to history and achieve the finest literary effects.

Part Three

THE HISTORIAN AND
THE SOCIAL SCIENCES

If historical studies are to play a significant role they must be sufficiently
appealing to the masses to reach a sizable segment of the population. So
Allan Nevins believed as he preached the popularization of the past and
penned his own stirring narratives and biographies. But Nevins was too
good a historian to elevate popularity above a search for the truth in his
scale of values. His ultimate goal—and the ultimate goal of all scholars
worthy of the name—was a complete understanding of the past. If this
meant sacrificing readership in the cause of accuracy, readership must go.
So it was that Allan Nevins, despite his crusade for well-written narratives
and his own penchant for narrative history, was a pioneer in advocating
the use of social-science techniques by his colleagues, as the essays in this
section reveal. The historian's use of these methods—borrowed from
economists, sociologists, anthropologists, political scientists, and social
psychologists—might repel the reader by overtaxing his capabilities or
offend him by the use of professional jargon, but that use was justified,
Nevins believed, if the result was better history.

10

What the Scientist and Historian Can Teach Each Other

Among the many manuscripts tucked away in Allan Nevins's files at the time of his death were two dealing with the interrelationship between history and science. The papers were obviously related; they were filed in the same folder, labeled with the same title, and contained a great deal of duplication. These have been merged to form the essay that follows, with paragraphs from the shorter manuscript inserted at seemingly appropriate spots in the longer. The result, although dated and preaching a message that seems embarrassingly obvious today, is still worth reading, partly because of the cogency of its arguments, partly because it admirably illustrates Nevins's early enthusiasm for the use of the tools of the scientist by the historian. The essay also reveals a great deal about Nevins's concept of history; whatever its borrowings from other disciplines, he believed, it would also remain an art rather than a science, never varying from its basic humanistic objectives.

Let us begin by a frank admission. Obviously the scientist and the historian have very little to teach each other in the field of method. We historians like to speak of some of our books as scientific in character; not a few scientists, conversely, now and then adopt a historical approach to special problems. In general, however, the historical method and the scientific method do not possess very much in common. Both science and history depend upon research in their explorations into the unknown. Both depend, in their higher reaches, upon an imaginative type of research. But that special possession of the research scientist, the controlled experiment, is unfortunately not available to the historian. Sometimes we wish that it were. We wish that in our investigations into the history of recent times, for example, we could call another Versailles Conference, with Woodrow Wilson, Lloyd George, Clemenceau, and all the other delegates attending, and with all the political, economic, social, and cultural factors of 1919 exactly reproduced, under conditions which would enable us to vary the elements at will. But this is impossible. In the field of method, the scientist and historian do have a little to teach each other, as I shall presently indicate, but we shall have to look elsewhere if we are to discover their principal importance to each other.

Where shall we look? It is in temper, outlook, and ideas that science has most to learn from history, as history has most to learn from science. If we examine the field of their possible interaction closely, we shall find that they possess a very considerable domain of knowledge and effort in common. That fact was hardly recognized at all fifty years ago; today many broadly educated scientists and advanced historians perceive it clearly.

In 1939, for example, the American Association for the Advancement of Science suggested that the Ecological Society of America take up a study of the relation of ecology to human welfare. The result was a symposium in December of that year on the position of ecology in the human situation. Just what could and should ecology do to increase the well-being of humanity? Dr.

134

T. S. Harding declared: "Science should have full equality with financial and administrative agencies in directing human affairs, but only when scientists are no longer the economic and social illiterates they tend to be today." He might have added, the historical illiterates. Dr. C. C. Adams, an eminent biologist, quoted this remark: It should be realized, he said, "that the financial and administrative agencies are generally equally illiterate of pertinent sciences!" But after this counterthrust he stated his general agreement with Dr. Harding. It is true, he admitted, that professional scientists tend to be illiterate in the realm of economic and social affairs. They should remedy this, he declared: "The scientist needs first to orient himself and put his own house in order, before advising all the world what to do."

In the summer of 1946, when I happened to be an officer of the American embassy in London, the seventeenth international physiological conference was held in Oxford. The attending delegates were each presented with a copy of a book by Sir Charles Sherrington called *The Integrative Action of the Nervous System*, not a new book, but a new edition of a work known for forty years. I believe it is regarded as a classic in its field. It contains a record of some wonderfully ingenious experiments into the workings of the nervous system; and it also contains a careful, speculative consideration of certain profoundly important questions which these experiments raise. Sherrington's special interest for a long lifetime has lain in the brain and nervous centers. He took as one starting point the theory of the nervous system based on the reflex action of the spinal column. This action has often been regarded as mechanical and deterministic, and some men have not hesitated to found on it a mechanistic view of human beings and human society. They say that men are simply a bundle of mechanical and chemical reactions. The essential doctrine of these students is much that of Descartes, who wrote centuries ago:

I regard the human body as a machine so built and put together that still, even if it had no mind, it would not fail to

135

move in precisely the same way as at present, since it does not move by the direction of its will, but only by the arrangement of its organs.

This mechanistic conception of man has a great many applications. It has given rise, for example, to a large and important school of modern novelists and poets who hold that men respond to brute impulses. Treating man as a product of natural determinism, without independent volition or reasoned ideals, these novelists have given us a grim series of novels and plays. Frank Norris in *McTeague* and *Vandover and the Brute*, Theodore Dreiser in *Sister Carrie* and the shabby, ill-fated protagonist of *An American Tragedy*, Robinson Jeffers in some of his abnormal creations, and a whole group of others from Jack London to Erskine Caldwell have drawn man as a product of mechanistic forces. The political application of the formula of Descartism has become even more important. A great many modern physiologists in totalitarian states have given their political leaders marked aid and comfort in pointing to human beings as essentially mindless and docile. Sir Charles Sherrington himself has remarked, with acid disagreement:

> Descartes' conception of the doings of man still finds its echo in official Russia. The citizen there, taken *en gros*, seems to be viewed as a system of reflexes. The State can "condition" and use these systems of reflexes. "Reflexology," as it is there called, becomes a science of Man on which the State leans. In "reflexology" Descartes would find Ivan Pavlov of Petrograd his greatest successor; and the successor was an experimentalist as Descartes was not.

Sherrington's own view of man is totally different from this robot conception. A student of history, sociology, and letters, as well as an experimental physiologist, he regards man as a higher being than a bundle of reflexes. In his later writing he declares that while the reflex is important, it is only part of the mechanism of the human nervous system. "Our inference," he writes, "has to

136

be that we are partly reflex, and partly not." That is, rational and
spiritual impulses exist alongside the mechanistic. There are some
processes that arise in the brain "intrinsically" by sensory activities. Presumably in a Shakespeare or Einstein the mental activities
which arise "intrinsically" are more numerous and important than
in an ordinary human being.

Let us turn from the physiologist to the historian, and from the
individual to society. Arnold Toynbee has given us in the six
volumes of his *Study of History* a survey of twenty-six civilizations.
That work reveals a vast knowledge of the facts of the human past.
It attempts a rigorous scientific approach to their analysis. To
what conclusions does Mr. Toynbee come? He tells us that
twenty-six civilizations have risen and declined or died, and that
one civilization remains in a flourishing estate—our own. What
has been the secret of the *rise* of these successive or overlapping
civilizations? Have they been the product of the innate characteristics of the people concerned? Did Babylonian, or Hellenic, or
Islamic civilization spring up and flower because of some inborn
and exclusive traits of the Babylonians, Greeks, or Arabs? Dr.
Toynbee dismisses that theory. Did some strong external stimulus,
on the other hand, produce these civilizations? That idea he
dismisses with equal vigor.

What then? If civilizations do not rise because of some strong
unconscious urge from within, or because of some stern determined thrust from without, what is the secret? The answer which
Toynbee gives for the society runs parallel to that which
Sherrington gives for the individual. He sees societies responding
to a combination of reflex impulses and creative impulses. Certain
environmental conditions produce a challenge, which is met by a
response. The challenge must not be too difficult, as it was with
the Eskimos; it must not be too easy, as it was with the
Polynesians. It must, in short, be a stiff challenge but nevertheless
a conquerable challenge. So much for the external impulse. The
response to this challenge is a kind of social reflex. But it is far
from being enough. In societies, as in individuals, *intrinsic*

137

impulses are also needed. Dr. Toynbee tells us that some element has to arise within the spirit of man if any great civilization is to be developed. It is not merely responsive; it is a creative element. He finds this element in the contribution of a few leaders who possess special endowments—in an elite. Usually, Dr. Toynbee finds, the special spiritual quality needed appears in one or more personages who have first withdrawn from the world and have then returned to it.

Here, as I have said, we find an eminent psychologist and an eminent historian following parallel paths. Both are concerned with fundamentally the same subject: the study of human behavior. Sherrington approaches it by experiments on the nervous system and brain, accompanied with much reading of Descartes, Gibbon, and Goethe; Toynbee approaches it by the inductive analysis of an overwhelming mass of data on the histories of twenty-six or twenty-seven different civilizations since the dawn of time. They reached somewhat similar conclusions. Sherrington found that mechanistic or deterministic reflexes are inadequate to explain the conduct of individuals. Toynbee found that deterministic reflexes are inadequate to explain the conduct of society in the great civilizations. Higher qualities—intrinsic qualities—have to be included in the equation. They amount to what a whole set of modern philosophers call creative evolution. It is evident that the disciples of a Sherrington and the followers of a Toynbee—and of a philosopher like Bergson—can exchange data and ideas with profit, that historians and scientists can join hands in one broad field.

The great defect of science, from the standpoint of the historian and the writer generally, is its aridity in all matters of the spirit and the emotions. It is not only narrow, but dryly narrow. Our New York neighbor of the Catskills, John Burroughs, wrote that he never went into a natural history museum without feeling that he was at a funeral. The birds and beasts were stuffed scientifically and fitted into neat glass cases; but this was dead, dissected nature, which had nothing to do with the bird in the tree, the fish in the lake, the wolf in the thicket. Emerson seems to have had the same feeling when he wrote disdainfully about "post mortem science." Thoreau made it plain that he, too, thought the scientific technique of dissection, record, and measurement rather valueless. He wrote: "It is not worth while to go round the world to count the cats in Zanzibar." This was what Wordsworth meant when he expressed his impatience with the cold mechanical exactitudes of the modern sciences. They had put us out of tune with the heart of nature and the human heart; he wrote:

Great God! I would rather be
A pagan suckled in a creed outworn . . .

The same impatience went into Walt Whitman's record of his evening at the astronomical lecture:

When I heard the learn'd astronomer,
When the proofs, the figures, were ranged in columns before
    me
How soon, unaccountable, I became tired and sick,
Till, rising and gliding out, I wandered off by myself
In the mystical moist night air, and from time to time
Looked up in perfect silence at the stars.

Science, when it is pursued for itself alone, without reference to the interests of humanity, tends to become excessively mechanical and to instill an aridly mechanical view of the universe. As a machine the world of the atom, or the biological cell, or the table of elements, are very exact and doubtless very wonderful. But a machine does not minister to the spirit or nourish the sense of beauty. It does not excite our highest interest.

Hence it is that the greatest literature (and history belongs to literature) has never had any close relation to science. Literature, indeed, has flourished best in times, places, and minds far removed from the cold scientific spirit. Dante could never have written his marvelous poem had he not believed in the universe of

139

concentric spheres, the *primum mobile*, the sun moving around the earth, and heaven, purgatory, and Hades all as next-door neighbors. His poem illustrates what Emerson meant when he said that astrology is preferable to astronomy, for it is closer to the human being. Shakespeare could never have written *Macbeth* so effectively had he not written for a people who believed in witches, as King James I believed in witches; he probably believed in them himself.

Science, as John Burroughs remarked, is full of the kind of knowledge gained by the head, but it offers very little of the kind gained by the heart. History—the true history of Macaulay and Parkman—is full of the knowledge gained by the heart and spirit. Hence it is that the scientist should take time to read history to broaden and humanize himself. When he reads history he comes closer to the Pascal who wrote the *Pensées* or the Huxley who wrote essays on Hebrew poetry. The scientist that the historian likes best—and that the world likes best—is the scientist who is also a great humanist. The perfect example is perhaps Humboldt, a scientist who was admitted to the Weimar coterie of Schiller and Goethe, who wrote his great work *Cosmos* to give not merely a graphic but an imaginative record of his explorations and investigations and who exercised an international influence upon letters and art.

The great defect of history, on the other hand, is that it tends to be too shallowly humanistic. In depicting the immense panorama of human events, the pageantry of city, camp, and court, the unceasing play of dramatic incident, it falls short of the penetration and exactness demanded by the scientist. The more literary it is, the less scientific it becomes; and ideally it should be a mixture of literary and scientific elements.

To gain penetration, it needs the digging implements with which science can arm it. It needs statistics, a science of very modern development which few historians can understand. It needs psychology, and especially abnormal psychology, which means something more than a popularization of Freud. It needs scientific geography, in that development from Ratzel's foundation to which a distinguished New Yorker, the late Professor Clarence Brigham, contributed so much. How can we understand the Mormonism that started in western New York without some economic geography? How can we understand Gerrit Smith, not to speak of John Brown, without some abnormal psychology? History needs the biologist. In fact, of all the ideas that have shaped historical writing in the past hundred years, those of the biologist Darwin have had the deepest impress. Subconsciously, if not consciously, most history is still written in the partial light of evolutionary theory.

Without these aids, as without economics, sociology, and political theory as well, history can never get beyond the surface of events. The probing spirit of the scientist is indispensable to it. From that spirit—with its cry of "Deeper! Deeper!"—history can never learn too much.

Let us try another approach. We might turn back to the time when Walter Bagehot, historian and economist in one, was stimulated by Darwin's *Origin of Species* to write his still valuable book called *Physics and Politics*—an effort to lay down social laws akin to Darwin's biological laws; but that is somewhat too remote a period. We can find a more recent illustration of the possibility of using history and science in such fashion as to throw light on each other. It has long been known that one science, geography, has a specially close relation to history. In the 1890s an English scientist named Halford J. Mackinder was teaching geography at various institutions, notably the University of London; at the same time an American historian named Frederick Jackson Turner was teaching history at the University of Wisconsin. The two men seemed as far apart in their pursuits as in their homes. Then both sprang into modest fame as the result of papers read before professional bodies. Turner in 1893 treated the American Historical Association in Chicago to his long essay on "The Frontier in American History"; Mackinder some years later delivered before the Royal Geographic Society his essay on "The

141

Geographic Pivot of History." It was many years before the two papers were compared. But when men finally did look at them together, they saw that Mackinder and Turner, the scientist and the historian, were treating of the same subject; they were treating of space and of the movement of men in space. Mackinder's ideas were so fresh and stimulating that they gave rise in Europe to a profoundly influential school, the school of geopolitics. Turner's ideas, equally fresh and stimulating, changed the outlook of millions of Americans upon history, politics, economics, and culture.

Nowadays nearly everybody is familiar with Mackinder's main doctrines, his restatement of world geography. In particular, everybody knows something about his theory of the four main divisions of the globe: the Heartland of Euro-Asia from Germany to Manchuria; the Midland Ocean with its bordering countries of western Europe and the North Atlantic; the tropical rain-forest country of Africa and South America; and the Monsoon lands of India and China. Most people know something about Mackinder's theories of an appropriate balance among the four. Similarly, nearly all reading people know something about Turner's theory of the shaping of American civilization by the moving frontier; a frontier important from the settlement of Plymouth and James-town down to the admission of New Mexico and Arizona, and important not because of what the settlers did to the wilderness, but because of what the wilderness did to the settlers. The frontier democratized them, it made them individualistic, it Americanized the alien born, it inculcated a fervent nationalism. Obviously both Mackinder and Turner were concerned with the movement and balancing of peoples in space; one thinking of migration and expansion in America alone, the other of migration and expansion in world space.

A closer resemblance could be traced between Mackinder and Turner. Both declared that modern society is face to face with the problem of closed space, that all the free land is gone, and that mankind must plan its future accordingly. Turner was inspired to

142

write his essay by the fact that the federal government announced in 1893 that the frontier had ceased to exist. Mackinder sees the earth already occupied and crowded, though he suggests that medicine and other sciences may yet make the Brazilian and Nigerian jungles as habitable as is tropical Java. Malthus, in his day, was equally influential on historians (Buckle) and scientists (Huxley). Another scientist, Henry Fairfield Osborn, has brought out a book elaborating this concept of closed space. Much of the globe is really overcrowded now, he declares: in China and India the old Malthusian principles are being reillustrated; and the scientist and the political administrator must join hands to conserve our horridly wasted resources of soil and minerals and to set limits on population growth, or mankind will suffer indescribable calamities. This carries us into controversial realms. Some technologists and scientists will doubtless be more optimistic. But the fact which I wish to emphasize is that a scientific geographer and a nonscientific historian hit almost simultaneously on this concept of closed space—this theory that about 1900 the whole useful surface of the globe became occupied, and that a human reorientation became necessary. To make the most of their ideas, Halford Mackinder had to study history and Frederick J. Turner had to study science. Their followers must form a partnership if they hope to vindicate their doctrines.

The fact is that as both develop, science and social theory come ever closer together. They do so in part because science has a greater and greater impact upon society. A recognition of the need for study of this impact has been growing in scientific as well as historical circles. Early in the Second World War the National Science Foundation took a poll of leading scientists on the question of the most important subject for postwar research, and a majority declared that it should be the study of human behavior. No department of science can now ignore that subject. Physics, which next to mathematics is nowadays regarded as the most basic of all the sciences, used to think that it had nothing to do with human action. The old classical physics of Newton indeed had

143

little concern with it. But the physics of today—the physics of Rutherford, Bohr, and Einstein, of Eddington, Planck, and Langmuir—is changing all the conditions of human existence. It is even threatening, under certain conditions, to make human existence impossible. It is high time that the physicist should concern himself with the conduct of those human beings who will have to manage atomic force. And where will one find so much data on human conduct as in written history?

The new physics has affected social theory in subtler ways than by fission of the atom. It has given science two new concepts, those of relativity and of discontinuity, which have greatly affected the general thought of the world. Both seemed to challenge all the old verities; both seemed to put an end to fixity and order. The Newtonian physics laid down exact laws, and it was reassuring to note that stars and planets obeyed them. But in the new physics light is bent, two parallel straight lines continued into space ultimately come together, and electrons within the atom apparently jump about unpredictably. One scientist, P. W. Bridgman, coined a bleak phrase for the result among thinkers— he termed it "an outbreak of intellectual licentiousness." It was actually noted, as the new physical ideas gained ground, that they gave a keener edge to the old philosophical disputes over determinism and free will, and over idealism versus materialism. It has been pointed out by one American historian, James Malin, that the modern quantum physics offered some theories which came into head-on collision with the religious philosophy that Catholics derived from Sir Thomas Aquinas. The spectacle of Aquinas of the thirteenth century and Planck of the twentieth in open battle was one which might well draw philosophers, religionists, historians, and scientists together as eager spectators.

The historian has his own beliefs as to the proper balance between the individual and the society or state, and his own evidence to support his beliefs. One of the greatest of the nineteenth-century historians, Lord Acton, planned a tremendous history of liberty; and what he wanted to do as a single grand synthesis many lesser historians, particularly of Britain and America, have done in detail. The general devotion of Anglo-American historians to the idea that human happiness and progress are best realized in conjunction with individual freedom is illustrated by long rows of volumes. Hence the distinct uneasiness of many reflective historians when they found, about 1910, that various schools of thinkers were evolving an "organismic" theory that might be interpreted as hostile to individualism. It was first applied to plant and animal life. F. E. Clements, the author of *Plant Succession* and other works, was typical of many other writers. He argued that concern with the individual plant was foolish; what was important was the vegetational unit, comprehending thousands of millions of plants. The whole plant cover of a given area at a given time behaved as a complex organism. Indeed a combination of vegetational cover units and the animal life of the area might be regarded as a biotic organism. This organismic theory of plant and animal life might be carried over to human society. We may think of the society of the Mississippi Valley, or the Virginia-Carolina Piedmont, as a vast, multicellular organism. André Siegfried pictured the limestone areas of France as supporting a radical culture, the granite areas a conservative society.

It would be particularly easy to carry this organismic theory over to human society if psychology lent its aid. Psychology is still a very young branch of science, and hence still torn this way and that by leaders who differ sharply among themselves. Speaking offhand or a priori, we might suppose that psychology would manifest an invincible attachment to the individual. How could it give aid and comfort to those who wish to divide mankind into herdlike organisms? Yet it did precisely that.

We need but briefly mention the behavioristic cult of John B. Watson, with its insistence that heredity counts for practically nothing in shaping human beings. Instead, say the behaviorists, environment and training—especially very early training—determine our characters. The clear inference from this doctrine is that education, begun early enough, will entirely remake any society, and that a managed society thus becomes possible. An organismic entity can be created. Under first Austrian and then German rule, the Czech people were notably individualistic, freedom loving, and averse to discipline. Their new masters believe that none of these traits need to be inherited. They believe that if children trained from the cradle in mass loyalties to Communist dictatorship, if all newspapers, radios, and magazines preach the same doctrine, if all political leaders instill it, if all pulpits preach it, a mass organism will be created. Behaviorism leads to the managed society. Even more important in this connection is the *Gestalt* psychology of the Germans, associated with the great name of Wilhelm Wundt. It, too, denies that human behavior is inherited. Indeed, it goes further: it denies that the individual has any proper existence except as part of the whole. Society is an organism; this organismic society is all-important; and it is the duty of the single person to merge himself or herself into it—for the individual by comparison counts for nothing.

When scientific or pseudo-scientific teachings reach such conclusions as these, the historian finds it his duty to step forward with his own conclusions. If history is sure of anything, it is that the individual is not exclusively shaped by education and environment. A great deal more than circumstance is involved. Make your discipline as rigidly uniform as you like; the product will vary amazingly. The stock reply to Watson and Wundt has often been quoted. It was furnished by George Lewes in his *Life of Goethe*. Lewes pointed to the immense variety of character in the governing class of Britain—a class all educated by the same process. What can be more deadeningly uniform than the training of boys who are born to prosperous middle-class parents, reared in early childhood in English country houses, sent to Harrow or Eton, thence sent on to Oxford or Cambridge, then turned over to politics. This process would destroy individuality if anything could. Yet men came out of it as different as the radical Fox was from the conservative Pitt. Franklin D. Roosevelt and Hamilton

Fish, Jr., were brought up a few miles apart in the Hudson Valley in equally rich homes, trained in the same way, sent to the same Harvard, put through the same law studies; but could two men be more unalike?

The historian knows, too, that if the past teaches anything, it is that love of liberty is an instinctive, deeply ingrained, and inherited human trait, and that in the long run attempts to repress it simply have one result—a violent explosion. The repression may go on for centuries, as in France; the final explosion is proportionately severe, as in the French Revolution. The chances for eradicating from the Czech people their sturdy love of personal freedom and national independence are substantially zero. The historian will be the last person to believe in the organismic theories of society. Taking his stand with Acton and Toynbee, not to say Emerson and Carlyle, he will insist that society advances through the contributions of countless individuals as individuals; and that among them, the work of natural leaders is indispensable. The role of the hero may as readily be undervalued as overvalued. An individual leader named Mohammed arises in a most unlikely time and a most unlikely place; and the history of the whole Middle East is altered. An individual named Robert Clive is born in a foggy, chilly island off the northwestern corner of Europe, and the lives of countless millions of Indians are altered for generations. The historian might say much, too, upon the comparative merits of free and regimented societies from the point of view of general human welfare and of efficiency; but that is another theme entirely.

Great spiritual elements, great moral impulses, great intangible forces—these must be considered in any theory of ultimate causation.

Some experts in science tell us that the next great chapter in its progress will be a biochemical chapter. They point to the way in which biology and chemistry, working together, have brought about the synthetic manufacture of vitamins and of certain hormones; they point to the experimental elimination of certain

147

disease viruses. Other experts believe that physics and chemistry, in combination, will write the next great chapter; and they can point to the epochal development of atomic energy. Now chemistry and physics are exact sciences, while biology, physiology, geography, and psychology are not. I have said that the vital difference between the historical method and the scientific method is that the latter alone can make use of rigidly controlled experiments. In the chemical laboratory every element in a problem can be rigidly measured and adjusted. So in the physical laboratory. But not so in other fields. Medical science, for example, has its controlled experiments—up to a certain point. In exploring the unknown its first step is to offer a hypothesis; let us say Dr. Carlos Finlay's hypothesis in Cuba that the stegomyia mosquito causes yellow fever. The second step is to test it by a series of carefully controlled experiments—bedding, food, dirt, and other elements. The third step is to draw the appropriate conclusion. The fourth step, as some scientist has said, is to accept this conclusion whether you like it or not. Unfortunately, many problems of biology, physiology, and psychology do not yield to such a procedure. Medical science finds that diseases vary inexplicably from patient to patient—particularly when they involve the action of mind on body—and that some ailments take a multitude of forms and phases. Three doctors are called to the bedside of a stricken patient. They make three different diagnoses. Later the postmortem shows that all were wrong. The three doctors are in a position to sympathize with historians who offer three or four main diagnoses of the causes of the fall of Rome or the opening of the American Civil War.

A number of physicians, perceiving this kinship, have made valuable contributions to both science and history in studies that connect it with physiology and psychology. One of the first such works was a volume by a noted English brain specialist, Dr. W. W. Ireland, entitled *The Blot on the Brain*. His essays on St. Francis Xavier and on the hereditary neuroses of the royal family of Spain are especially enlightening to historians. The Australian physician MacLaurin, author of those justly popular books *Mere Mortals* and *Post Mortem*, is equally effective in showing that in treating certain problems the research methods and the data of physician and historian are much the same. King Henry VIII profoundly affected the Reformation, English history, and by consequence our American development; Jean Paul Marat, perpetrator of some of the worst crimes of the French Revolution, greatly affected modern affairs. MacLaurin's evidence that much of King Hal's conduct sprang from long syphilitic illnesses, and all of Marat's from paranoia, is impressive. It is certain that a careful analysis of John Brown of Harper's Ferry, made by a skilled neurologist and physician, might throw a bright ray of light on a crucial turning point in our national past. Conversely, a thorough scrutiny of all the evidence on John Brown might help the present-day specialist with living patients.

It is altogether clear that history and science, both pursued with some real imagination and both studied with an attempt at profundity, disclose many common meeting points. The further they are extended, the more they will owe each other. Both the historian and the scientist are under constant temptation to oversimplify their methods and conclusions. The historical biographer can tell the scientist how very far Freud is from explaining Savonarola, or Bismarck, or Woodrow Wilson. The scientist finds the historian trying to explain the downfall of eighteenth-century Poland by its vicious constitution and the bad character of its governing class; and, in the person of the trained geographer, he points out how largely the downfall was attributable to the flatness of Poland, with no natural barriers against invasion. The infinite complexity of the past and the infinite complexity of the present both need emphasis. The more we know of history and the more we know of science, the less we are likely to accept simple monistic explanations of what must be highly complicated phenomena.

In addition, the historian has a special lesson to learn from the scientist in the latter's dedication to impartial and unprejudiced methods of study. When prejudice and ascertained fact come into conflict, when theory and data clash, the scientist never flinches. The historian must learn to imitate him. Conversely, the scientist has still to acquire from the historian that sense of perspective in which all research subservient to human well-being should be conducted. We begin to fear that science is going too fast. When we contemplate the awful possibilities of the atomic bomb, when we hear a British scientist say that one poison has been perfected so powerful that three pounds of it will wipe out the human race, we feel like begging the scientists to stop and read a little history. They need to think of society, its long past and we hope longer future, and not merely of scientific results. They might ponder the medieval tale of the sorcerer's apprentice who learned the magic word that brought buckets of water from the river into the house, but failed to learn the word which stopped the water. Perhaps it is history that has that word.

Finally, we may state one less commonplace conclusion than the mere fact that the historian and the scientist need each other. It is this: they both need the philosopher—the metaphysician. They both push their truth finding to a point where they find great spiritual elements—great intangible forces—great questions of ultimate causation—involved in their studies. Then it is that they want not only the wisdom of Thucydides and the insight of Newton, but the further-piercing vision of Spinoza.

11

Advances in the Social Sciences

That Allan Nevins kept well abreast of historical trends, even in his later years, is well illustrated in this address, delivered at Hofstra University, Hempstead, N.Y., in 1967, nearly a decade after his retirement from the classroom and only four years before his death. In it he urged his listeners to adopt social-science techniques then still in their experimental stage—sociological analysis of class structures, psychohistorical interpretations of individuals, econometric structuring in the solution of demographic problems. Yet Nevins was not quite sure that these tools would paint the brilliant pageant of the past that was his goal. He was, he told his audience, "profoundly shocked when, called upon to look at a page of modern exposition, he finds that it has no resemblance whatever to the kind of page that John Stuart Mill or Francis Parkman or Vernon Parrington wrote." That a man repelled by "horizontal lines of digits and rising or falling curves of graphs" should promulgate the cause of demographers, econometricians, and behaviorists demonstrates his dedication to the use of any device that would help unveil the past—whatever its effect on the melodious rhetoric that he loved.

Reprinted with permission from *The Hofstra Review* (Autumn 1967), 24–26, Hofstra University, Hempstead, N.Y.

A former student of mine, who is laboring earnestly to push back the frontiers of the social studies, is addressing himself just now to a study of classes in American society. This subject has at various times deeply interested Joseph Schumpeter, Charles A. Beard, Adolph A. Berle, and a long list of lesser economists, political scientists, and sociologists. But, as in many undertakings of this sort, the student has encountered baffling problems of definition. What *is* a class? Approached by Schumpeter's road, "class" demands attention not to the individual but the family. In the definition of *aristocratic* class (what Thomas Jefferson in Virginia called the Patrician Order), family is important. But if we approach the idea of class in strictly economic terms and rate the middle class, or what John Adams called "the middle rank of people," as much the most important element in our society, family ceases to mean much. Then too, class may be defined in terms of political power; or in terms of psychological attitudes, with pride—or at least a sense of separateness—as an essential ingredient; or in terms of legal privilege.

The study of so simple a subject as class, in short, involves us at once in economics, sociology, group psychology, and wide reaches of government and law. History is full of the classes, and so is political behavior. The relationships of literature to class, from Walter Scott at one extreme to Theodore Dreiser at the other, are multifarious. The social studies have become a vast and ever more closely woven web. We need only touch one strand—conceptualize the study, as the phrase goes—and the whole fabric trembles. Yet the relationships are so varied that it is often difficult to say what is an advance, and what is not. A certain forward thrust in economics may excite the social anthropologist and yet have no value or equivocal value for students of demography. The American Civil War seems a breakdown of political rationality to Mr. Avery Craven, who thinks highly of psychological inquiries; but that idea is repugnant to Mr. Bruce Catton, who thinks little if at all of them and approaches the war from other angles.

The rapidity with which the social studies now grow and the

specialization of research they involve are astonishing to anybody who tries to follow a few even in elementary fashion. No man pretends to be truly expert in more than two or three. We scarcely finish scanning an analysis by Simon Kuznets of postwar economic growth (Cambridge, 1964) before we are called upon to look into D. E. Apter's treatise *The Politics of Modernization* (Chicago, 1965). Barbara Ward's *Nationalism and Ideology*, which can best be classified as recent history, calls to us as urgently as Frank Riessman's *Mental Health of the Poor*, which hovers between psychology and sociology.

The very best minds of our time have a wonderful versatility, both in subject matter and in method. I need only mention Arnold Toynbee or Raymond Aron as examples. The late Ernest Jones, to offer another example, was a leading British figure in psychoanalysis, and he wrote a famous essay on the nightmare; but he was also widely known for a study of Shakespeare's *Hamlet*, and he finally launched upon a three-volume biography of Freud—a biography that covered a great segment of the nineteenth century. Freud himself had a hobby in archaeology and was a conscientious student of literature.

So much is now required of readers and workers in the wide field of the social studies, in fact, that some observers question whether individual inquiry should now be encouraged. Should not the important subjects be turned over to team-workers, to groups and associations? One answer to this question is plain: a Schumpeter in economics, a Freud in psychology, and a Winston Churchill in historical writing will always find opportunity to exercise their highly individual talents. But can lesser figures any longer work effectively alone? Should they even try?

The most spectacular recent advances in the social studies (though nobody can say they're the most important) have been made through the use of mathematics, and especially statistics, as new conceptual tools. We have been given a "fresh focus," the experts tell us, through the employment of numbers. Economics,

sociology, anthropology, and history can all be profitably transformed by a searching and skillful use of figures.

We should, say the experts, use tables of figures and arrays of
graphs to give ourselves an understanding of the true importance
of steel production in American development; or to comprehend
the real social significance of birth, marriage, and death as
Professor Roy Ladurie tries to understand them; or to get at the
significance of the median length of life in Victorian times as
compared with the far shorter life span of Elizabethan days (a
problem of demography that Peter Laslett of Cambridge, England, has brought home to us). We are told that a more skillful
use of mathematics can establish new and illuminating relationships among the main social disciplines. Nay, even in areas where
no statistics exist, they can be called out of darkness; the gaps can
be bridged; economic models can be built and tested.

All this is both impressive and depressing. Anyone who believes,
as I do, that such social studies as economics, anthropology,
sociology, and above all history ought to have a close relationship
with the humanities is profoundly shocked when, called upon to
look at a page of modern exposition, he finds that it has no
resemblance whatever to the kind of page that John Stuart Mill or
Francis Parkman or Vernon Parrington wrote. Instead, it flashes
before our eyes horizontal lines of digits and rising or falling
curves of graphs.

We must not be unjust, however. We shall lose heavily if we do
not try to grasp the new ideas and improved tools.

The first important deployment of quantitative techniques was
in the field called "econometric history," and it had a dramatic
effect. In April, 1958, two scholars, Alfred H. Conrad and John R.
Mayer, published in the *Journal of Political Economy* an essay
entitled "The Economics of Slavery in the Ante-Bellum South."
With startling efficiency and completeness, the essay made some
important points, in part old, in part quite original, respecting the
economic history of the South. We had long known that slavery
might be regarded as a labor system, as a livestock system, or as

154

both. As a labor system, it was of dubious economic utility. The Virginia or Alabama planter might find, when he sold his cotton or tobacco, that the return did not pay his bills for the slaves' food, clothing, housing, medical care, and (above all) capital costs. But the sale of Negro progeny often tipped the scale. Northern antislavery men pointed this fact out in the 1850s. William Cullen Bryant, as editor of the New York *Evening Post*, scornfully expatiated on the fact that the annual wheat crop in Virginia was worth much less than the annual pickaninny crop, for in a few years the pickaninnies could be sold to the Southwest.

It was this whole subject that Conrad and Mayer explored. And they brought out proof by the new econometrics that slavery just before the Civil War was *not* becoming unprofitable and hence moribund, as many scholars once declared. On the contrary, female slaves, producing an average of five to ten children apiece, made their owners an annual 7 or 8 percent return on capital.

This proof produced a sensation. So did another econometric paper published immediately afterward—a paper demonstrating that the construction of railways in the newly opened West did not have the indispensable connection with the profitable development of the land that had long been attributed to it. By econometrics, proof was assembled that nineteenth-century railroad construction in America was often pushed beyond necessity, and that a fuller use of natural waterways and canals could have obviated much of the outlay, without hardship to the settlers. As I have said, the result was dramatic. Only a few scholars had attended the meetings at which econometric papers were first read. They began flocking to later meetings, where strident contention gave way to reasonable debate.

Such veterans of economics as Edwin F. Gay, former head of the Harvard School of Business Administration, regarded the new method with suspicion. Professor Fritz Redlich of Yale declared that it produced not economics nor history but quasi-economics, quasi-history. Yet it has made astonishing progress. It is obviously important not so much for its disclosure of specific new truths as for its demonstration of the utility of a whole new method. If economics could find this unused key, why could not other disciplines find their own untouched keys?

Some larger questions are left, however. When a new key is found, its limitations as well as potentialities must be studied. The first impulse of some enthusiasts is to claim too much, and this impulse must be resisted. One of the best authorities on the so-called "mathematizing" of knowledge, on the application of the new quantitative techniques, has warned his associates of "the great hidden danger of subjective interpretation" of statistics—yes, even of statistics. And various scholars have been quick to point out what vast areas of life and knowledge have no responsiveness whatever to figures or graphs or any form of quantitative concept. As Henry David Thoreau wrote, there's no use going around the world just to count the number of cats in Zanzibar.

It used to be that a student in any of the various branches of technology or science could pursue his education in the faith that his specialized knowledge and skill would be useful for the remainder of his life. No such assumption is possible today. The advances in technology and science are so multitudinous and sweeping that the engineer has to be retrained for a fresh approach to his professional work every few years, or at least once a decade. Thus various branches of science and technology now place a higher valuation upon a recent graduate of M.I.T. or Cal Tech than upon an older man, despite the greater experience and more mature judgment of the latter.

A similar situation obtains in the social studies, where again obsolescence of knowledge is rapid. The inexorable command is that of the old emigrant trains in the West at dawn: "Catch up! Catch up!" How can we catch up? By attending professional meetings, by taking short courses, by such devices as the university seminars for Columbia University faculty members, by such agencies as the behaviorist center at Stanford, by other implements as yet untried. But catch up we must!

We must also realize that in our field of the social studies the fragmented pieces of human knowledge have constantly to be rescued from untidiness and confusion, and cemented together—cemented at new and ever higher levels.

12

The Explosive Excitement
of History

Believing as he did that reading history was a sovereign remedy for the ills of mankind, Allan Nevins was always eager to share with a wider public not only his own massive doses of historical narrative but also the prescriptions that he used to create his masterpieces. In one of his last essays, published in the *Saturday Review* in 1968, he discusses the techniques that have revolutionized historical studies since World War II and recalls his own excitement as he sensed their possibilities. The expansion of areas beckoning investigators, he suggests—both in time (with anthropological innovation opening new vistas on the distant past) and space (where newer interests have brought into the mainstream of history hitherto neglected areas in Africa and the East)—has offered new challenges to scholars, just as has the opportunity to probe more searchingly into man's behavior by using the tools of the demographer and sociologist. Professional historians will find little new in Nevins's appraisal, but they will be struck by his desire to make the whole world aware of the "explosive excitement" of history that he himself felt so strongly.

Reprinted with permission from the *Saturday Review* 51 (April 6, 1968): 13–15, 62.

What would one of the older American historians, such as George Bancroft or John Fiske, say if he saw on a student's desk a volume entitled *History of the Origins of Modern African Thought?* Or if he saw lying beside it a publisher's circular announcing: "Our latest and most important work in the history of demography, *A Historical Atlas of Religion in America*"? He would exclaim, "Is there really such a thing as modern thought in Africa—and is it worth study?" In the same breath he would demand, "What is demography, anyway—and need historical workers keep up with its latest atlases?" If proper explanations were given him, he might utter the angry comment, "Well, this is not history as my generation knew it!" He might add the rueful remark, "I see that great changes have occurred. But according to these explanations, I see that Carlyle was totally wrong when he wrote, 'All knowledge is the product of history.' He should have reversed the statement and written, 'All history is the product of new knowledge.' "

If our historian said this, he would find a host of young teachers, writers, and students of history warmly applauding him. "Old man, you have hit the nail on the head," they would say. True, history *is* the product of new knowledge, and as much of it as we can get. When you learn more, you will endorse another statement by Carlyle. He once wrote, "I don't pretend to understand the universe. It is a great deal bigger than I am. People ought to be more modest." Just so, our constantly expanding knowledge, all tributary to history, is a great deal bigger than we are. Historians ought to be more modest about their discoveries and achievements.

Many powerful new forces are at work in the field of history as it is now being written and studied, and few men understand half of them. This fact affects us all, for history is fundamental to our interests, ambitions, and comprehension of the world about us; to our opinions about ourselves, about other peoples, and about our common future.

History is constantly, inexorably growing. It extends itself in time, for more history is made every day, week, and month, with a rapidity that our fathers would have found bewildering. Meanwhile, new studies, from archaeology, epigraphy, and carbon-dating to astronomy, uncover more and more of the far past. History extends itself in space; new geographical units come constantly pressing upon the stage of events—not only fresh extensions of our Occidental world, such as Australia, New Zealand, Indonesia, and Japan, but Antarctica and the reclaimed deserts of Asia, Africa, and America. These spatial extensions invoke changed attitudes and outlooks. African history has been with us since Pliny remarked in consternation, "Always something new out of Africa!" But an African past now changed! Yesterday, African history, shutting out the colored man and all his cultures, began with Livingstone, Stanley, Cecil Rhodes, and the great partitions; today, beginning with the arts of prehistoric peoples, it mentions explorers and European annexations as but tiresome, trivial interruptions.

Dealing with time, history now forces us to accept the strangest materials. New methods of dating Folsom points have pushed the human occupation of America back to 14,000 B.C. or earlier. Dealing with space, history crowds upon our attention a whole host of startling interests. The Fall 1966 issue of *Daedalus*, published by the American Academy of Arts and Sciences, contained studies of fiction in Arabic lands, in Israel, in Poland, in Japan (with a special examination of trauma—i.e., the wounding effect of recent world convulsions—upon the Japanese novel), in India, and in other lands. We are invited elsewhere to compare West Indian fiction with Egyptian fiction, and to analyze *émigré* influences in thought—the impact of expatriate students and authors who leave Spain, Malaysia, or Vietnam to go to Oxford, Moscow, Roberts College, Petrograd, or the University of California, upon the lands to which they return.

The broadening of studies of all kinds—political, economic, social, and intellectual—in space, must eventually be carried to include all countries on the roster of the United Nations; and all these studies must in time be regarded in their historical aspects. But the steady extensions of history in time and space are of small importance compared with its momentous extensions in depth. Of this fact many illustrations might be given.

The impact of exact science in deepening historical inquiry in recent years has obviously been tremendous. Ecology, for example, was an old science when Huxley and Alfred Russel Wallace began writing. But the conservation movement that Theodore Roosevelt aggressively supported and that our national and state governments have so earnestly vitalized has given it fresh significance. Whether it touches chemistry in its research on pesticides and air and water pollution, or psychology in making "the sense of impending scarcity" a potent spur to action, or history in its light upon political and sociological obstacles to the progress of the movement, ecology is a study of large public importance.

Or, we open a learned journal and encounter an essay of unquestioned authority on "The Uses and Abuses of Thermodynamics in Religion." Upon examination, it turns out to be a historical analysis of the effect of twentieth-century physics upon philosophy and religious faith.

Meanwhile, the influence of the so-called social sciences in deepening history is clearly more pervasive and powerful than that of the exact sciences. No one can doubt that the role of psychology in history has been transformed by the ideas of Freud and Jung, just as the role of economics has been transformed by those of John Maynard Keynes. Many of the new ideas are debatable. But one happy effect of their transfer to history is to give students and the general public a sense of the continuing vitality of history.

Some of the rising generation feel much as Maxim Gorky, in *My University Days*, tells us that he felt when he undertook to convince fellow undergraduates that the old Russian thinkers were outdated, the old writers archaic, and that they must turn to better illuminants. He was encouraged by another enthusiast who spoke glowingly of Buckle, Lowell, W. E. Hartpole Lecky, Mill,

Spencer, Darwin, and the intoxication of their ideas. "He stroked the books with his palm as if they were kittens," writes Gorky, "and he explained excitedly, 'Good books, these are. This is a very rare one. The censor had it burnt. You must read it.' He handed me Hobbes's *Leviathan*." Some such excitement can be gained from certain of the latest treatises in the social sciences.

New excitements in history are needed—the excitement that some think can be drawn from the economics of Keynes and Schumpeter, the mass-psychology that Nietzsche thought would be the master science of the future, and the latest studies in sociology, anthropology, and behaviorism. Ingenious new tools are available—computers for handling lists of names, rows of numbers, and even word differences and word resemblances that track down the authorship of every written work; sampling techniques; fresh modes of processing data and calculating statistics. A sense of sailing like Drake and Columbus into new worlds can be highly valuable. The future historian should face all the new possibilities open to him intrepidly and hopefully.

But excitements—especially new excitements—have to be carefully controlled if they are to be useful. In facing novel concepts and using revolutionary interpretive theories, the historian must not blindly surrender to them, but seek to adapt them to classic models and improve them. They can always be improved by the use of imaginative and spiritual elements of inspiration, as a striking modern example may help to demonstrate—the example of a man who made bold use of new scholarly possibilities while clinging stubbornly to old humanistic values.

Any list of examples of scientific-minded historians who did much to accept new fields of inquiry that threw light upon the past, present, and future would carry us back as far as Thucydides and Herodotus, for Thucydides had a clear understanding of the sociology of the Hellenistic and the Oriental worlds, and of the social psychology of his own era; while Herodotus, with his unquenchable curiosity about the customs, manners, and beliefs of the different people of Europe, Asia, and Africa—primitive or advanced—was always anxious to put ethnology and archaeology at the service of history. His volumes are still a mine of information for the ethnologist and the student of comparative institutions no less than for the historian. And for illustrations of boldness in facing the new studies and courage in pushing into unexplored territory, we may well turn to a man who stands in the direct line of descent from Thucydides and Herodotus, one of the most fascinating of modern American historians: James Henry Breasted, an eminent scholar and archaeologist who was also a philosopher and the foremost modern apostle of the idea that man has followed "a rising trail" from the darkness and savagery of the remote past to a greater and greater elevation in civilization.

His was a life of struggle that might well be an example to later scholars. The son of a small hardware dealer in ailing health, he entered an undistinguished little college in Naperville, Illinois, went to a school of pharmacy, and served for a time as a mere prescription clerk in a drugstore. Possessing a strong religious instinct, he resolved to turn to the ministry, enrolled in the Chicago Theological Seminary, and soon engrossed himself in a study of Hebrew. When he developed doubts about dogma, his teacher advised him to seek a career in the Oriental languages, including Egyptian. Before long, he was studying in the Yale Graduate School under William Rainey Harper.

When Harper went to the new University of Chicago, he suggested to Breasted that he equip himself for a professorship of Hebrew there. A new day was dawning in the field of ancient history, as it is in wide historical fields today. Adolf Erman had lately founded a school of Egyptology in Berlin, applying the newest scientific methods to the study of Egyptian culture and lexicography, and encouraging a deeper investigation into all phases of Oriental culture. Breasted, taking his doctorate with Erman, was by 1895 fully launched upon his career, teaching

Egyptology and the Semitic languages, and helping direct the Haskell Oriental Museum in the University of Chicago. In 1905, this hardware dealer's son became the university's first full professor of Egyptology.

He began lecturing all over the United States on the story of human progress in Egypt, his fluency of speech and vitality of presentation charming all his hearers as he unfolded with warm enthusiasm what was a new chapter of history to Americans. German institutions cooperated in asking him to copy and arrange the Egyptian hieroglyphic inscriptions scattered through European museums, a task which he performed with fine precision, profound scholarship, and ardent zest in interpretation. The grand result of his labors was the publication in 1905 of his *A History of Egypt*, which remained standard until his death thirty years later; and the appearance in 1906–07 of his five volumes of *Ancient Records of Egypt*. He was then put in charge of University of Chicago expeditions in 1905–07 to copy further Egyptian inscriptions. He wrote a textbook, *Ancient Times: A History of the Early World*, which did justice to the Oriental and Egyptian phases of ancient history. The Rockefellers in 1919 enabled him to found the Oriental Institute of the University of Chicago.

It is important to note that Breasted, in developing his pursuits, never allowed himself to become a narrow specialist. He remained a humanist, and he was too astute and cultivated to neglect literary history. He thought he had detected clues to the development of conscience and religious idealism in Egypt. In 1912 he brought out his important volume, *The Development of Religion and Thought in Ancient Egypt*, a new chapter in the history of human ideas. He showed that the Egyptians had at first been materialists, with limited moral ideas. But in time they had developed a sense of moral values and a feeling of personal relationship with the Deity. And in 1933 he published *The Dawn of Conscience*, which expounded his doctrine of the progress of mankind along "a rising trail." He presented a hopeful new idea of the future of humanity; as he once wrote: "In the splendor of that buoyant life of the human soul which has come up out of the impenetrable deeps of past ages, and risen so high, modern man may find a glorious prophecy of its future."

He had not only shown courage in exploring new paths; he had cultivated his own aesthetic and philosophic gifts.

Some of the greatest breakthroughs in history in the near future will undoubtedly lie in the rewriting and reassessment of the histories of leading African and Asiatic countries. Men acquainted with the work being done in England at Oxford and the University of Birmingham are anxious that beginnings made at Harvard, Columbia, and the Universities of Wisconsin and California should be pushed further; promising activities are also under way at African institutions in Ibadan and Nairobi. The historic records being largely unwritten and traditional, an adoption of novel methods is imperative. In Asiatic history, Russia, Britain, and the United States must compete in giving direction and aid to Indian, Near Eastern, and Japanese institutions. We shall have a reoriented world history to write.

Apart from these geographical changes, a large future undoubtedly lies with the before-mentioned study closely related to geography; that is, demography, which deals with the growth and decline of populations, necessarily in geographic terms. Of late, the best work in demography, defined in A. B. Wolfe's words as "the continuous inventory and analysis of the human population and its vital processes," has been done by Peter Laslett and others at Cambridge University, where an active school of analysts and writers has sprung up, using the abundant parish and county registers of Britain as a source and enlisting a host of researchers. A long list of demographic factors must be studied: rates of births, deaths, and migrations, with the effects of average age-levels on various types of activities. Demography involves a scientific study of all kinds of human tendencies and processes, from the laws which control marriages to the facts regarding population mobility, and to the morals as revealed in illegitimacy rates. The disclosures which demographic studies make are sometimes star-tling—for example, the apparent revelation that the population of France has been more "moral" than that of Britain.

Recently, students have recalled that much pioneer work has been done in America. As Dr. Louis Hacker reminds us, in 1843 the political economist George Tucker brought out a work called *Progress of the United States in Population and Wealth in Fifty Years*, which overcalculated the future growth of population, but explored various social problems in the light of population statistics in a stimulating way. Another early American writer on demography attracted attention by his defense of urban compared to rural life. This was Adna Ferrin Weber, a country boy of upper New York who went to Cornell to study population and statistics, and then to Columbia, where he published his doctoral thesis, *The Growth of Cities in the Nineteenth Century*, in 1899. Although he saw the faults of urban life, he used many observations and sources to buttress his contention that the intellectual as well as the economic advances of mankind were closely related to the expanding power and energy of the cities. He even showed that the countrysides had more infanticide, more feeble-minded people, and more such defectives as deaf-mutes than the towns.

Much demographic ground remains to be explored in America as in Europe: for example, the composition of political parties and of voting totals in critical elections; and the important question of whether progress rests primarily on an elite, or on the varied contributions of the plebeians, the common people. Just where has social mobility been high, and just what have been its results? We may not like what the Frenchman Levasseur called the science of populations, but it is a safe prediction that historians will have a great deal more to do with it in the next few decades.

Demography may help answer a question which some scientists consider vital for the future of mankind: "Can genetic research improve the intellectual and moral quality of peoples?" It may help answer another tremendous question: "What are the population contexts which will best enable peoples to communicate with each other across borders and will best promote an exchange of ideas among intellectuals?" For surely Lyndon Johnson was right when he said at the Smithsonian bicentenary, "Ideas, not armaments, will shape our lasting prospects for peace."

13

Is History Made by Heroes?

Allan Nevins's friends must have wondered how he, as one of the nation's most successful biographers—of Grover Cleveland, Hamilton Fish, John C. Frémont, John D. Rockefeller, Henry Ford, and others—could plead so effectively for the study of the social forces underlying mass behavior. Did not his crusade for the use of sociological and demographic techniques suggest that the individual was less important than the group? Was the hero, of whom Nevins wrote so well, actually an insignificant force in shaping the stream of history? He attempted to answer that question in an essay published in the *Saturday Review* in 1955, just as he was writing his two-volume biography of Ford. Leaders, he tells us, have been important, but in instituting and pioneering change they have only responded to energizing changes in the body politic. In democratic nations the true instrument of progress has been the popular will, which in turn has been shaped by the massive forces governing social behavior. This is the theme admirably argued in this essay. Nevins was a superb biographer, but he was so only because he was a good enough historian to rank "forces" above "heroes" and to understand the underlying pressures to which they responded.

Reprinted with permission from the *Saturday Review* 38 (November 5, 1955): 9–10, 42–45.

When Archbishop Laud was put on trial by the Puritans for treason he was able to prove his innocence of the major crimes imputed to him. His accusers then said he should be put to death anyway. He had committed so many minor crimes that, all added together, they amounted to the major crime of treason. Laud was outraged. "This is the first time in my life," he roared, "that I ever heard men declare that 200 black cats make one black horse!" His remark has its application to the relations between biography and history.

Anyone can make an interesting experimental approach to history by taking a volume of the Dictionary of American Biography and reading several hundred pages. He will quickly perceive that, much as America has owed to its great men, it owes incomparably more to a host of useful men who achieved a lesser distinction. Indeed, any student of history must be troubled by the deceptive legends that gather about a few towering names. It is the fashion to credit almost every Union achievement in the Civil War, directly or indirectly, to the genius of Abraham Lincoln. It is the fashion to credit most of the accomplishments of the New Deal and half our exploits in the Second World War to the inspiration of Franklin D. Roosevelt. In government departments the secretary gets credit for the work of bureau chiefs; in business corporations the president is praised for the successes of his subordinates. But the twenty-one volumes of the Dictionary of American Biography show what a host of inconspicuously useful men and women we have had, and how remarkable were the contributions that thousands of them made.

The bitterness with which thinkers have fought over the issue of "heroes" vs. "forces" is explained by its deep philosophical implications and its relation to current politics. Hegel, with his dialectical theory of history, believed in forces, and inspired Marx, who inspired Lenin. Carlyle, with his frank exaltation of the hero—"I say great men still are admirable; I say there is at bottom nothing else admirable"—has been quoted by all believers in "greatness." Herbert Spencer was on the side of the forces; to him history was social evolution, a march from the "primitive undifferentiated social aggregate" to complex social heterogeneity. But Emerson expressed the spirit of American individualism: "The search after great men," he wrote, "is the dream of youth, and the most serious occupation of manhood."

The debate has been carried into our own time by such figures as James Harvey Robinson, with his "New History," and Arnold Toynbee, with his cyclical and religious interpretation of the past. Robinson, like his friend John Dewey, argued for the genetic approach to history; that is, for seeking in bygone forces and events the causal clues to the present. The explosion of the atomic bomb at Hiroshima was a bead in a long chain. Trace the chain back along its multiplying threads and then we can partly understand the epochal explosion; but the student must take into account geography, economics, sociology, psychology, and archaeology, for they are all bound into the causal nexus. Robinson's history took little note of individual heroes. Yet we cannot ignore on the other side the weighty authority of Arnold Toynbee. His picture of rising and fading civilizations discloses a vigorous belief in the power of the elite, and of great leaders among the elite.

Beyond doubt periods of crisis and convulsion bring the great man into such strong relief that impersonal forces seem to drop into the background. Today, after forty years of war and turmoil, during which we have fixed our eyes on such commanding figures as Stalin, Hitler, Mussolini, Churchill, and Roosevelt, we may be in danger of overestimating the role of the hero. These men certainly never underestimated themselves! It is one of the paradoxes of this stormy time that the Communists, who in theory regard the faceless proletariat as supreme and who trample the aristocrat under foot, have in practice glorified Lenin, Trotsky, and Stalin more than Rome glorified Caesar. But the question whether all the dominant figures of the two world wars had legitimate greatness and really shaped the course of history is not easily answered. We must not forget that Lincoln late in the Civil

War frankly confessed that he had not controlled events; "Events," he said, "have controlled me."

In certain fields of human action the social theory of history—the theory of impersonal forces enunciated by Herbert Spencer, Taine, and James Harvey Robinson—has special strength. In economic history as written during the last generation in America and England the individual seems unimportant and often quite disappears. Supply and demand, natural resources and machine power, cycles of boom and depression are what make economic history; and it must be added that they make much of it as dreary as an Arctic steppe. Once invention was treated as gloriously personal, and hearts thrilled to James Watt observing his mother's teakettle. But nowadays the social theory of invention and technological change reigns supreme, and if individuals are mentioned it is only to show how many men in how many countries almost simultaneously devised sewing-machines, telegraphs, and electric lights.

The history of exploration might at first blush seem strikingly individualistic. What of the feats of Columbus, of Livingstone, of Nansen? Could anything be more uniquely personal? But examined in detail against the full background of the times the work of Columbus himself becomes again part of a vast partnership of ideas, techniques, and experience, until even the importance of the most famous of Italian navigators grows dubious. In the American West our Clarks and Frémonts had the aid of a cohort of scouts, Indian-fighters, traders, and mountain-men. Exploration is as social an activity as invention. And this generalization applies to the exploration of thought. In the field of science we need think only of what is implied by the simultaneity of the discoveries made by Newton and Leibniz, Darwin and Alfred Russel Wallace. Why should the planet Neptune be discovered at the same moment by the Frenchman Leverrier and the Englishman J. C. Adams working independently, and why should two Americans quarrel over the honor of first using anesthetics? Obviously these claimants were riding the same rising common denominator of general knowledge. Indeed, the whole history of thought may be called a social history.

But there are other categories of human action in which the leader theory, the idea of Carlyle, James, and Toynbee, seems specially tenable. One is literature and the arts. Here it is the most original spirits, the iconoclasts and innovators, whose handiwork shines brightest. Thoreau broke from the herd; Whitman's prosody (though it had traceable origins elsewhere) was essentially unique in form and spirit. If Emerson, Hawthorne, Melville, James do not count as individuals they do not count at all. Similarly, the spiritual force that makes a potent religious leader can hardly be credited to Race and Environment; it must be more personal. I doubt if Puritanism can be understood except in the personal ardors of such men as Richard and Cotton Mather; or the Great Awakening except in the truly heroic fanaticism of Jonathan Edwards and the transcendent eloquence of Whitefield; or the peculiarly American marriage of religious fervor and organizing capacity except as displayed by Brigham Young and Mary Baker Eddy.

In American business, too, the leader unquestionably explains much in our national development that impersonal forces do not touch. The entrepreneur is by definition a path-breaker, a deviant from tradition, a man who remolds existing economic institutions. The most striking common characteristic of McCormick, Carnegie, Rockefeller, James J. Hill, and Henry Ford was their readiness to defy accepted economic law—not to speak of statutory law! Except for such men our business history and economic development would have been much slower, tamer, and in certain ways feebler than it was. In contemplating so bizarre a figure as Henry Ford we may well exclaim, "God moves in mysterious ways his wonders to perform"—but Henry nevertheless had a personal genius that assisted in the wonders. As for politics, that assuredly is the department of American life in which individual leadership has been most picturesquely arresting. Since the days when

Hamilton gave our republic its strong impulse toward centralized efficiency and Jefferson its zeal for individual liberty our best political leaders have truly shaped history. Few countries have owed as much in 150 years to five men as ours has owed to Washington, Lincoln, Wilson, and the two Roosevelts.

In the field of politics, certainly, Americans have always dearly loved a hero. Yet the judgment may be ventured that this is almost wholly an emotional, not an intellectual, attitude. In throwing up coonskin caps for Andrew Jackson, in apotheosizing Lincoln, in cheering Al Smith we may even suspect Americans of applauding themselves—of making these men into images which typify the American masses. At no time has the Carlylean idea of the hero as a highly superior being found currency among us. American democracy would pronounce that idea repugnant. We have always believed in the diffusion of opportunity; in the capacities of the common man for indefinite self-betterment; and in the special virtue of our institutions as distinguished from personal leadership. Our government, we say, is one of laws, not of men. It is true that we are proud indeed of Washington and Lincoln, and that even economic royalists feel a certain thrill when they see statues of Franklin D. Roosevelt in London and Oslo. But subconsciously most Americans feel that our democratic system deserves most of the credit—a system which in times of dire crisis will always throw up such great captains.

In short, for all our hero-worshiping tendencies we regard our chief leaders as essentially folk-products. We can point to the fact that we have responded to minor crises by producing minor captains like James K. Polk and Harry Truman, seemingly commonplace men with latent capacities far from commonplace. Of course, democracy must take the discredit for letting itself fall into dire extremities. It was partly because we trusted the Republic to that erratic nincompoop Franklin Pierce and that pusillanimous dotard James Buchanan that we were faced with the necessity of bringing forth a Lincoln or perishing. The point, however, is that we do tend to think of our eminent political leaders as projections of democracy and the common man, rather than as heaven-sent heroes, and we tend to think of them in emotional terms. Much of the admiration for Jackson and T. R. was strictly visceral—it had nothing to do with the mind. Hence the special emphasis of American mythology on personages with folksy traits—Davy Crockett, Lincoln, and Henry Ford. A more creditable side of our attitude toward heroes is our instinct to value character above intellect. That sound instinct, common to all Anglo-Saxon people, largely accounts for our success in government. In Washington, Lincoln, Lee, and Cleveland force of character counted for vastly more than subtlety of mind.

Altogether Americans ought to feel disposed to emphasize the social interpretation of history. As our national record grows longer and more complex I believe we shall be inclined to do so. We shall accept the fact that our main achievements are truly democratic achievements, and that the forces at work in the mass are far more important than instances of personal thrust and innovation. Where, then, will this leave the study of American biography?

The advantages of biography as a tool for examining the past are not to be underrated. A good biography humanizes history. Most people are not much interested in past times as a huge impersonal machine; they are interested in how human beings like themselves acted. Carl Sandburg's "Lincoln" is a telling example of the humanizing power of biography. Its scale is large; hundreds of people play parts in it; but each is presented graphically as a human being.

Biography, moreover, can be legitimately dramatic in a way denied to history. The past as a complex of forces is almost never dramatic; the past as the experience of one man can be a succession of dramas. In the life of Franklin one tableau follows another, from the hour when he walked up from the boat in Philadelphia, munching a roll, to the moment in the Constitutional Convention in 1787 when he made his apt remark about the orb on the President's chair: "At last I know it is a rising and not a setting sun." Some careers are in fact one long melodrama, like that of Lawrence of Arabia.

We may add to the partial credit of biography that it breaks up the illimitable detail of the past into simple and comprehensible units; for the biographical structure necessarily imposes a pattern. Douglas Freeman wrote four large volumes on Lee, but he nevertheless laid upon himself the strictest limitations. He refused to treat all of the Civil War; he did not treat even all of the war in Virginia; he described simply that part of the war which Lee himself saw. Because it lends itself to economy and design biography at its best is Art—even high art; while history, alas, or at any rate scientific history, is seldom artistic.

Nevertheless, for understanding the past in general, and that of democratic America in particular, biography can never be adequate. Insofar as we wish to gain a full comprehension of the past we should throw the emphasis of our study on groups and masses, on trends and impersonal forces. The reasons for this are varied.

For one, biography takes short views, and in fact is seldom good for anything but short views. The span of human life projected against the secular march of a nation's history is short, and the span of most active careers shorter still. Lincoln's really significant public leadership extended from 1854 to 1865, eleven years. Even in taking short views biography is likely to be disjointed and, from the historical standpoint, non-consecutive. James Truslow Adams gave us an excellent study of the Adams family from 1765 to 1920; but he had to admit that the Adams family separated from the mainstream of American history about 1830, with the rise of Jackson; thereafter its affairs throw little light on our history. Gladstone's long career was remarkable down to about 1880 as a close reflection of the British spirit in the age of *laissez faire*; it was equally remarkable after that date for its failure to recognize the new socio-economic forces that were assuming command toward the close of the century. Any proper study of the past demands a closer attention to what James Harvey Robinson called "genetic forces" than biography allows.

Again, while biography humanizes the past it often overhumanizes it, carrying an excessive amount of trivial detail. The Jacksonian era, I think, was not really exciting in the way in which Claude Bowers presents it; its true excitement, which was nondramatic, resides in the conceptions of it presented by Arthur M. Schlesinger, Jr., and his opponents. The conflict was rather of ideas than men. Then, too, biography unescapably takes partial and onesided views, and consciously or unconsciously almost always magnifies the role of its central figure. Biography states that an institution is the lengthened shadow of one man; but, actually, in ninety-nine instances out of 100 an institution is the lengthened shadow of many men.

Above all, biography is in too many instances superficial in its view of the past. It is superficial because its form forbids it to make intensive use of ideas; and only penetrating interpretive ideas based on facts and insights furnished by all the social studies can give us a grasp of history. The art of the Netherlands, as Taine wrote, can be better explained by Dutch landscape, atmosphere, and national character than by any theory of Rembrandt's personal genius. The fall of Rome, Robinson suggested, probably owed more to bad public health—malaria, lack of sanitation, malnutrition—than to the degeneracy of Nero and Tiberius. Poor price tendencies for peasant production may have had more to do with the Crusades than the preaching of Peter the Hermit. Certainly economic forces had a heavier impact on the American Constitution than any individual political ideas of James Madison; and certainly the sociology of race relations does more to explain the Civil War than the theory of a conspiracy by Yancey and Barnwell Rhett.

Let us consider two historical occurrences of very different character, the Battle of Second Manassas and the creation of the complex entity known as mass-production. In the Battle of Second Manassas the Union forces in Virginia were caught at a heavy disadvantage, with McClellan's large army slowly and sullenly returning by water, in various segments, from the James River front after the failure of the Peninsular campaign while John Pope's smaller army stood on the Rapidan. Feeling between the two Union armies was bad. McClellan and his chief officers hated Pope more than they hated the Confederate cause, and Pope expected to show how much abler he was than McClellan. Cooperation would have been poor even if the two forces had been close together and well concentrated. Robert E. Lee saw his opportunity to fall on Pope before McClellan's troops came up. He boldly divided his inferior army in the face of the enemy; sent half of it under Stonewall Jackson around to Pope's rear; took that general by surprise; and utterly defeated him before he could recover his balance. For a time Washington seemed in danger of capture.

Obviously, the history of that battle can be written from the standpoint of McClellan and his corps commanders, disgusted by Pope's incompetence. It can be written from the standpoint of Lee, whose masterly strategy wrecked Pope's army; Douglas Freeman has so written it. It can be written from the standpoint of Jackson, who had to do the rapid marching and effect the surprise in Pope's rear; and the British biographer of Jackson, Henderson, has written this graphic account. It can be written from the standpoint of Lincoln, waiting in agony in the White House, unable to understand why the jealous McClellan did not move more rapidly to Pope's aid, and unable to understand why Pope blundered at every step. To an artist looking for a literary opportunity it could best be written from the point of view of John Pope, who illustrated perfectly the workings of the Greek *hubris*. He was all boastfulness and arrogance before the battle; his swagger was incredible—he was a veritable Captain Bobadil; and when the curtain fell his ruin was complete. From any of these standpoints a simple and fascinating narrative might be penned.

But actually the only true history of Second Manassas would be one from the standpoint of the American Republic. It would have to embrace elements from all these special points of view, and avoid partiality toward any. It would have to deal with those traits in the American character which explain Pope's braggart vein, McClellan's petulant jealousy, and the general failure of Union *esprit de corps* in a critical moment. It would have to consider political factors in the background, for McClellan never forgot for a moment—nor did Lincoln—that a general who put a quick end to the war might easily win the Presidency in 1864. Questions of supply and transport on both sides, of logistics, would have to be treated. Then, and only then, would we have an understanding of Second Manassas, which almost brought about foreign intervention and the division of the American nation.

The birth of mass-production offers a different type of problem. Few people really understand mass-production, which they confuse with quantity production. In mass-production it is not quantity that counts; it is method. It means the focusing of seven elements upon production: power, accuracy, economy, system, continuity, speed, and repetition. The three chief among these elements are accuracy, which means standardization and interchangeability of parts; continuity, which means a system of moving confluent lines in assembling these parts; and speed, which means a carefully-timed correlation of effort in material handling and manufacture. Before mass-production came to birth cheap manufacture of complex wares in tremendous volume was impossible. After it came into existence automobiles, tractors, airplanes, tanks, and even ships could be manufactured with a speed, economy, and accuracy that has changed the whole human economy in peace and war. It first came into full existence in the Highland Park factory of the Ford Motor Company in the year 1913.

The old story of its birth was simple. Henry Ford conceived it; he gave his orders; moving lines, carefully timed according to the Taylor system, appeared in the Ford factory; and the miracle was accomplished. This story was accepted as authentic, because Henry Ford told it himself, with graphic detail, in "My Life and Work." But the actual history was very different. Research in various sources, including the recollections of employees, proves that in this instance the seminal ideas did not percolate from the top down; they rather moved from the bottom upward. A number of men, subordinates of Ford, first tried the combination of accuracy (standardization), continuity (moving lines), and speed (careful time-study) on the complicated assembly of the magneto. The saving in time and effort astonished them. They and others then used the same method in assembling the motor; and from that they turned to the assembly of the transmission. Again their success was astonishing. Three different segments of the automobile were being produced with such rapidity that they flooded the central assembly line of the car itself; and it became necessary to apply the method to the whole automobile. The Ford factory then became an intricate complex of moving lines, accurately timed, scientifically interrelated, and fed by continuous streams of standardized parts. A score of men were responsible. Two deserve the most credit, and neither was named Henry Ford. They were William Klann, a fertile-minded mechanic, and Clarence Avery, who had been Edsel Ford's instructor in a manual-training school and had brought a fresh set of ideas into the factory.

What must be our conclusion? Biography is one of the keys of history but only one, and excessive dependence on it easily distorts history. Social and economic forces are similarly a key, but only one; excessive dependence on them leads down the road of historical determinism, and would make man a mere automaton. The molding elements of history include ideas, forces, great men—and chance. A monistic picture of the past which exaggerates the role of any of these four is as unsatisfactory as an Egyptian painting without perspective. We have many reasons for reading good biography; but let us never forget that 200 black cats do not make one black horse—that a complete understanding of the multiple elements of the past cannot be gained from single lives. When Douglas Freeman had finished his "Lee" he was so impressed by the injustice his story had done the great array of subordinate officers that his conscience gave him no rest till he had published "Lee's Lieutenants"; and even that fell short of presenting the whole picture. A well-written biography is like a sonata finely played; but a well-planned history is like a great symphony, blending many themes, ideas, and insight into one tremendous whole.

14

The Old History and the New

Allan Nevins was seventy-seven years old when on January 16, 1967, he delivered the Gertrude Clarke Whittall Lecture before a prestigious audience at the Library of Congress. This occasion, he recognized, offered a unique opportunity to voice once again his often-expressed plea for the sound but readable history that he felt essential to mankind's progress. He also addressed himself, however, to the notion that modern techniques of research, often borrowed from the social sciences, were essential to the accurate interpretation of social behavior, whatever their damaging effect on literary narratives. In the pages that follow, Nevins, mellowed by both years and experience, displays few of the prejudices that he had earlier voiced against "dryasdust" pedants. Instead, he praises the social scientists who have contributed so significantly to the "new history" which has revealed so much about past societies, cautioning, however, that their findings are useless to society unless narrative historians ("humanistic historians," he prefers to call them) endow their discoveries with the breadth, vision, and stylistic distinction needed to capture a popular audience. In effect, Nevins urges a marriage between the "new" and "old" history, between the social

Reprinted with permission of the Library of Congress from *The Art of History: Two Lectures* by Allan Nevins and Catherine Drinker Bowen (Washington, D.C.: Gertrude Clarke Whittall Poetry and Literature Fund, 1967), 1–19.

scientist and the humanist, with each leaning on the other to beat back the forces of ignorance. His sound advice has seldom been better expressed.

It is recorded that when the British Empire went to war in 1914 one of its outlying dependencies astonished the Cabinet, sitting anxiously in Downing Street, with a crisp message. It read: "Barbados is behind you!" I am here in a humbler role than Barbados held in 1914. If I seem to have come to assure the august muse Clio that I am behind History, its writing, its reading, and its future growth, actually I appear only to raise a question; and for this even the least of us may sometimes be heard. When James Ford Rhodes delivered the presidential address to the American Historical Association in Boston in 1899, he remarked that he would be vain indeed if he thought he could say anything new about historical pursuits. Perhaps I may echo the deprecatory sentence that he added: "Yet to a sympathetic audience, to people who love history, there is always the chance that a fresh treatment may present the commonplaces in some different combination, and augment for the moment an interest which is perennial." Particularly is there reason to speak when history is in such a troubled position as it holds today.

Like everything else, the writing of history is always in a state of change. If slow, the change is evolutionary; if abrupt and drastic, it is revolutionary; and today I think it is plainly revolutionary. In the wake of two wars, and in the midst of the vast scientific innovations inaugurated by the unlocking of nuclear power, nearly every department of thought has been subjected to revolutionary stresses. Written history, as all have agreed from Thucydides to Mommsen, is largely an effort to chart lines of force. The entire outlook of history has been disturbed by the two global wars. As the French Revolution brought the common man for the first time under the lens of history, so the politicoeconomic upheavals of the last half century have brought a large number of neglected peoples and societies under continuous historical examination. At the same time, as Newtonian and Darwinian advances in science once changed the outlook of all students of history, so the advances of the age of Einstein have again sweepingly altered our interpretations of the past. Relativity reigns not in physics and astronomy alone, but in writings upon the development of society.

We will be unable to comprehend fully the present revolutionary changes for some time to come. Nevertheless, we can confidently affirm that our view of the history of Alabama is being perceptibly altered by the recent transformation of Africa. The facts of the past do not change, but our view of them does. Similarly, our view of the history of national states and regional alignments is being jarred into new angles of vision by the recent strides in communication and transportation that give mankind enlarged capacities for interaction. Some of them are beneficent; some are not. But they do bring us nearer the one world of which Wendell Willkie spoke. When Britain and France went to war in the eighteenth century, wrote Macaulay, red men scalped each other on the Great Lakes, and black men clubbed each other to death on the Niger. Still, the slaughter was then limited. But if the United States and Russia threaten each other with nuclear weapons today, all continents, all countries, all cities not only *feel* endangered but *are* endangered; and this fact gives us a compulsive new outlook upon the past as well as the future.

History becomes a more formidable subject every year. Once its tools were simple, the most important being diligence and accuracy in research, judgment in interpretation, and force in style. Once it concerned itself with themes that might be called majestic, but which were plain and understandable. These subjects, for the English-speaking peoples, were primarily political, constitutional, and religious. History was regarded as largely a training for lawyers, legislators, administrators, and the clergy. Political order and constitutional regularity were counted the two proudest contributions of the British and American peoples to society. They were lofty historical themes in themselves, and still loftier if viewed as tributary to the history of freedom, our proudest word, or of freedom and equality, our proudest phrase. The word sociology had not then been invented by Herbert Spencer, and economics in pre-Marxian days—or in England before R. H. Tawney and in America before Thorstein Veblen— was not discussed as the historical determinant that many later concluded it to be.

Henry Adams, one of the ablest figures in the old historical tradition, believed that the grand central theme in studying the past ought to be national character, its sources, its growth, and its results. That is, he believed this before he became fascinated by the Gallery of Machines in the Paris Exposition of 1900 and the 40-foot dynamos humming there; before, as he writes, his "historical neck [was] broken by the sudden irruption of forces totally new." He had written his nine-volume history of the administrations of Jefferson and Madison, he tells us, to delineate the character of the young Republic, although only six chapters in the first volume and four in the ninth dealt directly with the subject. His basic idea was better than George Bancroft's conviction that history is the will of God working through events, or John Fiske's that it is the will of God working through events and Social Darwinism. Most later historians, however, have pronounced Adams' theme at once too broad and too narrow: too broad, in the sense that it was too vaguely subjective, for anything can be read into the national character; and too narrow, in that character, however defined, is only one strand in the complex web of human development. The modern historian insists upon studying society as a whole, in its entirety and its constant flux.

His attitudes and tools have therefore become nearly as complex as society itself. He wishes to know as many facts about social structure as Sidney and Beatrice Webb mastered in England, or John R. Commons on this side of the Atlantic, and more. He would like to know more about psychology in relation to historical change than William James knew. He hopes to learn as much as R. H. Tawney learned about the way in which political doctrines, religious beliefs, and economic interests are all knit together by a thousand threads, and to display his knowledge as lucidly as Tawney did in *Religion and the Rise of Capitalism*. The modern historian wishes also to be as alert to new implements as the graduate students who are declaring today in scores of American and European universities that much as they would value a working command of another language, they would prize still more a full knowledge of computers. That is, they would prize an understanding of the way in which the most expert numerical techniques, the mastery of statistics, and the ability to frame complex problems for computer solution can cast new light upon a hundred subjects from poverty in Calcutta to voting patterns in Chicago.

In brief, the modern student of history feels that he must know something of a broad array of new conceptual tools—economic, sociological, anthropological, numerical, psychological—in analyzing the development of society as a totality. This he calls the "conceptualization" of history. He believes that we move forward in our mastery of the past not alone by old-fashioned fact finding and factual analysis, but by the use of quite new bodies of knowledge and new interpretations based mainly in the new social studies. (They are not really social *sciences*, though often miscalled that.) The rise of these studies, antedating and paralleling the changes just mentioned as stemming from two global wars and new scientific discoveries, has added to their revolutionary force. What may be called a new history seems to many to be emerging. When James Ford Rhodes delivered his presidential address of 1899, which *The Atlantic Monthly* published in February 1900, its laudation of Herodotus, Thucydides, and Tacitus carried a distinctly old-fashioned air. Its concepts were few and simple. The modern student would say that we have passed beyond them.

Rhodes, for example, clearly had no idea that a great new historical study called demography was already being born. He

185

had little realization that a new connection between psychology and history was appearing, tinged by the ideas of Freud and Jung, which would in time enable young American scholars to explain the personalities of the slave and the slaveowner—men in whom James Ford Rhodes was deeply interested—in more acute and complete terms.

Rhodes could not foresee, any more than you and I could only a quarter century ago, that numerical studies of society—that is, numerical analyses of population at different age levels, of epidemics and mortality, of food production and the incidence of malnutrition, and other subjects—would soon become important. Two years ago we had Peter Laslett of Cambridge University with us in the Huntington Library. He first opened my eyes to the extent to which the whole thought and outlook of a society in which the average life-span of its members covered only 30 years, as in Elizabethan days, was unescapably quite different from the thought and outlook of a society in which the average life-span reached 60 years, as it had by the time of Elizabeth II. This is one of the most interesting facets of demography. When I read Mr. Laslett's book, *The World We Have Lost*, a broader study of the social structure of preindustrial Britain, he opened my eyes again.

As for social anthropology and cultural anthropology, they were alike unknown, in their present-day meaning, when James Ford Rhodes wrote. For example, the blood feud as it was known in the old antebellum South, and was pictured in Mark Twain's tragic chronicle of the battles of the Shepherdson and Grangerford clans in *Huckleberry Finn*, cried in vain for an analysis by the cultural anthropologist. Mark Twain tells us that Baldy Shepherdson, like his enemy Colonel Grangerford, was a patrician and in his own eyes a gentleman. He could nevertheless shoot down a defenseless 14-year-old boy in cold blood and feel happily proud of the feat, a fact that only the social anthropologist and the psychologist could properly explain.

All advanced historians rejoiced when one social anthropologist, Mrs. Ruth Benedict, just after the last great war, produced her historical study of the Japanese character entitled *The Chrysanthemum and the Sword.* Her title emphasized the evident contradictions in the national character: the contradictions displayed by the Japanese, who are, as she wrote, "to the highest degree, both aggressive and unaggressive, both militaristic and aesthetic, both insolent and polite, rigid and adaptable, submissive and resentful of being pushed around, loyal and treacherous, brave and timid, conservative and hospitable to new ways." So eminent a historian of Japan as the late Sir George Sansom, the best historian any oriental nation has had, tells us that he had often felt impatient and confused because of his failure to grasp the national character; that he had almost concluded that only the creative artist could do the job. Sansom thought perhaps such an artist could illuminate the problem by flashes of insight, as Somerset Maugham seemed to him to have illuminated the Spanish temperament in his novel *Don Fernando.* But when Sansom read *The Chrysanthemum and the Sword* he took heart. He saw how well anthropological insights could serve history.

"It is a valuable book," he writes, "for not only does it give in very clear language an accurate picture of certain dominant features of Japanese life, but also it encourages one to believe that, in skilled hands, the technique of the social anthropologist may presently be applied with success to the study of other great societies." And we know how high a valuation General MacArthur, approaching the book from another point of view, set upon it.

As the new tools are applied, and as fresh conceptual analyses of old historical problems are developed out of constant advances in all the social disciplines, we catch at least glimmerings of a broader outlook upon history. The new tools do not themselves guarantee breadth. We might search for that particular quality in vain in the work of such a revolutionary experimenter with fresh techniques as Sir Lewis Namier. Unquestionably Namier was an expert in political behaviorism and in what is called "career-line analysis." Yet for all his ingenuity and penetration in the exploration of British political history, Sir Lewis achieved a

187

singularly small popular following in Great Britain, and none at all in the United States. Although he founded a distinct historical school, he never showed enough breadth, vision, or stylistic distinction to capture the public mind or be read outside the universities. While Tawney had breadth, as did Mrs. Benedict, most specialists in social-study interpretations are too specialized to cultivate it, and too narrow to garner its fruits. They are all too often just monograph writers.

It is a fact that in the United States the three historians who have made the deepest impression in recent times have done so through provocative new ideas broadly—not narrowly—related to the social studies. The three are Frederick Jackson Turner, who demonstrated the significance of the frontier as an evolutionary molder of the American people; Vernon L. Parrington, who in treating the history of our literature chose to follow what he called "the broad path of our political, economic, and social development, rather than the narrower belletristic" path; and Charles A. Beard, who in his *Economic Origins of Jeffersonian Democracy*, which is a better book than his *Economic Interpretation of the Constitution*, demonstrated that after the Constitution was ratified it still had to be filled in and given life, that this had to be done by an active, well-organized party, and that under Hamilton's leadership this party acted on economic lines for purposes mainly economic. All three historians provoked acrimonious controversies. And all three would have subscribed to an aphorism I once heard uttered by Hugh Trevor-Roper: "All historical developments, including religious developments, are meaningless except in their social framework."

This aphorism requires an illustration, which can be picked up anywhere. One is found in Robert Heilbroner's recent book on *The Limits of American Capitalism*. How, he asks, can we explain why in the early decades of the industrial revolution the British aristocracy, so proud, exclusive, and conservative, formed strong alliances with the rising leaders of manufacturing and trade, while the French aristocracy placed itself in disastrous antagonism to them? One part of the complex explanation doubtless lies in the role of the British younger sons. But the story takes meaning only in the whole social framework.

Yes, a comprehension of the possibilities of the new studies ought to give history greater versatility and breadth. In this broader outlook, with a social orientation and a constant use of such disciplines as economics, anthropology, and psychology, some of the old controversies that have troubled historical work will tend to disappear. The hoary disputation over the place of the hero in history, for example, may grow dim. More attention will be paid to the psychology of the masses, to the drift of the age, and to great formative movements; less attention to individuals who are supposed to have towering stature and to play cataclysmic parts in history. That such cataclysmic personages do appear from time to time nobody can deny. The greatest religious leaders— Buddha, Jesus, Mohammed; the greatest scientists—Copernicus, Darwin, Einstein; the greatest political leaders—Caesar, Napoleon, Churchill—will always hold their places as men who have deepened the flow of history.

It is surely a clear truth in advanced Western countries that while superficial aspects of society change rapidly, its fundamental character alters but slowly and gradually and changes more often through mass action than by individual leverage. Tocqueville declared that this was true of the United States, and it is true of other nations as well. It is another important fact, although discovered only in the last century, that in advanced Western societies ideas more often percolate upward than downward. This was not at all the belief of Froude, Carlyle, or Francis Parkman. It has been very much the belief of the best later historians of culture like George Macaulay Trevelyan and of sociologists like Pareto. In this realization by the newer school, also, some old controversies will tend to fade. And the maxim that history is past politics, a statement that Johns Hopkins University once inscribed on its walls, can no longer be accepted if we throw emphasis upon the history of integrated society.

A quite false idea of history is inculcated by such misleading labels as the Jacksonian Era, or the Age of Theodore Roosevelt, whether we think of men or parties. Leaders of great force of character like Jackson, or of great ability combined with force like Roosevelt, do in certain circumstances become the captains who head important movements. But are they truly the creators of an era? Seldom is this the fact. They may take charge of impulses that had their roots far back in the past and were growing powerful when they seized the helm, as Jackson did. Or they may become catalysts of vaguely defined bodies of opinion to which they give clear shape and direction, as T. R. did. They often fill an important third role in becoming centers of legend. Myths accumulate about them, and the myths invented by partisan followers, heightening their stature, become powerful in themselves. Any student of Jefferson has to distinguish between the real and the legendary Jefferson, a task that Henry Adams found difficult. Still more, a student has to distinguish between the actual Lincoln and the Lincoln that Carl Sandburg, among others, turned into so appealing a mixture of poetry, fable, and solid worth. Economics, sociology, and psychology do history a service in helping shake us free of these old misconceptions.

Thus far I have spoken respectfully and appreciatively of the new approaches to history and the new tools available in writing it. The new history is introducing fresh winds into a stuffy room, and these breezes should be welcomed. We need a spirit of cooperation. No true scholar should be a partisan of the new history, treated as one of the social studies, as something hostile to the old history, treated as one of the humanities; or a partisan of the old literary history as something hostile to the new scientific history. Properly viewed, they are not antagonistic to each other; they are complementary. Our task is to set proper metes and bounds to each and find just how they can be mutually helpful. This is the question I said I came to raise.

What disturbs me most is the tendency of many workers in the social studies to arrogate too large a field to themselves, to overrate their expertness, and to forget the towering achievements of their elders and contemporaries in the humanities. As Arthur M. Schlesinger, Jr., remarked, some men think that "social science" methods are not one of several paths to social wisdom, but the central and infallible path. They fling out challenges upon the necessity of using something called "integrated theory construction" as if this invalidated all previous writing. When they speak of history it is in condescending terms. C. Wright Mills, for example, in suggesting a genetic approach to sociological problems, warned students against "that dull pudding called sketching in the historical background." They plainly wish to see history become so specialized and scientific that it will lose all relation to literature. It will possess so few of the age-old attractions we have associated with the arts of narration, description, and personal portraiture or characterization, that few people will deem it worth reading.

This attitude, if given full rein, would destroy history as art—for it is an art. It would eliminate all the color and drama we have associated with history as *story*—for it is fundamentally a dramatic story. It would reduce historical writing to a narrow set of topics seldom related to any broad framework of meaning. Many of the subjects presented by sociology to the historian are highly interesting within fixed limits: a study of the mobility of population at a given time and place, for example; a study of mass religion; a study of working hours and leisure employments. To treat them expertly, however, requires complicated new principles that are hard to explain to readers and a new vocabulary that easily degenerates into an alien lingo, while they must be digested into a general narrative or they will mean little. The economist has *his* principles and poses the same problem of digestion into a larger whole; so does the psychologist; and what historian can master *every* such specialty?

This danger of losing touch with the intelligent reader, the

191

inquisitive general public, and everybody else but one or two fellow specialists is recognized by champions of the new approaches. One of them, Keith Thomas, the author of the opening article in the issue which the *Times Literary Supplement* devoted to the new history last April, indicates that it will be hard to swallow the new fare, but that the dose must be taken. "Sociological thinking," he writes, and he might have added anthropological thinking, psychological thinking, and the rest, "has usually been pioneered by rootless intellectuals, foreign observers and immigrants. It does not come easily to the English academic, who has always been more closely involved with the established social order. It involves cooperative scholarship and organized research, a world of seminars, workshops and graduate programmes, which is alien to the individualist, prima donna tradition in which most English historians have been reared. It brings with it the risk of jargon and obscurity, whereas history has always been regarded as a subject which should be intelligible and attractive to the layman. In the age of the historical factory some nostalgia is inevitably felt for the simpler days of the domestic system. But it is misguided to resist . . . professionalism." This champion of what we may call multispecialized history implies that "the coming revolution," the overthrow of history as written in the past, must and will be accepted.

All this would be highly alarming if we did not realize that the mainstream of history will sweep on in the old channels. History has always been written primarily on a humanistic basis, is today so written, and by every index we can measure will continue to be thus written. What are the histories of recent years that we keep on a convenient shelf? Are they books memorable for social-science expertness? Or are they histories that Mr. Thomas may hold in contempt because they are written by "individualist, prima donna" writers in a manner "intelligible and attractive to the layman"? As I read a list of ten American books the question answers itself:

James Truslow Adams, *The Epic of America*
Carl Becker, *The Heavenly City of the Eighteenth-Century Philosophers*
Van Wyck Brooks, *The Flowering of New England*
Bruce Catton, *A Stillness at Appomattox*
Margaret Leech, *Reveille in Washington*
Garrett Mattingly, *The Armada*
Samuel Eliot Morison, *The Maritime History of Massachusetts*
Barbara Tuchman, *The Guns of August*
Carl Van Doren, *Secret History of the American Revolution*
Edmund Wilson, *Patriotic Gore*

The *Times Literary Supplement* essayist was good enough to tell us that even when possession is taken of the historical field by its new masters, a place will be found for writers of the old school. They can find employment as popularizers of the invaluable stores of new knowledge brought them by the social-science experts. "If history is to maintain a deserving place in the affections of the reading public," he states, "it is essential that those with a gift for popular exposition should master the new techniques, so that, even if they do not themselves contribute to knowledge, they may at least be able to evaluate the contribution of others." That is, men of literary attainments and traditional attitudes will never be able to write books that have any originality or add anything to the world's libraries. But they can use their "gift for popular exposition" to make the really valuable histories by the specialists palatable to the masses. They can "evaluate the contribution" of the real writers and tell people what to think of them. Such condescension, such magnanimity! In this adjustment the old-fashioned historians will get a place—a footstool seat. They will be given a little piece of pie—humble pie.

Such a statement does grave injustice to the great majority of economists, anthropologists, and sociologists, who feel, just like the great majority of historians, that we are all partners in the search for an enlarged truth; that we can adjust our pretensions amicably; that no true worker looks down on another; and that least of all does he look down upon an august, rich, and continuously vital tradition. One of my oldtime students, Dr. Edward Saveth, recently edited an illuminating volume entitled *American History and the Social Sciences.* Largely made up of essays by men learned in the social disciplines, it is instructive in content and refreshing in temper. Dr. Saveth dedicated the book to me as a narrative (he meant a humanistic) historian, not because he saw that in my ignorance I badly needed to read it, but because he knew I would like its outlook.

One reason why specialists in the social studies seek a proper definition of their place in our partnership lies in their realization that for vast areas of historical study their skills have little or no value. They do not aim at the effects of a Clarendon in character study, or an Acton in the dissection of events, or a Lecky in painting social canvases. They know they cannot. One contributor stated frankly that while certain areas are amenable to social science concepts—community studies, entrepreneurship, political leadership—many are not. Another writer admitted that many social concepts, like status, class, and image, are vaguely defined. Even Turner never satisfactorily defined "frontier"; 17 different definitions of "power" have been listed. Various critics have noted that although Carl Becker said a great deal about the importance of the social-science approach to history, when he wrote his *Heavenly City* he scarcely touched upon one of the really central aspects of the eighteenth century, namely, its social science. Arthur Schlesinger, pointing out that Namier dismissed a whole range of historical issues because they were not susceptible of quantification, commented: "I am bound to reply that almost all important questions are important precisely because they are *not* susceptible to quantitative answers."

The social scientists who count are for various reasons as humble-minded as the historians who count. They know that their ideas and methods must be pooled in history with other ideas and methods, and they cannot be too dogmatic. They know that much of their material is likely to be so dull to lay readers that active minds will balk at it. Above all, if they have been properly educated, they have a reverence for the greatest humanists. They know that the writing of a sound piece of history possessing literary distinction demands high talent and sometimes calls forth touches of genius. There are plenty of substitutes for the opaque prose that the social scientist can furnish; there is little substitute for high literary talent, and none at all for genius.

Why and how are the best historical works written? They are planned because the author has a vision, or an approach to one. The subject takes hold of him, inspires him, and lifts him to a plane where he sees as in a golden dream the volume he intends to write. He sees also that it must be written in a particular way: in precisely *his* way and no other, with *his* selection of facts and *his* point of view.

To take one example in many, why did Lytton Strachey write *Elizabeth and Essex*, a masterpiece of compressed and highly dramatic narrative history? The chances are ten to one that Strachey wrote it because, after prolonged reading and reflection, he suddenly said to himself, "What a superb subject is embedded in that particular stretch of English history! What histrionic qualities the boastful, impetuous Essex, the sly Francis Bacon, the enigmatic, cautious Elizabeth revealed!" Or why did George Macaulay Trevelyan write *Garibaldi and the Thousand*? Again, no doubt, because after travel and long study Trevelyan said to himself: "I can make this one of the most enthralling tales of daring, fortitude, and patriotic devotion to be told in our time." These men did not write their books because they saw an opportunity to make unprecedented explorations into the field of psychological analysis or the sociology of rebellion.

The quality which good historical writing most demands, wrote James Anthony Froude, is—what? Social awareness? economic expertise? No, he replied, "Imagination." To my mind, Froude was absolutely right. Imagination is essential to re-creation of the past, and it is re-creation at which the historical artist aims. The imagination here invoked is not invention: it is the imagination that enabled Livy to *hear* the clash and jingle of the peck of rings, stripped from Roman knights on the bloody field of Cannae, that a Carthaginian emissary poured out on the senate floor in Africa after Hannibal's victory; the imagination that enabled Francis Parkman to *feel* the warmth of the turbid Mississippi off its Arkansas shore as La Salle, drifting downstream, plunged his arm over the side of the canoe. Other historians might give a different answer from Froude to the query as to what quality is most needed by the historian, but they would name some intellectual gift or trait, not some department of learning.

When Kipling wrote that there are a hundred different ways of writing tribal lays, and every single one of them is right, he stated a primary truth about history. A good historian sees how a certain subject can be shaped to make the most of the particular materials he possesses, the talents and experience he has accumulated, or the legitimate demands of public taste—demands that change sharply from time to time. This is right and proper. Especially is it right and proper for a writer to shape his book according to his talents. If he has great gifts, as my friend Bruce Catton, for example, had in approaching the Civil War, he does this by intuition and an inner compulsion. If he alters his design to make room for economic factors, or anthropological factors, that do not come naturally to him, he spoils it.

Ah, says the social scientist, but look at such a famous piece of literary history as Carlyle's *French Revolution*. How can you defend its manifest historical inadequacies? It should be studied by classes in English literature. But who would recommend it for study by earnest and informed students of French history? It contains nothing about the financial crisis that set the Revolution in motion. The economic specialist would throw it out of his library for that deficiency. It says almost nothing about the social changes that accompanied the Revolution, and nothing about the new civil institutions that grew out of it. Sociologists and governmental specialists would condemn it for that. What does it say about patterns of voting behavior, or mob psychology? Is it more than a fossil remnant in history?

The true historian catches up this challenge at once. What *does* Carlyle's *French Revolution* offer? he asks. Little that the social-science specialist values, everything that the humanist values. Are not historians humanists? It has passages of as tremendous moral force as were ever written, reminding us that Goethe told Eckermann that young Carlyle would produce masterpieces of moral insight. It has passages of superb pictorial vividness, reminding us of Lecky's comment that Carlyle saw the French Revolution as by lightning flashes. It has a burning intensity few writers can match, a fervent sincerity bursting from a hot heart and a sleepless brain, so that, as Carlyle himself put it, his writings rushed up "like rockets druv by their own burning." On the strictly historical side, it has a perception that the best French authorities have admired; for Carlyle, as François Aulard writes, perceived that the common people of France were the true heroes of the epic struggle. It has a command of the psychology of both individuals and masses that possesses almost unique value. As J. Holland Rose states, Carlyle "shows us the workings of the human heart as no other historian of institutions and no microscopic analyst, like Taine, has ever done or ever will do." It is for the social-science specialists to annotate Carlyle, as they have done, not for modern Carlyles—if we are fortunate enough to produce one—to annotate or popularize the books of the specialists.

One of the greatest attractions of history as a study lies in its endless variety, a variety that time cannot wither nor custom stale. The true historian does more than tolerate its versatilities; he admires its protean richness. The intolerance of a few social scientists, whose specialization too often gives them a mole-like vision, seems to me a sin that can do grievous harm to historical writing. Carl Becker, at whose side I taught for a year in Cornell University, was a historian I warmly admired. He had a wide-ranging love of historical reading; I used to see him move slowly across the sleet-swept campus above Lake Cayuga, with a great armload of books he was carrying from the university library to his home. He wrote one of the best books on our craft in *Everyman His Own Historian*. Yet, under the influence of Frederick Jackson Turner, Becker once yielded to a spirit of intolerance. He declared that Turner might well boast of the fact that his contributions to history and the social sciences had been set forth only in monographic studies, essays, and occasional addresses, that his collected works did not fill much space, that he had never yielded to the demand of his disciples and publishers for a "great work."

"Seven volumes at the very least they seem to demand," wrote Becker, "in stately leather-backed tomes for preference, something they may point to with pride as an achievement, a life work, one of those 'comprehensive' and 'definitive' histories no doubt which posterity may be expected to label 'standard,' and straightway shelve with Gibbon and Grote behind glass doors, rarely opened."

In this statement it is not the commendation of Turner for restricting his best work to short monographs that jars upon us. That eminent historian had every right to shape his work according to his own talents and vision, and it is because he did just this that *The Frontier in American History* is one of our assured classics. The jarring note is in Carl Becker's intolerant reference to Gibbon and Grote. These writers do not reside behind glass doors seldom opened. I doubt if any historian in any country is more frequently reached down from the shelves than Gibbon, or, even after nearly 200 years, read with more profit. I doubt if a survey would not show that every day some thousands of people in the United States and Great Britain, in Canada and Australasia, in South Africa, India, and the isles of the sea, can be found looking into *The Decline and Fall*. Grote holds a lesser place. But if Carl Becker could have read the admiring essay on Grote just written by the Italian historian Arnaldo Momigliano, dedicated to his friends of the Hebrew University of Jerusalem, and published in England and America, he would have done more justice to the continued vitality of a writer as well known in

198

French, German, and Italian translations as in English. There is a place for the writer of a multivolume set as well as for the monograph writer; a place for Mommsen and Prescott, McMaster, Francis Parkman, and A. T. Mahan, as well as for the best authority on econometrics.

The first requirement of the true lover of history is that he shall delight in its endless varieties—that he shall be tolerant of all themes, all approaches, and all styles, so long as the work under examination meets two tests. First, it must be written in a patient search for truth about some phase or segment of the past. Imagination must go into this search, imagination as a literary as well as a historical tool. In the second place, its presentation of truth must be designed to give moral and intellectual nutriment to the spirit of man, just as our most ambitious poetry, fiction, and philosophy should be so designed. This is essentially a literary design. Why did Thucydides describe so graphically the terrible plague which shook the Peloponnesian army and paint so faithfully the public attributes of Pericles? For precisely the same reason, I take it, that Aeschylus wrote the great drama of *Agamemnon*, and Euripides, the drama of *Medea*. They wished to probe spiritual and moral situations in a search for truth, and they intended to provide moral and intellectual nutriment for the spirit of man.

Or to take a modern instance, why did our own Henry Charles Lea write in such richly documented form his *History of the Inquisition of the Middle Ages*, probably the most important contribution any American has made to European history? Why did he present all the horrors of the Inquisition with calm, judicial pen? Because he felt that the truth would carry sweeping moral lessons. When far back in college days I read those three volumes, I had a teacher at hand, Guy Stanton Ford, who could tell me how controversial they were. Lord Acton, a Catholic, took some different views of the Inquisition. Happily, I did not linger over the adverse criticism. I pressed on to devour what is to me the most memorable of Lea's works, his depressing and yet exalting

199

book on *The Moriscos of Spain, Their Conversion and Expulsion*, which finds its climax in the forcible exile of the Hispanic Moors who had built so richly attractive a civilization. This masterly study of the brutalities of political and ecclesiastical intolerance, and the ensuing material and moral losses that crippled the Spanish nation for generations, was but a faraway, awesome story to the sophomore in the University of Illinois. Later it did not seem so far away. When the Nazi persecution of the Jews repeated the story with terrible additions, I was writing a great deal for the press. The fierce truthfulness of Lea's history and its profound moral and material lessons could then be remembered in that full force which had made his book a work of literature.

The list of works that meet the tests I have named—tests of literature as well as history—is long and slowly but steadily grows longer. Something could easily be said of a third test, the test of style. The nature of style, however, is often misconceived. Style is the man; that is, style is most important when it reflects the rich, full personality of a writer of intellectual power and fully developed character, and, through this writer, something of the temper and outlook of an era. So it was with Gibbon and Parkman, with Macaulay and Prescott. Their style was not impressive because of cadenced phrases, ingenious tropes, and well-climaxed chapters. It was memorable because the full personality of the author, and the spirit of the age, shone through. Certainly prose style is never given striking distinction by anything that the apparatus of the social scientist can impart to it; indeed, such scientists are likely to corrupt and debase it. William Makepeace Thackeray once wrote a piece of history, *The Four Georges*, of surpassing stylistic merit. Experts in economics, sociology, and anthropology could perhaps add a good deal to the content of those historical essays—but at the cost of depriving a classic work of all its vitality.

If anyone doubts that the spirit of an age counts nearly as much in the production of a distinctive style as the mind and character of the author, let him ask whether the outlook and attitudes of an exuberantly romantic and optimistic young America do not appear in the spirited, highly colored narratives of William Hickling Prescott, John Lothrop Motley, and Francis Parkman. Or let him consider what Maynard Keynes writes, in his essay on Malthus, about the British tradition of humane science, the spirit of a long age. Keynes speaks of "that tradition of Scotch and English thought, in which there has been, I think, an extraordinary continuity of *feeling*, if I may so express it, from the eighteenth century to the present time—the tradition which is suggested by the names of Locke, Hume, Adam Smith, Paley, Bentham, Darwin, and Mill, a tradition marked by a love of truth and a most noble lucidity, by a prosaic sanity free from sentiment or metaphysic, and by an immense disinterestedness and public spirit. There is a continuity in these writings, not only of feeling, but of actual matter." If this could be said of the thinkers of a long scientific age, could not a parallel statement, with an equally impressive list of names, be made about the historians?

If any social scientist will look with candid eye at the world's great treasury of historical writing and consider how much of the best of this writing is narrative, descriptive, and expository, and how little of it is analytical, he will rise from this examination with chastened temper. If he will further consider how well the best narrative and descriptive histories have endured the tooth of time, and how rapidly once-famous pieces of analytic history have become dated and empty, he will have further food for thought. A humble temper befits all historians, and the social scientists will do well to cultivate it. No one will deny that they can give us valuable new patterns of thought, useful new insights, and large bodies of original new facts. They can stimulate our mind, widen our vision, and whet our appetite for deeper truths. Like every study, history needs constantly to face new fronts and absorb novel ideas and techniques; as today we have a new painting, a new music, and a new poetry, we unquestionably need in some fields a new history.

These fields, however, are limited. Look at the important

historical works of our time, and ask how many of them would have been improved by specialized elements drawn from the social sciences. Could Van Wyck Brooks' half dozen volumes on American cultural history, beginning with *The Flowering of New England*, have been so improved? Could Samuel Eliot Morison's series on naval history, beginning with his *Maritime History of Massachusetts* and ending with his record of the Pacific war, have been so improved? Or could Walter Prescott Webb's book on the application of the industrial revolution to the conquest and settlement of the trans-Mississippi country, *The Great Plains*, published a generation ago (1931), be made more interesting to the general reader, or more essential to the student, by application of the newer concepts? Not in any significant degree.

We have come a long way since Bancroft could write about God working by examples, and Motley could intimate that a complicated century in European history should be viewed primarily as an 80 years' war for liberty. The old theological and political prepossessions have largely vanished. They have given way to our scientific age. Experts in the social sciences can help us gather more of the fruits of this age. Frederick Jackson Turner was right when he declared that data from "studies of politics, economics, sociology, psychology, biology, and physiography, all must be used." Nevertheless, the grand outlines and vital principles of history as it has been written down the ages still stand. The newer studies have no application whatever to wide areas of history and, when they do apply, should usually be regarded as adventitious and subordinate. Let the social scientists, in presenting their discoveries, remember that history, ever since Herodotus settled down in his native Halicarnassus to write chapters based mainly on his personal observation and reflection, has been greatest when it is viewed not as a branch of science but as a department of literature. Let them remember the truth that Henry David Thoreau put into a pregnant sentence: "It is not worth the while to go round the world to count the cats in Zanzibar."

15

The Limits of Individualism

Allan Nevins was recovering from a long and painful illness when in 1967 he was invited by Norman Cousins to submit this article to the *Saturday Review*'s "What I Have Learned" series; he had slashed his leg while chopping wood, and with his usual disdain for his own physical well-being neglected the wound until a serious infection forced him into temporary inactivity. "I wrote this article under difficulties," he confessed when it was submitted. "If you can make suggestions for its revision, I shall attend to the matter at once." Happily no such suggestions were made, for the essay reveals a great deal about Allan Nevins's changing attitudes toward scholarship. Contrasting the ineffectiveness of his father's individualistic labors as a farmer near Camp Point, Illinois, with the remarkable achievements he had recently witnessed when visiting a cooperative *kibbutz* in Israel, he concludes that cooperation will speed the progress of mankind—even in historical studies. His plea, then, is not only for a mass assault on the ignorance of the past, but for a vast common endeavor by labor, capital, agriculture, science, technology, and industry to achieve the worldwide "better society" that progress had brought within the reach of all mankind.

Reprinted with permission from the *Saturday Review* 50 (November 25, 1967): 25–27, 78.

The main lesson of life for me has been large and emphatic. It is partly moral, but I think more essentially spiritual. It is the lesson that in all walks of life the outdated tendency of Americans to maintain a stubborn independence limits in the most deplorable way their usefulness to themselves and to society, and sometimes totally negates this usefulness. The values in what Herbert Hoover called "rugged" individualism were once very real, but their relevance for American life passed away long ago.

Looking back, I can perceive that I was reared in an environment that was singularly well adapted to nurture a proud self-sufficiency, one which had validity in the nineteenth century but which today, I believe, should be subjected to a sharp, but discriminating, reappraisal. My paternal grandfather was a Scottish immigrant. Arriving in America without money or special skills, like most immigrants, this John Nevin (for the patronymic in 1850 had no final letter "s") had fought his way in Ontario, Pennsylvania, and Illinois to the accumulation of enough capital to purchase a small farm. His struggles were very similar to those of the father of John Muir in Wisconsin at about the same time. Like Muir's father, he obtained his farm, and a supply of farm machinery and livestock. He also obtained the usual mortgage on his acres, so that in later years he had to sell corn at 10 cents a bushel to pay the interest rate of 10 percent a year on his mortgage. But he took pride in his little farm, and found in it a much-prized independence. Readers of Burns's immortal poem, "The Cotter's Saturday Night," will discern in it something of the spirit that animated my grandfather. Like the miller of the Dee, he might be poor, but he would stand firm on his own two feet, caring for nobody who tried to issue him orders—no, not he!

Of course, the small farmer in the United States, even though he owned his acres, his horses, cattle, and pigs, and his tools, was far indeed from being fully independent. He had to face threats from a hundred quarters. He was largely at the mercy of the weather, with its recurrent droughts and floods. He had to withstand the hostile onslaughts of insect enemies—cutworms in

204

the corn, chinch bugs in the wheat, and multitudinous other pests. His orchards were afflicted with borers. Various scale diseases took their toll of his produce, and the word "rust" might mean that this specially insidious antagonist was ravaging his pear trees, his apple trees, his pines, and his promising stand of timothy hay.

And all the while, the dark shadow of the moneylender in Quincy, Illinois, fell across the farm. This lender got his funds in the East—in New York or New England—and transmitted them to the Middle West with a heavy charge for the service. The London moneylender had presented American farmers and planters with a dread image in colonial times, the image of the Boston moneylender had been malign in the Berkshire Hills in western Massachusetts in the 1780s, and, even in our own day, the Eastern moneylender has a bad name in Oklahoma, Idaho, and California. One of the many reasons why I hold the name of Woodrow Wilson in high regard is that, during his first administration, and with his support, legislation was enacted giving the toiling farmers of the country the benefit of federal credit in borrowing money for their operations. The power of the private moneylender, who not only charged 10 percent a year but collected it in advance, was thus curtailed.

Theodore Roosevelt's Country Life Commission had offered a verdict in 1909 that the American farmer was then in a better position than he had held in any previous period. This was in all probability a sound judgment. The position of farmers both East and West during the hard times of the 1890s was bad indeed, as all readers of the immense literature upon the Populist uprising and the Free Silver movement know well. Some scenes and situations, comparable with those painted by Hamlin Garland in his eloquent book of short stories and essays called *Main-Travelled Roads*, came within my own boyish observation. My father could have added some poignant details to those given in Garland's tale, entitled "Under the Lion's Paw."

The worst hard times were gone by the date of the Farm Loan Act of 1916. Prices for corn, wheat, oats, cotton, and livestock were improving. The farmers' skies were brightened also by the free distribution of rural mail, the coming of the telephone and electric light, and the proliferation of automobiles and good country roads. The sharecropper still had a mean life. (Only very recently have farm laborers begun to organize themselves on the pattern of industrial unions.) But the "full owners" of farms had a better and better lot, which their toil-worn wives shared. There were 1,720,961 of these "full owners" in the northern states in 1930, one of them having been my father. These owners were not only a very free and independent set of men, but to a great extent were "separate" men—*too* separate.

The community of small farmers in which I grew up—some of them Scottish, some of them of German blood and descent, and many of them Americans of long lineage, either Yankee or Southern—had splendid traits. All the families were of necessity frugal and hardworking. They were, on the whole, a religious folk, the Scots clinging to Presbyterianism, and some of the Germans to Lutheranism, while the Yankees were likely to be Congregationalists, and the Southerners elected the more evangelistic creeds of the Methodists and the Baptists. These farming people were the most unswervingly honest folk I have ever known. My father leaned backward in his rigid honesty. Once when he responded to an advertisement in a farm periodical, the advertiser sent him a free sample. He at once procured a money order and sent the advertiser what was probably thrice the value of the goods received.

Yet, by 1908, when I was graduated from high school, farming people were well aware of the fact that their political and economic individualism or separatism had been carried too far. Industry, with men like Rockefeller leading the way, was more and more efficiently organized. The banking interests, the railroads, and the mercantile interests were fully organized. When urban dwellers felt a sense of grievance over some inequity, they lifted their voices in unison. The rural population, however, was comparatively disorganized and voiceless.

If the farmer was too much a separate man politically and economically, his separateness was even more marked in the social field. It was here that his deprivations were greatest. Farmers repeatedly traded labor with each other, and so did farm women. At the threshing season in midsummer an informal neighborhood union sprang into existence. Horses, wagons, and men from all the farms rallied to carry the shocked wheat, oats, or rye to the steam thresher that "separated" the grain from the straw. In one or several of the commodious farmhouses, the women of the neighborhood spread a meal that was bounteous even to the verge of the overwhelming. Such cooperative effort, however, was transient. It lasted but a day or two, and then individualism reestablished its sway. Our township had a cooperative creamery, but its operations were on a limited scale.

I first became keenly aware of the social aridity of rural individualism in the Middle West—the Illinois of the early 1900s—when, after the Second World War, some work for the government took me to Israel, which had recently established its independence. Friends from the Hebrew University of Jerusalem arranged for me a visit to one of the oldest, best established, and most respected of Israel's *kibbutzim*. This particular *kibbutz*, which stood on the shores of Lake Gennesaret, or the Sea of Galilee, had played a gallant part in the then hostilities with the Arabs that marked what the Israelis liked to call the War of Liberation. The *kibbutz* officers showed me their well filled library, and then, with pardonable pride, exhibited their museum of natural history, a truly remarkable collection of stuffed animals and birds, superbly mounted. Their collection of moths and butterflies was equally distinguished, and contained specimens, I was told, of great rarity. They told me tales illustrating the devoted heroism of *kibbutz* members—men and women alike—during the recent period of attack and heroic resistance. I was

207

deeply touched as well as impressed. Here were the Nathan Hales and Molly Pitchers of Israel.

That evening, the heat of the day past, and a good dinner with abundant fruit enjoyed, I sat on the deep porch with my hosts, listening to the murmur of many voices about me as the members of the community discussed their problems and interests. I could not but think how superior the genial and helpful atmosphere of the *kibbutz* settlement was to the rugged individualism and separatism of western Illinois. Not every aspect of *kibbutz* life, I may add, seemed to me completely admirable. The enforced removal of many young children from their mothers, for example, struck me as a hardship to the parents that might have been avoided. But the *kibbutz* on the Sea of Galilee was in general, I realized, a far more truly civilized community than the township of Camp Point, Illinois.

The admirably efficient life of the Israeli *kibbutz* with all its high aspirations and social warmth impressed me the more because I could readily contrast them with the uncongenial atmosphere in which my father had labored to nurture certain simple and rather rudimentary efforts at organization for mutual help in Illinois. He had been elected president of a farmers' mutual fire insurance company, for example, and I often saw him toil into the night inspecting and signing fire insurance policies, an unpaid labor which he discharged with care and punctuality.

He was once elected county superintendent of elementary schools, but because he had only a partial high school education and no college training, he soon abandoned the position. The untimely death of his mother when he was in his teens had broken off his attendance at the Quincy, Illinois, high school. He also served as president of his township's Farmers' Institute, a body which met regularly to hear lectures by faculty members of the agricultural college of the University of Illinois, to hold informal discussions of farm problems, and to encourage the farmers to write letters on agricultural topics to *Wallace's Farmer, Hoard's Dairyman*, and the weekly *Farmer's Call*.

The state of Illinois was by no means devoid of scientific talent of a high order. The biological work of the Gennesaret *kibbutz* could have been critically appraised by Professor H. B. Ward of the biology department of the university; the geological work of the *kibbutz* could have been expertly weighed by Stephen Forbes, the state geologist, who might even have ventured suggestions for its improvement. But in those years, just before and after 1910, antedating the organization of the Farm Bureau Federation, and the emergence of an energetic chain of county farm agents in Illinois, the machinery for the transmission of the latest and best scientific knowledge to the ordinary farmer tilling his 160 or 240 acres was still defective. Socially, the existence of the farmer of Illinois or Iowa was far bleaker than it should have been. The Grange had never developed into a rich and stimulating social organization.

These were the contrasts which I pondered as I sat on the porch overlooking Lake Gennesaret, watching the beautiful sunset, and listening to the talk around me.

It was when I came into the full stream of my activities as a journalist and as professor of history at Columbia University and other seats of learning that I was taught my most forcible lessons in the superiority of cooperative effort to individualistic activity. Writing editorials for *The Nation*, the *Evening Post*, and the New York *World*, I could plainly perceive that the type of individualism engendered by Calvinism, the rough adversities of the frontier, and the possibility of seizing upon large stores of natural wealth, had emphasized physical and moral exertions at the expense of intellectual planning and action. I saw that historical writing also needed more thought and fuller organization. A variety of forces and stimuli in the historical world of the 1920s and 1930s impelled me to the conclusion that history needed one great new adjunct in its unceasing exploration of the past—that is, of yesterday and the day before yesterday—and also required a new adjunct in carrying the results of its researches to the public, for history can never be healthy without public interest

209

and support. That is, I concluded that it was important to set on foot a movement for the systematic and continuous creation of a first-hand, well documented body of personal memoirs, better planned and better secured than those which H. H. Bancroft, in an earlier period, had created for helping him write the history of pioneer California.

I concluded also that it was important to establish, if possible, a monthly or semimonthly magazine that would present historical events, developments, and personalities in a colorful, vigorous, yet authentic way to the great body of people who, I knew, were hungry for such fare. How did I know this? Because I had observed year by year the large sale of vividly-written books by such skilled writers and able, if not profoundly erudite, scholars as Marquis James, Carl Van Doren, Henry Pringle, and Margaret Pulitzer. Because, too, some of my own historical and biographical volumes and articles had found a wide and appreciative market. Movements set on foot to meet these needs resulted, in the end, in the establishment of the successful Oral History Office at Columbia, since then imitated all over this country and in a number of foreign lands, and in the establishment also of the bimonthly magazine, *American Heritage*, which now enjoys a circulation of about 330,000, and is widely influential.

But what heavy labors went into these efforts—and how slow and partial were their fruits until we placed them on a basis which enlisted a cohort of earnest workers instead of a handful! We had to find a place in this larger cooperative endeavor for the specialist with expert training and skills, and with some particular talent for organizing mass effort. It was when I drew to my side, at first as a paid assistant, Dean Albertson—an alert young man who is now a professor at the University of Massachusetts, and who was specially conversant with the latest technological advances in wire recorders and tape recorders—that the full potentialities of oral history could be realized. And it was only when a combination of fate or luck and persistent effort brought to our organization for the founding of a historical magazine the experience, sagacity, and skill of a gifted group of young men trained on *Time* and *Life*, and in Western journalism, that *American Heritage* began to evolve from a dream into a reality.

The roots of American individualism run deep into our past. Tocqueville and Bryce have related our individualism to the whole course of American history. But the direction of the stream has changed. We have entered the Age of Welfare-Concern, to borrow a phrase from the expert panel reports published by the Rockefeller Brothers in 1961 under the title *Prospect for America*. Concurrently and somewhat paradoxically, our era is also called the Age of Affluence.

We must here ask an important question: Have elements of moral strength been lost as society has turned from its old-time individualistic path to one of more cooperation and social-mindedness? No doubt all surviving believers in rugged individualism would say yes. But such strengths can easily be overvalued. When Tom L. Johnson, rising in Western politics, laid heavy emphasis on the traditional virtues of honesty and enterprise, he found that Clarence Darrow laughed at his limited view, calling him "the man who believed in honesty." And Lincoln Steffens, originally a reformer of traditional type, decided that Darrow was right. "Honesty is not enough," wrote Steffens in his autobiography. More was needed than the virtue which an individualistic and acquisitive society had drawn partly from Puritan tenets and partly from the harsh competitive struggle to get on in a rough environment.

Steffens pointed out that the young republic needed, in addition to virtue, qualities of an intellectual sort—intelligence, some knowledge and theoretical understanding of economics, resolution, humor, and leadership. I realized how right Steffens was when writing my biographies of Abram S. Hewitt and Grover Cleveland; I saw that a whole complex of qualities was needed to meet the stormy changes of their times. The stubborn courage of Cleveland and the enterprising thrust of Hewitt were important,

211

but the era demanded also some of the social vision of Henry George and the idealism of another public servant whose papers I edited—Brand Whitlock.

It was not until 1901 that all the main qualities of statesmanship required by a truly progressive and social-minded America were joined in one great national figure—Theodore Roosevelt. He himself could be called an aggressive individualist, but he also had a vision of an America built on cooperative lines without sectional, class, or economic divisions. He had to confront all the problems posed by an uncontrolled capitalism. He saw instinctively that a country reorganized on principles of social justice would have a great future. Just as J. Pierpont Morgan had succeeded largely because he was a "bull"—consistently optimistic in his view of the American industrial future—Theodore Roosevelt was an optimist in anticipating the future greatness of the country in national and international fields. Like Abram S. Hewitt and Woodrow Wilson, Theodore Roosevelt viewed politics as exciting and alluring because of his vision of the possibility of organizing society along lines of social justice. Brand Whitlock and Tom L. Johnson believed that the business of running the cities of Toledo and Cleveland was far more exciting than any private business.

But before a true social welfare state could be created in America, large new lessons had to be learned by its leaders in the art and practice of organization. Some of these lessons came from the states and the cities. LaFollette's outstanding success in Wisconsin, in persuading a whole commonwealth to overcome social inertia in order to improve the lot of the underprivileged, provided a primer that was much applauded by such historians as Turner, Beard, and Parrington. Other lessons were learned from the great industrialists who often became eminent philanthropists. It was not until I became immersed in an exhaustive study of the life of Rockefeller that I realized this contribution. Far more than a great businessman or a philanthropist, Rockefeller was a great organizer. After reducing the most chaotic segment of American industry—the petroleum business—to the orderliness of an absolutist state, he took the new and erratic domain of philanthropy in hand and gave it a set of working rules and aims that multiplied its effectiveness. Like his opponent, Theodore Roosevelt, he was an innovator, and like him, he proved that the application of intellectual power was of the first importance and a prime ally of honesty.

Lincoln Steffens and Brand Whitlock decided that in city, state, and national politics, honesty is not enough. Just afterward, Edith Cavell proclaimed to the world that patriotism is not enough, but that larger ideas of international planning and organization were required. We are still in the midst of a gigantic effort to organize international life on a firm and hopeful basis.

In the age that lies ahead of us, international cooperation will be vital. The countries of the world must learn to pool their efforts not just for security or economic betterment, but for the higher interests of mankind. In recent years I have toiled upon a history of the period of sectional division and civil war in our American past. The chief factor uniting Americans, I concluded, was the memory of past cooperation in the struggle for a better society. They were held together in large part by the recollection of their common effort in the Revolution, in their battle for a balanced and viable Constitution, in their fight for freedom of the seas in the War of 1812, and in their united effort against Indian perils and other difficulties in their great westward movement. It was this bond of union to which Lincoln appealed when he spoke in his Second Inaugural of the mystic chords of memory stretching from every battlefield and patriot shrine to every heart and hearthstone in the land.

What the world most needs today is the creation of a new battlefield of common endeavor and the rise of new heroes in the struggle to advance all mankind morally and spiritually as well as materially.

The United States, as a nation of fifty states and 200 million people, occupying a great part of the world's most favorable areas, changes economically, socially, and politically every few years. The holding of quadrennial elections in which the great political parties propose interesting platforms of action accelerates this process of change. But the importance of national unity and of what we may call a "consensus of sentiment" remains constant. Labor, capital, agriculture, science, technology, and industry must all act in harmony. This action must be carefully planned and must embody the newest ideas and the best conclusions of society. Contemporary Americans, unlike those of Lincoln's day, live in and for the future. It is not the loyalties of the past that hold them together so much as their common hopes for the future. Hence, social idealism, embracing the whole nation, is an absolute requisite.

The United States of the year 1975 will be an entirely different country than that of 1967, a part of an entirely different world. But we have the power, if we act with due forethought and employ our great latent capacities for planning, to ensure a better country with its varied groups acting amicably and constructively together. For this we need not only new leaders like the two Roosevelts, Woodrow Wilson, and John F. Kennedy, but a great body of well educated and truly thoughtful citizens determined to make the great republic greater still, and to see that it plays a worthy part in international life.

Part Four

TOOLS FOR THE HISTORIAN'S KITBAG

If historians are to write the sound, readable history necessary for the education and enlightenment of the nation's millions, Allan Nevins believed, they must use every possible tool that their ingenuity can contrive. Some of these can be borrowed from the social scientists, and this he urged throughout his academic lifetime. Others—autobiographies; diaries, letters, newspapers, and manuscripts—he believed to be often neglected or misused. Because he could never rest until every possible technique that might better understanding of the past was in the command of every scholar capable of its use, Allan Nevins spent a sizable amount of time and energy describing the many tools available to historians, explaining their use, and urging his contemporaries to employ them whenever they would result in better history. In the following essays he deals with a variety of these tools—biographies, autobiographies, diaries, manuscripts, newspapers, local records, oral history transcripts, and who's-who compilations—always rendering sound advice on the advantages and dangers in the use of each.

16

The Essence of Biography

Allan Nevins will probably be best remembered for his monumental studies of the Civil War, but he contributed almost as much to our knowledge of a galaxy of the nation's great and near-great as he did to our understanding of that tragic conflict. Certainly his biographies of John Charles Frémont, Grover Cleveland, Abraham S. Hewitt, John D. Rockefeller, Hamilton Fish, Eli Whitney, Henry Ford, Herbert H. Lehman, and James Truslow Adams would have won him a place among the immortals had he written no other books. Their writing forced him to think a great deal about the problems and methods of composing in this medium. These thoughts are summarized in this previously unpublished essay, apparently prepared late in his life (it was written on the back of Huntington Library stationery), in which he gives some very sound advice on how best to practice the biographical trade. In doing so, he also tells historians much they should know about the reliability of the biography as a source for their use.

What is it that makes a novel great? What makes a biography great? Clearly, in both literary forms style counts for a great deal; but no novel and no biography ever achieved greatness by richness or vigor of style. Some great novelists, like Dickens and Balzac, did not really have much style in the sense in which Matthew Arnold or Henry James would have used the word. In the work of some others, like Fenimore Cooper, the style is often positively bad. Again form and symmetry count for much. But they alone will not make a biography or novel a supremely rewarding experience. How unsymmetrical is Boswell's Johnson, how formless are *Les Misérables* and *The Brothers Karamazov*! What confers greatness upon any piece of literature is that creative element in it. There is nothing creative in style or form. Both operate marvelously as preservatives once the breath of life is put into a distinguished novel or biography. But vitality resides elsewhere; in the art of creation, or resurrection.

This creative requisite, difficult to define but easy to illustrate, is identical for the biography and the novel. It is met in every classic and enduring book, and is missing in the general average of volumes that gain brief attention and then die.

A fusion of inner and outer vision enters into the creation of characters who impress us with a sense of their complete reality. We speak of Anna Karenina, or Mr. Micawber, of Becky Sharp, of Babbitt, as if they were living people whom we have known, watched, and found conversable. Indeed, they seem more real than most of the flesh-and-blood people about us. I recall how in childhood I closed the pages of *David Copperfield* and *Dombey and Son* with much the melancholy pang of bereavement I should have felt if compelled to leave my community and friends. I was saying farewell to a group vividly alive to me. Some biographers produce this same sense of rounded reality in character: Lockhart's Walter Scott, Mrs. Gaskell's Charlotte Brontë, Trevelyan's Macaulay, and with all its defects, Sandburg's Lincoln. They recreate the central character and his or her circle so that they do more than speak and act: they live.

But a second test of biography is only less important. It is this:

Has the author the power of relating his characters in not only a significant but a poignant way to the universal laws of human experience? That is, he should have a story to tell, a set of experiences to describe, which harmonizes with and deepens our own sense of the mingled comedy and tragedy of life; the story being all the more effective if tragedy predominates. Every great novel tells a story which engages our fervent emotion. It may be as simple as *My Antonia*, as realistic as *The Old Wives Tale*, as commonplace in action as that neglected masterpiece *The Last Chronicle of Barset*, as abnormal as *Wuthering Heights* or most of Faulkner. At any rate, it must be a story which has a compelling and haunting quality. Some sense of an imperative force detaches itself from the page; we feel that Hardy *had* to tell the sad life chronicle of Tess, Balzac that of Père Goriot, and Mrs. Wharton that of Ethan Frome.

So it is with the great biographies. We see Dr. Johnson struggling with disease, with poverty, with his constitutional indolence, with his fits of overwhelming melancholy, with slights in youth and loneliness in age; or we see Mark Twain leaping in the audacity of his genius from continent to continent, basking in international renown, enjoying his exuberant wit and humor—and then suffering bankruptcy, bereavement of daughter and child, loss of faith in his country and human nature; or we watch Lytton Strachey's Queen Victoria as the bright years of romance with Prince Albert are followed by the iron years of widowhood and conscientious labor; and we see that all these narratives do touch a universal chord. They are interesting as a series of events; they are more deeply interesting in their relation to the human problem. Where is a sadder story than Carlyle's, so effectively told by Froude, or Woodrow Wilson's, his sword struck from his hand on the battlefield, as yet untold.

The principal challenge and delight in the art of biography is the task of characterization. No imaginative man ever began to write the life of another without saying to himself: Here is a person who once moved, thought, felt, and spoke, who was alive to his fingertips, who seemed to some people about him—his wife at least—the most interesting man in the world. How can I recreate that character? I must understand him myself first. Then by deft touches, or piled detail, I must build up such an understanding in my reader. Alas, how few biographers accomplish that first task of understanding the man they portray. Nothing is more difficult. Charles A. Beard once told me that he had never undertaken a biography because he despaired of understanding any man's thought and motives. Indeed, a full understanding is impossible, for no man really understands himself.

We all remember what Dr. Holmes says in the *Autocrat* papers about the three personalities of John. There is first the real John, known only to his Maker; there is second, John's own idea of himself, never the real John, but usually an idealization; and third, there is the world's idea of John, which corresponds to neither of the others. As Dr. Holmes points out, there are also three Thomases, so that when John and Thomas talk six persons are involved. It must be remembered, too, that the John of thirty, in all three of his characters, may be very different from the John of twenty; the John of forty very different again; and so on through life. John's character may change overnight if he is religiously converted, falls in love, or is inaugurated as president. The task of understanding a character bristles with difficulties, and at best only an approximation to the truth is possible. General Sherman said after a long friendship that he never understood that strange creative General Grant and believed Grant never understood himself.

It is evidence of the fascination which the task has immemorially presented that character study is one of the oldest elements in literature. The first true biographer, as we are often told, was Plutarch; and his forty-six *Parallel Lives* of Greek and Roman heroes are primarily studies in personality. I find the Romans better drawn, for Plutarch was closest to them. He was deficient as a storyteller, and few of his narratives relate the subject in a significant way to universal human experience. He was diligent in research, but knew nothing of scientific method, and made little distinction between tradition and valid evidence. His biographical work is also marred by one irritating fault; he was keenly interested in the ethical aspect of his heroes' lives and tinges his sketches with a great deal of moralizing. Still, he was a master of powerful effects; few scenes in literature surpass his compact account of the murder of Cicero.

And he did have a keen eye for character. He tried hard to understand his personages, and he evinces a striking talent for illustrating his conception of character by use of revealing human traits. He was able by a few deft quotations, a little group of incidents, to make the man real, human, convincing. His interest in human nature was curious and catholic, and he well understood the fact that the private qualities of a leader influence all his public actions; that as he behaves in small intimate matters, so he will behave in great. In reading Plutarch's lives of Antony and Brutus, we see at once that we are in the presence of the same *characters* who appear in Shakespeare; that is, the humanizing power of Plutarch fired Shakespeare with the desire to present them in the theater. Especially happy illustrations of Plutarch's method may be found in his lives of Alcibiades, Caesar, and Pompey. How well he shows Pompey's mixture of strength and weakness, and how graphically he brings out Pompey's most appealing traits, his humanity and magnanimity! Modern writers have added little to Plutarch's depiction of the fundamental traits of these men.

We may take as a telling specimen of Plutarch's talent for graphic characterization his twenty pages on Marcus Cato the Elder. He describes the man's arresting personal appearance: his fiery complexion, penetrating gray eyes, wiry figure, and battle-scarred breast. He emphasizes Cato's pugnacious qualities: his grim, ugly, ill-tempered face; his harsh, thunderous voice; his unflinching strokes. When he marched against Hannibal he went on foot, carrying his own arms, with one servant to bear his

221

provender; he cooked much of his own food and drank nothing but water, perhaps mixed with a little vinegar. On his farm he toiled with his own hands among his slaves, ate their coarse bread, and wore but a loose frock. His farmhouses were unplastered huts; his breakfast never saw the fire; his clothes were of the cheapest quality. When someone left him a piece of Babylonian tapestry, he sold it. He got rid of his slaves when they grew old, for he wanted nobody useless about him. When he governed Sardinia he walked that desert land without a carriage, dispensing justice in a rough, sententious manner. He rebuked all luxury, saying in Rome that it was hard to save a city where a fish sold for more than a work ox. Chiding an old man caught in an evil act, he growled: "Friend, old age has of itself blemishes enough; do not you add to it the deformity of vice." When the Samnite ambassadors, finding him boiling turnips in a chimney corner, offered him a present of gold, he retorted that a man content with such a supper had no need of gold. Detesting philosophy, he abused Socrates as an idle, prating fellow. After these twenty pages, we dislike Cato heartily, but we feel that we grasp his character.

In English biography, too, we meet skill in characterization long before thorough and accurate research or ability to tell a full life story. No better illustration of this fact can be named than Nicol Smith's admirable volume of *Characters in Seventeenth-Century English Literature,* a collection of brief but pungent and effective character sketches taken from Clarendon, Bishop Burnet, and similar writers. Or we can find illustrations in such authors as John Aubrey, Isaak Walton, and Roger North, three men who belong clearly to the school of anecdotal writers, concerned chiefly with the illumination of personality, which can be traced back to Plutarch.

Lytton Strachey has expatiated upon the contribution which John Aubrey's *Brief Lives* made to the art of biography, for he [Aubrey] had a keen eye for significant detail as well as a relish for a significant story. To him an illuminating incident was worth far more than a long train of facts. Nor did he hesitate to blurt out the truth. As he wrote a friend, he gladly set down many an incident "that would raise a blush in a young virgin's cheeks." He liked to bring out an idiosyncrasy. Thus he tells us that Francis Bacon liked to have music played in the next room while he meditated; that he strewed the table at every meal with sweet herbs and flowers; and that his restlessness of mind made him so wakeful that he often drank strong beer just before going to bed to quiet his intellect. From another thoughtful man, Thomas Hobbes, he quotes a memorable sentence. "If I had read as much as other men," said Hobbes, "I would know no more than they do." Still another thinker, William Harvey, discoverer of the circulation of the blood, had peculiar ways. He thought best in the dark, and when he built a house at Combe he constructed some caves in which he could sit and think. All this tells us more about personality, if not character, than the fact that Milton pronounced the letter r "very hard," but not more than the story that Sir Walter Raleigh, who had rough ways, once took a perpetual talker, grabbed a handful of hot sealing wax, and smeared it into his beard and moustache to shut his mouth.

It is indispensable for a biographer, after prolonged study and reflection, to make up his mind what his hero's character was, not merely in its basic elements, but in its changes between twenty and forty and between forty and sixty. Having done this, he must seek out ways of illustrating the main aspects of character in the most effective fashion possible. He will find the task easier if his main figure is extroverted; Walter Scott was easier to portray than George Meredith, Andrew Jackson than J. Q. Adams—though Mr. Samuel Bemis's portrait of Adams is admirable. It will help also if the hero has plenty of peculiarities, eccentricities, and picturesque ways; of what Macaulay called the anfractuosities of Dr. Johnson's character and mind. Some personages spill "revealing incidents" out of their lives as spendthrifts spill coins. Their biographers need only scramble over the pavement for them. Franklin did so, from the day he walked up Market Street in Philadelphia eating a roll to the day he stood in the Constitutional Convention pointing at the sun emblazoned on Washington's chair and remarking that at last he knew it was a rising, and not a setting, sun. Charles James Fox did so. Lincoln did so. But other men go through their lives without exploding a single incident which yields illumination.

An eye for matter which illuminates character is rare; it is given to few men. It does not do to assert, for example, that your hero is generous; that means nothing. It is useless to illustrate the statement by saying that he lent money to friends, carried the baby when his wife tired, and pitied the starving Chinese. Boswell had something memorably to the point when he related how Dr. Johnson carried a stricken prostitute through the streets on his back to his lodgings to succor her. The illustration ought to be unforgettable in its perfection. Albert Bigelow Paine, for example, in the biography of Mark Twain which deserves higher rank than it has gotten, tells us that Mark always kept an adolescent outlook upon life: "What a child he was!" How shall he prove it?

He offers a few simple bits of evidence: Mark Twain's delight in gaudy costume, expressed in exuberant admiration of the court dress of some Indian princes in Oxford; his pleasure in throwing sticks into an Alpine torrent, and then running alongside to see them foam over a waterfall; his preference for paintings of the Edwin Landseer variety and for music of the Jubilee Singer level. This is commonplace. But then Paine furnishes an incident of boyish exhibitionism that lights up Mark Twain as if a locomotive headlight had been suddenly turned upon the man. He relates how the two of them visited Washington so that Mark might speak for international copyright. They drove to the Willard Hotel and put on full dress for dinner. Writes Paine:

> I supposed he would want to go down with as little ostentation as possible, so I took him by the elevator which enters the dining room without passing through the long corridor known as "Peacock Alley," because of its being a favorite place for handsomely dressed fashionables of the

national capital. When we reached the entrance of the dining room he said:

"Isn't there another entrance to this place?"

I said there was, but it was very conspicuous. We should have to go down a long corridor.

"Oh, well," he said, "I don't mind that. Let's go back and try it over."

So we went back up the elevator, walked to the other end of the hotel, and came down to the F Street entrance. There is a fine, stately flight of steps—a really royal stair—leading from this entrance down into Peacock Alley. To slowly descend that flight is an impressive thing to do. It is like descending the steps of a throne-room, or to some royal landing place where Cleopatra's barge might lie. I confess that I was somewhat nervous at the awfulness of the occasion, but I reflected that I was powerfully protected; so side by side, both in full dress, white ties, white-silk waist-coats, and all, we came down that regal flight.

Of course he was seized upon at once by a lot of feminine admirers, and the passage along the corridor was a perpetual gantlet. I realize now that this gave a dramatic finish to his day, and furnished him with proper appetite for his dinner.

A less observant biographer might not have noted this incident, a less perceptive man might have smiled over it and quickly forgotten it. But in Paine's hands it illuminates Mark Twain's perpetual adolescence, his delight in showing off, in incomparable style.

When the event and the incident incompletely reveal character, pungent speech will sometimes do it. One of the lesser ornaments of American biography is Thomas Beer's sketchy, overmannered life of Stephen Crane; a book of about two hundred pages upon a minor figure in our letters. The author found his materials scanty and contradictory. But the volume conceals rather than exhibits a larger body of research than the casual reader would imagine; its style is arresting in a way peculiar to Beer; and it presents many insights into Crane's intellectual and moral nature. This is done in great degree by apt quotation, supplementing the narrative of his acts. What distinguished Crane was his uncompromising courage, which includes the harshest candor. He exhibited a rigid, unyielding honesty in depicting the street girl and her Bowery associates in *Maggie*; in reporting the Spanish War, in which the privates who died impressed him much more than the generals who strutted about; in describing war in general in *The Red Badge of Courage*; in refusing to pretend any interest in a single showplace of Paris; in ignoring the lurid slanders about his private life; in toiling to support the idlers who made his house in England a veritable hotel; in telling snobs what he thought of them and defending the underdog; and in writing his last books between hemorrhages. It is his blunt assertions of what he thought truth which make his incisive mind and resolute temper most evident to us. Listen to his unblenching words:

Tolstoy's *War and Peace* is too long. "He could have done the whole business in one-third of the time and made it just as wonderful. It goes on and on like Texas."

Oscar Wilde was a mildewed chump. He had a disease, and they all gas about him as if there was a hell and he came up out of it. . . . Mr. Yeats is the only man I have met who talks of Wilde with any sense. The others talk like a lot of little girls at a Sunday School party when a kid says a wicked word in a corner.

Englishmen aren't as easily shocked as we are. You can have an idea in England without being sent to court for it.

I was a Socialist for two weeks, but when a couple of Socialists assured me I had no right to think differently from any other Socialist and then quarreled with each other about what Socialism meant, I ran away.

Frances E. Willard is one of those wonderful people who can tell right from wrong for everybody from the polar cap to the equator. Perhaps it never struck her that people differed from her. I have loved myself passionately now and then, but

Miss Willard's affair with Miss Willard should be stopped by the police.

The question of soundness or acuteness in all this is not relevant; the essential matter is integrity expressed with bluntness. Stephen Crane found Robert Louis Stevenson insincere, Henry James absurd. He put his own personal requirement into two sentences: "I understand that a man is born into the world with his own pair of eyes, and he is not at all responsible for his vision—he is merely responsible for the quality of his personal honesty. To keep close to this personal honesty is my supreme ambition."

In perhaps two instances out of three, letters are the principal foundation of a biography. They are almost never as vital as the best kind of recorded talk. Boswell and Albert Bigelow Paine were singularly gifted in drawing Dr. Johnson and Mark Twain out in talk; gifted, too, in their perception of what was individual and characteristic in their hero's utterances. They were so saturated in the *ethos* of Johnson and Mark Twain that they knew just how to reproduce the particular effect produced by the spoken words. But such writers, such talkers, and such opportunities for recording talk are rare. It is a pity nobody ever recorded the informal talk, a shade too pontifical, of Nicholas Murray Butler. It is a greater pity that although John Maynard Keynes has a competent biographer in R. F. Harrod, he did not find a Boswell, for he was by all accounts an incomparable talker. A friend once remarked that in any conversation when Keynes was present it was no use saying anything, because he always thought of a better remark before you had time to make your own. His wit was shattering, his capacity for rudeness unequaled. "Words," he once wrote, "ought to be a little wild, because they are the assaults of thought upon the unthinking." The authorized biography by Harrod relies primarily on letters. So too must most biographies: on letters, journals, reminiscent bits.

A letter has one superiority over most other materials: it is

227

authentic and firsthand. A record of a conversation may be inaccurate, in content or emphasis; the impression of a contemporary may be prejudiced or stupid. But a letter comes from the man himself and expresses his mind even when he tries concealment. Of course letters vary greatly in value. In writing a life of Grover Cleveland I collected materials for a 600-page volume of his letters. Cleveland had no literary faculty whatever. He could no more have penned a vivid account of his observations or an eloquent transcript of his thought than he could have played a sonata or painted a picture. Partly because of this lack of literary sheen, his letters were a singularly transparent medium for his blunt, downright, simple mind. Utterly incapable of evasion, subtlety, or sophistication, he set down just what he was thinking in the most direct way possible. Hence it was that although he never wrote a colorful paragraph in his life, his epistles had an elemental strength that makes them readable and impressive. They present the man much better than my biography does. John D. Rockefeller, however, fell into a different category. He told his associates that the golden rule for them all in letter writing was the maxim: "Expose as little surface as possible." That rule defeats the biographer. And anyone who reads the later correspondence of Henry Adams, much of it ironic, facetiously masked, and enigmatic, finds himself peering at Adams through a clammy fog.

Moreover, a letter pertains to two people, not one, and sometimes tells us more about the person to whom it is addressed than about the man who wrote it. Intellectual level, tone of mind, and sympathy or congeniality must be considered. James Russell Lowell poured out his heart when he wrote to Charles Eliot Norton, whom he loved and trusted, but when he addressed E. L. Godkin some distinct reserve became evident. As we read Ralph Barton Perry's admirable *Life and Thought of William James*, we find that James wrote with candid loquacity as well as brilliance to his father, his sister Alice, his brother Henry, and Josiah Royce; but that his remaining epistles, though often delightful, are restrained. And yet how many eminent letter writers use almost the same tone to everyone. Theodore Roosevelt wrote in much the same vein to all his adult correspondents—not, of course, to his children. He could be as briskly, outspokenly, robustly superficial to George Otto Trevelyan as to one of his former Rough Riders, as headlong to John Burroughs as to Henry Cabot Lodge. So, too, Morley's Gladstone shows that the great British statesman wrote to intimates and strangers in much the same weighty, pompous manner. Queen Victoria is said to have remarked that he always spoke to her as if she were a public meeting; and he composed his letters as if he were addressing them to the *Contemporary Review* for publication.

Altogether, the biographer in using letters must weigh carefully the circumstances of their composition, the persons to whom they are sent, the fact that the most important letters have often disappeared, and all other circumstances. Letters fit best into the specious chronicle biography, of old called a "life and letters." One additional caveat may be entered. It is not impossible that the main body of a man's correspondence will actually belie his character, for some people change their personality when they pick up the pen. My old friend Conyers Read, sweet as summer in personal intercourse, became waspish on paper. Henry Adams became sardonic. Wilfred Ward, in the interesting life of his father called *William George Ward and the Catholic Revival*, tells us:

> The mass of the letters . . . [I used] . . . not only failed to illustrate my own knowledge of the personality, or the picture given by his contemporaries, but in general went in the teeth of such authentic evidence. Dean Church in his history of the Oxford Movement characterizes my father as "the most amusing and most tolerant man in Oxford." The bulk of his letters, it is not too much to say, would give the very opposite impression. . . . My father with his pen in his hand became an argumentative and dialectical machine.

The greatest danger in using letters is that they will give us an *inadequate* view of the writer. The greatest danger in using impressions, anecdotes, and reported sayings is that they will furnish a one-sided view.

While some men are one-sided, most men who play large roles in the world are not; and in political life particularly we can see that leader after leader suffers from the distorted observations and stories set afloat by thoroughly honest observers who see but one aspect. Lincoln is as good an example as any. He first loomed up as an important national figure in 1858, the year of the Lincoln-Douglas debates, and from that hour numerous eastern newspapermen and politicians set down their impressions. The preponderant testimony of casual observers from 1858 through 1862 was unfavorable. Henry Villard, then a press correspondent, saw the railsplitter at close quarters in 1858, and was offended by Lincoln's use of stories that were undeniably vulgar. The two took shelter once to avoid a shower. "Some people are talking of me for President," said Lincoln, and laughed. "Just think! A sucker like me President!" Charles Francis Adams talked with Lincoln in the White House just after the inauguration. He was convinced that Lincoln totally failed to comprehend the magnitude of the crisis, brought to public affairs a deplorable levity, and showed in his deportment not merely awkwardness but vulgarity. W. H. Russell, correspondent of the London *Times*, was more perceptive, but thought Lincoln far from impressive. Stanton, later Secretary of War, told McClellan that Lincoln was the original gorilla, and that the explorer Du Chaillu need not have gone to Africa to investigate the animal. Much more evidence might be piled up, for it was not until the fall of 1862 that Lincoln's essential greatness became evident to any but his close associates.

Some great men lend themselves readily to biographical caricature. Their image can be distorted by an accentuation of certain traits in the way in which Dickens distorted certain of his personages. G. K. Chesterton thinks that the people Dickens presents were real people, whom he had studied carefully, but that he saw them with boyish eyes of utter naïveté. That is, he concentrated on those peculiarities of Mr. Micawber, Squeers, Fagin, Mr. Dombey, Mme. Mantalini, and others which would delight an acute and rather impish youth. Walter Bogehot has a more convincing theory; he asserts that the great genius saw far better than others into the depths of character and delighted in exposing its quintessential elements, converting the individual into a type. Thus Samuel Weller is the quintessence of smart Cockney servants; thus Mr. Pecksniff is the humbug rural architect raised to the nth power. Dickens's method was legitimate in fiction, but improper for a careful biographer. Biography nevertheless is full of Dickensian volumes: particularly the portrait-biography. Frank Harris's *Oscar Wilde* is distorted; so is Paxton Hibben's *Henry Ward Beecher*; so, a little, is André Maurois's Shelley *(Ariel)*; so are even Lytton Strachey's masterly but hostile depictions of "Chinese" Gordon, Florence Nightingale, and others in *Eminent Victorians*.

Consider how easy it would be for a biographer who wished to present a Dickensian, or Stracheyan portrait to do so with Charles Sumner, a striking figure who was without a good modern biographer until David Donald brought out his fine recent study. He would begin by emphasizing the decorous correctness of Sumner's upbringing: Harvard College, law study, travel abroad, with sly touches indicating that Sumner was a prig. He would relate Carlyle's harsh dictum on Sumner: "The most complete nothin' of a man that ever crossed my threshold—naught whatsoever in him but wind and vanity." Emphasizing Sumner's pedantry, he would quote what his secretary, Moorfield Storey, said of the man: he "treated his mind as a reservoir, and into it steadily pumped learning of every kind." He would illustrate Sumner's complete lack of humor by apt anecdotes. For example, when a young woman just entering society told the senator, at a Washington party, that she loved to see lions breaking the ice, Sumner after a moment's pause solemnly remarked, "Miss Blank, in the country where lions live, there is no ice." Similarly, he would illustrate Sumner's pomposity. We would hear of Lincoln's comment: "I have never had much to do with bishops where I live; but do you know, Sumner is my idea of a Bishop."

Of course the intolerance of this man of conviction would be brought out. The tale of Brooks's attack upon Sumner in the Senate would be rehearsed with emphasis, as in Beveridge's life of Lincoln, on the provocation which Sumner had given by his outrageous insults to South Carolina and her leaders. We would hear again of President Grant's caustic thrust when he was told that Sumner did not believe in the Bible: "No, he didn't write it." His conceit might be presented in Lowell's little picture. Lowell tells us that Sumner used to say, when talking about himself, as he usually was: "Now listen to this: this is History." We would hear of his quarrel with Lincoln, his worse quarrel with Andrew Johnson, and his truly horrifying quarrel with Grant. The biographer would not miss giving an account of Sumner's autumnal marriage and his wife's abandonment of him after the briefest experience. In fact, she endured him but six months; and William Cullen Bryant observed that no wife could be content "with a husband who is too exclusively occupied with himself and his own greatness." Our biographer might close with the remark attributed to one of the Quincys when he was asked whether he was going to Sumner's funeral: "No, but I approve of it."

Now all this would be true as far as it goes, but it would be less than half the truth. There was another Charles Sumner altogether. This was the Sumner who wrote some of the most charming travel letters in the language; who was liked and admired by a long list of eminent men of letters in America and Britain; whose simple amiability in private life made him beloved of servants, children, and constituents; who had a fine enthusiasm for art as well as literature; who never evaded a duty, however disagreeable; who never failed to exhibit a high kind of moral courage; and who was capable also of rare magnanimity, as he showed in his great gesture late in life toward the South. Mr. Donald's carefully planned and deeply researched life of Sumner presents both his happy and unhappy traits, rightly emphasizing the former. It does special justice to his inborn rectitude, his serene endurance of social martyrdom, and his deep devotion to the Negro race. The result is a mixed, a complex, and to that extent a difficult portrait, but one truthful in detail and in general effect.

Of course I have here presented an extreme instance, but the caricature I have sketched is hardly less poster-like than some in print. Christopher Herold's life of Mme. de Stael (*Mistress to an Age*) and Garrett Mattingly's life of Katharine of Aragon are subtle, balanced, and scholarly. Lytton Strachey's briefer portrait-biographies gave too much encouragement to the school of caricaturists. Every person he treated in *Eminent Victorians*—Arnold of Rugby, "Chinese" Gordon, Cardinal Wiseman, and Florence Nightingale—has been the subject of a new biography since he published his book in 1918; and every biography has proved him essentially wrong in his malicious denigrations. One of these biographies, Cecil Woodham-Smith's *Florence Nightingale*, will outlast Strachey's own best book, his *Queen Victoria*.

A veracious biography involves thorough research, and the finest hand in selection and presentation. Human character is nearly always complex, is never to be penetrated at a glance, and is easily misjudged. Moreover, nearly all human acts and traits have a significance that varies with the sympathy or antipathy of the observer. Is Jones a shifty, wavering, uncertain man? Or does he simply see both sides of an issue, so that his apparent vacillations are simply proof of openmindedness and tolerance? Is Robinson a mean man, or a man of wise thrift? And the changes in the character of some men, from decade to decade, are sometimes startling. A long study of John D. Rockefeller convinced me that he scarcely changed at all from youth to age. He was the same man as a clerk earning $6 a week, as the architect of the Standard Oil empire, as superintendent of Sunday School, as founder of the University of Chicago, as octogenarian golf-player, and as landscape architect at Pocantico Hills; his unity, his integrity, was perfect; he always stood there like a piece of granite. But the mercurial Henry Ford, who could show ten moods in the same

day, went through at least three incarnations. The Ford of the first
heyday of success was an ardent idealist; he was the Ford of the
Peace Ship, of the Five Dollar Day, of the mass-production
complex which opened on the world as a new dawn, of that
remarkable welfare agency in his factory which he called the
Sociological Department. Then, as his idealism was chilled by
ridicule and misunderstanding, his final impulses warred with
darker qualities, his "mean streak," as intimates called it, the
outcome uncertain. And lastly, after a stroke he suffered in 1939,
during his final eight years the worse side of his nature triumphed,
so that he committed great wrongs against labor, against his son
Edsel, and even against the colossal industrial structure he had
reared.

Perhaps it would be well for the biographer to think that he is
dealing with various layers, or strata, in human personality and
character. The outward layer consists of stature, form, and
features, the tone of speech, the mannerisms of acting and talking.
The second stratum consists in the obvious tastes of a man in
books, in friends, and in work or amusements, along with his
response to such simple moral tests as breaking the Sabbath and
the lesser commandments. A third and deeper layer pertains to
elements of character which only the closest associates—wife,
business partners, bosom friends—can divine, and alas, which they
sometimes conspire to conceal. Finally, we may distinguish a
fourth or innermost stratum, which is called into manifestation
only by some great crisis; a crisis in which a man's conduct may
astonish even himself, for he will reveal a streak of heroism or
cowardice, of principle or falsity, of which he was ignorant. To
penetrate into this ultimate core of character is the biographer's
greatest triumph.

We can seldom be quite sure; but we seem to get at this core of
character when we see John Adams deciding to wreck his own
Federalist party to make a last attempt at preserving peace with
France; when we see the filibuster Crittenden in Cuba facing the
Spanish firing-squad, which asked him to kneel, with the defiant

words, "A Tennessean kneels only to his God"; when we see Ulysses S. Grant, dying of cancer at Mount McGregor, toiling at the memoirs which were his only provision for his family, dictating aloud while he could speak and struggling on in a whisper when his voice failed; when we see Grover Cleveland, faced at the outset of his campaign for the presidency by the devastating public revelation that he is father of an illegitimate son, bidding his panic-stricken friends, searching for plausible evasion, "Tell the truth!"; and when we see Mark Twain writing his terrible thoughts as his daughter Jean is borne to the grave. Psychoanalysis might be of great use to the biographer, in ways which Leon Edel indicates in his book on *Literary Biography*, if we had enough evidence to sustain its use; but we almost never do. Happily for the biographer human beings in their vicissitudes not seldom encounter tests which light up, as by a lightning flash, the innermost recesses of their souls.

17

The Autobiography

In this brief essay or lecture, found among his literary remains and apparently incomplete, Allan Nevins deals pleasantly with autobiographies as sources for the use of historians, demonstrating both their merits and their defects as reliable windows onto the past. His method, as usual, is anecdotal; he makes his points by describing a large number of published autobiographies, old and new, emphasizing the wide differences in their nature, and explaining how those differences tell us a great deal about the character of the writers. Any modern reader is certain to be struck by the breadth of Nevins's reading in this relatively obscure literary form and by the computerlike ability of his memory to produce exactly the right illustration for each of his points. If, as seems probable, this paper was delivered as a lecture to one of his Columbia University classes in historiography, his students were obviously favored with learning and advice all too rare among teachers.

At first glance the potentialities of autobiography, particularly in the way of character analysis, would seem to be enormous. For it is clear that the autobiography presents facts as to a man's

236

life, impulses, and motives which nobody but himself can know, given with the intimacy of the closest witness. Some autobiographies, of course, relate only to the external events of a lifetime. General Grant's *Memoirs* are a case in point. They tell us how he acted; they throw little light upon the psychological forces behind the act. But if a man does try to make his autobiography an intimate record, to make it what Richard Jeffries called "The Story of My Heart," it ought to surpass any other conceivable record.

The fact is that sometimes it does, but more frequently it does not. We need only look at the long list of autobiographies in print to see how imperfect most of them are; and these imperfections spring from certain basic defects of human nature. The fact is that if biography needs to be approached with a critical mind, autobiography requires much more caution. It may be far more deeply misleading. We may catalog the reasons for this under half a dozen heads:

(1) To produce a truthful record of a man's thoughts, feelings, and motives, two innate qualities are essential—self-knowledge and complete candor. A great many people, however, never attain real self-knowledge, but constantly deceive themselves as to their real traits; a great many others are seriously deficient in candor. Not a few men are anxious to produce an entirely false picture of themselves. Those who write apologias can seldom be trusted.

(2) For good autobiography a fresh and vivid memory is indispensable. Probably not one elderly man or woman in a thousand has the clear indelibility needed. People who pride themselves upon the accuracy of their recollections almost invariably find, upon referring to diaries or other records of transactions long past, that their memories are in some essential respects confused or erroneous. The best autobiographies are usually those written with the aid of fairly complete memoranda of the past. If these are lacking, the record is untrustworthy.

(3) If a man's memory is keen and vivid, or if he possesses fairly full memoranda of his life, the array of facts upon his career is

likely to be immense and overwhelming. In the nature of things, it is greater than the array of facts available for most biographies— perhaps any biography. To use these multitudinous facts well, the writer has to have an exceedingly just sense of proportion. Those who lack this give us an undigested mass of detail and may even perpetrate a work as prodigious and otiose as John Bigelow's five volumes of *Retrospection*.

(4) Anyone who writes of his state of mind in a period long past is almost certain to give us a view of it through lenses colored by the present. It would be difficult indeed for anyone now to recall with real precision what he or she thought of Hitler in 1934 or Charles A. Lindbergh in 1936. A new screen of emotions has been built up between us and those figures; and if we were to describe our past emotions toward them, we would unconsciously falsify the image. We forget how rapidly our views alter. We forget also how opinions change from a confused, inchoate state to a firm, definite shape. Once they assume the latter form, we tend to think that we always held these opinions—to forget that we were once very hazy about what may now seem a vital matter. And changes in taste always tend to elude us. Men become very censorious at one stage of life toward weaknesses which they once regarded quite indulgently. Dr. Johnson spoke of the fact that a young man is quite impatient of a boy's liking for tops, and an old man is quite condemnatory of a young man's liking for his mistress.

Now the first qualities listed above, self-knowledge and candor, are those most absolutely vital for a spiritual or intellectual autobiography of the highest quality. If we look at the greatest autobiographies, we see that they were all written by men of honesty, and in most instances of great moral earnestness. They were written to exhibit the mind and soul, not to conceal it. That certainly is true of St. Augustine's *Confessions*. It is true of John Bunyan's *Grace Abounding to the Chief of Sinners*. It is true of John Woolman's *Autobiography*, the first important American contribution to this department of letters. It is true of Benjamin Franklin's book; he tried to give an unadorned account of himself and his acts, he left out none of the "errata" that had marked his very imperfect career, and if he plumbed no great depth in his self-revelation it was because his sagacious, practical mind had little profundity. John Stuart Mill's autobiography is equally honest. As we read it, we can understand why Gladstone called him "the saint of rationalism." He was too rational to exhibit much spiritual depth and richness. But he was so much a saint that he is painfully conscientious in telling the whole truth about himself. A similar veracity appears, I think, in G. K. Chesterton's autobiography. It is almost excessively clever; it tells us more of Chesterton's remarkable mind than of his heart; but it is stamped with veracity on every page.

The best kind of autobiographical candor, I think, has something more than mere honesty, mere transparency of heart, in it. It is the candor that springs from a strong moral impulse or strong spiritual impulse. Men do not go to great limits in self-revelation unless they are impelled by some inner demon. In St. Augustine it was a horror of sin which made him confess so fully his past transgressions. In John Woolman it was an abounding love of God and fellow men which made him write a complete exposition of his attempts to serve both. How about Rousseau, it may be asked. But here some would question whether the record is as sincere as it appears—whether it is not decidedly artificial in places. And where it is sincere, there really is a strong inner impulse—an artistic, not a religious or moral impulse.

Let us look at some of the best recent American autobiographies and examine their qualities. As it happens, we have a singularly interesting roster of titles. They include works by distinguished novelists: Mary Austin's *Earth Horizon*, Theodore Dreiser's *A Book About Myself*, Herbert Quick's *One Man's Life*; books by men of action, ranging from Will James's *Lone Cowboy* to General Pershing's *Memoirs*; books by unimportant people, such as Thomas Emerson Ripley's *A Vermont Boyhood*, and by men of national renown, such as Calvin Coolidge and William Allen White; autobiographies as placid as Henry Seidel Canby's

239

The Age of Confidence, being his memories of youthful days in Wilmington, and as stormy and impassioned as Ludwig Lewisohn's *Up-Stream: An American Chronicle.* It is a varied and entertaining list.

It is at once evident that the purely objective autobiographies are on a much lower plane of interest than the works which are highly subjective, which attempt an extensive self-analysis, or which at least try to lay bare the heart and mind of the writer. Will James's *Lone Cowboy* is an excellent adventure story, but nothing more. It tells how he was born in Montana, his father a Texas cowboy and would-be rancher; how when hardly more than a baby he became an orphan; how he was adopted by a French fur trapper named Jean Beaupré—"Old Bopy"; how he was taken on long, long hunts and endured many perils; how his foster father was lost in an icy river and he was thrown upon his own resources; how he embarked upon a long drifting career as cowboy and bronco-buster, wandering all over the western country from Canada to Mexico; how he developed a passion for drawing and found that he had a genuine talent for it; and how finally—after he had served a term in jail—he began writing the self-illustrated books which made him modestly famous—*Smoky, Cow Country, Cowboys North and South.* It is a most beguiling story, for James tells it picturesquely in his own simple, honest language. But we hardly see the narrator any more distinctly than we see Old Bopy, or some of the sheriffs, sheepherders, and cowmen of the plains. He does not make us an intimate participator of his thoughts and emotions.

The same is of course true of the autobiography of Calvin Coolidge. It is a more self-revealing work, but its self-revelation is unconscious. We have to read between the lines for its spiritual confessions; and they are the confessions of a rather thin as well as self-repressed nature. I must say that I have never quite been able to understand why Mr. Coolidge wrote it. Certainly no strong impulse of any kind stands back of it. When we turn to Pershing's autobiography we of course find a work which, equally objective and impersonal, has a better excuse for being. For Pershing filled a unique place in one of the world's great crises; he was the only American who has ever led a great army to fight in Europe, and he knew more about the policies and acts of American headquarters than anybody else. By comparing his autobiography with that of Coolidge we can see that there are distinct degrees of intimacy in even objective biography. For Coolidge, discreet in everything, the soul of caution, tells us practically nothing of his acts and aims as president; he reveals nothing, he explains nothing, he justifies nothing. He is intent upon exposing no surface, upon provoking no controversy. Pershing, however, gives a full if by no means satisfactory exposition of all his activities as commander of the AEF. His book is valuable to the historian; Coolidge's is not very valuable to anybody. It leaves Silent Cal as much and as little of an enigma as it found him.

Neither Coolidge nor Pershing seems to have possessed great personal warmth, and neither was actuated by any strong feeling of any kind in writing his memoirs. We find more both of personality and of purpose in such an objective autobiography as that of James Weldon Johnson, entitled *Along This Way*. It is the story, as everyone knows, of one of our most successful American Negroes. He has made himself known as poet, song writer, journalist, and above all, as secretary for eleven years of the National Association for the Advancement of Colored People. He writes a modest and restrained book; but it is given a vitality that lifts it above the ordinary work of reminiscence by his deep feeling for the American Negro. He himself had suffered a good deal from the disabilities of his race. He gives a vivid and dramatic account of the time when he faced death at the hands of a mob which would actually have killed him had he turned his back—on the frightful charge that he had been alone in a Jacksonville park with a white woman! Only his own dauntless courage and the humanity of one of the leaders of the white group saved him; that, and the fact that the woman in the matter was ascertained after all not to be white, but colored. But the book is made moving by

241

his feeling for his race, not for the insults and injuries he himself has experienced. He believes strongly that Negroes should retain their racial identity, and not amalgamate with the white race. He thinks that if they preserve their self-respect they will be given better and better treatment by the remainder of the population. In the South, he writes, a new generation will arise which will be "moved consciously by a sense of fair play and decency, and unconsciously by a compulsion to atone for the deeds of their fathers." This strong emotion for an abused race breathes into his book, as into the far more eloquent works of W. E. B. DuBois—for example, his *Souls of Black Folk*—and into the autobiography of Booker T. Washington, a quality that ordinary memoirs will lack.

We reach a higher quality still, I think, in Herbert Quick's very characteristic and thoroughly delightful autobiography called *One Man's Life*. It is the work of a brave, buoyant, extremely active spirit, interested in a wide variety of facts and ideas, gifted with imagination, and actuated by a set of strongly altruistic purposes. His mind is more cultivated than Mr. Johnson's; his outlook is broader; and his aims are just as high. Quick was a true patriot and a devoted public servant, who did as much as any American to improve farm life. As teacher, editor, and federal official he made permanent contributions to rural prosperity. At the same time, he had a vital sense of the drama and color that went into the settlement of the West, and of the importance of the western spirit to the future of the United States. A great deal of all this goes into his autobiography. It is as bright, cheerful, optimistic a volume as one could hope to find. The author has poured his essential spirit into it, and we see that it is a rare spirit. He has also put into it his understanding of a whole section and his insight into the principal qualities that have made our republic grow great.

From beginning to end the work is subjective. In essentials, it is the story of the unfolding of Quick's mind, imagination, and aspirations. The great events in it are intellectual and psychological; and, grasping at once the healthiness of the young man's nature, the elevation of his spirit, we read of these events with intense sympathy. Quick, just entering manhood, came into contact with the radical movement of the Grangers, rising in the seventies against the abuses of the railroads. He saw the rise of the antimonopoly party after the panic of 1873; his family were followers of Peter Cooper. Out on the Iowa prairies, he heard the farmers talking excitedly of the reforms they would carry through at the state capital. Later came other awakening influences—school teaching, journalism, law study, a timid venture into politics. The book closes with his introduction to Henry George's *Progress and Poverty*, and the bursting upon his brain of a dazzling new illumination. It is all delightful; we are swept along by the enjoyment of the tale and by the excitement of seeing Quick's mind open into one range of ideas after another. Back of it, too, there is a unifying emotion: a faith in the sanity, justice, and hopefulness of American life at its best. The book has bits of poetry, bits of heroism, bits of humor. But it is an inspiring story because it takes us to the innermost recesses of the mind and heart of an aspiring personality.

A darker hue mantles the story of a man of darker and deeper nature: Theodore Dreiser's *A Book About Myself*. It is now an old book—it appeared in 1922; but it is a singularly apt volume to compare with Quick's. It covers his years of young manhood as a newspaperman in St. Louis, Chicago, Pittsburgh, and New York; it describes his first encounters with both the happy and the seamy aspects of American life—but above all the seamy side. He includes some exciting stories of his adventures while covering gruesome crimes. He gives us an acid impression of the dishonesty, intellectual and sometimes financial, which characterized a good deal of American journalism. He describes his conscientious and thorough investigations of political corruption, of vice, and of poverty, with their many interconnections. This story too, while full of incident, of biting bits of social description, of wise and tolerant sketches of human beings, is essentially subjective in interest. It describes how Theodore Dreiser's mind and spirit unfolded—and did so in a very different way from that of Herbert Quick. As he tramped his round in gathering news, as he talked with the lowly and struggling, as he sadly observed the crooks and scoundrels who exploited social injustice, a feeling of revulsion grew within him. He was collecting material for those novels which, describing with pedestrian realism the darker phases of American life, would in effect be eloquent propagandist pamphlets, incitements to revolt. He tells us how he tramped around the shacks and hovels of the slum district of Pittsburgh, and talked with the hunkies of Homestead, battened upon by the *padrone*, the labor spy, the company store, and the employers of child labor; how he compared these aspects of American civilization with the wealth and splendor of Carnegie, the Phippses, and the Olivers living in their grand mansions in the east end of Pittsburgh. A strong emotion pulses through this autobiography too. It gives the book unity and poignancy. It is curiously unlike the emotion that runs through Herbert Quick's volume; and yet both are authentically American.

We have a very different subjectivity when we turn to Mary Austin's *Earth Horizon*. It is the story of a life of struggle. Girlhood in a little house in southern Illinois; early religious experiences; attendance at Blackburn College; marriage, and a married life in which, as she writes, nothing turned out as she expected it; her husband's failure and his sudden disappearance, leaving her stranded in the West; her money troubles; her breakdowns in health; her struggles as a writer, and final success— this is the binding narrative thread of the book. The outer story is enriched by some striking incidents and many interesting personalities, for she knew William James, Ambrose Bierce, Jack London, and all the writers who lived in and visited the Southwest. It contains a number of fertile digressions upon various topics. In compressed sentences and paragraphs Mary Austin expresses her ideas, offers her perceptions, upon a wide variety of subjects. But the book is given strength by one powerful element—her feminist

244

convictions. It is given depth and richness by another strong element, to which the title *Earth Horizon* is an allusion; her mystical and fervent belief in the earth as a source of spiritual and artistic strength.

It is a much greater book than Quick's breezy, cheerful, sociable volume, or than Dreiser's sad and quietly angry work. The feminism is perhaps not altogether pleasant. It is evident that Mary Austin's experiences with the male world had been bitterly unhappy, and her bitterness runs like an astringent current through the chapters. It became part of her very temperament, this bitterness; I have never read her novels, but it must have disabled her from filling the part of a great novelist. The wonderful element in the book is the mystic attachment to the earth, to the land she was always celebrating in her better books—the *Land of Little Rain*, the *Land of Journey's Ending*, the *Lands of the Sun*. When she was twelve she learned at a Chautauqua meeting of Hugh Miller's book *The Old Red Sandstone*. The title had what she terms "a calling sound." She saved her pennies; the book was soon her own. It stirred and awakened some basic quality in her temperament. Hugh Miller had written of the geological history of his native Cromarty district in Scotland, with a strong feeling for the people and nature allied with the geology. His book created in Mary Austin a sense of the grandeur of the ancient earth, the wealth of its moods, the immensity of its pattern; it struck a chord that no American nature writer, no Thoreau, Burroughs, or even Muir, could have awakened.

It was this mystic sense of the grandeur of the earth which made Mary Austin a great writer. She caught a new apprehension of scale and synthesis, proper to Americans in "the breathless experience of owning a new country." She was carried by fate into the wide Southwest, where the earth is most impressive and overwhelming, its shapes endlessly striking. It was far better for her purposes than the rich bottom country of southern Illinois. She has written of the Mohave country, of the mountains about

Taos, of the deserts and hills, of the sheepherders and vaqueros who inhabit them, as nobody else has done. And the same mystic feeling flows into her book, giving it life and eloquence. We feel, as we read the volume, how the earth has dominated her life, and how it has transmuted all her experience with a creative touch. We shall have many American autobiographies. Some will be like Quick's; some will be like Dreiser's; but we shall never have another quite like Mary Austin's.

Nor shall we ever have one quite like *The Education of Henry Adams*. It is one of those books of self-revelation which seem to be attempting to conceal thought, passion, and personality, but which instead express it with extraordinary force—even with passion and eloquence. Henry Adams was unquestionably a genius, but a genius who never quite realized his own capacities. In his autobiography he seems intent upon "debunking" his own life—upon making himself appear smaller than he really was. Why? I think it was in part because he never comprehended his powers and never made quite the fullest use of them; because to the end he deceived himself about his own nature. He would have liked a life of action. He wished to control power as his great-grandfather John Adams, his grandfather John Quincy Adams, and even his father Charles Francis Adams had controlled it. That is, he wished political power. All the time he should have known that his talents lay in another direction. He was fitted by nature to play a commanding role in quite another realm than that of Congress or State Department; in the realm of the scholar, teacher, thinker, critic, and historian. Of this we have the fullest proof in his writings. But he never himself quite perceived the fact—or if he did, never reconciled himself to it. His genius was at war with his ambition; he was at any rate unwilling to submit to his genius; and his great book is a record of the resulting conflict.

18

Why Public Men Keep Diaries

To Allan Nevins the stuff of history could be found
everywhere: in government records, in local archives, in
business documents, in autobiographies and reminiscences, in
diaries kept by the great and near-great of the past. He
recognized, however, that each of these media is warped by
the circumstances of its origin and must be used with caution
lest the user be misled by the purposes or prejudices of the
author. In this article, published originally in the *New York
Times Magazine* in 1952, he comments briefly on the rash of
diaries of public men then appearing, then dwells at greater
length on the nature of the diary as a historical document and
sketches the guidelines that historians should follow in its use.
Here, as in dealing with the proper employment of the variety
of materials needed to explain past behavior, his concern is
with the accurate re-creation of the life and thought of the
nation, freed from the distortions of either past or present.

A generation ago it was the fashion to ridicule people who

247

kept diaries. They were suspected of being too self-conscious and naïve; the egotism that is inseparable from a diary was pronounced offensive. Besides were not most diaries rather stilted and affected—rather Victorian? Pepys, of course, was immortal—but what a price Pepys had paid for his fame. For who would want his soul pried into, his deepest secrets flaming scarlet under the vulgar gaze.

Today the diary is back in full fashion. President Truman keeps a diary, and last week entries from it appeared in a book, *Mr. President*, and stirred up a furor. Books of other public men come from the press—the Forrestal diaries, the Hopkins diaries, the Stettinius diaries, the Bonsal diaries. Ambassadors like Joseph Davies in Moscow and Joseph Grew in Tokyo have vied with war correspondents all over the map in diarizing. Generals kept pace with them. Busy as he was, even Eisenhower (who had told friends how an overwhelming sense of history overcame him when he went to Gibraltar for conferences and planning) not only directed his naval aide, Harry C. Butcher, to keep a full diary record but supplemented it now and then with notes of his own.

All this, of course, is simply in the line of a great tradition, or perhaps we had better say in the line of an irresistible human impulse to record great experiences and powerful emotions.

Most students of recent history know something of the highly impressive journal of former Secretary of the Treasury Morgenthau. It is almost a diary to end all diaries. Including a verbatim report of innumerable conversations, and the text of countless documents, it is so voluminous that it would take almost as long to read every word of it as to live through the years during which it was compiled! But it is a great public service none the less. For generations to come, men interested in government and politics will recall Mr. Morgenthau's name with gratitude.

The diarist was busy among the fathers of the Republic. To name but three men, Washington himself kept a fairly assiduous if often brief record; John Adams was still more industrious; and Gouverneur Morris left two volumes which, valuable for American affairs, are simply priceless for the French Revolution. In Civil War days pens again scratched busily. Young John Hay as Lincoln's secretary, chatting with the "tycoon" in the White House and seeing all the important figures of the time, set down their words almost as they were uttered. Secretary of the Navy Gideon Welles labored into the night over his cantankerous but fascinating journal, one of our great source books of history. Thus the stream has flowed on.

Beyond question, the diary will play a larger and larger part among the records of history. The telephone and airplane have to a considerable extent annihilated the letter as a preservative of facts and opinions. Political and business leaders who do not write many letters find it all the more important to fix their position by memoranda and diary notes. The very pace at which events now occur favors the keeping of journals. Arthur Ponsonby in his study of British diaries remarks that the four greatest incitements to a daily record are religion, sports, war or a similar crisis, and frequent contact with great people.

But what is the precise value of the diary in the eyes of the historian? What makes a good diary, and how is it to be distinguished from the bad?

It should be said at once that, just as the diary is a unique literary form, it often possesses unique historical attributes. It holds its special place not merely because it offers an intimate running view of events, and not merely because it furnishes much unconscious self-revelation, but because it can be—and often is—more artless, unstudied and utterly honest than any other form of evidence. It is this because it presents a witness talking not to others but to *himself*.

Outwardly, the diary looks much like a memoir or autobiography. Actually, a world of difference exists between Ben Franklin's autobiography and John Woolman's journal. The vital distinction is that an autobiography is always intended for somebody else's eyes, even if only that of the family, and is therefore dressed up; the diary is half the time kept for the diarist alone. Why did Pepys make his incomparable record? Simply, it is generally agreed, to enable himself in later years to relive the joys and sorrows—the good meals, wenchings, hard efforts to save and quarrels with Mrs. Pepys; the theatrical performances, gaudy sights and good company—of his early manhood.

Even if the diarist has posterity in mind, his rapid daily jotting is bound to be franker than a carefully planned autobiography. Gideon Welles after the Civil War tried to conceal some of his blindnesses, his errors of opinion and less creditable exhibitions of spleen by editing his diary.

Stephen Bonsal wrote his diary of the Paris Peace Conference at the behest of Woodrow Wilson, who declared: "You can't be too indiscreet for me. I give you full absolution in advance." When the time came to publish it as "Unfinished Business," mistaken judgments and errors of action were plainly evident. But Bonsal was too honest to edit them out.

The same vital distinction holds between the diary and the letter. Here again the two forms often look a good deal alike. But the letter is meant immediately for another eye; the diary only remotely that, or not at all.

No, the diary is unique in its immediacy and frankness. It is further unique in this: that it can be written by the illiterate or semi-literate as well as the most cultivated. Since social history is just as important as political, literary or diplomatic history, the coal-heaver's or seamstress's diary may be worth more than the statesman's.

One of the great merits of Washington's diaries—historically—lies in their simple, casual frankness. If he knew that posterity had its eye on his pages, he almost never gave evidence of the fact. The present-day reader sometimes wonders why he wrote at all! In May 1775, he was attending the Continental Congress in Philadelphia. The colonies were moving rapidly toward revolt and independence. All about him were interesting and important men engaged in work destined to affect all humanity. And what did George confide to his diary?

May 12 Dined and supped at the City Tavern.
May 13 Dined at the City Tavern with the Congress. Spent the evening at my lodgings.
May 14 Dined at Mr. Wellings and spent the evening at my lodgings.

Washington's record for the Constitutional Convention of 1787 is almost equally colorless. The daily line or two was simply a sort of personal bookkeeping; it was for himself, not posterity. But its honesty is all the more compelling whenever he does state a conviction, bare an emotion, or deal with a controversial situation.

In fine, the best diary for the purpose of history (assuming weight or color in the contents) is that which is least self-conscious. Only the honest, unstudied diary carries a stamp of strong character.

The diaries of John and John Quincy Adams are not really violations of this cardinal rule. Taken together, these massive works cover American history and international relations from the earthquake of 1755 (when John began) to November 1846 (when John Quincy, still a hard-working Congressman, made his last entry). They deal with almost every side of national life and thought.

These two Adamses kept diaries, it is plain, because they had to. Being men of the strongest convictions and fiercest emotions, they needed diaries to blow off steam, to purge their breasts of perilous stuff. Without their journals they would have exploded. John Quincy Adams, for example, coming into collision in Monroe's Cabinet with John C. Calhoun on the Missouri Compromise, would stifle his anger until he could hurry home to tell a sheet of paper what he thought of Southerners:

March 3, 1820. The discussion of the Missouri question has betrayed the secret of their souls. In the abstract they admit that slavery is an evil***But when probed to the quick upon it, they show at the bottom of their souls pride and vainglory in their condition of masterdom. They fancy themselves

251

more generous and noble-hearted than the plain freemen who labor for subsistence. They look down upon the simplicity of a Yankee's manners, because he has no habits of over-bearing like theirs and cannot treat Negroes like dogs. It is among the evils of slavery that it taints the very sources of moral principle.

Prejudiced, partisan, intolerant, vain, freakish—the Adamses were all that. They were also extraordinarily able, clearsighted, earnest and elevated; their integrity and their patriotism were almost perfect. Their journals are candor and honesty throughout. An American history would lack many of its most glowing pages if we did not have John Adams's picture of the sober Quaker merchants of Philadelphia shedding tears over the breach with the mother country, of his own nomination of Washington to be Commander in Chief, of the flight of Congress in 1777 from Philadelphia, and many other striking occurrences.

It would be a still greater loss had John Quincy Adams not given us his lively sketches of Jefferson telling "large stories"; of Henry Clay sitting up all night over cards at the Ghent Conference; of W. W. Crawford threatening President Monroe with his cane and calling him "You damned infernal old scoundrel"; of John Randolph of Roanoke, "drunk with bottled porter," making a ten-hour speech "in raving balderdash of the meridian of Wapping"; of W. H. Harrison's inauguration, a "showy-shabby affair"; and of his own heroic battle for the right of petition.

Almost equally honest is another type of diary common in official life: the diary that serves as a daybook in which the income and outgo of action are scrupulously set down against the possibility of a hostile audit. That is the kind of diary that James K. Polk wrote. He had never kept a journal until he became President. He ceased keeping one the moment he left office. Obviously, he believed he needed a record to refresh his own memory, help keep his course straight, and confound critics.

A similar daybook was begun by Hamilton Fish when he entered the State Department in 1869, and abruptly discontinued when he left office in 1877, our best single source of inside knowledge for the Grant administration—it was begun for the same precautionary reasons that actuated Polk. Secretary Fish wished to be certain that when the self-righteous, fanatical Charles Sumner, who mauled facts to suit his own purposes, challenged an act or statement, an answer was at hand. He wished to be sure that when Russian minister Cataczy told milder lies than usual, they could be refuted.

Even the diary frankly kept for publication, however, if used with due caution, may be priceless. Both the great social and political diary of a Mayor of New York, Philip Hone (1828–1851), and the still greater diary of George Templeton Strong (1835–75), soon to be published, were written for posterity. So was the gossipy diary of Charles Greville, with its mass of detail on Georgian and Victorian politics; and so of course was the "Cabinet Interior" of Gideon Welles—though he nominally left the issuance to his son.

The question whether some diaries do not reproduce conversations intended to be confidential—do not "violate the sanctuary," as Lord Morley said—opens a wide field for discussion. They certainly do so no more frequently than books of memoirs and letters.

After all, both the law and public sentiment offer certain safeguards. In any event, historical-minded people will sympathize (within limits) with Wilson's behest to Bonsal to be indiscreet, for from the right kind of indiscretion rises truth. The triumphant emergence of the diary into new life is on the whole a happy fact. It is a department of letters that humanizes the past. It interlocks the personality of the individual with the great blind processes of history as nothing else can. Better than the letter or memoir, it reproduces the atmosphere of the fleeting moment. The larger the number of diaries, the closer our links with other eras, and the warmer our sense of the continuity of human sorrows, efforts, and aspirations.

19

The Role of the Manuscript Collector

When the Manuscript Society held its annual meeting in Los
Angeles during the autumn of 1965, an inevitable feature of
the program was a visit to the Henry E. Huntington Library
and a talk by Allan Nevins, the brightest star on its
permanent research staff. Nevins chose to speak on the role of
the manuscript collector as not only a preserver but also an
engenderer of historical documents; the collector, he insisted,
should not only save and interpret the records of the past; he
should stimulate the production of diaries, letters, and
memoranda for the use of future scholars. For the manuscript, he made clear, was uniquely important in interpreting
the past, clothed as it was in an intimacy lacking in published
records. His address is reproduced here from the manuscript
that he left behind at his death, with only a few pages on
diary writing that he had borrowed from another talk
omitted. It was also summarized, and praised, by Linda
Turner in the Winter 1965 issue of *Manuscripts*.

Thomas F. Madigan published his book *Word Shadows of
the Great: The Lure of Autograph Collecting* in 1930. The book

254

begins with some quite needless apologies for autograph collecting, when it would have sufficed to quote the statement of Goethe that he took pride in possessing a considerable collection of autographs, and often paused to examine or reflect upon them; or a couple of sentences of Edgar Allan Poe: "Next to the person of a distinguished man of letters," wrote Poe, "we desire to see his portrait; next to his portrait, his autograph. In the latter especially there is something which seems to bring him before us in his true idiosyncrasy—in his character of scribe." Madigan's volume seldom rises above the anecdotal level, but the anecdotes sometimes contain useful historical or literary material.

In his first pages, Madigan pauses to extol Henry E. Huntington and his library. "I had the pleasure of a most interesting interview with the amiable bibliophile and man of affairs . . . shortly before his death," he writes. "I visited him at his beautiful home set among the orange groves at San Gabriel, California [nomenclature has changed]. On my way to his room on the second floor I paid my respects to Gainsborough's Blue Boy and other great English masterpieces which hung on his walls. The great financier sat comfortably in a huge easy-chair from which he might look out over his sloping lawns and sweet-smelling orange groves." Those were pre-smog days. "Illness had not impaired his geniality nor his interest in collecting."

Huntington was a collector with a sharp differentiation from other collectors. He entered the field early; he entered with a very large fortune; and he entered with a plan. He therefore formed much more than a collection in the ordinary sense. The institution that bears his name is rather an aggregation of several hundred collections merged into one. The Stowe Collection, to name but one of its treasures, contains about 800,000 items; matching it, in value if not in scope, are the Ellesmere Collection, the Huntington Collection, the Pizarro-La Gasca Collection, the Montague Collection, and numerous others. And still the library grows; the S. L. M. Barlow Collection, obtained not long ago, is just attracting the scholars needed to explore its values.

Collectors of autograph material deal with manuscripts of books and lesser literary works; with letters by and about famous people; with journals, diaries, and autobiographies or reminiscent memoirs. They deal with them as rescuers and preservers of manuscripts, as sorters and arrangers expert in the combining of materials, as students and interpreters, and as discoverers of previously unperceived values. The novelist Bulwer-Lytton once made an acute remark about the art of interpretation. The best criticism, he wrote, is enlightened enthusiasm; and most manuscript collectors can lay just claim to that quality—enlightened enthusiasm. They receive a great deal of praise for their labors, and lovers of history and of literature will agree that they deserve all of it. They sometimes reap more material rewards also, as prices reported from the auction rooms remind us.

If collectors receive some criticism as well, that is right and proper. One valid criticism is implicit in a recent report of the chief of the manuscript division of the Library of Congress. "For many years," he writes, "the bulk of the manuscript material acquired by the library has been classifiable as personal or family papers. That is, it consists of bodies of documents created or received by individuals and preserved by them or their families to serve as a record of thoughts, activities, and transactions that concern them. Such groups of papers are analagous to the archives or official records of governments, organizations, or institutions, and in both cases the maintenance of their integrity as groups is essential if they are to tell their full story." This is commonplace. But, the Library of Congress report goes on, the gatherings of most manuscript collectors are too miscellaneous in character to have proper value. Personal and family papers "differ markedly from 'collections of manuscripts' assembled by a collector, whether an individual or an institution, for such collections, usually consisting of documents originally preserved as items in many different groups, ordinarily have significance as groups only for the light they throw on the interests and activities of their collectors."

This criticism loses its point as the activities of collectors become more specialized, as they concentrate their efforts upon one man or subject. Under the pressure of high prices such specialized collecting takes the place of miscellaneous purchasing. A man by sheer necessity becomes a Shelley collector, or a Franklin collector, or a Lincoln collector, or a Roosevelt collector; and what he gathers is correspondingly more valuable.

A more pertinent criticism of the collector, to my mind, is that he neglects one large field of possible usefulness. He rescues manuscripts from oblivion, he assorts them, he studies and interprets them; but he does singularly little to help produce them. That, he says, lies beyond his function. He takes manuscripts where they occur, as gifts of previous generations, of luck, or of the gods. He prizes immensely a well-written letter, and would pay a fortune for even a badly written note by Poe; he values beyond ordinary price a diary with some of the qualities of Pepys or Evelyn; he would give all that he has to possess the autobiography of Lord Byron that impious hands—those of the widow and John Cam Hobhouse—perhaps consigned to the flames. The letters, the diary, the memoir came down from past generations. What of future generations?—what creative provision can be made for them?

Well-written letters—letters as spontaneous as Mrs. Carlyle's, as full of color, vitality, and acute observation as those of Lady Mary Wortley Montague (women rank among the best letter writers), as richly vigorous as Byron's—are not written to order. Letters (I mean letters of literary value) are nothing without a strong personal element, and the personality must be that of a Charles Lamb or Edward Fitzgerald, a Mark Twain or William James (William James the pungent, not Henry James the bore) or Brand Whitlock. No means exists of creating potential letter writers of keen insight and powerful personality; they must create themselves. But can they not be inspired and helped? Were I a manuscript collector interested in providing good manuscript letters for collectors of coming generations I would buy volumes of good letters; mail them to friends; scatter them about in public libraries; and talk about their delights.

The good letter writer has to have an ear cocked for the apt and illuminating remark, an eye open to the arresting scene, a gift for storytelling. I open Brand Whitlock to three of his pages and on them I find three instances of the flash that the good letter writer must train himself to transmit. On one he reports lunching with Edith Wharton, and telling her with happy gusto of the novel he has begun to write; he sketches the plot with enthusiasm; and then Edith Wharton with her hard realism swiftly takes him down. She says, "Do you know where you are getting off?" That searching remark sets Brand Whitlock to thinking so hard that he gives up his novel. He abandons it. On another page Clarence Darrow, an old crony, comments on current literature in the year 1932. Everybody, he remarks, is writing his autobiography nowadays; everybody is standing on a street corner beating a bass drum, and saying: "For God's sake, look at *me* a moment!" And on a third page Brand Whitlock reports still another encounter as only a very perceptive man can tell a good story. He recalls that he had seen an unusual man at the 1912 Baltimore convention. He got up early one hot day to see Bryan in a hotel dining room:

> On a large round table there was the debris of the most enormous breakfast I ever saw—a perfectly gargantuan breakfast . . . the scooped out shells of grapefruit, the empty shells of innumerable eggs, morasses of porridge hardening in their bowls, meat bones, and cups still swimming in cold coffee. I sat down as far away from this display as I could, and found that I had seated myself beside a man who was smoking a cigar and reading a newspaper. I thought his face was familiar; he had long hair and a drooping mustache, and presently he spoke to me and said he was Murray of Oklahoma.
> "You were president of the constitutional convention out there, weren't you," I said.
> "Yes," he replied. "I am Alfalfa Bill."
> We fell to talking and he asked me whom I was for for

President; I told him Wilson. He said that he was for Wilson too, and I, perhaps a little surprised, said:

"May I ask why you are for Wilson?"

He turned and looked at me very seriously and said:

"I will tell you. I am an ignorant man. I never had an education, or a chance to get one, but I want to see a scholar in the White House."

It was rather touching that, don't you think?

The man who can put these bits into three pages is a good letter writer; and the girl or boy who sees copies of the poet Cowper's letters, and Shelley's (which have the best criticism of Keats for the time in them), and Theodore Roosevelt's, and Mayor Gaynor's lying about, will have a good chance of becoming another good letter writer.

Diaries are a different matter—manuscript diaries. They are numerous as the sands on the seashore. William Matthews's volume listing American diaries, published by the University of California Press, fills nearly four hundred pages with a partial record of the diaries or journals that have been published in whole or in part, omitting whole categories as well as all unpublished diaries. It would be safe to estimate that ten thousand diaries have been kept in the United States, good and bad, short and long. Really good diaries, from either a literary or historical point of view, are, however, as rare as really distinguished letters, for they demand the same rare gifts. Countless diaries are begun and presently discontinued. They are dropped for two good reasons: first, because maintenance of a diary requires unusual pertinacity and industry—it is an acid test of perseverance; and second, because nobody can keep a diary long without realizing that he is presenting in it his whole mind and character, and many therefore abandon what they realize is indecent self-exposure. However, the historian believes that we can never have too many diaries, even if imperfect; even the worst ones may contain valuable historical grains. The writing of a manuscript diary is therefore much to be encouraged. Incidentally, if kept with care it may become a possession with genuine cash value.

The encouragement of diary keeping is somewhat easier than the encouragement of letter writing on a high level; it is a little more readily brought within the province of the manuscript collector; and it will in the end pay a larger return. The instinct for attempting and maintaining a record of this kind is deeply implanted in the human breast, as Professor Matthews's volume tells us. This is a subject on which I speak with special feeling, for I have had much to do with diaries; I have edited versions of the diaries of Philip Hone, John Quincy Adams, James K. Polk, Hamilton Fish, Brand Whitlock (he called it a journal and it matches his letters in quality), and George Templeton Strong. In their different ways they are all fascinating.

Just how can the keeping of diaries be encouraged? A little more directly than the composition of distinguished letters. Again and again we have met men who have had remarkable experiences; our society is full of them. We ought to say to them, when we hear of this or that arresting occurrence, "You ought to keep the same kind of record that old Samuel Sewell kept." Particularly should the expert in manuscripts say this. Again and again, too, we meet men who hold responsible public or semipublic office. We ought to say to them, "You know that when Hamilton Fish became secretary of state he found it of the greatest importance to keep a daybook of all that went on in his office; a clear matter of fact record of what President Grant directed him to do, what the British minister Thornton amicably worked out with him, what the arrogant Senator Sumner tried to force him into, and what the scoundrelly Spanish minister attempted in Cuban affairs." Particularly should the manuscript collector, the friend of scholarship, say this. . . .

Any perceptive, diligent, and truly literate man or woman can lend his or her hand to the production of manuscript material that posterity will pronounce valuable. Usually it will fall into one of three categories: a body of letters, a diary, or an array of historical and geographical memoranda. The letters need not deal with transactions of striking historical importance; it will suffice if they are observant, witty, or vividly descriptive. The diary need not be that of a figure high in the state, like Samuel Pepys of the admiralty, or John Adams, or Gideon Welles of Lincoln's cabinet; an Ezra Stiles, a plain Congregational clergyman (though he rose to be president of Yale), or a Philip Hone, or a George Templeton Strong, can write a more valuable diary. The collector of historical or geographical memoranda who pens his own commentary on what he collects, like Benson J. Lossing, the author of the once well-known field books on the Revolution and War of 1812, or Henry Howe, the compiler of historical handbooks of New York and Ohio, has a peculiarly difficult task, for he must travel widely, conduct careful interviews, and observe minutely; but he will obtain a large reward in entertainment as well as instruction, and his manuscript work and his collections will alike be invaluable to the historian.

Very few men will undertake such production unless they are stimulated to approach life with resolute curiosity, with unflagging alertness, and with literary assiduity. The collector of manuscripts is the beneficiary of men who in the past have felt such a stimulus; he usually thinks his duty done if he brings zeal and scholarly expertness to reaping the harvest thus sown. He is a devoted servant of the past; is not that enough? But he should be more than a collector of past products; he should be a creator of new productions.

How remarkable it is that a man, whether an autograph dealer, or a librarian, or a historian, who spends years fingering old manuscripts of the Tudor age, or the Stuart era, or Jacksonian times, or the days of Calvin Coolidge, never says to himself: "Why can't I do something to get such materials made for history in this year 1965; in the administration of Lyndon B. Johnson; in the days when nuclear energy is just beginning to make cheaper and more abundant power possible; when we are beginning the conquest of space; when the economic concepts of Keynes are revolutionizing our outlook more than Adam Smith revolutionized the outlook of the old mercantilistic society."

261

How can we do it? By whetting men's curiosity, by opening men's eyes—that goes without saying. By making the fact plain to all that the record made by the man on the periphery is as important as that of the man at the heart of great events—the periphery is a better station for seeing it all; and the fact that the present is just as dramatic, as picturesquely colorful, as richly fascinating as any past age—probably more so. These are facts that should be vividly present to the consciousness of everyone concerned with manuscripts, more vividly present to him than to anyone else.

20

History and the Newspaper

Originally prepared as a lecture, and probably delivered to a Columbia University class during Allan Nevins's first years on the campus (internal evidence suggests that it was prepared in 1929), this hitherto unpublished paper reflects neither the author's literary skill nor his profundity as a scholar. It had obviously been hurriedly prepared, with an abundance of typographical errors, abbreviations, and other evidence that its ultimate destination was not the printed page. In it Nevins discusses at some length the importance of a medium he knew well—the newspaper—as a source for historians, using his own experience to illustrate its virtues and defects and giving sage advice on the features entitled to the greatest trust. Hence it deserves a place among his essays on the tools of history as still another illustration of his concern with the accurate re-creation of the past.

In the last three or four years no historical or biographical works have been more popular than four which have not been produced by professional or academic historians: Albert J. Beveridge's *Lincoln*; Claude Bowers's *Jefferson and Hamilton* and his

Party Battles of the Jacksonian Period; and Mark Sullivan's *Our Times*. Two of these writers are prominent newspapermen. All of these works, or groups of works, are distinguished by their exceptional use of newspaper sources. Beveridge's second volume in particular is based far more upon the contemporaneous press than upon books or manuscripts. There are numerous pages in it where the footnote citations contain references to ten or twelve different newspapers. Claude Bowers's volume on *Jefferson and Hamilton* deals with a much earlier period, when our press was in its infancy. Yet we find it full of references to the *Columbia Sentinel*, the *New York Evening Post*, the *Gazette of the United States*, the *American Minerva*, the *Philadelphia Aurora*, and many more. As for Mr. Sullivan's opus, his chapters on "Dewey," on "Mr. Roosevelt Gets a Start," on "America in 1900," and on "The Emergence of the Automobile" are obviously composed of materials drawn more largely from newspapers than from all other sources combined.

Here we have three highly popular and successful works: one dealing with the period from 1789 to 1801; one centering its intensest interest upon the decade 1848–58; and one concerned with the years 1898–1904—all relying largely if not mainly upon the newspaper for their facts and for the vitality of the general treatment. Other illustrations could easily be named.

This is a comparatively new although already well-established tendency in the writing of history. Fifty years ago such books would have filled the professional historians with astonishment and no little dismay. Twenty years ago, when James Ford Rhodes read a paper on newspapers as historical sources to the American Historical Association, he said that "the impulse of an American writer in justifying the use of newspapers as historical materials is to adopt an apologetic tone." Nobody apologizes now. Mr. Beveridge and Mr. Bowers, like a half-dozen other of our best historical writers, would never think of apologizing.

The use of newspapers as historical sources has grown steadily greater and bolder during the last generation. The first writer of

American history to use the newspaper on any extensive scale was Herman Von Holst, in his *Constitutional and Political History of the United States*, of which the first volume appeared in 1877. Von Holst was a foreigner. He was striving hard to obtain an understanding of the inner essence of American institutions and life, and he turned naturally to the press for assistance. He was the first to use *Niles' Register*, the *New York Tribune* and *New York Herald*, and the *Washington Globe* with considerable thoroughness; and he often used smaller papers—for example, the *New Orleans Picayune* during the Mexican War.

He immediately had a successor who went much further than he did. In 1883 John Bach McMaster brought out the first volume of his *History of the People of the United States*. The readers of this volume found it bristling with materials drawn from our early press. The first reference to an authority or source given in its pages was to a magazine, *De Bow's Review*, upon slavery in 1784; the first long footnote, found on page 12, is a description of the Boston bridge over the Charles River drawn from the *Boston Gazette* and the *New York Gazette* of 1786. Succeeding volumes of McMaster demonstrated the tremendous use which might be made of this kind of material. Newspapers were drawn upon to furnish historical details; to illustrate, by their advertisements no less than their news, the life of the common people; to demonstrate the currents of public opinion; to make vivid the whole period. Even yet many readers regarded the use of the newspaper by such writers as McMaster as suspect. They distrusted newspaper evidence; they felt that there was something loose and unreliable about it. It was not until 1895, when James Ford Rhodes brought out the first volume of his *History of the United States from the Compromise of 1850*, that this attitude was definitely dispelled.

Just what did James Ford Rhodes do with newspaper material, and for the popular conception of the newspaper as an historical source? His history differed fundamentally from McMaster's. Whereas McMaster centered his attention upon the life of the

265

people, Rhodes was interested chiefly in politics. McMaster was primarily descriptive; Rhodes was primarily analytical. Rhodes's history seemed to be more dignified, and to be more scientific. Yet it made quite as full use of newspapers as McMaster's successive volumes had done.

Rhodes stated frankly that when he began his studies of the crowded and exciting years from 1850 to 1860, the tense decade before the Civil War, he was struck with the scarcity of materials for an animated narrative. The main facts—the bare bones—were in the state papers, the law books, the Congressional debates, the records of party conventions and platforms. But where was the flesh and blood to clothe these bones and give them life? There was little private correspondence available. There seemed to be few biographies and reminiscences. But Rhodes had himself lived through those exciting years. He had a vivid boyhood recollection of the great part which newspapers had played in politics; of the eagerness with which men had read Greeley's *Tribune* and Bryant's *Evening Post*, and later George W. Curtis's noble editorials in *Harper's Weekly*. He at once set to work upon the newspaper files; and he at once found that they were invaluable. No one could understand the history of the period without them. He found much there which could not possibly have been gotten elsewhere. For example, when he was hunting for data upon the Whig Convention of 1852 and was at a loss to understand why Webster had been defeated while Winfield Scott was victorious, he came across an inside account of the convention from the *Boston Courier*. It proved to have been written by a Massachusetts delegate to the convention. It explained everything in that dramatic story. It explained why, when the great Daniel Webster ardently desired the nomination, when Rufus Choate advocated it with thrilling eloquence, when Webster was easily the greatest available figure in the Whig Party, the antislavery men of Massachusetts and Maine stood coldly in opposition to the orator.

Again, General Winfield Scott, after his nomination, stumped the western states for the presidency, making the first campaign tour in our history. It was a factor in his overwhelming defeat. Yet Rhodes found that no adequate account of it was available outside the newspapers. The story of it was well worth preserving. He found, again, that the newspapers corrected many errors of dates and even names in biographies and earlier histories of the period. He found, more importantly, that they corrected many logical assumptions, especially those put forward by public men of the period. By a logical assumption he meant the assumption that a given fact or event would be followed by a certain cause. Thus a contemporary of Rhodes declared that the Pottawatomie massacre of 1856 had been one of the reasons for the defeat of Frémont that year. It will be remembered that while Frémont was running for the presidency on the Republican ticket, the border war of proslavery and antislavery men was raging in Kansas. On May 24, 1856, five proslavery men were foully murdered by John Brown and his followers on Pottawatomie Creek. The authority of whom Rhodes speaks declared that this bloody massacre of proslavery men was excitedly used as ammunition by the Democratic orators and Southern leaders, and that it turned the scale of the campaign against Frémont. But an examination of the Democratic and Southern press showed that no use was made of the Pottawatomie massacre in the campaign, that few references to it appeared anywhere, and that it had no effect upon the voters. Study of the newspapers in this case dispelled an unfounded assumption as to cause and effect.

Many writers who have made extensive use of newspaper files in preparing an historical work could supply still another illustration of services which the newspaper performs. It will often overturn, by indisputable contemporaneous evidence, some tradition or accepted story which has become embedded in history. History, says Fontenelle, is a *mensonge convenue*—a lie agreed upon; but old and tattered newspaper files will sometimes expose the long-accepted fiction. A few years ago it fell to me to write a history of the *New York Evening Post*, which is one of the oldest and most renowned of American journals, and whose line of editors, beginning with the founder Alexander Hamilton and running down through Bryant, John Bigelow, Parke Goodwin, Carl Schurz, E. L. Godkin, and Rollo Ogden, is certainly the most distinguished. In this work I found some striking exemplifications of the point I have just mentioned. It had long been agreed, for example, that the founder of Central Park in New York was Charles Downing Law, the noted landscape architect. He was the editor of a monthly magazine called *The Horticulturist*, he spoke often in favor of public parks, and it was always believed the plan originated in an editorial of *The Horticulturist* in 1849. But I found that the real originator of the plan was William Cullen Bryant. He had traveled much abroad and been struck by the parks of Paris, London, and Madrid. As early as 1836 he proposed reserving land for a central park; on July 3, 1844, he commenced an editorial campaign in the *Evening Post* for its establishment. It was because of this campaign that in 1850, when Fernando Wood ran for mayor against Ambrose C. Kingsland, both came out in advocacy of a Central Park—and Mayor Kingsland carried the plan into effect in 1851. Again, it had always been supposed that the first complete and well-edited edition of the *Federalist Papers* by Hamilton, Jay, and Madison, that was issued in 1802, had been edited by William Coleman. Henry Cabot Lodge in his edition of Hamilton's collected works says that Coleman brought out the volume. But I found in the *Evening Post* files an editorial statement by Coleman himself that he was not the editor, and that the *Federalist Papers* were first brought together in fairly complete form by a New York attorney named John Wells.

Behind all these salient aspects of newspaper usefulness, of course, lies the broader fact that the press forms an unrivaled source for the study of opinion, and for gaining some insight into the spirit of the age. Motley says that to read the autograph letters of William of Orange and Philip II gave a "realizing sense" of the time. One can best gain the "realizing sense" of the Civil War by reading the bound volumes of *Harper's Weekly* and the *New*

York Tribune; by thus feeling, day by day and week by week, the impact of the news from the front, the alternations of hope and despondency; by absorbing from the minor items, the pictures and the very advertisements an understanding of what life was like in those tense days.

So much for the virtues and the utility of the newspaper for the student of history. But what of its limitations and defects? The newspaper can easily be misused by the historian. It is a sense of this fact which makes many writers apologetic about using it at all, and many readers suspicious of its use. Great numbers of people have a low opinion of the credibility of newspapers. In fact, society might be divided into people who say, "You can't believe anything you see in the papers," and those who say, "I know that's a fact: I read it in the papers." What are some of the rules to be observed in the use of the newspaper? This is a subject on which, it seems to me, an enormous amount of nonsense has been written.

The nonsense springs in the main from disregard for a fairly obvious fact. The fact is that when we speak of the newspaper as material for history, we cannot speak of it as a unit, a single entity. It is not a unit but a combination of highly diverse units or elements. A hundred and fifty years ago, when the newspaper was all written by one man, it was truly a unit. Ninety years ago, when James Gordon Bennett got out the first issue of the *New York Herald* in his cellar in Wall Street, working at first entirely alone and then with only two or three helpers, it was still a unit. One part of it resembled another and was as accurate or inaccurate as another. But nowadays the great metropolitan newspaper is a highly departmentalized institution. It consists of many elements, not of one. Failure to note this primary fact leads some writers to try to discuss "the authenticity of the newspaper" as a whole, which is fatuous; what can be discussed is the authenticity of its various parts.

Anyone who examines carefully an issue of the New York *Times* or *World*, or of the London *Times* or *Manchester*

269

Guardian, will see at once that it consists of twenty main departments and fifty subdepartments. It carries political news, which is supplied for the most part by specialists, who in dealing with subjects of major importance sign their names. It carries financial news, written also by experts, who more frequently remain anonymous. It carries building and real estate news, again in the best offices the work of experienced men. It has college and school news; the old *Evening Post* used to have a special college editor. To an increasing extent it has scientific news, which the press once avoided because it could not find experts, or if experts were available they could not write for the general public. One bureau, Science Service under Dr. Slosson, now supplies expert scientific reporting in genuinely readable form. There is society news. There is labor news; at least one labor specialist, Mr. Leary of the *World*, is regarded by labor circles as an invaluable interpreter and even guide. There is sporting news, and such experts as Mr. Grantland Rice are among the most highly paid men in journalism. There is foreign news, again the work of experienced men, often specially trained. There is news of exploration, and the *Times* has attached a special correspondent, Mr. Russell Owen, to the Byrd Antarctic Expedition. There is an array of critical departments: drama, with names as well known as St. John Ervines; literature, with names sometimes as distinguished as those of Stuart P. Sherman and Henry S. Canby; and music. There are the editorials, the letters, and by no means last, the advertisements and paid notices. There you have a modern newspaper. The newspaper is almost as complex as modern society itself, and in their steadily increasing complexity the two keep fairly equal pace.

Obviously, it is futile to talk of accuracy or inaccuracy, authority or lack of authority, with reference to the newspaper as a whole. The newspaper cannot be dismissed with either a blanket endorsement or a blanket condemnation. It cannot be used as if all its parts had equal value or authenticity. The first duty of the historical student of the newspaper is to discriminate. He must weigh every separate department, every article, every writer, for what the department or article or writer seems to be worth. Clearly, a great part of what is printed in every newspaper is from official sources, and hence may be relied upon to be perfectly accurate. The weather report is accurate; so are court notices, election notices, building permits, lists of marriage licenses, bankruptcy lists. Though unofficial, other classes of news are almost totally free from error. The most complete precautions are taken to keep the stock market quotations minutely accurate, both by stock exchange authorities and by the newspaper staffs. An error in stock quotations may have the most disastrous consequences, and mistakes are hence excluded by every means within human power. So with shipping news, news of deaths, and a considerable body of similar matter—sports records, registers of Congressional or legislative votes, and so on.

Thus one great division of material in newspapers can be treated as completely authentic. There is another large division which may in general be treated as trustworthy and authoritative. This is the news which is prepared by experts under conditions exempt from hurry and favorable to the gathering of all the significant facts. The weekly review of a real estate expert is a case in point. The sporting news of the best newspapers, prepared by experts under conditions which make for accuracy, is singularly uniform, and this uniformity is the best evidence that it is truthful and well proportioned. Society news, industrial news, and similar intelligence, especially when it appears in the form of weekly surveys written by known specialists, is worthy of the utmost reliance.

But in dealing with news which contains a large subjective element, and which is prepared under conditions of hurry and strain, the critical faculty must be kept constantly alert. Every conscientious correspondent at an inauguration, or a battle, or a political rally, or in an interview, tries to report the facts. But not one of them can help reporting, in addition to the facts, the impression that he has personally received of them. The most

271

honest and careful observer ordinarily sees a little of what he wishes to see. It is through failure to make critical allowance for this fact that the historical student of newspapers is most likely to be led astray. Beveridge in his life of Lincoln remarks upon the striking difference between the Democratic reports and the Republican reports of the Lincoln-Douglas debates. At Ottawa, Illinois, for example, these two great leaders held their first joint debate on August 21, 1858. Lincoln came on a special train of fourteen cars crowded with shouting Republicans. It arrived at Ottawa at noon and, according to the Republican papers, when Lincoln alighted a shout went up from a dense and enthusiastic crowd which made the bluffs of the Illinois River and the woods along it ring and ring again. Lincoln entered a carriage; according to the *Chicago Tribune* men with evergreens, mottoes, fair young ladies, bands of music, military companies, and a dense mass of cheering humanity followed him through the streets in a scene of tumultuous excitement. But according to the *Philadelphia Press* and other Douglas papers, Lincoln had only a chilly and lackadaisical reception. "As his procession passed," stated the *Philadelphia Press*, "scarcely a cheer went up. They marched along silently and sorrowfully, as if it were a funeral cortege following him to the grave." On the other hand, the Democratic papers declared that the reception of Douglas was perfectly tremendous; the cheers were so thundering, said the *Philadelphia Press*, that they seemed to rend the very air. But the *Chicago Tribune* said that Douglas had no reception of consequence; that the only cheers he got came from the Irish Catholics. Yet both reporters were probably fairly honest. They saw what they wished to see.

A still more striking illustration may be drawn from Rhodes's history. He described the memorable debate in 1850 on the Omnibus Bill, or the Great Compromise; a debate which, including as it did Clay, Webster, and Calhoun, was a battle of the giants. He pictures the impressive scene when Calhoun, swathed in flannels, was carried into the Senate Chamber and, already at death's door, too weak to deliver his own speech, listened while Senator Mason of Virginia read it for him. "Calhoun," says Rhodes, citing Charles A. Dana's report for the *New York Tribune*, "sat with head erect and eyes partly closed, immovable in front of the reader; and he did not betray a sense of the deep interest with which his friends and followers listened to the well-matured words of their leader and political guide." That is, Dana, writing for the antislavery *Tribune*, pictured Calhoun as too nearly gone to show any animation. But the reporter who described the scene for the proslavery *Charleston Mercury* saw a very different Calhoun. "Calhoun's step as he came in seemed almost as firm and elastic as ever," wrote this reporter. Calhoun remained seated during the reading of the speech, he continued, but he sat erect and alert, with "his eyes moving about the audience to note its effect. The most interesting spectacle was presented after the Senate adjourned. There were Clay, Calhoun, and Webster standing together for some time near the speaker's desk and conversing about his speech." That is, the *Tribune* reporter saw Calhoun crawl into the chamber and sink back in his seat with his eyes closed as one dead. The *Mercury* reporter saw him enter the chamber alert, listen to his speech with sparkling and roving eyes, and go forward afterward to stand erect with Clay and Webster discussing the subject. Yet both reporters were probably honest. They simply carried a different subjective attitude to their interpretation of what happened.

It is necessary to bring to a large part of each day's news a critical frame of mind. It need not be said that the same critical tests which the historical student applies to newspapers written years or decades since might profitably be applied to all general readers of the newspaper written yesterday. Properly used, the newspaper may be a liberal education in itself. A great newspaper of the more intellectual and serious kind, like the *Springfield Republican* under Samuel Bowles, or the *Tribune* under Greeley, or the *Evening Post* under Godkin, or the New York *Times* today, will furnish the alert, thorough, and critical reader a broad and in some respects also a deep training in every department of

273

present-day life. But it must be read alertly and critically. The critical reader will seek out what he knows to be the most expert and authoritative. He will form a careful estimate of the strength and weakness of this newspaper or that newspaper, this department and that department, this writer and that writer. He will make a conscious effort to go to those sources which are best.

21

History This Side the Horizon

When Allan Nevins was invited to address the Vermont
Historical Society in the summer of 1950, he elected to
disabuse its members of the all-too-common belief that
everything significant or glamorous had occurred in distant
places or in the remote past. Too seldom, he insisted, do we
recognize that the daily occurrences that seem commonplace
to us today will fascinate historians of the future; we can serve
those scholars of tomorrow by collecting and preserving the
records that they will use, even if those records seem
insignificant to us at this time. While Nevins voiced no
revolutionary ideas on collecting to the collecting-conscious
Vermonters, he did underline the importance of preserving
even the seemingly unimportant records of the present,
documenting his point with excellent examples. "A moving
and thoughtful address on vital issues of historical interpretation and understanding," the editor of *The Vermont Quarterly* branded it, and with justice.

Reprinted with permission from *The Vermont Quarterly, The Proceedings of the
Vermont Historical Society* 18 (October 1950): 153–62.

We have all, at some time or other, wished that *we* had been placed where we might see great epochal events pass before our eyes, and record them in the glowing prose of an excited onlooker or participant. If only *we* had been at Waterloo to see Napoleon's Old Guard falter and retreat before the British squares; if *we* had stood in the Hall of Mirrors at Versailles to witness the German acceptance of the peace treaty painted by Orpen! Henry W. Nevinson in *The Dark Backward* has vividly depicted a series of memorable scenes from history: the ten thousand battered, exhausted warriors of Xenophon reaching the shore of the dark blue Euxine; grim Diocletian at Spalato watching the martyrdom of a group of Christians; Prince Hal's forces on St. Crispin's day in fierce onset against the French knights, the incessant blows on armor sounding like hammers on a thousand anvils; Napoleon at Jena, triumphant as the cuirassiers swept by him. If only, we think, we could have seen such events! Or, better still, if we could have had the chance that John Hay and John G. Nicolay had when they were chosen secretaries to live and work with Lincoln throughout the Civil War. Instead, we seem never to see or hear anything of true historical significance, of dramatically memorable quality; we never talk with the great personages of our time, and know nothing of state secrets.

In this view of the past there lurk two fallacies. The first is our exaggeration of the advantages possessed by men at the heart of great events. It is true that a Winston Churchill does now and then appear, a leader who not only participates in great events, but sees them with the eye of an imaginative historian while they are being enacted. It is true that more frequently a man can play such a role as that of John Hay, who sat with perceptive eye in the White House during the four years of Civil War and wrote about it afterward, or Ray Stannard Baker, who went with Woodrow Wilson to Paris and in due course dealt in historical prose with the events he had witnessed. It is a fact, however, that in general the participants in great historical events or the onlookers at memorable historical scenes know much less about them than those who come afterward. They are too busy and excited to observe, or they see only one facet of a many sided transaction, or they are precluded by their special routine duties from taking note of the activities about them. It was not the men in the front line of Pickett's charge who understood most fully the battle of Gettysburg. When we think enviously of the opportunities that a British or American Cabinet officer has for knowing what is going on, that man may frequently be complaining that he knows less than a newspaper reporter.

It is literally true that some members of Lloyd George's Cabinet (not the inner War Cabinet which directed affairs but the outer general Ministry), working night and day, knew less about World War I than the freely observant man in Regent Street or Pimlico. Nor is this situation unusual. I have lately seen a manuscript letter written by the Secretary of the Treasury in Lincoln's Cabinet, Salmon P. Chase, to Senator Zachary Chandler of Michigan in the late summer of 1862, at the very time that the Emancipation Proclamation was being issued. Chase declared that he knew nothing about public affairs. Day after day he toiled at his Treasury desk over figures of revenue and outgo, over plans for raising money and checks upon expenditures. But a broad picture of the colossal conflict then raging he never obtained. He wrote:

Maryland has been rescued and Pennsylvania saved from invasion. But the rebel army has suffered far less than our own in the battles of the last two weeks, and has strong positions which it should never have been permitted to win. What now? Who can tell? I, though charged with the responsibility of providing for the enormous expenditures entailed upon the country, have no control over—no voice even—in deciding on the measures by which the necessity for them is created. In fact, I know about as little of what is being done as any outsider.

Neither credit nor responsibility for what is done or decided outside of the Treasury Department belongs to me. . . . There is . . . at the present time no Cabinet except in name. The heads of Departments come together now and then . . . nominally twice a week; but no reports are made; no regular discussions held; no ascertained conclusions reached. Sometimes weeks pass by and no full meeting is held. One can get some information about military matters if he will make due inquiry at the War Department or about Naval matters at the Naval Department: but full systematic accounts of the progress of the struggle; the purpose entertained; the means and modes of action by or against us, are neither made nor given, nor required.

In short, when Secretary Chase wished to know how the Civil War was being conducted, and what the government in general was doing, he had to send out for a copy of the New York *Herald*.

The second fallacy is the idea that we ordinary men and women have no opportunity to observe matters of first-rate historical interest. The fact is that history lies all about us if we have eyes to see it. It lies about us not merely in times of war and crisis, but in everyday humdrum times. Everyone sees immediately that if he had been an English village priest in the days of Crecy and Agincourt, even in a quiet hamlet of Surrey or Norfolk, he would have had matter to record that would greatly interest twentieth century students of history. Everyone realizes that if he or she had been a plain yeoman farmer or a housewife in Revolutionary days, living anywhere—in Virginia, in the Brandywine or Wyoming Valley, in the district between Saratoga and Bennington—and had possessed even a crude use of the pen, a record would have emerged upon which readers of our day would pounce with avidity. But a century hence, five centuries hence, *our* descendants will think of us as living in the most romantic, the most colorful, the most exciting of times; and they will wonder that we did not leave multitudinous records of the fascinating changes, the tremendous innovations, which swept and swirled all about us.

"Just think!" they will say. "Those hardy Vermonters dwelt in the era of the last decades of the railways, with their great express-trains thundering along roads of steel, and first decades of the airplane, then so primitive that people marvelled at air-lines that crossed the Atlantic in twelve hours—not twelve minutes, but hours—and at craft that carried a hundred—not a thousand, a pitiful hundred passengers. They dwelt in a time when radio had just lost its novelty, and when in many a humble village people could yet be found who had never seen a television screen. Synthetic fabrics were yet so new that millions still used the quaint cotton and woolen garments of their forbears; and synthetic foods had not yet transformed the old-style grocery stores with their thousand curious and odorous products based on the land. Countless men vividly remembered the uncomprehending awe with which, as a hundred thousand people lay dead in faraway Hiroshima, they heard the epochal announcement of the birth of atomic energy—the announcement that heralded a new era far more distinctly than the fall of Rome or the discovery of a New World by Columbus."

Our extraordinary advantages as observers of living history in this tempestuous year 1950, in the very center of the most terrible and wonderful century mankind has up till this time known, would be perfectly clear to us if we could stand for a moment at the vantage point of (say) the year 2100 A.D. It would be clear because time would give us a perspective which now only imagination can supply—and few of us have very much imagination. Few have even the elementary type of imagination which would enable us to comprehend that the most vital elements of history are not the hey-rub-a-dub events taking place in the Senate in Washington, or at No. 10 Downing Street, or in the offices of the Kremlin; they are instead the humble day-by-day events which register the impact of sweeping economic and social changes upon the masses—the events which exhibit our growing utilization of the air for communication or transportation, of synthetic chemistry for clothing and food, and of the atom for energy. Emerson once congratulated Thomas Carlyle on his imagination as a historian. "I think," he wrote, "you see as pictures every street, church, parliament house, barracks, baker's shop, mutton-stall, forge, wharf, and ship and whatever stands, creeps, rolls, or swims

279

thereabout, and make it all your own." This is a good kind of imagination; but better still is the imagination which sees all these commonplace scenes changing, evolving, taking on new shapes and glowing with fresh life.

Macaulay penned a famous passage upon the nature of history which I have sometimes felt could aptly be turned into modern American phraseology. He was pointing out the inadequacy of the stiff brocaded history which Hume, Gibbon, and Robertson had devoted to wars, monarchs, and state events. This left out the homely life of the plain people, which only the historical novelists had theretofore touched. "A truly great historian," wrote Macaulay, "would reclaim those materials the novelist has appropriated. We should not then have to look for the wars and the votes of the Puritans in Clarendon, and for their phraseology in *Old Mortality*, for one half of King James in Hume and the other half in *The Fortunes of Nigel*. . . . Society would be shown from the highest to the lowest, from the royal cloth of state to the den of the outlaw, from the throne of the legate to the chimney corner where the begging friar regaled himself. Palmers, minstrels, crusaders, the stately monastery with the good cheer of its refectory, and the tournament with its heralds and ladies, and trumpets and the cloth of gold, would give truth and life to the representation."

Convert this passage into terms appropriate to our own time and place, and we can see what an opportunity the townsman of Rutland, the officeholder of Montpelier, and the rude farmer of Windham possesses to record materials for history, or to write history itself. "A truly great historian," we would say, "must reclaim those materials which Dorothy Canfield and Robert Frost have appropriated. We should not then have to look for wars in Parkman and Douglas Freeman, and for the struggles of Republican and Democrat in James Ford Rhodes, while we searched for the customs of the hill farmer in Walter Hard, the speech of the north-country Yankee in Edith Wharton's *Ethan Frome* and *Summer,* and the tricks of the Concord or Montpelier politicians in Churchill's *Coniston.* Society would be shown from the highest

280

to the lowest; from the marble mansions of Manchester and Woodstock to the den of the prohibition hijacker, from the quiet study of the university president to the blaring din of the corner drugstore as teen-agers feed the jukebox, from the college youth on the ski-tow to the lumberjack, from the proud Proctors to the despised summer resident. Palmers, minstrels, crusaders, Fuller brush men, the ornate resort hotel with the good cheer in its cocktail lounge, the State Fair with its heralds, ladies, two-headed pigs, the swing-bands and the nylons, would give truth and life to the representation." For in these terms we define the history that coming generations will cherish.

Too scornful of what is commonplace today, we forget that in half a century it will begin to seem romantic—"romance draws in with the six-fifteen"—and that in a century much of it will obviously possess transcendent social significance. And we are often misled by a plain, homely, even vulgar exterior into overlooking rich lodes of ore that lurk just under the surface. At Columbia University we have lately made a prolonged, carefully planned, and adequately financed effort to expose and quarry some of the veins of historical material that branch all about us. Our Oral History Project, as it is termed, has undertaken to interview in systematic fashion, according to a well-studied pattern, scores upon scores of men and women whose lives seem of significance to the community. They are asked, before it is too late, to pour out their reminiscences into the faithful ear of a wire recorder; these memoirs are then transcribed; the persons interviewed carefully edit, and if they like, expand their story; and the result, duly signed, is placed in the University Archives under whatever restrictions the donor wishes to impose. Already, within the space of a year and a half, we have obtained the stories of men who have taken their memories into death's dateless night. We rescued from oblivion Burton J. Hendrick's account of how he, Ida Tarbell, Lincoln Steffens, and others made *McClure's Magazine* great in muckraking days. We preserved the late Dr. Joseph Collins's narrative of how he treated Henry James and other distinguished men for mental ailments, and how he founded the Neurological Institute. Some 110 life stories, aggregating more than eleven thousand typed manuscript pages, have now been taken down from the lips of more or less distinguished people. It is obvious that the memoirs of Norman Thomas, for example, or Judge Learned Hand, or Walter Lippmann must have enduring historical value. But it is extraordinary how frequently a person of outwardly ordinary antecedents and appearance, who might seem to have lived an uneventful life, has a record of striking originality and value to relate.

Suppose yourself travelling from Chicago to New York with the author of that shrewdly perceptive but somewhat supercilious volume called *The Man Who Knew Coolidge*. In the smoking car the attention of Mr. Sinclair Lewis and yourself is drawn to a gentleman who might very well have known Coolidge. He looks like the type. He is clearly a prosperous businessman. He is reading not Homer or Shakespeare, but *The Nation's Business*. He is plump, bald, bespectacled; Mr. Lewis would call him pudgy. He looks a bit like Mark Hanna's pictures. His conversation betrays the fact that he is an advertising man; worse still, he has for many years been a Chicago advertising man. As he speaks of his acquaintance with Herbert Hoover, Sinclair Lewis draws back in repulsion.

But Mr. Lewis would be missing one of the many exciting men in our business-minded nation; for the materialistic, obese, ordinary-looking fellow-traveller has played a leading role in several important events and developments. His name, A. D. Lasker, might not mean much to us. His ordinary conversation, while showing wisdom and breadth, might not seem highly impressive. It is only when the lens of Oral History is turned upon him that the significance of his busy life becomes plain. For Mr. Lasker, as head of one of the two or three greatest advertising firms in America (Lord & Thomas), did more than any other man to transform the nature of American advertising. Its guiding principle until he came upon the scene had been "Reiterate the name! Keep the name of the product before the people!" His labors gave it a new guiding principle: "Explain just what your product will do! Educate people in its specific merits!" For senseless iteration ("Mellen's Food: Babies Cry for It") he substituted education ("Ivory Soap: It Floats"). To name but one of Mr. Lasker's feats, he was the man who, more than all others combined, made it permissible and popular for women to smoke cigarettes. And further use of the lens of Oral History showed that Mr. Lasker had other significant pieces of history to reveal. As head of the Shipping Board just after World War I, he was on intimate terms with Warren G. Harding and was able to study shrewdly that president's character. He had encouraged Walter Teagle of Standard Oil to carry to Harding advance information of the dishonesty of Albert B. Fall in the Teapot Dome lease. As an associate of Walter Wrigley in the ownership of the Chicago White Sox, he had been in the midst of the famous Black Sox scandal, and had himself drafted the plan which made Kenesaw Mountain Landis the autocrat of baseball.

Not every community has in its midst an Albert D. Lasker; or a Jackson Reynolds, able to tell at length the history of the founding of the Bank for International Settlements; or a Reuben Lazarus, able to expose (for posterity, not for the present day) the inner workings of Tammany Hall, and to relate how he served as defense counsel for Jimmy Walker at the dramatic hearings before Governor Franklin D. Roosevelt which ended in Mayor Walker's resignation. But every community does possess men and women who, though they often do not realize it themselves, have stories to tell which posterity will find significant and engrossing.

One token of our failure to recognize that history lies this side the horizon, and indeed all about us, is found in the excessive preoccupation of Eastern historical societies with the Revolutionary epoch, and of Western historical organizations with the pioneer era. The two greatest and richest historical associations in America, the Massachusetts Historical Society and New York Historical Society, were established one just before and the other just after the year 1800. Their chief founders, Jeremy Belknap and John Pintard, had lived through the Revolutionary period. It was natural that these societies should long devote themselves to the heroic age of the struggle for independence and for a durable Constitution—to the years 1765–1800. In due time the concentration of historical attention upon the late Colonial and Revolutionary epoch was somewhat mitigated by the occurrence of another great heroic era, that of the Civil War, which excited men's imagination and aroused their commemorative instincts. But too much of our organized historical activity still appertains to the infancy and adolescence of the republic. It is too seldom recognized that we have enacted a fuller, prouder, and more complex history in the fifty years from the installation of Theodore Roosevelt to V-E Day than in any other period of American past; that we have made in this fifty years our richest record of martial, political, social, and intellectual achievement; and that our descendants will think us fortunate to have lived in this era as Englishmen hold fortunate those who lived in the age of Elizabeth, and Frenchmen those who shared in the glories of the age of Louis XIV.

In making this plea for a realization that the stuff of history is not something altogether remote in time and distant in place, I do not wish to be misunderstood. No one has a higher respect than I have for the dignity of history. That our best written history requires a perspective which only time can impart; that it is necessarily the fruit of long and wide research; that it is seldom composed except by men who have undergone long and arduous training; that it demands literary talent of a high order; and that it must be invigorated and ennobled by a strong moral impulse— this I fully believe. What is history? Theodore Roosevelt said that history is a vivid and powerful presentation of scientific matter in literary form; and it would be difficult to improve upon this statement. I do not believe that Tom, Dick and Harriet can write history in this sense, or should annoy the world by trying. John Burroughs once remarked that not one man in five hundred can make any observations upon nature that are worth recording. He might have added that not one in five hundred thousand is capable of recording them as Henry Thoreau or Gilbert White of Selborne did. So it is with history conceived in the austerest sense.

But history is a house of many mansions. I do believe that many persons now inert or timid might record historical matter of enduring importance; and that they would do so if they disabused themselves of the notion that history is far away beyond the blue horizon. The fact is that the garments of Clio float about us and by resolutely putting out our hands, anyone of us who is shrewd, observant, and careful can grasp them. Particularly is this true of the great field of social and cultural history—a field in which the village, the provincial town, and the state capital are as important as Washington or London.

Let me quote from another unpublished letter; a letter written almost precisely a hundred years ago by a historical craftsman who believed that history lay all about him—Benson J. Lossing. Mr. Lossing, who belonged to the race of itinerant scholars exemplified by Henry Howe and John W. Barber, wrote three works now too much neglected—his *Pictorial Field Book of the Revolution, Pictorial Field Book of the War of 1812,* and *Pictorial Field Book of the Civil War.* Upon the first-named work Lossing expended more than eleven thousand dollars, then a fortune, before he received a cent of return. He wrote on November 27, 1851, to David L. Swain, president of the University of North Carolina, of his patient, self-sacrificing, laborious efforts to obtain historical materials from the lips of men who had witnessed great events and changes, from traditional family narratives, and from visits to interesting scenes and old buildings:

> The fact is, my dear sir, I visited the various important localities of the Revolution, under the great disadvantage of being an entire stranger in person and name, and "utterly unknown to fame." I sought out the various places with patient perseverance, and the men from whom I might obtain information, I looked for upon the ground of each

event. I know not, personally, a single individual in North Carolina, and I had but one solitary letter of introduction to a gentleman in your state, and that was to the excellent Dr. Wilson of Hillsborough. Even that letter was from a hand, personally unknown to me. Under other peculiar disadvantages, I made the long journey, not the least of which was the claim of the business of my profession, my source of livelihood. Yet, through God's providence, I have accomplished the journeyings, and trust that I have not omitted any place of great general importance. . . . I know that our general histories have given comparatively little of the Revolutionary struggle in the Carolinas, and would lead one to think that they were only the cockpit in which the combatants fought, without furnishing much of the *sentiment* of the Revolution. I have no such appreciation of the matter; on the contrary, I see in the Carolinas, and particularly in the "Old North State," patriotism as deep and abiding, and as early and efficiently manifested as in Boston, Boston the boasted "Cradle of Liberty." . . .

My greatest difficulty has been to discriminate as to what material was most essential to be used and what to omit, so that my work should not be prolix, and too voluminous for popular circulation; for to make the work too large and expensive for the mass of our reading population, would defeat one of the prime objects of my efforts—the placing of a topographical and historical view of our Revolutionary struggle, in a simple manner, before my countrymen. But in this condensation I have not been partial, and my narrative of events in the South will be found quite as minute as of the North.

I like also to think of Henry Howe, the author of the *Historical Collections of New York*, and similar books upon Virginia and above all of Ohio, jogging over a country road in his plain buggy, drawn by his old white horse, pausing at every hamlet and town to talk with the older inhabitants, and record their recollections of historic men and events; collecting newspaper clippings, letters and other materials for the delightful historical grab-bags that he compiled. The methods of such men as Howe and Lossing left much to be desired; the spirit in which they worked was altogether admirable. History to them was not to be found only in remote times and places, beyond the blue horizon; it lay all about them and they gathered it up as eagerly as ever Argonaut gathered a bag of treasure.

Be assured that many of us have a similar opportunity to collect and lay by historical gold. The most difficult part of history to obtain is the record of how plain men and women lived, and how they were affected by the economic, social, and cultural changes of their times; the most fascinating part of history is this same record. The Rev. Willian Gordon of Roxbury, Massachusetts, struck in 1776 "with the importance of the scenes that were opening upon the world," resolved to write a big bow-wow history of the Revolution. His work is now so dead that few know it exists; but the humble diaries of everyday events by Ezra Stiles, William Bentley, and others of the period are immortal. George Bancroft's biography of Martin Van Buren is utterly forgotten, but Philip Hone's prosaic everyday record of eating, drinking, talking, reading and travelling in Van Buren's time is a perennial joy to readers, and an ever-fresh depiction of life in oldtime New York. We may have many excuses for not setting down historical material, and some of them may be valid. But we do not have the excuse of never seeing matter of enduring historical importance, for it lies around us as the sea lies around the mariner.

22

Oral History: How and
Why It Was Born

When the editors of the H. W. Wilson Company's *Wilson Library Bulletin* decided in 1966 to devote a special issue to oral history, their first step was to invite Allan Nevins to describe the beginnings of that exciting new device for preserving today's records for the use of future historians. Well they should, for if any man deserves to be called the "father" of any innovation in historical method, Allan Nevins has earned that title for oral history. As early as 1938 in his *Gateway to History* he called for an organization "to obtain, from the lips and papers of living Americans who have led significant lives, a fuller record of their participation in the political, economic, and cultural life of the last sixty years." A decade later—on May 18, 1948—Nevins conducted the first oral history interview at Columbia University, plying George McAneny with questions about his civic activities in New York, while a graduate student's pencil vainly tried to record the answers. From these small beginnings emerged the Oral History Office of Columbia where hundreds of thousands of pages of reminiscences have been tape-recorded and tran-

Reprinted by permission from the *Wilson Library Bulletin* 40 (March 1966): 600–1. Copyright © 1966 by The H. W. Wilson Company.

scribed; from those beginnings, too, evolved the dozens of oral history projects that today function in universities, libraries, and historical societies throughout the world, all recording the masses of data that future historians will use in interpreting today's civilization. In this brief essay, Allan Nevins describes with justifiable pride his major role in launching this movement and lists some of the records it has preserved.

"A curious thought has just occurred to me," Dr. Johnson once remarked. "In the grave we shall receive no letters." Despite such volumes as *Letters to Dead Authors*, that is indubitably true. It is equally true that from the grave no letters are sent out to the most anxious inquirers into old history or old mysteries. We can take a few precautions to prevent Time from putting too much as alms for oblivion into the monstrous wallet on his back; that is all. Oral history is one of the latest and most promising of these precautions, and already it has saved from death's dateless (and undatable) night much that the future will rejoice over and cherish.

In hardly less degree than space exploration, oral history was born of modern invention and technology. "Miss Secretary," says the President, "take a letter to the Prime Minister of —. No, stop! I'll just telephone him; quicker, easier, and above all safer. We know he has no recording device." What might have been a priceless document for the historian goes into the irrecoverable ether. The head of the great Detroit corporation, who wishes to get information on finance from several bankers, and important scientific facts from several laboratory experts, catches a plane to New York. The graphic letter that the student of social progress would prize is cut short—a telegram will do. The news-behind-the-news that a Wickham Steed once sent *The* (London) *Times* from Berlin or Bucharest does not even go on teletype; it is put on a confidential telephone wire.

All the while the hurry and complexity of modern politics, modern financial and business affairs, and even modern literary and artistic life slice away the time that men need for methodical, reflective writing. What wonderful letters Theodore Roosevelt gave the world, so full of his endless zest for life, his incredible energy, his enthusiasms and his hatreds. To go further back, what a shelf of delightful comment on a thousand subjects from the Western mastodons to the iniquities of European diplomacy, from decimal coinage to Watt's new steam engine, from slave management to Ossian's poetry, we find in the massive volumes of Jefferson's writings. No doubt great letter writers still exist. But their numbers are fewer, and the spirit of the times is hostile to them.

It was something more than a sense of these considerations that inspired the planners of oral history. It was natural that they should be rooted in the history department of the greatest university in the largest and busiest city of the continent. It was right that they should have some knowledge of what the California publisher H. H. Bancroft had done to preserve a picture of the life, lore, and legends of the youthful years of the Golden State by interviewing scores of pioneers, and getting their dictated reminiscences down on paper. The planners had a connection with journalism, and saw in the daily obituary columns proof that knowledge valuable to the historian, novelist, sociologist, and economist was daily perishing; memories perishing forever without yielding any part of their riches. They had enthusiasm, these planners. It was partly the enthusiasm of ignorance; the undertaking looked deceptively easy.

Anyway, they set to work, at first with pencil and pad, later with wire recorders, later still with early tape-recording machines. They found that the task needed a great deal of money, and money was hard to get. It needed system, planning, conscientiousness, the skill that comes with experience, and above all integrity. It was more complicated and laborious than they had dreamed. The results were sometimes poor, but hard effort sometimes made them dazzling.

And the work was adventurously entertaining. At every turn they met a new experience, a fresh view of history, a larger knowledge of human personality. They would never forget the eminent New York attorney who had once collected a million dollars in a single fee, and who interrupted the story of his career to exclaim, "This is the most delightful experience I have ever had, this reminiscing." They would always remember the labor leader who in the course of an engrossing story suddenly laid his head on the desk and burst into tears; he had come to the point where he had been sent to prison for alleged racketeering. They would always keep a picture of Norman Thomas singing a pathetic song composed by the harried tenant farmers of the Southwest, and of Charles C. Burlingham, still active at almost a hundred, recalling how as a mere urchin he had seen a Negro hanged in front of his father's parsonage in downtown Manhattan during the raging of the Draft Riots.

The original ventures had been modest, but they rapidly expanded into large national undertakings. With elation the managers watched Henry Wallace record for posterity about two thousand typed pages of reminiscences, with large diary excerpts to illustrate them; with elation they heard Mrs. Frances Perkins, who possessed an approach to total recall, record what (with additional matter she contributed) came to a memoir of five thousand typed pages. Governors, cabinet officers past and present, industrialists, and distinguished authors and editors lent themselves to the enterprise. Many of them had been badgered for years by their families to set down recollections that history would need; not infrequently they had long felt a desire to furnish their own account of an important transaction or controversial period, but had lacked time and opportunity until suddenly seated before a tape recorder with a well-equipped interviewer before them. This interviewer, upon whom half the value of the work depended, had prepared himself by reading files of newspapers, going through official reports, begging wives for old letters or diary notes, and talking with associates. Sometimes a subject possessed a fresh and copious memory, as did Secretary Stimson; sometimes his memory had merely to be jogged, as that of Governor Rockefeller; sometimes it had to be helped by extended work, as that of former Governor Herbert H. Lehman.

Now and then, too, the work originally done had to be revised and redone. This was true of the memoir prepared by that distinguished jurist and unforgettable personality, Learned Hand. His outspoken comment, his salty wit, made his original recollections remarkable. One or two sentences may be recalled. He commented on the reverence he felt for Brandeis: "I often scolded myself, when I was a young man. You eat too much, I told myself. You drink too much. Your thoughts about women are not of the most elevated character. Why can't you be like that great man Brandeis, who does nothing but read Interstate Commerce Reports?" Judge Hand's first version, however, lacked the depth and expertness supplied when a professor of law who had once been his clerk was induced to serve as a new interviewer.

Some of the anticipated obstacles never appeared. Even busy, important, and excessively modest men proved in many instances accessible; they entered into the spirit of the work. The mass of invaluable memoir material mounted. It proved possible to protect the reminiscences against intrusion; the integrity of oral history never came under suspicion, much less attack. Better and better equipment was purchased, better and better systems of interviewing, typing, and indexing were developed. About half of the memoirs were thrown open to students at once, the other half being kept under time restrictions. And the students appeared, first in scores, well-accredited and watched; then in hundreds; then in more than a thousand, not a few of them writing important books.

One difficulty, however, always persisted: the difficulty of finance. It proved impossible to operate even a sternly economical but efficient office for less than $40,000 a year, and costs rose. Work had begun on funds supplied from a happy bequest to Columbia University by Frederic Bancroft of Washington, a bequest upon which the head of oral history had a special claim; and the University itself contributed quarters and money. As the project grew, certain foundations gave generous help. Other corporations made use of its skills, giving oral history not only valuable bodies of reminiscences, but a fee in addition.

Thus the material accumulated by oral history grew year by year, both in bulk and in quality. Thus the work it accomplished attracted wider and wider attention, raising up imitative agencies in various parts of the United States, and even abroad. Because New York City is an unapproachably effective seat for such work, because the office spent the utmost pains upon its methods, and because its personnel counted brilliant young men (some of whom have now made their mark elsewhere), the heads of the office on Morningside Heights believe that their accomplishment has not been equaled elsewhere. They are glad, however, to see the type of activity they began in the preservation of priceless memories for the instruction of posterity copied elsewhere, and the tree they planted, like a banyan, creating sister trees in surrounding ground. May the work flourish and spread!

23

A New Horizon for Who's Who:
A Proposal

That Allan Nevins should have sent the following memorandum to the editors of *Who's Who in America* was almost inevitable. His concern throughout his busy academic lifetime was with both the writing and tools of history; the books needed to enlighten present and future generations could only be produced if scholars were provided with ever more revealing documentary evidence. This was the purpose that underlay his dedication to oral history programs. This was his purpose, also, when he prepared this proposal which was sent to the publishers of *Who's Who* in 1957. In it he urges collaboration with a group of social scientists to develop questionnaires that would reveal much about the nation's elite—questionnaires that would provide grist for future historical mills. The version that follows was found in carbon form among his literary remains.

The reference work of today is the historical, sociological, and economic source of tomorrow. Indeed, many such reference works as the *Statesmen's Yearbook* or *World Almanac* follow a curious sequence of life, death, and resurrection. Throughout the year of publication they are in constant use, leafed assiduously by journalists, students, and men of affairs. On New Year's eve they suddenly look deader than Darius, and, as alms for oblivion, go to the wastebasket or dusty top shelf. When a few years pass, however, the surviving copies awaken to a vitality new in kind and richer in degree.

The historian, with a murmur of joy, hales down the *passé* volume, and exhumes an election statistic of Detroit which enables him to pen an illuminating interpretation of the automobile workers' response to some Administration measure. The economist, scanning a paragraph on trade conditions in Nigeria, catches a shaft of light on the worldwide effects of Bank of England policy. Even the craggiest, most stonily factual reference book, when a little mellowed by time, becomes a quarry from which some perceptive scholar can extract handsome building materials, as John Stuart Mill did from the venerable *Annual Register*, and James Ford Rhodes from the *Tribune Almanac*.

Biographical compilations stand highest of all in this category of reference books which end a current use only to gain a perennial value. The presentation of what Leslie Stephen called national biography is pursued on three levels. The most fundamental is the basic yearbook of current biography, inaugurated by the British *Who's Who* in 1848, indifferently sustained on the Continent by *Qui Etes Vous?*, *Wer Ist's?* and the like, and vastly improved by *Who's Who in America*. Above this rises the biographical dictionary from time to time compiled under learned auspices. This was seriously begun in Britain with the eighteenth century *Biographica Britannia*, of which Cowper wrote that it was:

> A fond attempt to give a deathless lot
> To names ignoble, born to be forgot,

and in the United States with *Appleton's Cyclopaedia of American Biography*. It has given the two countries those noble works of reference, the *Dictionary of National Biography* and *Dictionary of American Biography*, not only indispensable tools but entertaining treasuries of human lore. Finally, as the pinnacle of national biography, we have our growing libraries of formal works from the ordinary one-volume life to the multivolume monument like Masson's *Milton* and Nicolay and Hay's *Lincoln*.

Now that *Who's Who* has reached its sixtieth year the time has come, in my opinion, to make a proposal for adding to its usefulness not as a biennial reference work—it is almost perfect in that area—but as an agency in assisting the future armies of scholarship in various fields.

In looking at the sheer bulk of *Who's Who*, with its 3,000 triple-columned pages and endless array of sketches, some thoughtless people may share Cowper's feeling. They may echo Leslie Stephen's admission, after editing the *D.N.B.*, that he had sometimes wondered what was the use of his "long procession of the hopelessly insignificant"; they may say that while Carlyle was doubtless right in calling history the essence of innumerable biographies, he was also right in groaning over the huge dustheaps, the mountainous "kitchen-middens", that dryasdust detail has accumulated. What is the value to posterity of these many thousands of condensed biographies? The answer falls into three parts.

In the first place, all conscientious students of the past must confess the force of the old aphorism that the world never knows its greatest men—or some of them. The differences in talent and character between those who attain eminence and those who remain on a commonplace level are often slight or nonexistent; mere accident raises one and represses the other. Behind the eminent cabinet minister stands the obscure undersecretary who supplies the real grasp of policy; below the famous captain of industry is the self-effacing staff of executives who really guide the business and score its triumphs. Most crises of history do not make heroes; they simply bring the theretofore unrecognized hero into light, to exert his latent powers. Many lives that appear commonplace, in short, are not really so; they are full of capacities potentially great.

In the second place, behind even the admittedly minor names we often find a bit of history—political, economic, or cultural—that has striking value. How many have ever heard of Issachar J. Roberts, an early nineteenth-century son of rural Tennessee who resolved to become missionary to China? On funds of his own, he sailed to Macao in 1836 to work as a saddler while preaching to lepers, "which connection ostracised him from his fellow-missionaries." In time, after work among British troops in Hong Kong, he turned up in Nanking as chief aide to Kan Wang, leader of the Taiping Rebellion, who made him minister of foreign affairs. All went well until he suddenly accused Kan Wang of murdering his servant; Kan Wang retaliated by dashing a cup of tea dregs in his face; and Roberts fled, to die of leprosy in Illinois. If we knew more of the details of this life, we would possess a good deal of light on China, the rise of Hong Kong, the bloody Taiping revolt, and the missionary movement. Sometimes, in fact, an obscure figure penetrates to the very heart of events. In Henry Adams's narrative of the Burr Conspiracy appears briefly one Daniel Clark, "the richest and most prominent American in New Orleans" in 1805, who played a telling but quite enigmatic role. He was a robust fellow: he fought a duel with Governor Claiborne, assailed General James Wilkinson as a traitor, and fathered two illegitimate children who inherited a half-century of litigation over his estate. Yet many facts of his life are so shrouded that the true character of his role in the conspiracy remains dubious.

And in the third place, even fairly famous men have often left in darkness the very facts upon which the modern *Who's Who* most rigorously insists. Everyone who consults the large biographical dictionaries knows how often a question mark is placed against dates of birth, marriage, and death. The rule of editors has been to exclude the phrase, "Place and date of birth unknown"; if such facts are not stated, inability to find them is implied. Take, for example, the American adventurer Gilbert Imlay, born "about" 1754 and died "perhaps" in 1828, who is remembered for various writings and for his heartless liaison with the celebrated Mary Wollstonecraft. His whole life from 1796 to 1828(?) is a blank. If he had but filled out a questionnaire for *Who's Who*!

It once fell to my lot to write the account of that unwearied social crusader T. S. Arthur for the *D.A.B.* He published some seventy titles. He edited five widely circulated magazines. He lectured and travelled. He was a leading Swedenborgian. His *Ten Nights in a Bar-Room* was the most celebrated and profitable polemic novel, next to *Uncle Tom's Cabin*, ever written in America. Yet some of the basic facts of his career, indispensable to an understanding of his personality and a knowledge of his importance to his times, had never been recorded. Fortunately I discovered descendants who had them. But what if he had left none? David Bennett Hill, long Democratic boss of New York, did not; and for an indication of how much mystery can remain in a recent striking career led largely in the public eye, we need only turn to the sketch of Hill.

No, in spite of Cowper's gibe and Carlyle's groan, we can never know too much about our national biography. The wider we cast our nets for information, the more varied and complete the body of facts we obtain, the ampler will be our means of understanding America past and present. The sociologist, the economist, the psychologist, and the historian of the future can all use additional sets of facts. We have few systematic agencies for collecting them, and in some respects the most efficient of them all is the office of *Who's Who*. It works carefully, methodically, and continuously. It gathers its data not as some suppose, every two years, but all the time, and embodies them in monthly supplements as well as biennial volumes. Its labors are not purely mechanical, but involve a great deal of precise collation, and even some interpretation. It is time, I submit, that experts in the social studies—and perhaps in science as well—awake to the possibilities of a useful collaboration. The late Mr. and Mrs. Wheeler Sammons laid the basis for such a partnership when in 1953 they turned their reference properties over to a public-service nonprofit corporation.

Already *Who's Who* has established an archive open to all honest students. Containing the mass of reference data brought together since the first issue in 1899–1900, it is naturally a narrow if not exactly meager archive. The facts gathered were purely skeletal. Some of the accompanying correspondence, however, has illuminating qualities. John W. Leonard, the first editor, has told us a little of his perplexities and tribulations. Again and again he was roughly commanded by distinguished persons to "Leave me out!" Others, only too anxious to be included, offered accounts of their achievements that would have made Baron Munchausen blush. Not a few were genially expansive. "Do you really invite women to confess publicly their age—and then expect them to commend your book?" demanded one woman author. Sometimes the owners and editors of *Who's Who* had to go to extreme lengths to get the information they wanted, and the results were even more instructive than they had expected. Thus the visit of Samuel Crowther to Henry Ford in behalf of Wheeler Sammons converted Crowther from a critic of Ford to the position of admirer and lieutenant, and furnished Sammons with a striking view of the industrialist.

Just how can *Who's Who* supplement the basic data it has gathered for sixty years? Just what kind of new dimension should it add to its work? These are obviously questions for the experts to answer. The economist would make one suggestion as specially beneficial to his studies, the sociologist another. Nobody wishes to increase the bulk of the famous red book; what is desirable is to build up a larger body of reserve material. A short new questionnaire, to be answered on an optional basis, with a guaranty that the response would be kept confidential for a certain time, might produce material that the next generation would pronounce invaluable. The persons listed in the current *Who's Who*, constituting one in every 10,000 or 12,000 of the population, are a cross-section not of the nation but of the best part of the nation. By and large, they offer the chief justification of American civilization. It is not enough that they list their parents, children, lives, and works; they should be given an opportunity, pointed by well-drafted queries, to add something more. We would not expect anything from Mr. Stevenson or President Pusey, who will have their biographers, but from John Doe we might expect something significant.

I cannot even guess what the economist or sociologist would wish included in the additional questionnaire. But I may venture to say what would interest at least some historians. If every contributor to *Who's Who* was invited to add to his published data a brief statement, for the archive only, of what he regarded as his most noteworthy enrichment of the life of his times, the replies might often be pretentious, but also often modest and illuminating. If all were invited to lend for copying any letter or document of special public interest, the result would be an immensity of chaff, but also some grain.

For example, the first volume of *Who's Who* offers a sketch of John T. Campbell, civil engineer. It tells us that he was wounded at the head of his Indiana company in the Civil War; that he was an Indiana leader in the Greenback movement; that he was the first to discover the peculiar slope of hills in the glacial-drift area; that he invented the game "Wabash"; that he· joined the good-roads crusade, and "introduced straw as a remedy for sandy roads." He had something to record, and the chances that he did it are about zero. No doubt Clio can survive without ever knowing just what was the game of "Wabash," and how far the strawing of sandy roads went. But seriously, the versatile Mr. Campbell had something to contribute to our knowledge of his times.

The ways and objects of getting the Mr. Campbells to contribute to a larger dimension of *Who's Who*—to a biographical archive—must be expertly planned, or the effort would be worthless. The inquiry, what data will be deemed most useful in 1975 or 2025 can be answered but roughly, even by panels of specialists. But a group of trained talents could assuredly come to some conclusions. The governing bodies of the American Historical Association, American Political Science Association, American Sociological Society, American Economic Association, and Modern Language Association (which all counselled the editors of the *D.A.B.*) might be urged to create a committee to consider the possibilities of a fact-gathering partnership with *Who's Who* and the best modes of preserving the fruits and making them available to research. In time regional committees might grow out of the national body, for the South, the Far West, the Northeast, and the Middle West differ greatly in problems and needs. Under such auspices, such aid as was needed from foundations should be readily attainable.

Properly carried through, such a program would leave the biennial reference volume unchanged; but it would use its machinery and prestige to build a steadily expanding biographical archive of value to widely different types of inquirers. The growth of this archive, which might be kept intact or might be distributed among university libraries on a regional basis, would realize the purpose which Wheeler Sammons had in mind when he transferred his property to a nonprofit corporation, intended to be perpetual, with the object of developing what he called "A Library of American Biography." Various difficulties, including company litigation, have delayed this undertaking. Mr. Sammons, farsighted as he was, seems never to have thought of enlisting the scholarly resources of the country in a broad partnership. Such a partnership, however, might be of great value on both sides. The archive might in time become one of the best-recognized research institutions of the land.

The United States has a future to which the three hundred and fifty years of our past are but the briefest prologue. We cannot too earnestly address ourselves to a better-planned assemblage of materials, on a broadly democratic basis, for comprehending the record we shall write, and on which we shall build. Here is one feasible way of contributing to that end.

Part Five

GREAT HISTORIANS OF THE NINETEENTH CENTURY

To Allan Nevins a great historian was a well-read historian; the author of the specialized monograph so burdened with professional jargon that it was readable only to a few fellow craftsmen he ranked far below the literary stylist in his hierarchy of heroes. This is made abundantly clear in the seven essays that follow. Most of these were apparently delivered as lectures in the course on "The Literature of American History" that he first offered at Columbia University in 1937 and that became in 1942 "The Great Literature of American History." They are of interest today, although dated, both for their acute summation of the merits and faults of the nineteenth century's most influential scholars and for what they tell us of Nevins's own beliefs and prejudices. All were found among the files of manuscripts he left behind upon his death in 1971.

24

George Bancroft

Allan Nevins's lecture on George Bancroft, probably delivered in his "Great Literature of American History" course during the late 1930s or early 1940s, admirably reveals his sound judgment and critical acumen. Never one to parrot the views of others, he ably summarizes the critical literature on Bancroft then available before drawing his own conclusions—most of them highly original for that day. In the end Nevins's indictment is more brutal than that of Bancroft's other critics; Bancroft failed to rank as a major historian, he concludes, because his task "demanded gifts beyond his endowment." Neither natural ability nor training equipped him to write the literary epic to which he aspired; his was not a "pen tipped with lightning." Yet he contributed more, in Allan Nevins's view, than many of the "puny scientific tribe" who had usurped historical writing in the twentieth century. This essay, then, is interesting not only for what it says of Bancroft, but for what it says of Nevins during his early teaching days before his dislike of "scientific history" was muted by greater understanding.

It was a crowded and fruitful life that George Bancroft lived. "You have both written the history of your country, and made yourself a part of it," Robert C. Winthrop wrote him on his ninetieth birthday. As his biographer M. A. DeWolfe Howe says, his work and his life together cover the whole history of America from the first English colonization to 1891. He was teacher, editor, writer, statesman, ambassador. He became a great national figure, and an important link between the cultures of the Old World and the New. If he is not still read as a historian—and he is certainly worth reading—he must be remembered as a versatile, able, and generous-spirited worker in many departments of American life.

Indeed, when we look at the range of Bancroft's activities, the eminence of the stations he occupied, and his prominence in the public eye, we can see why Americans of his own time looked upon him as Englishmen regarded Macaulay, and Germans Treitschke. A scion of New England Unitarianism, he received in the study of his ministerial father, in Phillips Academy, and in Harvard, Göttingen, Heidelberg, and Berlin, as excellent an education as anyone could ask. He added to his studies in German universities a European tour. He knew Goethe and Humboldt, Byron and Lafayette, Hegel and Manzoni. From Europe he brought back a romantic ardor which expressed itself in a small volume of verse, in an impatience of the pedantry encouraged by Harvard's classical courses, and in various extravagances of dress and manner which subjected him to much ridicule. With ardor he threw himself into the establishment of a school modeled upon the German gymnasium—the Round Hill School at Northampton. He wrote for the *North American Review*; he translated the treatise of his old master Heeren of Göttingen upon *The Politics of Ancient Greece*. He felt a natural bent, nurtured by travel and study, for democracy and egalitarianism of the Jeffersonian stripe. It has been noted that, delivering the Fourth of July oration in 1826 at Northampton, the day that Jefferson and Adams died, he eulogized the former—the Virginian and not the New Englander

—as the man "whose principles are identified with the character of our government, and whose influence with the progress of civil liberty throughout the world." Despite the federalism of his ancestors and the Whig beliefs of most of his associates, he entered the Democratic party of Jackson, Van Buren, and Benton at the very time it rose to power. He was soon collector of the port of Boston, and then in succession the unsuccessful Democratic candidate for governor, secretary of the navy under Polk, and minister to England.

The first volume of Bancroft's *History of the United States* appeared in 1834, having apparently been written in the two preceding years. The title announced that he expected to bring the work down to "the present time"; and this first step carried the story from the discovery of America to the restoration of the Stuarts in 1660, a long span. But as his canvas grew wider and more crowded, he found that it was enough to carry the work to the end of the Revolution; and this required ten volumes. Of the ten, three were written in the thirties; then, after a pause of a decade, five more came out in the fifties; and the last two were issued in 1866 and 1875 respectively. It is easy to remember that Bancroft was born in 1800. One-third of his work was therefore written while he was comparatively young—in his thirties—the remainder between his fiftieth and seventy-fifth years. In his later years he had to spend much time on revision. Great strides were being made by others in the study of American history; their works corrected or supplemented his own; and by ruthless editing he kept pace with the general advance of knowledge.

Few histories in any land have had so immense a success as Bancroft's. Commercially, it filled his pockets with money. His income from his books was not only large, but well sustained. But what was of far more importance to him, it obtained and kept the applause of two generations of Americans. Edward Everett wrote him in 1834 that the first volume was immortal. "I must tell you, that I think you have written a work which will last while the memory of America lasts; and which will instantly take its place

307

among the classics of our language. It is full of learning, information, common sense, and philosophy; full of taste and eloquence; full of life and power. . . . You give us real, individual, living men and women, with their passions, interests, and peculiarities." The history brought tears to the eyes of Emerson. The praise which it received in the thirties and even the fifties might be set down to American exuberance and the lack of worthy rivals. But even in the eighties it held its place. When Robert Louis Stevenson made his journey across the plains as an emigrant he carried Bancroft's history as his literary baggage. And in 1892 we find Charles F. Richardson, in his history of American literature, declaring that the history of the colonies had been so well treated in these ten volumes that later writers would find little to do. "To tell this story was Bancroft's task; and it will hardly need to be retold in full by other writers."

It is the fashion to treat Bancroft as a writer without important ideas, or rather, with only the one idea of democracy; but this is an injustice. He set forth his basic doctrines in his address of 1854 at the semicentennial of the New-York Historical Society. Some of these tenets were derived from Heeren; others were original with himself. History, he declared, is no chaos of unmeaning events; it is God working by examples. It is a unit—all civilized nations have a common history, and none can really be considered apart from the rest. As he put it in the preface to his first volume, "The United States constitutes an essential portion of a great political system, embracing all the civilized nations of the earth. The forces within this unity are constant; its totality is an organic whole. The great basic values of truth, morality, and justice are unchanging; they are born of God, and like all his creations are immutable. There is nothing relative or evolutionary about them. But there is a collective human will in history which is capable of evolutionary progress. It moves onward and upward, achieving better states of knowledge, and finer patterns of behavior. Society, therefore, constantly though slowly produces new organizations or states, in which freedom is fuller than in those which preceded it, and truth,

308

morality, and justice have better scope. As mankind improves in experience, education, and culture, it can set up stronger and more permanent governments; its opportunities and possibilities grow ever greater." Bancroft regarded the American democracy as the crowning achievement of mankind in this upward climb. He said of the United States in the preface to his first volume: "At a period when the force of moral opinion is rapidly increasing, they have the precedence in the practise and the defence of the equal rights of man." He went on from this statement, in his preface, to offer a long and glowing panegyric of American democracy. We may, if we like, regard Bancroft's philosophy of history as naïve and elementary; but we cannot deny that he had a philosophy, and that he had worked it out in rather full detail.

It is also often said that Bancroft learned his historical method at the feet of Heeren, but this is quite misleading. As a man, and as a teacher of Plato, Heeren undoubtedly influenced him. From Heeren he also drew his enthusiastic belief in the importance of original authorities, and his insistence upon minute research and verification. But otherwise he seems to have learned little from Heeren. The German laid great emphasis upon economic factors in history, and indeed was the first to attempt a large-scale economic history of the ancient world. But Bancroft cared little for economic currents. Heeren, again, insisted upon a rigid objectivity; but Bancroft was undisguisedly partisan. Heeren attached great value to the interpretation of masses of historical fact and paid no attention to a dramatic presentation, full of color and interest. But Bancroft was inexpert and superficial in his interpretations, while he excelled in giving dramatic form to his chapters, and vigor and vividness to his narrative. The principal elements in Bancroft's method were four. (1) He endeavored to go to original sources for his facts; believing that much error crept into American history through the indolent way historians had of repeating one another, he consulted the basic documents. To be sure, documentary collections were inadequate in his day. But he supplemented the libraries by making huge accumulations of his own. These, now in the New York Public Library, include many original bodies of papers—the Samuel Adams papers, the Hawley papers, the Riedesel papers, and others, together with 210 bound volumes of transcripts. (2) Bancroft carefully distinguished between original authority and second-hand authority, between eyewitnesses and hearsay witnesses; and in other ways exercised a discriminating choice of evidence. (3) He cast his narrative into as dramatic and gripping a form as possible. Since he was to show God working in examples, and since the American democracy was the culminating example of history, he threw into his writing a high fervor, a vibrant excitement. To him there was nothing prosaic in the story; it gripped his enthusiasm, and though he lacked imagination, he tried to make it as exciting to others as it was to himself. Necessarily, this dramatic form meant a certain amount of bias; he was always republican and antimonarchical, always democratic and antiaristocratic, always Christian and antipagan, always American and to some extent anti-European. (4) Though a rhetorical writer, he was never flatulent or verbose, and demanded a rigid condensation. He abbreviated quotations from documents, sometimes in a way that did them injustice. He strove to be eclectic instead of comprehensive; to pick out what was typical or representative from a crowded array of facts. His dry, crisp, nervous utterance, coupled with a certain ardor of spirit and an occasional bit of floweriness, gives his style a peculiarly hectic quality which sometimes becomes most irritating. Robert Louis Stevenson found it—as we should expect—intolerable.

But Bancroft's principal defects as a historian arise out of his philosophy, not out of his method. Indeed, his method was in general very good. Some of his incidental rules—for example, his maxim that an historical personage should always be presented from his own standpoint, but judged from the author's—are excellent. But his philosophy gave him an essentially uncritical attitude toward American history. The man who finds a divine plan in history, who relates it as God working in examples, necessarily makes himself an advocate rather than a judge. The idea that the collective man constantly evolves better forms of manners and culture, improved states of living, requires a weighting of the scales in favor of the latest age. In particular, the idea that American democracy is a vast improvement over all systems which have preceded it, and that the essence of American democracy is to be found in Jeffersonian or Jacksonian equality, is a most dangerous idea for a historian. In making his successive volumes vote for Jackson and explain God's purposes, Bancroft had to be excessively unfair to a wide range of forces, personalities, and institutions; he had to praise much that he should have censured. His method was not a bad one; his philosophy or basic set of doctrines was most pernicious. It makes his history today seem antiquated, distorted, and curiously parochial.

Bancroft's plan or arrangement of his work is open to some exception. The first four of his ten volumes cover 271 years. The last six treat of only 19 years. Since he wrote by chapters rather than by integral volumes or sections, his work often lacks progression and logic. It is surely absurd that he puts his chapter on Indian life into the third volume instead of the first. He did not solve with success the problem of passing easily from the Southern to the Middle Colonies, and from the Middle Colonies to New England; he has little of the lucidity or symmetry of arrangement to be found in John Fiske. It must be said also that his plan or scheme was basically defective in giving too much attention to politics, and far too little to social life, economics, culture, and institutional development. This fault left large areas of colonial history totally untouched and gave other writers an opportunity to open wide new avenues into the past. Indeed, it is evident that Bancroft never carefully planned his work as a unit. How could he, writing three-tenths of it in his thirties, five-tenths in his fifties, and two-tenths in old age? Compared with a carefully outlined and integrated work like Lecky's *England in the 18th Century*, it has something of the aspect of an improvisation.

If there are grave defects of plan, the work has still more serious faults of prejudice or of that type of superficiality which arises

311

from a firm prepossession, a prior assumption. No one can justly blame Bancroft for errors based on inadequate information when that information was simply not available in his day. He thought, for example, that Cabot touched land in Labrador; he did not have the facts that Harrisse, Prowse, and others have revealed. He thought that the scheming selfishness of the tyrannical James I was responsible for the dissolution of the Virginia Company; he did not know that W. F. Craven and others would reveal data putting an entirely new aspect on the matter. All historians are subject to revisions of this sort. But we can blame Bancroft for flaws which arise from bias—from his stern adherence to his philosophy of American history.

In describing the early colonists, for example, he treated them as nearly all zealots for democracy; he read back into their history a manifestation of Jeffersonian ideas of equality. The fact is, we know today, that colonial society was not democratic and egalitarian at all in its main trends; aristocracy called the tune in trade, in politics, in religion, in education, and in society. Bancroft glosses over many of the faults of the early Puritans, and understates the theocratic bigotry and tyranny of the time. It remained for writers like Charles Francis Adams, in *Three Episodes of New England History*, to give a truer view. Bancroft treated the founding of New Haven as another exemplification of the spirit of democracy and humanity; but the evidence, justly weighed, proves that Davenport and Eaton really believed in a narrower and more intolerant theocracy than that of Massachusetts Bay. Bancroft's treatment of Andros misses the whole point of the great experiment in colonial reorganization attempted under the last of the Stuarts. Because of his faith in democracy, he overlooked many of the defects of frontier society and the vices of self-governing commonwealths. He says little of the lawlessness of Americans, of their crudity and ignorance, of their restlessness, and of their intellectual superficiality. He tends to minimize the turbulence of popular assemblies, the intolerance shown by mob opinion, the craziness of many democratic ideas in the sphere of finance, and the amount of sheer selfishness which went into revolutionary movements.

Holding the prepossessions he did as to democracy and the position of the American republic as the ripest fruit of time, it was inevitable that he should treat the Revolution with a total lack of detachment. To his mind that great uprising had but one side. In the dispute of the colonial and English Whigs with the colonial and English Tories, the Whigs alone stood upon principle, and in every issue they were right. The last six volumes of his work are essentially a glorification of the Revolution. They are written in the best Fourth of July spirit; their temper is that of such oratorical glorifications of the heroes of '76 as Webster's Bunker Hill address. The schoolboy hero-worship of Bancroft's own enthusiastic youth is carried into the last volume. In the preface to this last volume he remarked: "It is good to look away from the strifes of the present hour, to the great days when our country had for its statesmen Washington and John Adams, Jefferson and Hamilton, Franklin and Jay, and their compeers. The study of these times will teach lessons of moderation, and of unselfish patriotism." His character sketch of Washington may be interestingly contrasted with McMaster's. Bancroft penned a sustained eulogy, in which not one critical word appeared. "In the perfection of his reflective powers," he writes, "he had no peer." "He never failed to observe all that was possible, and at the same time to bound his endeavors by that which was possible." "Divine wisdom not only illuminates the spirit, it inspires the will." "Integrity was so completely a law of his nature that a planet would sooner have shot from its sphere than he would have departed from his uprightness." "Washington . . . established a new criterion of human greatness." McMaster, on the other hand, correctly said that it was important to see Washington in his weakness as well as in his strength. He had magnificent self-control. "But we shall also hear his oaths, and see him in those terrible bursts of passion to which Mr. Jefferson has alluded, and one of which Mr. Lear has described." He was unselfish; yet we must see him "exacting from the family of the poor man the shilling that was his due." He was commanding; but "we shall know him as the cold and forbidding character with whom no fellow-man ever ventured to live on close and familiar terms." Such statements must have shocked Bancroft profoundly.

In all the quarrels between royal governors and provincial legislatures, Bancroft tended to assume that the latter were in the right. His discussion of the Navigation Acts rested upon the assumption that their object was tyrannical and their effect wholly pernicious; two assumptions that a little objective inquiry should have shown him were totally erroneous. He similarly assumed that the British Parliament had no legal authority whatever over the colonies. He took the attitude that the American colonists, when they fully realized the principles at stake, were practically unanimous in their demand for independence; the fact being, as he had ample means of knowing, that the revolutionists and patriots were almost equally matched, with a large body of Americans strictly indifferent and neutral. He thought that resistance to this united demand for independence was actually wicked—for the voice of the people is the voice of God. "Why should man organize resistance to the grand design of Providence?" he wrote in his first volume—later, it is true, striking the sentence out of a revised edition. In speaking of the opposition to the Port Bill by the Bostonians, he wrote that the populace knew "that they were acting not for a province of America, but for freedom itself. They were inspired by the thought that the Providence which rules the world demanded of them heroic self-denial as the champions of humanity, and they never doubted the fellow-feeling of the continent." The idea that the unity of the British Empire was an ideal worth struggling for—an idea that he could have found vigorously expressed by his hero Benjamin Franklin—never seems to have struck hold in his mind. As Bassett states, it is hard to see how a historian to whom Lord North's daughter gave all her papers could have used them, as he presumably did, without forming some respect for the British—let us rather say the loyalist—point of view in the great controversy.

Two other of Bancroft's prepossessions related to the Indian and to slavery. Of the savages he really knew little. He had none of that firsthand information which Parkman obtained, while modern archaeology and ethnology were hardly even in their infancy when he wrote the chapter on the Indians in his third volume. But he over-idealized the Eastern savages, painting a portrait of a "noble red man" which owes more to Cooper than to fact. In treating slavery he forgot his maxim that a man or an institution should be presented from the point of view of his or its own generation and adherents. He detested slavery and missed no opportunity to denounce it or those who profited by it. The attitude of the seventeenth and eighteenth century toward an institution which at that time probably had more beneficence than cruelty, so far as it affected the Africans, he completely misses. He attributes the African slave trade to the rapacity of the British merchant and to the desire of the British Government to "weaken the power of colonial resistance" by setting blacks against whites. The first of these motives is quite inadequate to explain the slave trade and very unfair to British interests; the second is fantastically unsound. When Bancroft came to treat the efforts of advanced Southerners to halt the slave trade, he applauded it as wholly noble and idealistic; forgetting the selfish grounds such a slave-breeding state as Virginia had for wishing its stoppage.

An enumeration of the defects of Bancroft's history is easy, for every passing year makes our perception of them keener. But to list and explain his services to historical writing is more difficult. He is so outmoded and outworn that some of us are likely to question now whether he ever really possessed great value; whether he was not brummagem metal rather than pure silver, not an *ignis fatuus* rather than a true light. William Milligan Sloane tells us that when Bancroft was in London, it was the habit of

H. H. Milman, H. Hallam, Macaulay, and Lord Mahon to breakfast together once a week, and that Bancroft was often with them. Of these five writers Bancroft and Mahon seem to stand bracketed together as lost to living literature. Everyone reads Macaulay; many people still read Milman's *History of the Jews* and Hallam's *Literature of the Middle Ages*. But who reads Mahon and Bancroft?

Yet as late as 1887 Sloane, who was not deficient in judgment, wrote: "In Bancroft's work there lies the quality of permanency, and so long has it been before the world, and stood the test of critical examination, that we might almost say the judgment of posterity has already been passed." When M. A. De Wolfe Howe, whose judgment was even better, wrote his summation of Bancroft's work at the close of his biography, he spoke of the "intellectual greatness" of the man; he noted Bancroft's vivid and impressive power in dealing with battles, campaigns, and political events; and he referred to "the sixty years of victorious labor upon a lofty enterprise" as if confident that Bancroft would remain a great star in the historical firmament. A recent writer in the *Jernegan Essays* agrees with Von Holst's statement that "every historian of the United States must stand on Bancroft's shoulders." And two New Englanders who "revalued" Bancroft for the *New England Quarterly* in 1933 tell us that "In several capacities and on many points Bancroft wrote history which has endured the test of time." The tendency to a scornful dismissal of Bancroft is strongest among those who have never really read any sustained part of his works and is not likely to find much countenance among those who have.

We must do Bancroft the justice which, following Heeren, he insisted all historians must do to personages of the past: We must present him from his own standpoint before we criticize him from ours. We stand in a period when the ideals which dominate historical writing are rigidly—indeed much too rigidly—scientific. We give our approval to what is scientific in Bancroft's work: to his careful distinction between original sources and secondary

316

aids, between Quellen and Hulfsmittel; to his thorough search for original documents; to his desire to place men and events in a broad frame; and to his understanding, gained perhaps from Humboldt and Buckle, of the role of geography in history. It is rather amusing to note that the two writers who "revalued" Bancroft in the *New England Quarterly* based all their praise of him upon scientific elements in his work. They declare that again and again one encounters in Bancroft statements which are not only excellent in their lucidity, but "so genuinely modern in their tenor that it is almost unbelievable that they were written almost a century ago." They point out how realistic is his treatment of Drake, how good a guess he made when he said that Father Hennepin was in the pay of William III, how acutely he criticized the leaders and battles of the Seven Years' War, and how intelligently he did justice to General Braddock. That is the tendency of everyone today, to appraise Bancroft from a scientific point of view and from no other. But it is not quite fair to a historian who never pretended to be scientific.

The fact is that Bancroft was a philosophical and literary historian. He seemed great to the generation living between 1830 and 1890 not because that generation did not know good historical work from bad, but because that generation believed in philosophical and literary history. He seems very defective to our generation because we do not believe in such history. If the pendulum turns—if new times bring back a taste for history rooted in a special view of the world and written with a keen eye to dramatic effect and rhetorical phrasing—Bancroft may be much better esteemed. It is by no means impossible that another generation will find Channing quite unread, utterly *passé*; but that it will find many readers still turning the leaves of Bancroft. Channing has no style, no gusto, no philosophy; indeed, when all is said, very little to recommend him except a distinct expertness of fact—and that is a very evanescent virtue. Bancroft has some qualities that are, as Sloane said, perdurable.

What Bancroft wished to do was to produce an historical epic of democracy, based upon fact but written in vivid and glowing language. He thought of his historical function as embracing some of the work of the poet and prophet. Was it an unworthy ideal? On the contrary, it was a very high and noble aim. And it was an ideal which he came near to attaining. His six volumes, in the edition revised in his old age, are truly an historical epic, and if we but read them through from beginning to end, as a poetically molded whole, we would understand the fervent enthusiasm which they inspired in millions of Americans during the nineteenth century. Viewed as an epic of freedom, the history is not so ill-proportioned as it seems when measured from the scientific point of view. We have the planting of the colonies; the conquest of the continent for the English race; and then as a grand climax, the struggle to attain freedom and nationality—a climax that is worthy of three volumes out of the six. Nor, if we look at the history as a prose epic, is the fervent exaltation of democracy and the consistent weighting of the scales in favor of the adherents of liberty such a defect as it might otherwise seem. To Bancroft, writing of heroic tendencies and events in an heroic way, there was much in his work which had a poetic truth even if it did not always have absolute truth in the prosaic sense. He focussed his attention upon the animating spirit which had brought a great population to the New World, hewed out homes and institutions in the wilderness, and created the United States of America, dedicated to freedom and equality. The spirit gave life where the word was death. He felt that he could write his history as a great philosophical and literary epic only if he used his materials freely, and he so used them.

Judging him by the criteria which he himself used—weighing him in the scales in which he wished and expected to be weighed—we can see that his greatest deficiency is a literary deficiency. If a literary and philosophical historian has the belletristic power of a Carlyle or a Michelet or even a Macaulay, who cares that his method is not rigidly scientific? Who would blame Bancroft for his factual deficiencies, his inability to estimate the Navigation Acts correctly, his failure to do justice to George III and Lord North, if he had written with the power and genius which went into Carlyle's *French Revolution?* The unhappy fact was that, while trying to write a great historical epic, he possessed only the equipment that is adequate for a scientific historian. The puny scientific tribe can always fall back upon their researches, their facts, their bibliographies—they do not need brilliancy of intellect and a pen tipped with lightning. Bancroft essayed a task which demanded gifts beyond his endowment. For all his education, his long preparation, his versatile experience, his intellectual power, there was not in him the light of genius that flamed in Gibbon, or Michelet, or Carlyle. He attempted to write a great philosophic history without having in any real sense a philosophic mind; he attempted to write a great poetic transcript of American experience and to seize the essence of the American experiment without having the power of divination required. Had he been willing to be another John Richard Green or another McMaster, he would today be more useful in the homely everyday sense in which any tool is useful. But let us honor him for the ambitious effort which he made and admit that in some of his chapters he did achieve effects worthy of the theme.

25

John Lothrop Motley

Allen Nevins's lectures on historiography would inevitably pay tribute, and highest tribute, to the triumvirate of literary historians—William Hickling Prescott, John Lothrop Motley, and Francis Parkman—whose works illuminated the Golden Age of American literature. These were men who brought the past alive to readers for a whole century, and beyond. They might lack the "scientific" exactness of twentieth-century scholars, but they possessed a far more valuable attribute in Nevins's eyes: the ability to write history, and good history, that would command a wide audience of lay readers. That he devoted a lecture to each is probable; unfortunately that on Prescott was not found among his papers, although his views on that historian are briefly stated in his introduction to Clinton Harvey Gardiner's *William Hickling Prescott: A Biography*, published in 1969. Sufficient to say that he ranked Prescott with Motley among the nation's greats. There could be no higher rung on the ladder of greatness, for Nevins saw John Lothrop Motley as virtually supreme among the world's literary historians, capable of breathing life into a record basically prosaic, and of endowing Holland's struggle for independence with all the drama of a mighty epic.

When we turn to John Lothrop Motley, we encounter a lesser figure than Prescott, and yet one admirably fitted to furnish a complement to the older historian's work. His personality contrasted in salient respects with that of the author of *The Conquest of Mexico*. Motley led a far more active, robust, and social life. Instead of blindness and invalidism, he had superb physical vigor. Instead of confinement to the state of Massachusetts, interrupted by only fleeting visits abroad, he was throughout his career a man of cosmopolitan contacts. After leaving Harvard he went to Göttingen, where he formed a friendship of lifelong cordiality with Bismarck, and there he took the keenest interest in Hanoverian life and manners. He naturally became acquainted with the best German scholarship in the field of history, reading Niebuhr, Von Ranke, and Sybel; so that far more than Prescott, he was affected by German ideas and models. But his European education was obtained less in the classroom than behind post-horses and on shipboard, for he traveled widely and displayed an omnivorous curiosity about all that he saw. It is to be noted that when he visited Rome, he thought not of research into institutions and laws after the German model, but of the tumultuous masses who had filled the Forum, and of the living waves of conquest which had broken over the city walls.

By temperament he was much more ardent and mercurial than Prescott. In times of good fortune he could be joyous and exuberant beyond measure; when adversity came, he was plunged into the depths of depression. He was a warmly sensitive, emotional, and expressive human being; his rich and varied nature had many facets, and it showed a different aspect to every observer. Responsive and cordial, he made innumerable friends in Europe and America in spite of his elegance of manner, his aristocratic pride of bearing, and his very distinct intellectual snobbishness. One of the handsomest of men, he was quite aware of the quick impression that he made upon cultivated and sensitive women. Genuinely imaginative like George Bancroft, Richard Hildreth, and Francis Parkman, he hoped at the outset that he might make his mark in pure literature. He wrote two novels, *Morton's Hope* and *Merry Mount*, which are rated by impartial critics as distinctly superior to Parkman's attempt in fiction, *Vassall Morton*, to Hildreth's early novel, *Archy Moore*, and to Bancroft's poems. An ambition to succeed in the more creative field of letters is by no means an unhappy omen in the early career of a historian. In *Merry Mount* Motley showed some ability to recreate the scenes of early New England life, and the training he received in writing of the jovial Anglicans who raised their Maypole at Wollaston Heights, the grim Puritans who so disapproved of their merrymaking, the old hermit of Boston, and other early colonial figures must have been valuable to him in his later work. But he soon saw that history was his forte. It appealed to his ardent mind as did nothing else. His lifework irresistibly forced itself upon him.

A singularly attractive and even captivating personage Motley was; and a singularly adventurous, interesting, and captivating career he led. No one has sketched it better in brief compass than Oliver Wendell Holmes. In the preface to his novel *A Mortal Antipathy*, the witty doctor offers a short autobiographical sketch. After glancing at the literary scene in New England and America during his young manhood, and telling how he came to begin the *Autocrat* papers in the *Atlantic Monthly*, he goes on to mention some of his other books. He speaks of the delight which he took in writing a memoir or short biography of Motley, a delight which arose out of the fact that he could thus live Motley's days over again:

> I saw him, the beautiful, bright-haired boy, with dark waving hair; the youthful scholar, first at Harvard, then at Göttingen and Berlin, the friend and companion of Bismarck; the young author, making a dash for renown as a novelist, and showing the elements which made his failures the promise of success in a larger field of literary labor; the delving historian, burying his fresh young manhood in the dusty alcoves of silent libraries, to come forth in the face of

Europe and America as one of the leading historians of the time; the diplomatist, accomplished, of captivating presence and manners, an ardent American, and in the time of trial an impassioned and eloquent advocate of the cause of freedom; reaching at last the summit of his ambition as minister at the Court of Saint James's. All this I seemed to share with him as I tracked his career from his birthplace in Dorchester and the house in Walnut Street where he passed his boyhood, to the palaces of Vienna and London. And then the cruel blow which struck him from the place he adorned; the great sorrow that darkened his later years; the invasion of illness, a threat that warned of danger, and after a period of invalidism, during a part of which I shared his most intimate daily life, the sudden, hardly unwelcome final summons. Did not my own consciousness migrate, or seem, at least, to transfer itself into this brilliant life history, as I traced its glowing record? I, too, seemed to feel the delight of carrying with me, as if they were my own, the charms of a presence which made its own welcome everywhere. I shared his heroic toils, I partook of his literary and social triumphs. I was honored by the marks of distinction which I gathered about him, I was wronged by the indignity from which he suffered, [I] mourned with him in his sorrow, and thus . . . I felt as if I should carry a part of his being with me so long as my self-consciousness might remain prisoned in the ponderable elements.

Motley, we have said, found his life work forcing itself upon him. He did not resolve to become a historian and then sit down to find a subject, as did Prescott. His general reading upon the European past and particularly upon the Renaissance and Reformation, fired his vivid imagination until he was seized by an ambition to undertake a subject which seemed to him one of the grandest themes of all that record. In 1846, after his short service as secretary of legation in St. Petersburg, he began to collect materials for a work on the grim sixteenth-century struggle of which Holland was the center. As he wrote to his friend William Amory, Prescott's brother-in-law: "I had not made up my mind to write a history, and then cast about to take up a subject. My subject had taken me up, drawn me on, and absorbed me into itself. It was necessary for me, it seemed, to write the book I had been thinking much of, even if it were destined to fall dead from the press, and I had no inclination or interest to write any other . . . It was not that I cared about writing a history, but that I felt an inevitable impulse to write *one particular history.*" And he went on to tell Amory of his famous interview with Prescott. The older writer, his fame long since secure, had himself determined to write the history of Philip II. But he generously encouraged the young man to enter the same field, as Irving had encouraged Prescott. Motley never ceased to feel the warmest gratitude. As he confided to Amory:

> Had the results of that interview been different—had he distinctly stated, or even vaguely hinted, that it would be as well if I should select some other topic, or had he only sprinkled me with the cold water of commonplace and conventional encouragement,—I should have gone from him with a chill upon my mind, and, no doubt, have laid down the pen at once. . . . You know how kindly he always spoke of and to me; and the generous manner in which, without the slightest hint from me, and entirely unexpected by me, he attracted the eyes of his hosts of readers to my forthcoming work, by so handsomely alluding to it in the Preface to his own, must be almost as fresh in your memory as it is in mine. . . . I fear that the history of literature will show that such instances of disinterested kindness are as rare as they are noble.

Like Prescott's writings, those of Motley show an instinctive taste for the dramatic. As a boy he had possessed histrionic tendencies, making miniature theaters and acting out his reading and his own invented stories. He had an irrepressible enthusiasm for grand scenes and heroic personages, to which he gave lifelike and artistic depiction. The vices and defects which are so unhappily inseparable from the German scientific method rolled

324

off him like rain from a water-proofed garment. Intensely interested in the flesh and blood of history, he cared nothing for its dry bones. Like Prescott, he was therefore a descriptive and narrative writer concerned with objective fact. But in his broad conception of his themes, his use of the past to teach great object-lessons to the present, he was more of a philosopher than Prescott. His history of the Netherlands was meant to go far beyond an eloquent and vivid record of the struggle of the Dutch people against civil and ecclesiastical tyranny. It was intended to illustrate certain great fundamental truths in government, politics, and religious development. In effect, it is a history of all western Europe during a crucial period—a history of the concluding phases of the Reformation, of the triumph of religious freedom over clerical absolutism, and of the emergence of Europe from the Middle Ages into the full light of the modern world. It shows the Protestant movement, after many vicissitudes, reaching its culmination, and the world well launched upon a new and more liberal era in religion, politics, and society.

Motley's titles, *The Rise of the Dutch Republic* and *The United Netherlands*, though not inaccurate, were unfortunate. They have led many people to think of his works as the history of a single small nation, when actually he deals with Spain, France, and England almost as fully as with Holland. He presents Philip II and William the Silent as the two principal antagonists of a complex struggle in which, directly or indirectly, a half dozen nations participated. A panorama covering most of the sixteenth century is unfolded. At the beginning of his history we see many elements of feudal civilization still persisting in Europe: Holland enchained, England weak, Spain gaining the sway over a vast empire; pre-Copernican ideas of this world and medieval ideas of the next in the ascendancy. At the close of his history, we see the modern lineaments of society, such as town life, distinctly marked; science making steady progress; Holland liberated; England, triumphant over the Armada, in the front rank of nations; France now the political leader of the Continent; and Spain sinking into decay. The great central event of the century under review, the axis and pivot of his seven volumes, was the establishment of Protestantism in northern Europe. After following Dutch history in these volumes down to 1609, he did not intend to go on with it in the seventeenth century and present the wars of Holland against Cromwell and Louis XIV. Instead, his plan was to write the history of the Thirty Years' War in Germany, a direct continuation of the great religious struggle, a mighty and tragic panorama.

The first part of Motley's history, the three volumes which are called *The Rise of the Dutch Republic*, and which have always been recognized as his best, met as enthusiastic a reception as Prescott's books. They were warmly praised by the best Dutch historians for their industry, conscientiousness, and grasp. British scholars, led by Froude, applauded them—though Froude thought Motley unjust to Queen Elizabeth. No one can deny that this work, if not always perfectly accurate and fair, is a tremendous story told with fascinating lucidity and ease. It begins with a description of the land, people, and civilization of Holland in the first half of the sixteenth century. After some pages upon Charles V, the narrative proper commences with his abdication in the year 1555. Motley relates how Philip II took up the reins of government in Spain and Holland, how the Reformation, the true cause of the Dutch revolt, spread steadily, and how the Inquisition, which he paints in somewhat too ghastly a hue, scattered oil on the flames it was meant to quench. From this point the familiar story proceeds with graphic and original detail, drawn by the author from every available archive. He traces the activities of Egmont, Horn, and the Prince of Orange; he tells of Philip's resolve to enforce the decrees of the Council of Trent; describes the popular storm aroused by his torturings and executions; relates how Alva was sent into the Netherlands to crush the revolt; describes the arrest of Egmont and Horn and their execution; and narrates the long years of war that followed, with the heroic feats of the Hollanders, the defense of Haarlem, the defeat of Alva's

326

fleet on the Zuyder Zee, and other stirring events, till, when freedom was in sight, William of Orange was assassinated. With this calamity of 1584, the first three volumes end.

It is a magnificent story, with half Europe for a background and some of the main forces of modern civilization hanging in the balance; and it is admirably told, for Motley's style possesses a force and a dignity that sometimes rises to eloquence. Yet it is marred by great faults. Motley was a less thorough workman than Prescott, and at numerous points his narrative has been radically corrected and improved by modern scholarship. He is too fierce a partisan, and throws his scenes upon the canvas in too lurid colors. William of Orange in his pages is the perfect hero; Alva and Philip are complete and utter scoundrels—or almost that. Of Philip he writes that "if there are vices—as possibly there are—from which he was exempt, it is because it is not permitted to human nature to be perfect in evil."

The four volumes of *The United Netherlands*, issued in 1860–67, cover the second great epoch in what he expected to be his story of "the eighty years' war for liberty." They begin with the independence of Holland virtually achieved, though not recognized, and extend from the death of William the Silent to the Twelve Years' Truce, or from 1584 to 1609. The first half of the work is as much a piece of English history as of Dutch. It deals with the period when the alliance of England and Holland against Spain was almost a political union, and the Earl of Leicester was governor of the United Provinces; and the narrative culminates in a stirring chapter on the defeat of the Great Armada. Motley never wrote anything better than his account of the tragic siege and loss of Antwerp, or his picture of the destruction of the Spanish fleet in 1588. The second half of *The United Netherlands* is inferior in interest. It contains no events which catch at the heart like the relief of Leyden or the inhuman massacre at Naarden, and no personalities which win our regard as William of Orange or Leicester do. Still, Philip and Elizabeth and Bloody Mary are involved, and the narrative comes to a logical conclusion with the triumph of the Hollanders in 1609. Motley carried the history on for a brief space with his *John of Barneveld*, which is ostensibly but not actually a biography. It presents a partial view of the causes of the Thirty Years' War, and has dramatic value in its picture of the struggle between the patriot martyr, Barneveld, and the ambitious soldier, Maurice the Stadholder, each determined to control the new Dutch state. But Motley never lived to complete his ambitious design by writing the history of the Thirty Years' War itself. He was drawn back into our diplomatic service, became minister to Austria and to England, and, after some years of ill health, died in 1877.

Motley's work, like Prescott's, was thus left unfinished. As a piece of historical tapestry, it has one superiority to Prescott's—its unity of pattern. Motley's books form a complete series, dealing with the very core of one of the great movements of civilization. The histories of the two conquests written by Prescott are, by comparison, mere colonizing episodes, detached from his main labors on Spanish history. But in other respects Motley is at a disadvantage. His strong prejudices frequently carry him away and make him unfair. Even Froude, as it has been said, saw the golden thread on the gown of the Dominican monk, but to Motley the gown seemed wholly black. He was weaker in analytical talent than Prescott, and his excellence in describing how events happened is often offset by his total inability to show why. He could not deal with a complicated situation, as in his chapters on Spanish diplomacy, with the perfect lucidity which Prescott usually commanded. Nevertheless, as long as men love a noble canvas, treated with sweep, color, and general correctness, if not with perfection of detail, Motley's books will continue to be read.

The principal ideas which Motley's works illustrate are, as we should expect, large and simple conceptions. If he held any beliefs as to the course of human history as complex as those which George Bancroft adumbrated, he nowhere states them. His principal tenets were his belief in human progress—a faith which he unquestioningly shared with most writers of his century—and his championship of freedom, political, religious, and intellectual, as the finest fruit of man's slow advance. This freedom, he held, found in democracy its strongest bulwark; and like Bancroft, he thought the American system of government the finest form of government yet evolved. "The more I see of other countries," he wrote in his diary in 1841, while residing in St. Petersburg, "the more I like America"; and he could have made the same statement in his last years in England and Holland. Naturally, he also believed that religious and intellectual freedom were better served by Protestantism than by Catholicism, but upon this subject he was not so narrowly dogmatic as to assert Catholicism irremediably bad. In economics, he was a typical Manchester Liberal, believing in free enterprise, unfettered trade, the restriction of governmental regulation or interference within the narrowest limits, and world peace. He was not so conservative as Herbert Spencer, but he was less advanced than John Stuart Mill. In all these respects, his mind was very much the mind of a highly educated American Protestant of his time; and though in writing to Holmes in 1867 he declared that the grand mission of America was "to uproot, not to conserve the dead and polished productions of former ages," and urged Holmes to see that his son became a "radical," Motley himself was always a conformist rather than a dissenter.

The successors of Motley have done far more to revise both his facts and his conclusions than have the successors of Prescott, or of Parkman. Not merely have scholarly monographs shed much new light upon Charles V, Margaret of Austria, Don Juan, William of Orange, Prince Maurice, and other great personages of his histories. Two comprehensive works on this period by Dutch historians have appeared, one written by Robert Fruin, the other by Petrus Johannes Blok; and both have done much to displace Motley as a trustworthy authority. In the eyes of these eminent Dutchmen, Motley was too romantic, too pictorial, and too dramatic. Fruin in particular objected that the American historian delighted so much in the spectacular that he lost sight of the distinctions between the important and the unimportant, and thus gave a distorted picture of the heroic period of Dutch history. Both Dutchmen also corrected a multitude of minor details in Motley's pages. In the pages of the Dutch critical review *De Gids* in 1859–60, Fruin, then about to be appointed the first professor of Dutch history since the restoration of the monarchy, pointed out many flaws in *Rise of the Dutch Republic*, as recently translated into Dutch with editorial notes by R. B. van den Brink, the national archivist. Fruin, in the preface to his third volume, later compared Motley with Schiller, the historian of the Thirty Years' War. "The work of these great word artists," he wrote, "entrance the reader rather than convince him of the justice of their presentations. Sound criticism, based upon comprehensive knowledge of the sources, did not come until after their time."

Today Fruin himself has been largely outdated. A comparison of the great synthesis by Petrus Blok, *The History of the Dutch People* (which has been translated into English by O. A. Bierstadt and H. Putnam), with Motley's histories, suggests that the American historian was defective on three main counts. In the first place, his passion for dramatic episodes and striking scenes did indeed, as the Dutch critics have said, lead to a certain distortion of historical truth. The actual events were less dramatic than his portrayal of them. More important than this was his exaggeration of the religious element in the great struggle of the Dutch for freedom. Both Fruin and Blok regard the Dutch revolt as a national upheaval against the Spanish oppressors, a patriotic rather than a Protestant movement; and they find in this interpretation a broader interpretation of its various phases. Finally, Motley was at fault—especially in his *History of the United Netherlands*—in paying inadequate attention to both economic and constitutional history. He lacked a thorough understanding of governmental and especially constitutional ideas on the continent of Europe in medieval and early modern times, and thus missed the true significance of some of the struggles which he narrated.

But it should be said that, after all subtractions have been made, Motley remains a historical classic to Dutch readers no less than to the English-speaking world. The translations of his volumes are in constant use in the Netherlands, and every literate person is familiar with them. Indeed, it may be said that he is now much more read in Holland than the first of his critics, Fruin; and that by virtue of his literary excellence he remains assured of general currency even though some of his conclusions have been rejected.

It is unfortunate that Motley still lacks a biographer. The thin memorial lecture or essay by Oliver Wendell Holmes is the only volume on his life. But he left a monument to himself in his warmly personal correspondence, which is worth the attention of anybody interested in nineteenth-century affairs.

In the two portly volumes of Motley's letters, edited in 1889 by George William Curtis, page ten brings us to his first voyage to Europe (1832); the last letter was written in 1877 from Kingston Russell in England. Almost everything between is European, for there were but flying voyages to Boston and Washington. There is much of interest about diplomatic life in its old stately character; much about the British intellectuals—Macaulay, Milman, Carlyle, Thackeray—a fine description of his lectures on the Georges and his appearance in 1858 ("a colossal infant, smooth, white, shiny ringlety hair, flaxen, alas, with the advancing years, a roundish face, with a little dab of a nose upon which it is a perpetual wonder how he keeps his spectacles, a sweet but rather piping voice")—John Bright, Disraeli, and others; a good deal about Bismarck. The Iron Chancellor, in his younger days, frisked about with Motley, enjoyed seeing him cock his heels above his head in the Yankee way, and learned that rollicking song, "In the good old Colony days." It is all urbane, pleasant, sunny and European. For a lazy evening before a fire it is amusing and not too stimulating reading.

But fortunately this placid current of European gossip is suddenly cut athwart by a torrent of real emotion, vigorous argument, conflicting hopes and anxieties—the Civil War has begun, and Motley is in an agony of sympathy with the North. There are argumentative letters to British friends—Mill, Bright, and the rest. There are heart-wrung letters of condolence to Lowell on the loss of his nephew and to Holmes on the wounding of his son. There are fierce denunciations of the South, fiercer expressions of devotion to the North. This cultivated cosmopolite suddenly awakes to find that he is after all an American, and that all his innermost convictions are bound up with American principles. As he writes his daughter from Vienna in the battle-autumn of 1864:

> For one, I like democracy. I don't say that it is pretty or genteel or jolly. But it has a reason for existing, and is a fact in America, and is founded on the immutable principles of reason and justice. Aristocracy certainly presents more brilliant social phenomena, more luxurious social enjoyments. Such a system is very cheerful for the few thousand select specimens out of the few hundred millions of the human race. It has been my lot and yours to see how much splendor, how much intellectual and physical refinement, how much enjoyment of the highest character has been created by the English aristocracy; but what a price is paid for it! Think of a human being working all day long, from six in the morning to seven at night, for fifteen to twenty kreutzers a day in Moravia or Bohemia, Ireland or Yorkshire, for forty or fifty years, to die in the workhouse at last: This is the lot of the great majority all over Europe; and yet they are of the same flesh and blood, the *natural* equals in every way of the Howards and Stanleys, Esterhazys and Lichtensteins.

This has the true American ring; and some day a biographer will arise to do justice to Motley's vibrant Americanism and his exuberant literary talents.

26

Francis Parkman

One might expect Allan Nevins to reserve his highest praise for Francis Parkman, the high priest of the literary historians of the Golden Age and by far the most enduring chronicler of his generation. That Nevins seems slightly restrained in his adulation is probably due less to a lack of enthusiasm for Parkman's writing talents than to a fascination with his methods. A historian who found his raw materials and atmosphere in the field rather than in books was bound to intrigue Nevins, who saw libraries and archives as temples of learning in which he spent most of his own life. Those who varied from this pattern, as did Francis Parkman, were worthy of comment. So Nevins deals much with his hero's career, but he also displays his usual good judgment in appraising and evaluating the various volumes in Parkman's monumental series on France and America.

The third in the trilogy of great Brahmin or Federalist-Whig historians of New England birth, Francis Parkman, was nine years younger than Motley and twenty-seven years younger than Prescott. Washington was still president when Prescott first saw the light, and Motley was christened in the midst of the second war with England. But Parkman was not born until 1823 and did not graduate from Harvard until, in 1844, Prescott had won international fame, and Motley, with two novels behind him, had chosen his great theme of the struggle for civil and religious liberty in sixteenth- and seventeenth-century Europe and embarked on his task. Parkman's career covered seventy years; he brought out the final volumes of his history in 1892 and died in the year of the Chicago World's Fair, of Cleveland's second inauguration, and of the great panic.

His lifetime thus covered the flowering of the old-style romantic and literary history in America and the first decades of the new period of specialization, minute research, and attention to scientific, rather than literary, effects. He himself owed his main allegiance to the old school of literary historians. Yet he possessed in much larger degree than Motley the new scientific temper of judicial impartiality and excelled even Prescott in his zeal for discovering primary sources and in the exhaustiveness and accuracy of his learning. So it was that the new scientific school claimed him for their own. John Fiske compared him in descriptive and narrative power with Macaulay or Froude, in objectivity with Gardiner, and in thoroughness of research with Stubbs.

Most historians are children of the library, and if they enter the great world, receive their training, like Macaulay and Irving and Motley, in political and diplomatic affairs. It is left for poets to consecrate themselves to nature, and for novelists to study the wide range of social life. The first fact which arrests attention in studying Parkman and his work is that he was a natural devotee of field, forest, and stream. His paternal grandfather was a Boston merchant, his father a wise and cultivated Unitarian clergyman of that city. The boy was not brought up in a city manse, however, but on the farm of his maternal grandfather at Medford, Massachusetts. Hard by Nathaniel Hall's farm lay the great forest of Middlesex Fells, some four thousand acres full of hills, cliffs, marsh, and pond, with wild animals and birds in abundance, as lonely, rough, and wild as the primeval forest. The imaginative boy saw in it a miniature version of the American wilderness; he became fascinated both by animal life—filling his pockets with reptiles and furry animals—and by mineralogy, beginning at a tender age a collection of rocks which he cherished and increased until old age.

Physically, he fitted the outdoors. He grew up to be a large man nearly six feet tall, square-shouldered, firm-jawed, and sturdily knit. He showed a robust energy, an intense love of hardship and adventure, and a vibrant manliness. When, as a student at Harvard, he undertook his rough journey in exploring those woods of northern New Hampshire where Rogers' Rangers had fought the Indians, he seemed ideally cast to be a historian of action and danger, of such subjects as western exploration and frontier warfare. Even after his health gave way, his friends always wrote of him as a person of vigorous pursuits rather than of the library and desk. "His whole carriage and expression," writes E. L. Godkin, "was that of a modest but resolute man, capable, in spite of whatever drawbacks and infirmities, of hard work and the persistent prosecution of difficult undertakings."

From his youth he showed the strong purposefulness, the determined will, that became so important a factor in his historical work. He chose his subject early; he prepared for it with more assiduity and energy than prudence; and he clung to his intention—which rapidly broadened as he grasped its full meaning—with grim persistence. While still in his teens he resolved to write the history of the final struggle between France and Britain for the possession of North America. As he first envisaged it, this apparently embraced little more than the French and Indian War; and what attracted him principally to the theme was the romantic character of the wilderness marches, scouts, and battles. "I decided," he later wrote, "to treat the history of the American forest; for this was the light in which I regarded it. My theme fascinated me, and I was haunted with wilderness images day and night."

335

But what began as a G. A. Henty or Cyrus Townsend Brady choice in historical composition was rapidly extended into an ampler, more dignified, and more philosophic theme—indeed, one of the grandest themes to be found in all modern history. He realized that he must carry the struggle back to its first beginnings, to the period of the Thirty Years' War in America, when in 1613 the English from Virginia almost wiped out the French in Port Royal, and when in 1629 an English fleet forced Champlain to surrender Quebec. He realized that he must bring within the panorama the whole story of French exploration, French missionary effort, French administration, the struggles between church and state, and the relations of both nations with the Indians. What was undertaken as an adventurous wilderness chronicle thus became the complex history of the ever-intensifying conflict, extending over 150 years, between two races, two cultures, and two religions, with the richest territory in the world as its prize. From Charles H. Farnham's brief and very imperfect biography it is difficult to make out just when, and by what degrees, this larger conception unfolded in Parkman's imagination; but it had certainly been completely realized when in the late 1850s he began work on *The Pioneers of France in the New World* (published 1865).

His self-imposed training for this task was as unique as his personality. He realized that his education could not be sought wholly or even principally in libraries. Apparently he felt a robust dislike of the still air of the book-room, an impatience that amounted to contempt for all mere pedants and scholars, a distaste for archives and dusty piles of manuscripts; he could discipline himself to work as hard as any Dryasdust, but he and his work had constantly to be aerated. Europe meant little to him in comparison with what it meant to Irving, Bancroft, Prescott, and Motley. The forest, the lake, the wilderness trail, and the prairie were his best school. Entering Harvard in 1840, he began his trips to the wilderness the following year, and had soon explored the wildest parts of Maine, New Hampshire, and the country about

Lake George and Lake Champlain. He took careful mental notes. As a mere freshman he wrote of his tramp up the Magalloway: "My chief object in coming so far was merely to have a taste of the half-savage kind of life necessary to be led, and to see the wilderness where it was as yet uninvaded by the hand of man." In his letters and notes he already showed that power in the vivid word-painting of natural scenes which was later so important a part of his equipment as historian. In a few sentences he could set a vista clearly before the eye:

From the high banks [of the Magalloway] huge old pines stooped forward over the water, the moss hanging from their aged branches, and behind rose a wall of foliage, green and thick, with no space or opening which the eye could penetrate. Soon the moon came up and glistened on the still river and half lighted the black forest. An owl, disturbed by the glare of our fire, sent forth a long wild cry from the depths of the woods, and was answered by the shrill bark of some other habitant of the forest.

Wherever he went he gathered notes on topography, impressions of untamed nature, and legends of frontier life and border conflict. In 1845 he explored the Great Lakes region to Sault Ste. Marie and Mackinac and in 1846 took the trip of 1,700 miles which enabled him to write his first book, *The California and Oregon Trail.* It is not one of his best works. It displays here and there an amateurish hand, and its interest is by no means unflagging. Yet it is a good adventure story, studded by fine passages of description. He had become an expert in woodcraft and an accurate shot with the rifle; he was a fine horseman; and he placed an excessive confidence in the power of his muscular body. Together with his friend and classmate Quincy Shaw, he passed several months with some friendly Sioux of the Oglallah family. He showed extraordinary power of adaptation to the wild habits and primitive fare of these savages, and gained a knowledge of the Indian mind that was invaluable to him in his later work.

Meanwhile, in his wanderings both east and west he cultivated his naturally keen zest for wild landscapes, for changes in weather and season, and for the life of bird and beast. An unspoiled forest or lake delighted him far more than the grandest scene of the Old World; and when he paid a visit to Italy for his health—a visit important for the knowledge of Catholic ways and ideas which it gave him—he wrote: "All here is like a finished picture; even the wildest rocks seem softened in the air of Italy. Give me Lake George, and the smell of the pine and the fir."

There is much in Parkman's character and temper which reminds us of a greater man and far greater writer, Sir Walter Scott. Both were highly cultivated, both suffered from severe physical handicaps, both made their fortune and fame by writing. But both were devoted to the outdoor world, to physical activity, to adventure in scenes of wild physical beauty; neither ever wrote a page which smelled of the lamp or of musty library walls. Both were stirred by peril and battle, and Parkman must often have repeated Scott's words—"Sound, sound the clarion, fill the fife; to all the sensual world proclaim; one crowded hour of glorious life, is worth a century without a name." Both loved the folklore, the legends, and the household tales of a vanished era; Scott of the border country between Saxon and Gael, Parkman of the still wilder border between French and English. The books of both are marked by the salient characteristic of *picturesqueness*; both have poetic sympathies and a high sense of color. Both were at heart Tories and aristocrats, and though Walter Scott had far more of warm social feeling for the common people than Parkman ever had, politically they held much the same convictions.

The parallel, of course, cannot be pushed to an extreme; the genius of Scott was a far richer, brighter flame than that of Parkman, while he had an ampler nature as well as a finer imagination. But there is nevertheless a real kinship between these two authors who disliked libraries and loved the blue sky, the tangled brake, and the gloomy mountain, who delighted in fiery action and in picturesque legend.

Parkman both essayed more and accomplished more than Prescott or Motley, for he had a stronger will and he suffered no real interruptions. The two older men left their work unfinished, but before Parkman died he had, by publishing eight different books in eleven volumes, wrought every part of his broad design. The undertaking occupied him during more than forty years, for he had begun composing *The Conspiracy of Pontiac* in 1848. The first volume in the sequence, when they are properly arranged, is the *Pioneers of France in the New World*. This is followed by *The Jesuits in North America* and by *La Salle and the Discovery of the Great West*, which complete the story of exploration and missionary enterprise. Then come *The Old Regime in Canada* and *Count Frontenac and New France*, which are concerned principally with the administration and internal development of French Canada, but which also begin the story of conflict with the English in King William's War, ending in the Peace of Ryswick the year after brave Frontenac's death (1698). In *A Half Century of Conflict* the tale is carried forward through the years 1700–48, with a spirited narrative of Queen Anne's War and King George's War—that is, the War of the Austrian Succession. Finally, in the two volumes of *Montcalm and Wolfe* we reach the masterpiece of the whole series. *The Conspiracy of Pontiac*, though the first written, furnishes a not very important crown to the whole design.

Parkman did not carefully plan his series of books as a whole and in detail; he simply plotted it in a general way and then allowed it to grow. He wrote *Montcalm and Wolfe* before he composed the *Half Century of Conflict*, which chronologically precedes it. If we look at his eight books as a general history either of New France or of the conflict between the French and the English, its design is in various ways radically defective. Some parts of the story are given excessive emphasis; some are very improperly slighted. Perhaps the work is best described as a history of French Canada which expands, when the year 1690 is reached, into a history of the struggle of the French and British for dominion in America. But even viewed in this light, the narrative is not altogether well proportioned or well arranged.

It was assuredly a mistake, viewing the series as a whole, to give almost half the first volume, *The Pioneers of France in the New World*, to an account of the abortive attempt of Ribaut, Laudonniere, and others to establish a French colony in Florida. That attempt, and the conflict with Spain which it provoked, is an interesting little tale; but it had no lasting significance whatever, it is connected neither with the history of French Canada nor that of the Anglo-French conflict, and it stands as a detached and rather pointless historical essay. It would have been better had Parkman, beginning with Jacques Cartier's voyages of 1534–35, given more space to them and to the French fishing and fur-trading enterprises in Canada which preceded the advent of Samuel de Champlain in 1603. Later on, Parkman grossly neglects the activities of the French in the Ohio and Mississippi valleys, and at points farther west, that is, he neglects it in the sense of giving it quite inadequate study and space. He tells most nobly the story of Marquette, La Salle, and Joliet. He is fairly satisfactory in treating of Detroit, if not of Michilimackinac.

But the whole history of Louisiana from its beginnings in 1697 down to the year 1750 receives only one chapter (in the *Half Century of Conflict*), which does not extend to thirty pages. The account of the establishment and maintenance of the chain of posts with which France, in the first half of the eighteenth century, joined her colony in Canada to her colony in Louisiana, is equally thin and unsatisfactory. And the history of the trans-Mississippi explorations of La Veredrye and others is not only inaccurate from the modern point of view, but is allotted insufficient space and emphasis. The West was of crucial importance in the conflict of France and Britain in the New World. Able leaders on both sides began to see as early as 1700 that the control of the interior was the vital point on which all else depended. Yet such is Parkman's apportionment of space that readers of his eight books would not readily grasp the fact.

The fact is that Parkman ought to have written nine different books—perhaps even ten—rather than eight. He begins well. The first epoch in the history of French Canada is that thirty-five- or forty-year period coterminous with the career of Champlain. He sailed up the St. Lawrence in 1603. He helped next year to found Port Royal (Annapolis) in Nova Scotia. Until his death in 1635 he labored to develop Canada as a French colony, to spur on the work of exploration—he himself reaching Lakes Champlain, Ontario, and Huron—and to make the fur trade profitable.

The second era in the history of French Canada is that of the missionary activities under the Franciscans, the Recollets, the Ursulines, and above all the Jesuits, an era which began to end when in 1649 the Iroquois virtually wiped out the Huron tribesmen among whom the Jesuits had met the greatest success. Commercially also the colony was a failure in these years. The year 1660 found not more than two thousand French people settled in the whole land. Parkman treats this heroic but by no means fruitful or triumphant period admirably in *The Jesuits in North America*.

Then came a third era. A new company was formed—The Company of the West Indies—to develop the colony; Louis XIV began taking a personal interest in it; fresh shiploads of colonists were sent out; New France became a royal province. A young churchman arrived at Quebec in 1659, Francois Xavier de Laval-Montmorency—best known as de Laval—who had resolved that Canada should be ruled by the church, and under a regime as strict and austere as that of the Puritan theocracy in New England. His mark is upon Quebec's life still. He came into conflict with governor after governor, but usually he had his own way. This is the era of which Parkman treats, again admirably, in *The Old Regime*. At the same time, in the years 1659 to 1682, the explorers were busy in the Far West—Radisson, Groseilliers, Joliet, Marquette, and above all La Salle. To them Parkman devoted one of the most fascinating of his books, *La Salle and the Great West*. The fourth era was ushered in by the arrival of the

341

Comte de Frontenac, in 1672, as governor of New France. He was a man of determination and iron strength. He asserted the dominance of the civil authorities over the church in ruling the province; he broke the strength of the Iroquois; he fought off Sir William Phips's expedition against Quebec in King William's War; and before he died at the close of the century, he had begun preparing New France for the desperate struggle which all men of vision saw must be fought out with the British. This story could not be better told than in Parkman's *Count Frontenac and New France.*

So far, in his first five books, Parkman has done admirably. *The Pioneers of New France* lacks unity, but that fault, arising from the attempt to treat both the Florida colony and Champlain's work, is the only notable defect. But Parkman, after giving five volumes to the first century of New France, or rather less than the first century (1603–98), essayed to cover a crowded half-century of Anglo-French history in America in the two volumes which he gave the most colorless and vague of his titles. Comprehending so much history, the *Half Century of Conflict* lacks unity, sprawling as does no other of Parkman's works. Its chief weakness, however, is its want of vigor, energy, and scholarly thoroughness. It contains fine elements. But too much had to be combined within the covers of one not very long work.

Here are interesting personalities to be drawn—Cadillac, Bienville, Vaudreuil, Iberville, and Charlevoix on the French side; Shirley, Pepperell, and Dummer on the English; here are two blood wars, those of the Spanish Succession and the Austrian Succession, with sieges, battles, and sickening border raids; here is the foundation of two great cities, Detroit and New Orleans, and the rise of the colony of Louisiana; here are fresh administrative changes in New France, and additional conflicts between church and civil authorities; here is the development of agriculture as well as the fur trade, with fifty or sixty thousand French colonists finally settled in the valley of the St. Lawrence and the maritime areas; here are the capture of Louisbourg, the deportation of the

Acadians, the founding of Halifax, and the colonization of Nova
Scotia; here is the establishment of the chain of posts reaching
from Niagara down the Mississippi, and the Far Western explorations already mentioned. The subject offers matter enough for
two books. Had Parkman, the sands of whose life were now
ebbing away, written those two books—had he closed the first
with the Treaty of Utrecht and its immediate sequels, and opened
the second with the outbreak of King George's War, making each
book full and thorough—his great series would be without the one
glaring weakness which it now shows.

But this one great defect ought not to diminish our admiration
for the volumes which precede the *Half Century of Conflict,* or
for the masterly work on Montcalm and Wolfe which follows it.
Parkman's search for material was so painstaking, his use of it was
so painstaking and so impartial, and the alembic of his concise but
eloquent style is so magical, that his best works are perdurable.
They are truly made—as Carlyle said permanent books would
have to be—of asbestos.

If in Prescott we are impressed by color and in Motley by
eloquence, in Parkman the abiding power is of vividness. Again
and again he gives the reader the sense of having all but watched
his scenes unfold. His powers of inward visualization were
apparently stimulated by his physical blindness, which compelled
him, listening to books and documents with eyes shut, to form a
distinct mental impression of his subject. Whereas Prescott and
Motley saw history as drama, Parkman saw it as a series of
pictures. His greatest gift lay in description, and his inspiration
was particularly fine when he had to deal with a wild natural
background. In these eleven volumes we constantly feel a sense of
the great wild shaggy continent as a setting for the conflict of race,
culture, and religion which the English so decisively won; while in
reading of a specific scene, such as La Salle on the Mississippi, or
Father Jogues penetrating the New York wilderness, or Robert
Rogers stealing through the snowy forest to a surprise attack,
Parkman's sense for form, color, and sound recreates the whole

drama before us. He sometimes reminds us of Michelet's famous remark that history is not narration, as Thierry thought, or analysis, as Guizot believed: "it is resurrection."

Like Motley, Francis Parkman tells the story of a momentous conflict between democracy and absolutism, between free institutions and a rigidly disciplined despotism; and many parallels might be drawn between the struggle of Holland and Britain against Spain and the struggle of the British colonists in America against New France. In both instances mighty consequences hung upon the issue of the combat. The extinction or survival of political, religious, and economic freedom in all Northern Europe was at stake in the resistance which the Hollanders under William of Orange and the Britons under Elizabeth offered to Philip of Spain. The ultimate sovereignty of North America and the whole character of the civilization of its peoples were at stake in the battles between the regimented forces of New France and the free, untrammeled, spontaneously vigorous forces of New England. In both instances the outcome of the tremendous grapple was heartening to those who believe in the superiority of a free society.

It would be difficult to say which historian had the grander theme. But it is Parkman's subject which, for two reasons, has the stronger appeal to American readers. It is our own history that he writes—the molding of our own institutions of which he treats. And in the second place, picturesque as sixteenth-century Europe is, with its steady emergence of modern ways of life from medieval ideas, laws, and customs, a greater picturesqueness attaches to seventeenth- and eighteenth-century America—to the vast rugged wilderness that was the setting for the conflict and to the barbaric stone age tribes who were caught up as participants in the long-drawn succession of wars.

Yet in the middle of the nineteenth century neither the weightiness of Parkman's theme nor the wild picturesqueness of his background was readily apparent to most Americans. His imagination seized upon the possibilities of a subject which others regarded disdainfully. Every educated man could see the tremendous importance of Motley's work, could realize that he touched the central elements in the battle of liberty against repression, of modern against medieval ideals. But at first few could perceive that Parkman had set hand to an equally imposing canvas.

John Fiske tells us that in 1865, passing the pleasant windows of the book shop of Little, Brown & Co. in Boston, he noticed a book called *Pioneers of France in the New World* and recalled the author as having written an older volume entitled *The Conspiracy of Pontiac*. He remembered also that he had once taken down this latter work "just to quiet a lazy doubt as to whether Pontiac might be the name of a man or a place." If that conspiracy had been an event of Merovingian Gaul or Borgia's Italy, he adds, he would have felt a twinge of conscience in not instantly recognizing it; "but the deeds of feathered and painted red men on the Great Lakes and the Alleghenies, only a century old, seemed remote and trivial." Fiske also tells us that in his early years he heard it said that the story of the French and Indian War was something of no more interest to later Americans than the cuneiform records of an insurrection in ancient Nineveh. That struggle was actually treated, late in the nineteenth century, in a book entitled *Minor Wars of the United States*. It was Parkman's genius that, as early as his college years, discerned at least indistinctly the epic proportions, the tremendous implications of his theme. Before he had completed it, the reading public of America, Britain, and France—for he was quickly translated into French—had comprehended it too.

Parkman was happy in his temperament and his time as well as in his literary gifts. His temperament, bold, adventurous, and romantic, with a passionate love of the wilderness which reminds us of John Muir, enabled him to make the most of his picturesque background of forest, mountain, lake, and torrent. Do we say background? The untamed forest, the stormy waters, the broad prairies, were active factors, impersonal participants, in the history which he recorded. To leave Nature out of the contest between

Britain and France in the New World would have been to omit one of the most powerful elements. No one could have done full justice to its role who did not feel a powerful sympathy for it; and Parkman delineated it with an affectionate understanding. He treats geography not as a cold scientific element in the flow of events, but as real and immediate force, as clearly envisioned as any human personage of the drama.

He was fortunate in his time because he took up the pen when it was still possible to study both the shaggy wilds of North America and the red tribes who dwelt amid them in something like their pristine state. By going into the pathless woods of northern New Hampshire, lower Quebec, and the Adirondacks, Parkman could see the country over which French and British armies and Indian war parties had marched much as they had seen it. By taking his summer trip to the West and spending months among the Sioux Indians, not without peril to life, he could study the aborigines as they had been for centuries past—he could realize accurately what the Chickahoming tribes seen by John Smith, the Mohawks known to Sir William Johnson, the Hurons converted by the Jesuit missionaries, had been like. A historian born a generation later would have had no such opportunity.

The treatment which he gave his materials was that of a romantic artist whose natural exuberance is held in check by a grimly powerful Puritan conscience. His first historical book, *The Conspiracy of Pontiac,* showed more of his unfettered bent than the subsequent works and was later condemned by him (with some justice) as turgid and rhetorical. Much might be said in this connection of the view which he took of the Indian. Cooper was one of his favorite authors; and it is clear from a hundred pages that he would have liked to romanticize the savage. But he resisted the temptation, and, aided by his personal knowledge of the Sioux, gave so cool and objective a portrait of the Indian that it has been criticized by philanthropic persons as lacking in sympathy. He regarded them as survivors of the stone age and, while not slighting their better characteristics, did not conceal

their squalor, ignorance, and vengefulness. Any practical frontiersman of the time would have endorsed Parkman's attitude. In his
treatment of wilderness scenes, of forest, lake, and mountain, we
find the same natural romanticism curbed by a dutiful restraint.
His bent was toward bold and striking effects; yet he learned to be
minutely realistic in his descriptions of persons and places, and he
mastered enough of geology and botany to give cold scientific
accuracy to his observations. This "passionate Puritan," as his
daughter called him, described the whole triple conflict of Indian,
Frenchman, and Briton under the sway of the same conflicting
impulses: an intense delight in the romance of it all, an eager
interest in the pictorial and adventurous elements, held in leash by
a cool scientific interest in analyzing the defects of French
institutions (notably in the Old Regime), and in showing how
Anglo-Saxon practicality, democracy, and strength of character
overthrew them. He painted a vivid panorama in colors that will
be undying, and that later writers, who must lack his special
knowledge of the forest and Indian, can never match. He told a
story with fascinating narrative power. But he also, no less than
Motley or Bancroft, taught a lesson.

The pages are full of examples which prove that if the French
idea failed of realization, it was not from any lack of lofty qualities
in individual Frenchmen. In all the history of the American
continent no names stand higher than some of the French names.
For courage, for fortitude and high resolve, for sagacious leadership, statesmanlike wisdom, unswerving integrity, devoted loyalty,
for all the qualities which make the heroic, we may learn lessons
innumerable from the devoted Frenchmen who throng in Parkman's pages. The difficulty was not in the individuals, but in the
system; not in the units, but in the way they were put together.
For while it is true—though many people do not know it—that by
no imaginable artifice can you make a society that is better than
the human units you put into it, it is also true that nothing is
easier than to make a society that is worse than its units. So it was
with the colony of New France.

347

27

Hermann Eduard von Holst

When Allan Nevins faced the task of appraising von Holst's contributions to American historiography for his Columbia students, he could summon little of the enthusiasm that added sparkle to his evaluations of Motley and Parkman. His apathy is understandable, for von Holst not only adjusted facts to plead for his own biases but made few pretensions to literary greatness. This, to Nevins, was the cardinal sin. George Bancroft might err in his over-glorification of God, country, and democracy, but at least he tried to compose a literary epic. Von Holst did not. Hence he was entitled to a less thorough treatment than allotted the giants; this treatment, moreover, would focus more on his sins than his virtues. In this brief lecture, Nevins spends perhaps more time than is warranted on von Holst's accounts of the Mexican War, the Dred Scott decision, and comparable episodes that deserve criticism than he does on others warranting commendation. He succeeds, however, in telling us a good deal about von Holst and something more about Allan Nevins.

There is little danger nowadays that we shall overrate the achievement of Hermann E. von Holst; there is great danger that we shall underrate it. To begin to understand its magnitude, we must fix clearly in mind two facts: first, his foreign birth and upbringing; and second, the earliness of the date at which he began to publish his seven-volume history of the United States. That large work, which he entitled *The Constitutional and Political History of the United States*, but whose publishers very improperly used only the word *Constitutional* on the cover, is now little used. Its chief value today lies in its careful use of a large number of pamphlets, monographs, legal papers, and Congressional speeches not readily accessible elsewhere. It has been superseded, though it still has a supplementary usefulness in connection with McMaster, Schouler, Adams, Rhodes, and other writers. But when published it was a monumental piece of history, it was highly useful to a whole generation which had nothing better, and it did much to smooth the way for subsequent writers.

Von Holst was the only Continental European to have written an extended work upon the history of the United States—a fact which in itself should entitle him to praise. His career had some heroic chapters. The son of a poor Estonian parson, he raised himself out of poverty. Born in 1841, he took his doctorate at Heidelberg in 1865; he earned his bread for a time as a private tutor in St. Petersburg; and then in 1867 he published a pamphlet in which he passionately indicted the Russian government. The result was an order for his arrest. He might have remained in Germany, where he had studied. But apparently America appealed to him as a land of perfect liberty, and in the summer of 1867 he landed in New York. He had no money, no friends, no clear idea of what he should do to make a living. At first he lived in one unheated slum room with three other men, working as a day laborer. But his education enabled him to become a tutor again. He began writing for a Cologne newspaper, and after two years he became assistant editor of a German-American Encyclopaedia (*Deutsch-Amerikanisches Konversations-Lexicon*). Even in 1868 he had gone into politics as an opponent of Tammany and a stump-speaker for Grant. Meanwhile, he maintained his personal connections with German men of learning, particularly Heinrich von Sybel of Bonn University. It was von Sybel who, when a group of Bremen merchants sought somebody to prepare an expert account of the operations of universal manhood suffrage in America, recommended von Holst; and the young man's labors on the subject fired him with a determination to write a long, impartial, and exhaustive history of the workings of democracy in this country.

This in itself was rather heroic—he was but twenty-eight or twenty-nine at the time, and the field he meant to enter had been largely unbroken. And still more heroic was the way in which he carried it through. At the age of forty he was stricken with a painful disease of the stomach. This he attributed to the poor food and hardships of childhood life in his father's parsonage, but his physical weakness had probably been accentuated by the privations he had undergone in his first winter in America. He showed grim endurance. "You would never learn from him," remarks a writer in the *Nation* for January 28, 1904, just after his death, "that he was most of the time in severe physical pain; nevertheless, the greater part of his intellectual work was done in such a physical condition that many men would have gone to the hospital and comfortably given up the ghost. Disease and suffering often laid him by for long periods together, but if he could sit at his desk at all, he worked with a thoroughness and application which were in themselves a lesson to the student." Resolute in facing difficulties, he carried through his history of democracy in America from the end of the Revolution to the beginning of the Civil War in almost precisely twenty years. During half of this period he was an ill man. Throughout all of it he was busy teaching. He had gone back to Germany to become professor in the new University of Strasbourg in 1872, and two years later went to Freiburg, making a great reputation as lecturer, writer, and public speaker. For a time he sat in the upper chamber of the

Baden Parliament, and in 1890 he was an anti-Bismarckian candidate for a seat in the German Reichstag. Yet in spite of his physical weakness and his many activities, he completed his history in 1892. It is clear that he was a man of iron will and vigorous personality.

The first volume of the history was issued in 1873—a date which itself tells us much. At that time no writer of any importance, save Hildreth, had entered upon the period of American history following the Revolution. Schouler was meditating his own work, but had not progressed beyond some note taking and some unsuccessful negotiations with publishers. McMaster was not to issue his first volume for a decade. Fiske was still immersed in philosophy and science. Von Holst had to hew his way through an untracked forest; and he had to compose a careful and satisfactory narrative while as yet few materials had been collected. He possessed a German thoroughness, and a true historian's appreciation for original sources. "Anyone," declared a friend, "who frequently went in and out of his house, sat at his table, and entered his library can bear testimony to the steady, unwearying use of sources which enabled the historian to come to his own conclusions." Because of his residence abroad, nearly all of these sources were printed; like Hildreth, he made slight use of manuscripts. But of the printed debates of Congress; of various newspapers, notably the *New York Tribune*, the *National Intelligencer*, and later the *Independent*; of Congressional and executive reports; of political biographies, memoirs, and pamphlets; and of the collected works of leading American statesmen, he made most full and careful use. His own library, while not enormous, was well selected, comprising some of the most important American sources; and while in Germany he made frequent trips to the British Museum, with its large American collections. "He was one of the first writers on American history to realize the wealth of fact and contemporary discussion to be found in the records of Congressional debates, and in the newspapers; and his patient and persistent labor among these different sources gave him his sureness of grasp on questions of political motive and tendency." His position as a pioneer ought never to be forgotten.

The great weakness of von Holst's history has of course been pointed out a hundred times. He began with a clearly formed set of preconceptions and made his facts conform to them. The character of these preconceptions is readily explicable. Reared in Estonia under a tyrannous Russian government, he became a natural devotee of political liberty. Reading Laboulaye on American institutions while still a student in Germany, he formed an exalted idea of the power and purity of free institutions in America. He came to this country immediately after the close of the Civil War, and settling in the triumphant North, found that everyone accepted as a matter of course the doctrine that the outcome of the recent struggle had vindicated all the Northern positions upon slavery. The intellectual atmosphere in which he moved from the beginning was the atmosphere made by Horace Greeley and Carl Schurz, William Cullen Bryant and Henry Ward Beecher, Charles Sumner and Thaddeus Stevens. He accepted the radical Republican point of view with regard to the South and its peculiar institution. Everyone regarded the Civil War as the natural consequence of the folly and stubbornness of the Southern people in maintaining and seeking to extend an immoral and anachronistic institution. In defending slavery, the Southerners had espoused utterly untenable principles of state sovereignty. A protracted moral and political struggle had finally culminated in the terrible conflict. In some lights this war had been a terrible calamity; but it had brought the republic certain invaluable benefits in extinguishing slavery, destroying extreme ideas of state sovereignty, and giving the republic a new birth of freedom.

Adopting this basic concept of the first period of American national history as a period of struggle between slavery and freedom, between nationalism and disintegrating state rights, von Holst wrote his seven-volume history about it. The sources of information from which he drew his facts and ideas, as his history proceeded, were primarily Northern. In using and appraising his materials, he gave emphasis to those which upheld the antislavery thesis and ignored or depreciated those of Southern tendency. When he quotes Calhoun, Cass, Jefferson Davis, Toombs, Douglas, and others of their schools, it is usually for the purpose of pithily refuting them. His history is so thesis-ridden that it is—from our present-day point of view—poorly constructed. Only three volumes are required to bring him down to 1850, for the slavery question was not of paramount importance in the first seventy years of national life. Then four more are required to carry the story from 1850 to 1860. No one would infer from the first three volumes of his work that the great topics of national dispute and agitation were territorial expansion, the embargo, the tariff, the United States Bank, internal improvements, the Treasury, the navy, the wars with France, England, and the Barbary pirates, the personalities of Jefferson and Old Hickory and William Henry Harrison, the appointments to office. No one would dream from these volumes that the United States in these seventy years had undergone an economic and intellectual development of the most astonishing character. What interested von Holst was slavery, viewed in the light of an advancing disease, finally extirpated by an operation which almost cost the life of the patient; and about that conception he has cast his whole book. It is, as we see now, an unscientific and misleading conception, and his whole work is vitiated in consequence.

Take, for example, his treatment of the Mexican War, the origins of which he both distorts and oversimplifies. The very titles of his chapters are unduly tendentious: "Polk Weaves the Warp of the Mexican War," and "The War of Polk the Mendacious." Biographers of Polk and the editors of his diary have substituted for the old Whig caricature of a mean-spirited, sinuous, and untrustworthy politician the portrait of a conscientious, laborious, and high-minded leader of statesmanlike views. Historians of the Mexican War have dispelled the idea that it was a discreditable enterprise of unscrupulous expansionists, eager for more territory on which to erect slave pens, and have shown that the greater part of the blame for the collision of the two republics rested upon Mexico.

Von Holst treats the annexation of Texas by joint resolution of the two houses of Congress as both unjustifiable and unconstitutional: unjustifiable on ethical grounds, unconstitutional because the Senate should have been allowed to vote on a treaty of annexation. He takes the view that the whole movement for making Texas a part of the Union was given its principal energy by a foul plot of the slaveholding South to add to its power. He insists that the ensuing war was a conflict of unblushing imperialism, premeditated by Polk, skillfully made possible by his diplomacy, and finally provoked by troop movements which he ordered. At the least, this can be pronounced a hopelessly one-sided view. American settlement in Texas was not part of a plot, but a natural advance of the frontier in which Southerners for plain geographical reasons and no others played the leading part. The revolt of the American settlers in Texas was a justified uprising against intolerable oppressions. The demand for annexation was quite inevitable, and in view of European interest in Texas, the American government would have been grossly remiss had it not made the most of the opportunity. After this annexation had been accomplished, the Mexican government showed less reasonableness of temper than the Polk administration. Mexican pride had naturally been wounded by the loss of the fair Texan province. In addition, many Mexicans of the upper classes feared that democratic ideas would spread from the United States into their country; most Mexicans felt a strong prejudice against foreigners, and especially Protestants, while they held Americans in contempt; Mexican politicians, anxious to display their patriotism and fearlessness, encouraged the feeling against Americans; Mexican army men believed that the United States was feeble in a military sense; they thought that Mexico, protected by her deserts and mountains, held a superior strategic position; and they hoped for assistance from Britain and France. As Justin H. Smith puts it, "the press clamored for war; the government was deeply committed to that policy; and the great majority of those who counted for anything, panting feverishly, though with occasional shivers, to fight the United States, were passionately determined that no amicable and fair adjustment of the pending difficulties should be made." Smith perhaps puts the case against Mexico not much too strongly when he sums it up in these words:

> Mexico, our next neighbor, on no grounds that could be recognized by the United States, repudiated her treaties with us, ended official relations, aimed to prevent commercial intercourse, planned to deprive us of all influence on certain issues vitally connected with our declared foreign policy, seemed likely to sell California to some European rival of ours, made it impossible for us to urge long-standing claims or watch over citizens dwelling within her borders, refused to pay her admitted debts to us, claimed the privilege of applying to our government publicly the most opprobrious epithets in the vocabulary of nations, . . . and proposed to assume such an attitude that, whether by foreign support or any other circumstances, she could open fire upon us without even giving notice.

Von Holst insists that the desire to annex California was one of the real mainsprings of the Mexican War. He dilates upon Polk's eagerness for that half-independent province, upon the newspaper articles calling for its acquisition, and upon Cass's speech in the Senate late in 1844 calling for action. But Justin H. Smith points out that when Polk sent Slidell on his fruitless mission to Mexico City, while he instructed that envoy "to obtain the cession of northern California, if he could," he directed that he "should not press the matter, if so doing would prevent the restoration of amicable relations with Mexico."

The attitude of the American people, in the eyes of Smith, was much less open to reproach than that of the Mexicans. To be sure, the motives of territorial aggrandizement and the belief in the "manifest destiny" of America to occupy the whole continent were discreditable. Many of those who strove to whip up a demand for war had an eye on their political advancement. But both Rives and Smith point to the solid grounds which the American people had for resentment. They had suffered a long series of grievances without redress; the American flag and American ministers had been insulted; property had been confiscated; our citizens had been maltreated; and as a climactic irritation, Slidell's mission had been inexcusably rejected. The country had some grounds, too, for feeling that Mexico might allow Britain and France to use her, or at least parts of her territory, for purposes of their own.

A fair view would seem to be that war began because both Washington and Mexico City miscalculated the situation. The Polk administration believed until near the end that a peaceful adjustment could be reached. It supposed that if pressure for the settlement of American claims and for the readjustment of the boundary was combined with conciliatory words and an offer of money, Mexico would yield. As soon as the government realized the gravity of the situation, it would recede and grant most of the American demands, even for the sale of California. Polk did not understand that Mexican blood easily grew heated, that an insult to the honor of anyone of Spanish stock is deeply resented. He did not sufficiently comprehend that the Mexican government was afraid of popular anger and a revolution at home if it yielded to humiliating conditions. The Mexicans, on the other hand, miscalculated with equal blindness. They did not realize that Polk could not and would not compromise on the boundaries of Texas—that he would insist on the Rio Grande as the southern limit. They did not understand how important it seemed to Polk, Bancroft, Buchanan, and the whole American people that California, a weak state attached to Mexico by a thread, should not be allowed to fall into British hands. They did not perceive that a long train of small injuries was irritating American opinion to the point

where war seemed proper. Hence it was that when Mexico made
the error of rebuffing Slidell, the Polk administration made the
countererror of ordering Zachary Taylor's army to march from the
Nueces to the Rio Grande. And hence it was that when a skirmish
occurred on April 24, 1846, both nations rushed to arms.

In dealing with the period following the Mexican War, von
Holst was as partial, prejudiced, and vituperative as in treating of
that conflict. Of the Dred Scott decision he writes that it would
"remain the greatest political atrocity of which a court had ever
been guilty even if the reasoning of Chief Justice Taney, who
delivered the opinion of the majority, was as unassailable and
convincing, historically and constitutionally, as it was in fact
wrong, sophistical, and illogical." One may feel that the Dred
Scott decision was a great error without ceasing to believe that
Taney's motives were high, and that once his premises were
granted, his historical and constitutional arguments had a great
deal of force. The fact is that the Constitution was highly
ambiguous respecting the limits of Congressional authority in the
territories, and on this ambiguity two honest opinions of diametri-
cally opposite character might be founded. Von Holst calls
Buchanan "train-bearer to the slaveocracy," adding that "once he
had lifted its train, he could no more drop it than could the boy in
the fairy tale tear away his finger from the feathers of the golden
goose." Slaveocracy is not the name for the Southern leaders, and
we may believe Buchanan excessively subservient to Southern
opinion without regarding him as its menial servant. Von Holst is
always ready to think the worst of Douglas. Even in the battle
over the Lecompton constitution, he writes, Douglas's "fidelity to
principle was much more like a worn-out and tattered garment
than an impenetrable coat of mail." Of Seward's "irrepressible
conflict" speech he states that the central sentence was "a phrase
of happy invention," when actually it was the most unfortunate utterance in Seward's life. Throughout the final volumes of
the history, in fact, the point of view is that of the *Liberator* and
the *Independent*.

357

It was natural that, tracing in detail the great sectional quarrel and keeping his eyes constantly fixed upon the dark blot of slavery, von Holst should seem to arrive at the conclusion that American institutions were less beneficent and wholesome than he had at first supposed. His reviewers accused him of belittling the republic, its leaders, and its political machinery. European readers, too, remarked that he was a harsh critic of the American way of life, giving its governmental aspects almost unqualified condemnation. But this he always denied. His attitude, he insists, is friendly. He states that when he first came to America, filled with the high expectations taught him by Laboulaye, he was disillusioned to find Tammany Hall what it was. But before long he adjusted his position. He learned, he writes, "that here was only an act of the one great drama, the history of western civilization; and that . . . the players in it, the principal ones as well as the great mass, were neither demigods nor devils, but *men,* struggling under many shortcomings, but with great energy, their way onward, not with startling leaps, but advancing step by step, just as all the rest of the great nations of the earth have had to do."

28

John Bach McMaster

John Bach McMaster, whose voluminous eight-volume *History of the People of the United States* was published between 1883 and 1913, hardly seems the sort of historian to stir Allan Nevins's enthusiasm. Largely forgotten today, and never popular in the sense of a Motley or a Parkman, McMaster made few pretensions to comprehensive research and fewer still to literary excellence; his organization was faulty, his interpretations insignificant, his sources largely newspaper files, and his style unpretentious. Yet Nevins views him with somewhat greater tolerance than he does von Holst and paints a surprisingly flattering picture of his influence on historical writing. He concludes that portions of McMaster's multivolume history are still usable today, but that his uncritical use of sources, his failure to recognize the importance of leaders, and his inability to fit his findings into a meaningful structure doom him to a minor role among the major recorders of the nation's past. This previously unpublished lecture, probably given to the Columbia students in the "Great Literature of American History" course, was found in manuscript among the papers left by Nevins on his death.

Few stories in the record of American scholarship are better known than that of the debut of John Bach McMaster as a historian. It is the story of a small, shy young man who, although by profession a civil engineer, had at an early age been fired with an ambition to do for the life of the American people what Macaulay had done for the life of England in his famous chapter on the kingdom in 1685; who had devoted the leisure of several years to the production of a bulky manuscript; and who one day in 1881 deposited it at the offices of D. Appleton Company. The response of Appleton's readers was chilly; but Mr. Appleton himself picked it up, took it home, and began to read it to members of his family. They were fascinated, and the next day young Mr. McMaster was offered a contract. Before long a multitude of Americans were reading the volume; and at Princeton, where the young man taught, President McCosh called him in, and with his dry Scots humor exclaimed: "Well, Mr. McMaster, why did ye na tell us that ye were a great mon?"

It is well known, too, that the publication of this brilliant volume brought young McMaster an offer of the second chair of American history to be established in any American college or university. The first had been established in 1881 at Cornell University, when President Andrew D. White called his old friend Moses Coit Tyler to fill the post where he produced his four volumes on the history of American literature in the colonial and Revolutionary periods. A mere instructorship in American history had been created at Harvard in 1883, with Albert Bushnell Hart as the incumbent. A new appreciation of history was making itself felt; the American Historical Association was founded in 1884. McMaster was to spend the rest of his active career teaching in the University of Pennsylvania. The mere fact that so active and original a writer was in their midst gave successive generations of students an interest in the American past. He was not a brilliant instructor. But, writes one disciple, "his assiduity in research, his honesty in the sifting of material and presentation of facts, his kindliness as a teacher and a friend, gave encouragement and inspiration to a host of young men, many of whom joined the teaching staffs of other colleges and universities to bear aloft and carry on the torch of historical learning."

The main significance of McMaster's career will be missed if it is not appreciated that he was much more than a good writer of history; he was much more than a hard-working university professor. He was the man who above all others in the period 1890–1910 interested and instructed the great mass of literate, intelligent Americans in their national past. When he appeared upon the scene George Bancroft was still active, but his star was unmistakably waning. John Fiske was bringing out his successive volumes, but they stopped where the national era began. Von Holst and James Ford Rhodes were busy; indeed, the year 1892 in which McMaster published his third volume in fact witnessed the issuance of von Holst's last volume and Rhodes's first two. But von Holst was merely the historian of the antislavery movement in its broadest aspects, while Rhodes was merely the historian of sectional conflict. McMaster had the whole broad panorama of American history from the end of the Revolution to the close of the Civil War to cover; and cover it he did in all its main aspects—political, economic, social, cultural, diplomatic—in eight bulky volumes. And these volumes had special characteristics of content and style which made them highly appealing to the broad mass of readers. They were a history *of* the American people addressed *to* the people. It is not strange that President Theodore Roosevelt called McMaster *the* historian of the American people.

The total sale of his eight volumes doubtless exceeded that of any contemporary writer of American history. Nor were his books bought to be set on shelves with their pages uncut. His interest in the daily life of the people, his keen eye for picturesque social customs, his sense for the dynamic energy of American life, and his industry in collecting information from newspapers, travels, memoirs, letters, and pamphlets, made each of his volumes a mine of interesting information. When in 1913 he completed his eighth volume, just thirty years after the publication of the first, the event was marked by a national observance. A committee of Philadelphians drew up a program; a reception committee was appointed which included Dr. S. Weir Mitchell, James Ford Rhodes, General James Harrison Wilson, ex-Governor Samuel W. Pennypacker, and other distinguished men; President Wilson and ex-Presidents Roosevelt and Taft sent their congratulations; and at the meeting in the hall of the Historical Society of Pennsylvania, representatives of various universities and learned societies offered their felicitations.

He was a teacher of American history in another sense: as a publicist, and as an author of widely used textbooks. He had no sooner won his reputation than he was besieged with invitations to write magazine articles, to give lectures, and to edit compilations of various kinds. He contributed to the *Atlantic Monthly*, the *Century Magazine, Harper's Monthly*, the *Outlook, Lippincott's*, and the *Forum*; he wrote for the *New York Herald* and *World*, and for Philadelphia newspapers; he contributed monographs to learned publications. He edited nine volumes of the Trail Makers Series—the editing, to be sure, not of a high quality. He wrote the articles on Freeman and Macaulay for *Warner's Library of the World's Best Literature*. He contributed three chapters to the *Cambridge Modern History*. A number of miscellaneous books came from his pen, the most important being his charming volume on *Benjamin Franklin as a Man of Letters* and his two-volume life of Stephen Girard. Indeed, the whole list of his printed writings and speeches fills seven duodecimo pages. Some of it was too ephemeral to be worth his time:

Among the historian's minor products [writes E. P. Oberholtzer] as a writer were an essay on the history of his country to serve as a preface for Baedeker's *United States*; an article on Garfield for the tenth edition of the *Encyclopaedia Britannica*; a history of the Johnstown flood and the relief work done at the time . . . ; a brief illustrated history of the University of Pennsylvania, in its colors, red and blue; and an oration for President McKinley to deliver on the occasion of the annually recurring Washington's Birthday celebration in the Academy of Music in Philadelphia, under the auspices of the University of Pennsylvania.

And no textbooks did so much as McMaster's to change the attitude of ordinary Americans toward our national history: to render it more critical and realistic, to broaden it outside the wonted political channels, and to rid it of myths and lies. His *School History of the United States*, issued in 1897 by the American Book Company, was designed as a grammar-school text, but was actually better adapted to high schools. He therefore followed it in 1901 with a *Primary History*, and in 1907 brought out an intermediate version of the *Brief History*. First and last, these texts sold more than 2,500,000 copies. A Spanish edition of the *School History* was issued for our insular dependencies. They involved McMaster in a sea of controversy—in disputes with patriots who thought that he did not give enough space to American heroes; with Southerners who thought him unkind to the Confederacy; with Masons on the one side and Catholics on the other; and not least important, with various editors who thought the author too subservient to the Grand Army of the Republic. But the textbooks were a success both commercially and educationally; they gave McMaster handsome profits, and they permanently altered the method and attitude of teachers of school history.

The principal new features of the *School History* were three: the generous space given to economic and social history; the reduction of attention to colonial history, with a concomitant enlargement of the attention to Western expansion and to Eastern industrialism; and the planning of the text as a continuous narrative instead of a disconnected series of topics. It was complained of the book that it still gave an excessive space to military affairs—not less than 24 percent of the work; that it dismissed some important political movements, such as Jackson's war with the Bank of the United States, in brief and vague statements; that it was not sufficiently explicit upon the "crooked thread of slavery"; and that a good deal of it was dull. Nevertheless, it was manifestly superior to any existing text, and it held that superiority for perhaps a decade. Brought home from school by hundreds of thousands of children, it doubtless caught the attention of a multitude of ill-read adults and taught them more of the American past than they had ever known.

Altogether, McMaster stands with George Bancroft as one of the great teachers of history to the American people. He made our history more of a popular force than any other writer of his time. He did for the United States much what John Richard Green— who was not one of his models, despite the similarity in title of their books—did for Great Britain. For a full quarter century he really was, as Theodore Roosevelt said, *the* outstanding historian of the United States. And it can be said that in its combination of detail and comprehensiveness, his eight-volume history (or nine volumes, if we add the rather weak work on the Lincoln administration) stands unrivaled among histories of America.

His admiring pupil Ellis P. Oberholtzer remarks that McMaster's method as a historian calls for no learned critical analysis. "He himself applied none to it, and was not greatly concerned with history as a science." As he himself viewed his function, it was simply to find facts and bring them out from the cover under which they had long lain. Writes Oberholtzer in a singularly uncritical and in some ways misleading paragraph:

> His idea of history was simply a description of past events. He could not confine himself to the election of Presidents, declarations of war, the fighting of battles, the making of treaties, about which more or less was known, but the thoughts, feelings, interests, movements of the people year by year, and make these explain events. He turned to the old newspapers. His critics have said that he attributed too much importance to the information which came from such sources. It is certain that he was a pioneer in the use of authorities which writers before him had neglected. The use

of the newspaper gave his narrative an order of sequence, a verbal swing, and a nearness to the life of the people which neither he, nor anyone else, could have gained by a mere study of Presidents' messages, Congressional reports, and the use of letters and diaries which alone are often held to be worthy of consultation.

The fact is that "order of sequence," or continuity, is one of the qualities which McMaster's history most glaringly lacks. It is true that his research was very wide—wide rather than deep. It is true that he tells a smoothly flowing story, collecting an immense mass of facts and arranging them in readable form. It is certainly true that he comes nearer to the life of the people than any other American historian—and that is a great virtue. But if his method has certain virtues, it makes also for evident faults.

Its principal fault is the total lack of any general plan. No historian of the life of the people, as distinguished from the life of the state, or the development of institutions, or the evolution of the national culture and mind, can present a definite pattern. The daily routine of the people has no pattern. That is why social history is usually so formless and chaotic. If it can be tied into the life of the state or of economic institutions, a pattern will emerge; but a year-by-year or decade-by-decade account of what men ate, wore, and drank, how they traveled, where they found their amusements, how they lighted and warmed their homes, what newspapers and magazines they read, and what standards of living they attained, can possess little system. A running description of these aspects of the national life, drawn from newspapers, travels, and memoirs, can have little real continuity or plan.

In a history like that of Henry Adams, or even James Ford Rhodes, a definite pattern emerges, giving connection to all the parts. A consistent purpose runs through all of Henry Adams's nine volumes; the last chapters are as inevitable as the first and fall into place like stones in a neat mosaic. But in McMaster's *History* his method gives each chapter an air of standing by itself, an integral, separate unit—or at most we get two or three chapters which form such a unit; while each volume again stands singly, having no organic connection with the volume which preceded it or the volume which follows.

In the fifth volume, for example, which covers the years 1821–1830, two of the thirteen chapters stand out with special vividness. One is a chapter on British travelers and critics, and on American rejoinders to their strictures. It is an able, learned, and acute summary of a large body of picturesque and amusing (or irritating) material. It might have been bettered by being connected with the struggle for political reform and an enlarged democracy in Great Britain; by being used to illustrate the great fact that the movement for a wider political liberty was worldwide, and that the American example was hated by many Britains, extolled by many others, because it bore upon that worldwide contest. Nevertheless, the chapter is illuminating and valuable. It might well be used as an essay in any magazine. But it stands by itself in the book. It is as isolated as such an essay would be in a miscellaneous magazine. The author passes from it to a very inferior chapter on the rise of the common school, or rather on the general failure of the public school to rise. No pattern emerges.

The other vivid chapter deals with the election and inauguration of Andrew Jackson. It is a vigorous, lively, entertaining story. The Randolph-Clay duel, the first nominating conventions, the scenes as Jackson was sworn in, and the ensuing scramble for office, make a colorful tale. Moreover, the chapter has enduring significance as a description (not an analysis, but a description) of a crowning success won by machine politics. That success was achieved by very disreputable methods, including an unblushing exploitation of charges of "bargain and corruption" against Adams and Clay which were totally false and were known to be false by the men who used them. But this chapter is not connected with any underlying idea about American political institutions and their development. It is not connected even with any general view of the successes and failures of the Adams administration; although it was the very virtues of that administration—its vigor in pushing certain large policies, its dignified refusal to use offices for political purposes or otherwise to play petty politics—which gave the Jacksonian forces their great opportunity. Once more we have a chapter that would make a good magazine essay, if properly condensed; but that stands alone in the book much as it would have stood alone in *Harper's Monthly*.

In this same fifth volume we have some excellent illustrations of another defect of McMaster's general method: the presentation of a body of detail which leads up to no conclusion at all, or at best a small and vague conclusion. We are given a mass of facts which possess some color and interest in themselves, but establish nothing. The ninth chapter of the book deals with the common school in the United States. Though the volume as a whole treats of the 1820s, a great part of the material pertains to colonial days, and much of the rest goes back to the years just following the Revolution. The chapter describes the early free schools of New England, the Lancastrian system and Sunday schools as borrowed from England, the abortive movement for public schools in the South, and the paper requirements of Ohio, Indiana, and Illinois, dishonored in the breach. Thirty pages of rather chaotic detail culminate in the statement that the common school as an important American institution was still unborn in 1830. We might find some fault with the content of the chapter. It contains nothing on the influence of French political philosophy; nothing on the educational ideas of Benjamin Rush. But our principal question as we close the chapter is why it was introduced into McMaster's *History* at this point at all. A long discursive essay, rambling over the whole map and the whole period from the seventeenth century to Jackson, is hardly justified when it concludes merely in a *negative* fact: the country had no common schools.

Similarly, a sixty-page chapter on political ideas brings us to a quite lame and impotent conclusion. Much of this chapter is concerned with the provisions of state constitutions written between 1776 and 1820. Suffrage is treated with numerous glances into the remote past. In tracing the history of judicial review we are brought into touch with the famous cases *Rutgers* vs. *Waddington* and *Trevett* vs. *Weeden*, in New York and Rhode Island respectively, just after the Revolution. The history of the president's cabinet, of the annual message, of the presidential nominating system, and like matters are reviewed for the whole period 1789–1830. The development and mutation of the doctrine of state rights in various sections are treated. And after sixty pages of ill-assorted facts, we come to—what? To the conclusion that dissatisfaction with the character of the presidency was widespread, and that many Americans by 1825 were weighing the idea of electing the president by direct popular vote, of confining him to a single term, and of forbidding him to appoint any member of Congress to office. Surely, we have a right to expect more from a review of the political thought of the 1820s, the period of J. Q. Adams's eclipse and Jackson's rise to power!

It should be said at this point that, taken singly as detached or semidetached essays, many of McMaster's chapters are highly valuable, and some may well be termed invaluable. His account of popular feeling in the era of the Confederation has never been bettered. In his fourth volume, describing the period of the War of 1812, the popular discontent with the war and the rising internal dissension as one executive blunder followed another are vigorously limned. Specially useful in this volume are the three chapters devoted to the banking system after the failure to renew the charter of the Bank of the United States (expiring 1811) gave irresponsible state banks an opportunity to corrupt the legislature and defraud the people, and to the national revenue system, including the tariff. The banking and revenue practices of the nation were closely connected with standards of public and private morality; and the historian ably pictures the effects of financial disorder upon the general population, lowering the standards of honesty and increasing the spirit of speculation. In the fifth volume the chapter on Western development, which includes an account of the Erie Canal and the Cumberland Road, is well worth reading; though it was surely an error to include in this same chapter a lengthy (and none too expert) account of Lundy, Garrison, and the beginnings of the abolitionist movement.

And if McMaster's work lacks plan, if his successive volumes have no pattern, if the separate parts seldom cohere, it must be said that his chapters of social description are often admirable. They furnish a picture of manners and conditions of daily life which, even since the publication of an extensive cooperative history of American society, is still indispensable. Such a sequence of social chapters as that in the seventh volume, where McMaster treats of "The East in the Forties," "Social and Political Betterment," "The West in the Forties," "The South in the Forties," and "The Movement for Expansion," is as instructive as it is fascinating. Here we have an excellent record of the rise of Mormonism, in which the author avoids any prejudice. We have a spirited summary of the many-sided reform movement of the forties, with its lunatic fringe in the Millerite excitement. We have a picturesque description of the growth of Chicago and Milwaukee. And in the treatment of the South, the brutalities of slavery are unsparingly delineated while at the same time McMaster does justice to some of the graces of Southern life. The eighth volume is not one of McMaster's best. He was beginning to tire, while the decade of the 1850s was too crowded with events and forces to be covered in five hundred pages. Seldom indeed does he get far beneath the surface. Still, as a mere description of surface phenomena, the account of the panic of 1857 and ensuing depression is well executed.

Various academic critics of McMaster have found fault with him for certain shortcomings which touch the form rather than the substance of his work. Writing so much, and under such a heavy pressure of academic and other duties, he yielded repeatedly to the temptation to paraphrase his sources, and sometimes copied them almost verbatim. Mr. Eric Goldman has shown that he levied upon the ideas and language no less than upon the facts of such works as William Cabell Rives's *Life and Times of Madison*, Edmund Quincy's *Life of Josiah Quincy*, and Dr. John H. Gihon's history of the governorship of John W. Geary in Kansas. McMaster even boldly borrowed a general passage from Macaulay. His attribution of credit to the sources from which he thus lifted material was inadequate. Dr. Goldman has also shown that in his paraphrasing of material from Congressional reports, from the newspapers, and from memoirs and letters, he often altered the sense, or but partially reproduced it. Another shortcoming of the historian was a gross laxity, amounting to carelessness, in the use of proper names in his text. Any reader who goes critically through the history can find scores of these slips. He will write (in speaking of the future Denver) of Aurania instead of Auraria; he refers to the civil governor of Utah as Cummings instead of Cumming; and so on. Nor was his use of footnotes as careful as it should have been. Unlike James Ford Rhodes, he had no expert research assistant and no adequate secretarial help; he did not verify his references any more than he verified his quotations—and only constant verification will preserve any writer from sad inaccuracies.

But these charges of textual borrowing, of inaccurate quotation, and of defective footnoting are after all of no great importance. In the main, McMaster was a thoroughly independent if not highly original writer, standing squarely upon his own feet. In the main, his quoted or paraphrased matter is sufficiently accurate to inspire confidence. In the main, his footnotes serve their purpose. No historians are exempt from criticism on these or similar headings, and if we challenge the writer who is without fault to throw the first stone, nobody will step forward. In view of the fact that McMaster's nine heavy volumes of the *History of the People of the United States* contain hardly less than two million words, while he wrote perhaps a million words of other historical material, the wonder is that he attained so high a standard of accuracy and wrote so many pages that withstand the severest scrutiny.

Much more serious are two general defects. One is the fact that newspapers are in general a highly tendentious source. Their editorial opinions, their correspondence, and their news stories are seldom objective; they have the coloring of a party or a class bias, sometimes faint, frequently very heavy. Any historical text based upon them is likely to betray at various points this coloration. McMaster had a deplorable habit of using newspaper material in such a way that the reader is often confused as to the source of a given statement; he does not know whether it is the journal or the historian who is speaking, whether it is John Bach McMaster or the *New York Herald* which is authority for a specific assertion. In a writer who follows his sources thus closely, the danger of a deviation from impartiality and objectivity is doubly great. It may be added that newspapers are seldom accurate in the sense in which government documents are accurate. They report much half-knowledge as knowledge; they furnish many statements which come near the truth but do not quite hit it. Produced under conditions of haste and pressure, they need closer scrutiny than McMaster gave them.

The other general defect of McMaster is that he seldom gives adequate weight to personal leadership or the influence of eminent men. In his fifth and sixth volumes, for example, we see much of the plain people of the United States; but how much do we really see of Monroe, John Quincy Adams, William H. Crawford, Clay, Webster, Calhoun, or Benton? They are names and little more. The author gives us none of those incisive thumbnail portraits which we find scattered through James Schouler; still less does he give us the finished depictions of mind and personality which we encounter in James Ford Rhodes. We need not believe in any Carlylean theory of the great man to believe that strong men do mightily affect the course of human events; that a Jackson, a Calhoun, a Wilson, or a Franklin D. Roosevelt may count for more than millions of ordinary folk.

371

When McMaster does pause to dissect a personality, he is often so sharply critical that the reader is left wondering that the man enjoyed the fame and influence that fell to his lot. Altogether, the element of leadership is inadequately presented in McMaster's narrative.

But as a history of the American people, the great work has enduring value. Some parts of every volume (except perhaps the eighth and ninth) must for many years to come continue to be used by all earnest students of the first seventy-five years of our national record. The massive compilation lacks the scholarly and literary finish which make the work of Parkman and Henry Adams true classics. But in interest, in human warmth, in panoramic scope, and in vitality, no historical work written in this country save those of Parkman and Adams, Prescott and Motley, surpasses it.

29

Henry Adams

Allan Nevins viewed the historical writings of Henry Adams with mixed feelings. On the one hand he greatly admired Adams's use of archival sources, his lucidity of expression, his regard for the canons of objectivity, his emphasis on accuracy, and the penetrating depth of his analysis. Like most students of history, Nevins would rank Adams's *History of the United States during the Administrations of Adams and Jefferson,* his *Mont St. Michel and Chartres,* and his *Education of Henry Adams* among the major classics by American authors. Yet he was plainly unhappy with Adams's move toward scientific exactness and his abandonment of the soaring literary style that enshrined Prescott, Motley, and Parkman among the immortals. Nevins correctly saw Adams as bridging the gap between the amateur and professional eras in American historical writing, and he never quite forgave him for the aid and comfort he provided the dryasdust historians who were to dominate from his day on. In this previously unpublished lecture, apparently another in his series on "Great Literature of American History," Nevins reveals enough of Adams's life to show its influence on his writing, then analyzes his several books with a keen eye to their strengths and weaknesses. Nevins is especially aware of the bias in Adams's works and underlines the manner in which many of his conclusions have been outmoded by later research.

373

For several reasons Henry Adams occupies one of the most interesting places in American historiography. A good though not a great stylist, and a man of thoroughly scientific temper, he does more than anyone else to cover the gap between the sweeping literary effects of writers like Parkman, Prescott, and Motley, and the colorless impartiality and analytical depth of the most recent school of history. He succeeded, as Schouler and Fiske never did, in satisfying both those who demand high literary felicity in historical writing and those who require the strictest regard to canons of accuracy, objectivity, thoroughness, and penetration. In the second place, he was by common consent of his students a great teacher of history. He not only instructed but inspired. Introducing the seminar method at Harvard, he imbued the young men who gathered about him in his private apartments with a zest for investigation, a critical temper, and an understanding of the difference between fruitful and unfruitful methods of research. "He had the power not only of exciting interest," writes Henry Cabot Lodge, "but he awakened opposition to his own views, and that is one great secret of success in teaching." For a third reason, Adams derives a certain importance from the fact that he was the American historian who tried hardest to formulate a philosophy of history—to explain the basic principles which give continuity and meaning to the human record, and which, if properly studied, might explain toward what goals mankind is headed. Finally, the historical work of Henry Adams is given a peculiar interest by the depth, the vivacity, and the sardonic quality of his personality. Professor Commager writes: "Of Henry Adams alone, among the major historians, can it be said that what he was is more significant than what he wrote." That statement requires modification: Parkman, Prescott, and Woodrow Wilson, for example, were greater than their books; but we can at least say that Adams's many-sided and enigmatic personality imparts a special interest to his writings, that we feel in his books undertones and overtones that are lacking in most historical works.

Adams's historical work was of course profoundly influenced by his ancestry, his early environment, and that prolonged process which he called his education. Great-grandson of John Adams, grandson of John Quincy Adams, son of Charles Francis Adams, he was brought up in an atmosphere redolent of history; from early boyhood he saw great personages and heard talk of weighty political and diplomatic events. His mother sprang from an old and prosperous Boston family, the Brookses, who also placed their mark upon him. "Had he been born in Jerusalem under the shadow of the Temple," Adams wrote of himself later, "and circumcised in the synagogue under his uncle the high-priest, under the name of Israel Cohen, he would scarcely have been more distinctly branded, and not much more heavily handicapped in the races of the coming century, in running for such stakes as the century was to offer." Most of us could wish that we had suffered from such handicaps! Yet certain disabilities he did indeed feel. One was psychological; his forbears had accomplished so much and had risen to such heights, that he believed he could never equal them, and was hence at times haunted by a sense of frustration. Another was intellectual. He was reared in a cultivated Bostonian community which in many ways looked backward rather than forward—which in social, economic, and governmental matters was often static and sometimes retrogressive; so that, though born in 1838, he pronounced himself a child of the eighteenth century, and confessed that he always felt difficulty in adjusting himself to the fast-changing world of the nineteenth and twentieth centuries.

From Harvard, where he thought that he learned very little and where he certainly gave but slight evidence of his brilliance, Adams went abroad to study in Berlin. His ambitions, it seems evident, were political, and he thought of preparing himself for the bar. As a born individualist, he disliked German methods of instruction, though years later he was to introduce the German seminar into New England. Travel over a large part of Europe broadened his tastes; he met Garibaldi in Palermo; he wrote newsletters to the *Boston Courier*. Deciding that he did not care for law, he returned to the United States to serve as his father's secretary in Washington in the winter of 1860–1861. He studied the swirl of passions and interests as the country was carried into war; and as the conflict opened, he finally gave up all ideas of a career at the bar. Though he was intensely eager to join the army, he yielded to his father's wish that he become secretary of the American legation in London. Thus far, he later wrote—perhaps not quite sincerely—he felt that his life had been a failure; and it was not until English society took him up and he found a new interest in science that his despondency left him. In London and at the country houses he met such men as Bulwer-Lytton, Robert Browning, and Herbert Spencer; he formed a close friendship with Charles Milnes Gaskell; and he fell under the spell of Sir Charles Lyell. His secretarial duties did not prevent him from writing for the *North American Review*. Particularly interesting was his long review of Lyell's *Principles of Geology*, on which he lavished great pains and enthusiasm. Like John Fiske, like E. L. Youmans, like his own brother Charles Francis Adams, he was fired by the new scientific concept of evolution.

When in 1868 he returned to the United States, his political ambitions were apparently still strong. Finding himself out of touch with American ways, he went to Washington as observer and journalist; made friends with such men as Adam Badeau and Moorfield Storey; wrote at length on politics, after British models, for the *North American Review*; and looked about for an opening. But all his fire and idealistic energy were quenched by the Grant administration. In the *Education* he refers to Senator Don Cameron as belonging to "the very class of American politicians who had done most to block his intended path in life." As Allen Johnson puts it: "American politics in 1870 offered no career to talent; and Adams, partly from natural sensitiveness and shyness and partly from long residence in England, could not or would not make the necessary advances to those in party conclave who had offices and favors to confer." Always an individualist, he would not conform to machine requirements. Nor had he any of the talents which would enable him to appeal to a popular constituency—to run for Congress as his father and grandfather had done. Feeling more than ever out of touch with the American world, he embarked on another trip abroad. It was while on this rather unhappy foreign tour that he received an offer from President Eliot of Harvard to become assistant professor of history. After some hesitation, he accepted. The story goes that when Eliot told him that he would be expected to teach medieval history, he replied that he knew nothing about it; whereupon Eliot retorted that nobody else did either. Writes Henry Cabot Lodge: "Mr. Adams has told me many times that he began his course in total ignorance of his own subject, and I have no doubt that the fact that he, too, was learning, helped his students."

Adams's seven years at Harvard were not, according to his own account, especially pleasant or fruitful. But we may discount his somewhat ironic depreciation of all his own work, his sardonic habit of dwelling on his ignorance and his failures. While he says that he was not a successful teacher, his students all assert that he was one of the most inspiring men on the faculty. Some, like Perry Belmont, positively worshipped him. He left a permanent mark on the educational system of Harvard by his introduction of the seminar—one of the first in the country—and his use of modern research methods. Recognizing that a new era in historical writing had arrived, he emphasized institutional history. "Society is getting new tastes," he wrote an English friend, "and history of the old school has not many years to live." He sent his students to original sources; he had a way of pitting a man who followed one authority against a man who followed another, and cheering them on in their battle; he put stimulating questions to his classes; and in 1876 students working under his direction published a volume entitled "Essays in Anglo-Saxon Law," which contained essays by Adams himself, J. Laurence Laughlin, Henry Cabot Lodge, and a student who died early, Ernest Young. As Herbert Baxter Adams states, this volume "was the first original historical work ever accomplished by American university students working in a

377

systematic and thoroughly scientific way under proper direction." It was a good enough book to be used and cited by British scholars like Sir Frederick Pollock. During these Harvard years Henry Adams married a Boston girl, Marion Hopper; while for a time he carried the boresome and time-consuming but useful burden of the editorship of the *North American Review*.

Before Adams left Harvard, he gave a course in the American period for the years 1789–1840. This perhaps did much to crystallize his interest in the early national era—an interest which would naturally be keen, for it was the era in which his family had played so central a part. Giving up his teaching and editorship just as the Reconstruction era closed and the Hayes administration opened a new epoch, he returned to Washington to devote his time to historical pursuits—and to society. He had good friends there—John Hay; Clarence King; Don Cameron and his beautiful wife; Henry Cabot Lodge and his witty wife Nannie. Possessed of leisure and ample means, enjoying a modest amount of fame and prestige, he could write as he pleased. There opened the middle period of his life, which was to be notable for four historical works: one a volume of materials, two biographies, and the last and greatest a broadly-planned history of sixteen years of the republic, 1801–1817.

Of Adams's *Documents Relating to New England Federalism, 1800–1815* (1877), it is necessary to say only that it is a useful collection of papers, with a very brief introduction. The second work, a *Life of Albert Gallatin* in one large volume and the *Writings of Gallatin* in two more (1879), was much more important. Mr. Commager remarks that the biography is the best in the field of American history. It is a good biography; but it is very far indeed from being the best. Its great fault is a lack of digestion. Adams let the letters of Gallatin speak for themselves, knitting those of biographical interest together with a neat and sometimes even brilliant connecting narrative of his own. He himself kept too far in the background, so that in the biography itself as well as in the two volumes of writings he appears rather as an editor and not as an author. This would have been more legitimate had Gallatin, who was a very amusing talker, been an extremely good letter writer. But as a matter of fact, his letters are poor; they are formal, wordy, and dry, and the parts of the book that are given up to them make most tedious reading. Fortunately, in two long sections Adams divorced himself from the correspondence of his hero and appeared in his own right as narrator and interpreter. The first of these is the section dealing with Gallatin's secretaryship of the Treasury under Jefferson and Madison, when he was a not unworthy successor of Alexander Hamilton. He had a well-defined policy: he intended to administer the revenues with systematic frugality, to spend less than the income, to pay off the national debt, and then to use the annual surplus in great projects of national improvement—or if this was not done, to remit it and reduce the taxation. How he earnestly tried to carry out this scheme, and how he failed, is a fascinating story. The other part of the book in which Adams allows himself free rein as historian is the section covering the Treaty of Ghent. This, indeed, is the finest part of the biography. It traces in detail the diplomatic labors of both Gallatin and John Quincy Adams; and Henry Adams was so anxious to avoid any show of favor toward his grandfather that he rather leans over backward. He is extremely hard upon the British in the negotiation, and modern scholarship has corrected him there. But he was quite right in assigning to the suave and wily Gallatin, rather than to the stubborn, high-tempered John Quincy Adams, the principal credit for the highly successful character of the American negotiation.

The *Life of John Randolph of Roanoke*, contributed to the American Statesmen Series in 1882, is rather a long essay—perhaps 60,000 or 75,000 words—than a true biography; and by common consent it is the weakest of Adams's literary productions. Why Adams ever undertook it is a puzzle, for he later confessed that he had found the task detestable. With Randolph, who had been one of John Quincy Adams's bitterest enemies, he had no sympathy whatever—and consequently no understanding of the man. William Cabell Bruce does not overstate the matter when he remarks of the volume: "In its pages, he has fully availed himself of the opportunity it afforded him to direct against the memory of Randolph the thrice-refined venom in respect to its subject which filtered into his own veins from those of his great-grandfather, grandfather, and father. The book is really nothing but a family pamphlet saturated with the sectional prejudices and antipathies of the year 1882. . . ." Nor does it contain much that even in 1882 was fresh and original. Most of it is simply a *rechauffé* of Hugh Garland's two-volume biography, to which are added certain materials drawn from letters of Randolph to Gallatin, Monroe, and Nicholson which Garland did not have. The book is written in popular style, which in places seems brilliant, but which lacks depth and weight; while it is totally undocumented—no footnotes, no bibliography, not even a preface. In the first chapter a few pages on the social and intellectual life of old Virginia stand out above the rest of the volume, while the pages on Virginia politics have merit. But as a whole the book is a failure. It is not even convincing; for it displays John Randolph as "grotesque," but it does not explain the reasons, some physical, some psychological, which made him so. At about this same time, according to John T. Morse, Adams also wrote a short life of Aaron Burr. It was rejected by the publishers of the American Statesmen Series on the sound principle that Burr was not a statesman; and the manuscript seems since to have disappeared.

All of this writing was the prelude and preparation for Adams's principal work, to which he devoted the greater part of the 1880s. He had been collecting material ever since he left Cambridge; he had been maturing his plan; and he commenced work with what he later called a "wild interest." The suicide of his wife in 1885 interrupted his labors, and sent him on a long trip to Japan to recover from his grief and loneliness. That tragic event was a maturing experience, which left its mark upon his mind and personality. On his return from the Orient he set to work again and in 1889 published the first two volumes. Four more appeared in 1890, and in 1891 the final three. By intelligent students of American history the work was at once hailed as one of the greatest thus far produced in America; and though the general public paid little attention to it, Adams had a *succès d'estime* which should have satisfied him more than it did.

One section of Adams's history has excited general admiration. In six chapters of social and economic history, crowded with facts and illumined with philosophical comment, he constructs "a fitting portal through which the reader may approach the Jeffersonian epoch." In these chapters he describes the physical, commercial, and industrial state of the country as the nineteenth century opened; the principal characteristics of the American people at the time—moral, intellectual, and spiritual; the peculiarities of the New England culture, the Southern culture, and the culture of the Middle States; and finally, the ideals which were insensibly but steadily transforming the republic and converting a raw social order into a more mature and responsible society. It was unfortunate that to these six chapters Adams did not add a seventh. His book would have profited had he given room to a chapter on the political structure of the country; to the doctrine, nature, and objects of the great parties, explaining the antithesis between the old Federalists who had set up the Constitution and operated the government under Washington and John Adams, and the Republican party which under Jefferson had accomplished "the revolution of 1800." As the work stands, the reader has to grope his way to an understanding of party principles and party differences.

Beginning his narrative with the day when Jefferson walked to the Capitol to take the oath of office as president, Adams treats all the political and diplomatic events of the next sixteen years in careful and illuminating detail. That he confines himself too closely to state affairs is unquestionably true. It is not until the final four chapters of his last volume that he returns to economic, social, and cultural history; and when he does return, his description of these elements is too brief, his analysis is not sufficiently searching. The book is thus not in any full sense a history of the United States, or at least of the American people. But as a piece of political history, the work—though not without blemishes—is admirable. It is founded upon a mass of materials which Adams was the first to draw to light; for he used not only the manuscripts of leaders of the time, but the diplomatic archives of the French and British as well as American governments. In this way "the springs of many a movement which were before obscure are . . . brought to sight, and . . . the reader is helped to follow the logic of events with an order which has gained lucidity from new discoveries, and . . . with a philosophy which has gained new insight from a widened historical perspective." The grasp of materials is always vigorous; the style is dignified, lucid, and graceful. On the whole, too, a careful balance is held between the Federalist and Republican points of view. Knowing that he would be suspected of a family bias, Adams attempted a rigid impartiality, and at times practised this virtue even too strenuously. If he does not quite sympathize with democratic tendencies—and by nature he was far indeed from a democrat—Henry Adams at least recognized their potency and wholesomeness. He declares that as modern science developed more and more the capacity of man to control the forces of nature, the old-fashioned conservatism of the Federalist period naturally disappeared from American life. Jefferson, "the most active minded and sanguine of Virginians," who had invented a new plow and other improved appliances, foresaw clearly the democratic tendencies which were destined to unfold themselves in a larger and larger trust in the capacity of the people for self-government. Remarking that "every foreigner and Federalist agreed that Jefferson was a man of illusions, dangerous to society and unbounded in power of evil," Henry Adams hastens to add that "if this view of his character was right, it only proved that there was a vein of idealism in the national character of the American people; for it is very certain that Jefferson's opinions, in one form or another were shared by a majority of the American people."

382

In short, Henry Adams recognizes that Jefferson and the Republican party represented the great dominant forces of American development; that Alexander Hamilton, crying "Your people, sir—your people is a great beast!" and Fisher Ames, asserting that "Democracy cannot last," and George Cabot, declaring that "I hold democracy in its natural operation to be the government of the worst," and John Adams, remarking that liberty can accomplish nothing for the good of man unless it is "constantly supported and improved by a few—that is, by the nobility," were out of touch with the great forces of American life, and while not unpatriotic, quite wrong. To this extent, Adams in his history takes the side of Jefferson and republicanism and gives his verdict against Adams and federalism. At the same time, he denies Jefferson's statement that the Revolution of 1800 "was as real a revolution in the principles of our government as that of 1776 was in its forms." He is at pains to point out how far it fell short of any such significance. Jefferson, entering office with a set of egalitarian state rights principles, was forced by events to adopt a practical policy which was the very antithesis of what he taught. Adams writes that it is hard to see "how any President could have been more Federalist than Jefferson himself"; that he used vigorously the very executive powers which in preceding administrations he had denounced; that by the Louisiana Purchase he gave a death blow to strict construction, converted the Constitution into blank paper, and opened the way for the eventual consolidation of vast powers in the federal government; and that finally, "he who nearly dissolved the bonds of society rather than allow his predecessor to order a dangerous alien out of the country in time of threatened war, made himself monarch of the new [Louisiana] territory, and wielded over it, against its protests, the power of its old kings." It was only in a social sense, according to Henry Adams, that Jefferson's democracy was "final and sweeping"; in a governmental sense it simply did not work. This is of course too harsh and sweeping a judgment—though it has partial force.

It is the great defect of Henry Adams's virtues of objectivity and impartiality that he also shows lack of feeling; that his analysis, if fair, is so coldly—nay, frigidly—fair that it often bears an aspect of hostility. Edward Channing remarks that "the author is out of sympathy with the actors in his story, and loses few opportunities to sneer at the theories and performances of Jefferson and Madison, who, whatever their faults may have been, represented the thoughts and aspirations of the majority of their countrymen." As we have just indicated, he did not fail to see that they represented popular feeling, and to praise them for the fact; but he never felt even a passing warmth of regard for them—no compassion for their failures, no exultation in their victories. It is doubtless true that Macaulay sympathized too strongly with the Whig chieftains, that Motley spoke too eulogistically of William the Silent; but we could wish that Henry Adams now and then showed at least a faint flush of sentiment for his major figures. He seems to have been puzzled by the mind and character of Jefferson. He concedes that the third president, according to all standards in such matters, must be pronounced a great man; he concedes that in world affairs he took a place near Pitt and Bonaparte, while in home affairs for eight years he was "the government itself"; he concedes that while holding this great place, he practised with success "the austerity of Cato and the simplicity of Ancus Marcius"; he concedes that he embodied an "ideal purity" in American politics. Yet Adams cannot bring himself to like or strongly praise the man. An aristocrat by birth, Jefferson seemed to him "excessively refined" in his tastes for a democratic chieftain. He delighted in intellectual studies, yet was "superficial in knowledge and a martyr to the disease of omniscience"; he had a strong feeling for artistic and literary form, which even in itself Adams hardly allows to be a virtue—it was "the sure mark of intellectual sensuousness"—yet he seldom wrote a page "without exposing himself to attack"; he played a strenuous part in affairs, yet was so feminine in his personality that he "yearned for love and praise," and he was so theoretical that he was ready "to risk the fate of mankind on the chance of a reasoning process which was far from certain in its details." His practical measures are strongly criticized: Adams holds that his reforming zeal was too soon exhausted, that he played too timid a role in his relations with France and Britain, that the mode in which he carried through the Louisiana purchase placed a "final" bar against all attempts to "restrain the government from doing whatever the majority should think necessary." In treating Madison, a much weaker figure, Henry Adams is equally chill and severe. And in his estimate of the two great parties he is never betrayed for a single chapter into showing warmth or sympathy for either. Both Federalists and Republicans, it appeared, repelled him. If subtlety is one of the great merits of Adams's work, he is often over-subtle; if objectivity is another great merit, he is often excessively austere and Olympian.

In his judgments upon specific events, Henry Adams evinces a shrewd insight that has in most instances been supported by the studies of subsequent investigators. At some point he was led by intellectual bias or by inadequacy of data into mistaken conclusions. His judgment upon the Kentucky and Virginia Resolutions of 1798 is excessively severe, for he fails to take into due account their historical background, while he uses his attack upon them to sharpen his indictment of Jefferson's statesmanship. That Jefferson, after conferences with George Nicholas of Kentucky and W. C. Nicholas of Virginia, drafted the Kentucky Resolutions, there is no longer any doubt. These resolutions set forth that the union of the states was a compact, that whenever the general government assumed undelegated powers (as in passing the Alien and Sedition laws) its acts were "unauthoritative, void, and of no force," and that in all such instances "each party"—that is, states and nation—"has an equal right to judge for itself as well of infractions as of the mode and measure of redress." Adams holds Jefferson to the strictest responsibility for these assertions, so potentially destructive of national unity—although the legislatures of both Kentucky and Virginia softened the language, and that of Virginia struck out the word *void*. Jefferson's own intent, it seems clear, was by no means so extreme as Henry Adams assumes. As he wrote Madison (November 17, 1798), it was to put matters in such a train that the Republican leaders should not be committed to push their views to extremities, and yet should be free to push them as far as events rendered prudent. Adams's indictment of these unhappy documents, and of their authors (Madison having written the Virginia Resolution) is altogether too harsh and (for once) unrestrained.

The story of the acquisition of Louisiana was for the first time told in Adams's pages with completeness and accuracy; for he supplied many details which furnished missing links in that great transaction and made it understandable. He showed that Santo Domingo occupied a pivotal position in the matter. "St. Domingo was the only centre," he writes, "from which the measures needed for rebuilding the French colonial system could radiate." It was necessary for Napoleon to crush Toussaint l'Ouverture before he could make sure of his grip on Louisiana—and crush him he could not. The heroic career of the black leader is narrated with graphic circumstance and with even a faint semblance of feeling. Toussaint, writes Adams, "exercised on our history an influence as decisive as that of any European ruler." Turning to the diplomatic history of the transfer of Louisiana, Adams brings before us the whole galaxy of men and women who figured in it: Napoleon and Talleyrand; Don Carlos IV of Spain, Queen Doña Maria, and Godoy; Leclerc, Rochambeau, and Laussat; Addington and Lord Whitworth; Jefferson, Madison, Monroe, and Chancellor Livingston. With many a new document, he illuminates the whole sequence of cause and effect leading to the momentous sale; a sale which, as he is quick to assert, changed the whole social, economic, and political equilibrium of America.

But masterly as is Adams's account of the sale of Louisiana, it is not without its defects. He realized clearly that to Americans the Spanish retrocession of Louisiana to France in 1801 was intolerable. But he fails to give Secretary Madison due credit for his history which is expounded in general terms in the concluding chapters of his *Education*, and more specifically in his "Letter to American Teachers of History." Lord Kelvin's law of the dissipation of energy was applied to the movement of human forces and events. The stream of history became a demonstration of the hypothesis of entropy: the gradual running down of the universe. To illustrate his ideas he produced two complementary works: the *Mont St. Michel and Chartres*, to portray the idea of medieval unity; and the *Education of Henry Adams*, to present the idea of modern multiplicity. What is the relation between these two great books, and how do they—taken in combination—develop his theory of entropy?

First, he assumes that in human experience two great forces have always existed and always competed. One is an inner force, a subjective impulse, which has through the centuries clothed itself in religious forms, or in a devotion to God; and this force makes for unity. The other is an outer or objective force, which in older times was known as Nature, and in our day is most powerfully expressed as science. It makes for multiplicity.

Second, he declares that if we look at history, the first phase of force reached its culminating expression in the era of medieval unity. Mankind then attained, spiritually speaking, its highest degree of unity. In the absolute dominance of faith (if it was absolute) and of the church, civilization had more simplicity, more of integralism, than it had before or since. But a great change quickly supervened. The use of the inductive mode of thought, the application of experiment to physical science, opened a new phase of force. Man and his spiritual life ceased to be the center of the universe. Nature and science became the focus of all interest. Thus unity was challenged and the world began to move toward multiplicity and diversity. That is, it moved toward disintegration and chaos; by a law of accelerated entropy which threatened a dissolution of society by the middle of the twentieth [century]. At any rate the emergence of a new and unpredictable

quick enunciation of this American attitude. Madison's instructions to Livingston, he says, are "remarkable for their mildness." Mildness! The fact is that on September 28, 1801, Secretary Madison, taking note of the rumored transfer from Spain to France, wrote Livingston that this cession was a matter of "momentous concern"; that it had already received "the most serious attention" from Jefferson; that the transfer would be likely to cause "collisions" which would endanger peace between France and America; that it would alarm the South for the safety of its slaves; that it might well turn the thoughts of Americans toward "a closer connection" with Britain; and that it could easily lead to a "crisis" in which Louisianians would be exposed "to the joint occupation of a naval and territorial power"—Britain and America. Henry Adams pays insufficient attention to the instant excitement of public opinion in America, and particularly in the South and Southwest. And he makes a needless mystery of Napoleon's motives in the sale of Louisiana. War between Britain and France was imminent. As Addington frankly told our minister, Rufus King, one of the first steps of Great Britain when it began would be to seize Louisiana. Nobody in Paris believed in Napoleon's colonizing schemes. A sale in anticipation of war was practically inevitable. Livingston knew that it was so, and some months before the cession he wrote Madison that he felt no uneasiness, because he was sure that the whole affair would end in a transfer of the region to America. Lord Whitworth, the British ambassador in Paris, shared this belief. Why, then, should Adams say that it is difficult to penetrate Napoleon's motives in relinquishing what had been one of his darling objects? He had no choice.

Henry Adams's treatment of the conspiracy of certain Federalist leaders in 1804 for the dissolution of the Union is one of the finest bits of narrative in his history, distinguished also for its masterly analysis of evidence. Much of the material was familiar to those who had read Adams's documents on New England federalism, the life of Plumer, and Henry Cabot Lodge's *Life of*

Cabot. But new facts were brought into view, and all the data was arranged in a compact and beautifully finished monograph. The story is defective only in failing to draw as much evidence from the newspapers of the time—evidence of a corroborative nature—as it might have done. But Adams lays his finger upon the precise meaning of the conspiracy. It was not a plot of men greedy for power or pelf; it was not a reckless or thoughtless enterprise. On the contrary, it was the work of men who believed they were acting for the country's good at their own heavy peril; and it was undertaken not in hardihood of spirit, but after long heart searching and with melancholy forebodings. It was the product, as Adams says, of despair—despair of saving in any other way the social, the moral, the religious, and the political scheme of things which the conspirators identified with American welfare. One man alone, Aaron Burr, was conspicuously self-seeking and reckless; the New Englanders moved in a very different spirit. And the heart of the plain people of New England never responded to the machinations of these leaders.

In treating of the Burr Conspiracy, Adams made effective use of materials which his industry for the first time dragged to light from the Spanish and British archives. But he was excessively certain of his very dubious conclusion—the conclusion that it was Burr's definite intention to raise an army of adventurers, descend the Mississippi, seize New Orleans, and wrench Louisiana from the Union. Later research, and particularly that of Walter F. McCaleb, has placed Burr's intentions in doubt. According to Mr. McCaleb, the real object of Burr was to recruit an army in the Southwest, and then lead it to the overthrow of Spanish authority in Louisiana and Mexico City, setting up his own empire in that area. The historian Channing, after investigating the topic, decided that it is impossible now to divine Burr's real intention. Possibly, according to Channing, Burr had both objects—the detachment of Louisiana and the conquest of Mexico—in view; possibly he waited upon events to determine which would be most feasible; possibly he had never quite made up his mind what he

would undertake! At any rate, it is impossible to accept Adams's treatment of the affair without serious reservatio

Thus we might follow the *History* down to its co exposing weaknesses at one point and errors at anothe whole it is a magnificent piece of work—magnificent i of new facts, in its lucidity and grace, in its genera statement, and in its philosophical insight. It is mor general tone than readers of Adams's later works find it; for if the first six and the last four chapte attentively, it will be seen that the author sets American ideals, and believes that these working their way toward some grander fr weaknesses of the *History* are its refusal to the economic strands in American life—ref ate, for Adams felt himself unequipped forces—and its general frigidity, which the author's temperament.

The books of Henry Adams's secon the *History*—are much the most im have said that they alone deserve t period, as he and his brother Bro 1893. The panic had broken; the he was summoned home to Brooks spent several weeks in Brooks had just planned his tion and Decay," a pre-T civilizations have followed the course of our own c told by Brooks, approve From these conversatio a great effort of thoug out a science of histo the present in the l

Rejecting existi boldly into the

type of civilization. All history thus falls into a dualistic frame-work.

The two illustrations of this view of civilization are unquestionably masterpieces of imaginative reconstruction of the past. Studying medieval times to gain a comprehension of the period in which unity was most powerful; reading history, poetry; the medieval philosophers from Abelard to Aquinas; conning medieval architecture, painting, and tapestry, Adams evolved a pattern which centered in the Virgin. She was not the Mary of the Catholic Church; she was the Lady of Chartres as a creation of the medieval mind. In Mont St. Michel he gives us a penetrating study of this medieval mind as a key to general human history to that point. He divides his book into three parts: first, the slow ripening of thought in the "dark ages" and early medieval period toward its great successful effort at synthesis in the twelfth and thirteenth centuries; second, the achievement of emotional and aesthetic unity, as expressed in the Cathedral of Chartres; and third, the achievement of rational and philosophical unity as expressed in the writings of Thomas Aquinas. He shows how for a brief period, in a special place, Chartres of the thirteenth century, mankind met its need for inner harmony and repose.

Turning then to the study of multiplicity, Adams found his central theme in his own life and personality. He called his *Education of Henry Adams* "a Study in Twentieth Century Multiplicity." Here he shows the shattering impact of science on modern life. This book, too, falls into three parts, not so clearly defined as in the first. He begins with an account of the great difficulties and disabilities of the generation he knew as a young man—the generation he saw in Boston before the Civil War, in London during the Civil War, in Washington just after it—a generation inadequately prepared to meet the great challenge of modern science, expressed in the geology of Sir Charles Lyell and the biology of Darwin. The second part of the book presents the effort of one fairly typical individual, Henry Adams, to adjust himself successfully to the world of multiplicity, with all its chaos

GREAT HISTORIANS OF THE NINETEENTH CENTURY

of facts and forces, all its centrifugal and disintegrating tendencies. The third outlines the formula on which he lighted for this adjustment: his adoption of the dynamo, first seen at the Chicago exposition of 1893, as the symbol of the modern age. As the Lady of Chartres raised the religious idea of unity to its highest power, so the dynamo raised science and mechanistic force to its most efficient level.

The two books can be understood only in combination, and the full relation between them can be understood only in the illumination of the three large volumes of Henry Adams's *Letters* already published. What place they give Henry Adams in the world of ideas is still uncertain. Unquestionably, however, they—far more than his *History*—give him a place in the category of master artists of American letters.

30

James Ford Rhodes
as Man and Historian

Nothing could have been more fitting than that Allan Nevins, whose multivolume *Ordeal of the Union* is one of the nation's finest monuments to the Civil War, should have been asked by the University of Chicago Press to edit an abridged edition of James Ford Rhodes's *History of the United States from the Compromise of 1850*. Rhodes's seven-volume history of the war, published between 1893 and 1906, played the same role for its generation that Nevins's monumental study does for ours; each typified an era of historical interpretation—Rhodes, the "scientific" approach current in his time; Nevins, the interdisciplinary stress with its emphasis on social forces. In performing the herculean task of compressing the work into one volume, Allan Nevins made a thorough study of Rhodes's background, career, and impact. The result, published in 1966 as an introduction to the one-volume edition (printed by the University of Chicago Press in its *Classic American Historians* series), is a penetrating appraisal of one of the nation's master scholars.

Allan Nevins, introduction to *History of the United States from the Compromise of 1850*, by James Ford Rhodes (Chicago: University of Chicago Press, 1966), pp. vii–xxvi. Reprinted with permission.

The career of James Ford Rhodes was quite remarkable. He was a successful businessman who, at the height of his lucrative enterprises, gave up moneymaking, and although he possessed no special training for literary work, threw off all commercial connections, changed his residence, immersed himself in books, and embarked upon a deliberate and persistent effort to make himself a historian. Charles W. Eliot later remarked that by this very unusual shift from trade to letters, a shift completed in 1885 at the age of thirty-seven, he "rendered great service to American scholarship and the country." It was an example which might more frequently be followed. He himself took some pride in it. He wrote Frederic Bancroft that he ought to be given credit for withdrawing from business when he was rapidly accumulating a fortune, because "I thought I ought to devote myself to something higher"; and equal credit for the fact that, having withdrawn, "I did not become an intellectual dawdler or a European sojourner." He had worked hard in managing his coal and iron business, but he was pleased to record that, without any spur of necessity, he later worked much harder upon his history.

In this abandonment of pelf to pursue a higher ambition we may see the strain of idealism which not infrequently mingled with the hard practical realism of sons of the Western Reserve, who were Puritans at a second remove. Many strains went into Rhodes's character and training. His father, Dan Rhodes, was a Vermonter by birth and a cousin of Stephen A. Douglas. All accounts emphasize his roughness of tongue and manner, but they likewise credit him with ability and character. Certainly he made a success of his various enterprises in coal, iron, and lake shipping; certainly he showed a marked respect for education and spent money generously to school his son. The mother, Sophia Lord Russell, was a serious-minded woman of Connecticut origin, who gave much time to church and charities. Rhodes never forgot that he was of pure New England stock, a fact to be remembered in appraising his history; and when he took up literature it seemed more natural for him to go to Boston than to New York or Washington.

Yet he had imbibed at an early age the hustling, progressive, hopeful spirit of Cleveland. Mark Hanna became a brother-in-law; John Hay was a friend; he knew and admired John D. Rockefeller. He also imbibed from his early surroundings a spirit of breadth and tolerance in both politics and religion. Although his school-mates were chiefly Republicans, his father was a staunch Douglas Democrat. His mother was an Episcopalian, his father was a Deist, and his early teachers were fervent Congregationalists.

This breadth of outlook was a fortunate element in the training of the future historian; nor was his rather desultory education without great value. In grammar school and the very superior Cleveland high school he found two men as teachers whom he thought inspiring. In the University of the City of New York, where he studied in 1865–66, he met another, Benjamin N. Martin, who specially fostered his taste for history. Rhodes and the other students mastered Guizot's *General History of Civilization in Europe*, a text with a high concentration of facts and liberal ideas, so completely that they could have given a full abstract of the book. Another text they employed was George Weber's *Outlines of Universal History*. Martin not only encouraged wide reading, but insisted that his students give much time to essay writing. He introduced young Rhodes to Macaulay, whose essays delighted the lad, and to Tocqueville, whose analysis of the democratic system in America and France, and defense of it as a historical necessity, were equally pleasing.

"And," wrote Rhodes later, "I read two books that mark an epoch in my intellectual life—Buckle's *History of Civilization*, and Draper's *Intellectual History of Europe*. I shall never forget the interest and even excitement with which I turned the pages of Buckle's two volumes. Such purely intellectual emotion does not often fall to one. I was mastered. In my mind I became a disciple of Buckle. How I regretted his untimely death! But it seemed to me that earth had no purer pleasure to offer than to be able to produce such a book; and death seemed robbed of its terror after having achieved such celebrity. The story was then current that Buckle's last words were, 'Oh, my book, my book!' And under the influence excited by those two volumes no story could have been more pathetic. As I read the last words of the second volume, May 16, 1866, I resolved some day to write a history."

Not completing his course at New York University, Rhodes spent the following year at the old University of Chicago, where he read the Scottish philosophers, heard Robert Collyer preach, gained his first acquaintance with Herbert Spencer's ideas, and was given a warm love for English literature by another inspiring teacher, William Matthews. Here, too, he was captivated by the brilliant political articles and scholarly reviews of the *Nation*, recently founded by E. L. Godkin. Then came six months in Paris, where he saw the Exposition of 1867, listened to a course of lectures by Edouard Laboulaye, and wrote some letters on French affairs for the *Chicago Times*. A short period of study at the School of Mines in Berlin followed, after which he made a tour of the principal iron and steel works of western Germany and the British Isles. When he came home to Cleveland in 1868, his father lost little time in packing him off to investigate the coal and iron resources of North Carolina, Georgia, and eastern Tennessee (1869), a horseback journey which took him into the heart of Reconstruction unrest. It is clear that although Rhodes's training was unsystematic, it was remarkably varied, practical, and stimulating, and that even as a boy he learned much outside books— much of men, of affairs, of different scenes and social environments.

The fifteen years of business life which occupied him from 1870 to 1885 were clearly irksome—he spoke of letting his partners bear the main burden—and might have been intellectually deadening. But he refused to give up mental stimuli. He laid out a systematic course of reading in which the historians bulked large; he devoured novels and plays; he joined the Vampire Club, a literary group in which John Hay was the dominant figure; and he continued to train himself in writing. His ambition gradually became fixed. "One evening in 1877," he states, "while reading Hildreth's *History of the United States*, I laid down my book and said to myself, Why should I not write a History of the United States? From that time my reading, though desultory and often interrupted by the pressure and anxieties of business and the claims of society, had this end in view. I began making notes. I resolved that as soon as I gained a competence I would retire from business, and devote myself to history and literature. This resolution was sometimes shaken, and sometimes lost sight of, but it would not entirely down." When in 1885 he crossed the Rubicon, he began contributing articles and reviews to the *Magazine of Western History*. Meanwhile, he gave nearly a year and a half to rest and travel. Then, returning temporarily to Cleveland in 1887, he began reading for his first two volumes, and on November 30, 1891, submitted then to Harper & Brothers.

Rhodes was always explicit in stating his historical aims. He meant to write a great narrative in the style of Thucydides and Macaulay, trying to delve broadly into the sentiment and spirit of his period, and to present its principal figures and scenes with memorable power, but not desiring to penetrate to the economic and philosophical roots of events. The idea of a philosophy of history did not attract him; he distrusted historical laws. He copied into his first notebook a sentence from George William Curtis: "In writing history the vital necessity is the historical sense, the ability to conceive the spirit of a time and to interpret it with candor." His models in English letters were Gibbon, Macaulay, and Lecky rather than Freeman or Stubbs; in American letters he thought that Motley's *Rise of the Dutch Republic* and Fiske's *Discovery of America* were the two greatest books produced up to 1892. He defined his ambitions rather carefully in 1907, when his work was practically done, in a letter to Charles Francis Adams:

You owe me no apology whatever for saying that "no well and philosophically considered narrative of the [Civil War] struggle has yet appeared," as the remark did not disturb me in the least. For a philosophical narrative was not my aim. There is use for the philosophy of history, and it will ever have an attraction for busy and profound thinkers, and addiction to it does not necessarily preclude good narrative work. Lecky did little but philosophize in his History of Morals, but that did not prevent his writing a good narrative of the Eighteenth Century. You yourself who are given to philosophy wrote a gem of a biography in the life of your Father; and that and your essay based on the Fish papers show that you need yield to no American historian in the matter of a narrative style. But a purely narrative historian should, so far as he can, put all philosophic conditions aside. His aim is to tell a story and leave philosophy to others. One great merit of Macaulay, said Justin Winsor, is that his narrative carries his philosophy along with it. This was not strictly true of Macaulay in all cases, nor is it of my volumes, but such was my aim, and what little philosophizing I have indulged in has diminished as my volumes have grown.

He added, referring to a criticism which Adams had just written in the *Proceedings of the Massachusetts Historical Society* (October, 1905) of the fifth volume of his history:

A concrete case will show why one with my method should avoid if possible all philosophic theory. Did I believe with you (which I do not) that the "blockade was the controlling condition of Union success," that "the blockade was the determining factor, as cotton was the dynamic factor of the struggle," I would not have "woven the narrative over this philosophical skeleton." For had I done so, such is the constitution of the human mind, at any rate my own, that as I went through the mass of my material I would have seized upon all the facts that made for my theory and marshalled them in its support while those that told against me I would have unconsciously and undoubtedly quite honestly neglected. As William James said of H. Spencer, he has a great avidity for facts that support his theory and amasses them in a surprising manner; but he has no eye for the others. My aim was to get rid so far as possible of all preconceived notions and theories.

In short, Rhodes wished to analyze historical transactions and to appraise historical personages, much as he would have analyzed business affairs and appraised contemporary figures in the Cleveland business world; to present a straightforward, objective, and if possible vivid story of events, without much theorizing and no use whatever of abstract ideas; to avoid tendentious and dogmatic writing on the one side, and writing detached from reality on the other. The principal engines in his arsenal were his hard common sense, his honesty, and his immense industry. He warmly prized Theodore Roosevelt's commendation of him as "a great historian who understood practical affairs," and one "in such wise superior to Lecky." He frankly admitted that in his *History* he avoided writing on subjects for which he lacked special and expert competence, skirting the question of sea power because "I have not the basic knowledge," refusing to go into considerations of military strategy because he lacked the "competence," and abstaining from any discussion of fine points of international law.

He stood squarely on his position as a judicial-minded, hard-headed, shrewd-eyed, and perfectly candid narrator, who founded his story—and it was always first and foremost a story—upon diligent labor by himself and trained assistants in the available sources. His principal helpers were Professor E. G. Bourne of Western Reserve University, Miss Alice Wyman of the Boston Athenaeum, and Mr. D. M. Matteson of Cambridge, Massachusetts, and he knew how to employ their talents to supplement his own. They contributed to his masses of data, and sometimes to his interpretation, but never to his dominant ideas or style. Matteson has testified: "Whatever went into the melting pot, the gold that came out—and it was gold—was all Rhodes."

Rhodes is properly to be judged as a historian in the light of his avowed aims, and in the light also of the materials that he was able to use. When he began writing his *History* in 1887, the events of 1850–60 (covered in the first two volumes) were as near him as the events of the decade 1940–50 are near Americans today. Many valuable works on the period had been published, but they were naturally for the most part political and military; other works did not appear until after Rhodes had completed his writing, and books furnishing social and economic materials, in particular, were delayed. In one postscript after another, as his successive volumes came out, Rhodes lamented the fact that various writings had emerged too late for his use.

Thus at the close of his second volume he remarks that when W. P. Trent's valuable *Life of William Gilmore Simms* and Thomas Nelson Page's less useful but colorful book *The Old South* had been published, his printer's work was so far advanced that he could not levy upon them. He tried to look fairly on the Southern side, but Trent and Page presented some considerations that he had missed; and he particularly commended to his readers Trent's chapter called "Romantic Dreams and Political Nightmares," and three chapters by Page on the social and intellectual history of the South. In his volumes on the war, Rhodes was prevented from giving due space to naval operations by the fact that the *Naval Records* had not been published. Rhodes had the benefit of Nicolay and Hay's *Lincoln,* but not of any of the more thorough and candid work on Lincoln which was inaugurated by Miss Tarbell's two volumes in 1900. He had the benefit of Jefferson Davis's *Rise and Fall of the Confederate Government,* but not of any biography of Davis worth mentioning. Gideon Welles's *Diary* was not published until long years after Rhodes had passed Welles's period of service (1911). An immense mass of memoirs, including such indispensable items as the autobiography of Carl Schurz, and the reminiscences of Jacob D. Cox, James Harrison Wilson, and Henry Villard, was poured out after Rhodes had finished. Indeed, that stream has continued into our own day. What good use Rhodes might have made of the classic *Diary* of George Templeton Strong, for example!

When he came to the Reconstruction years, Rhodes labored under an even greater disability in the thinness of his sources. The fifth and sixth volumes of his history appeared in 1906. Everyone could see that they emphasized political history, omitting many topics of cardinal importance on the economic and social side; and some of their deficiencies in this respect were rather glaringly revealed when in 1906–7 W. L. Fleming published his *Documentary History of Reconstruction*, a two-volume work which comprehended the cultural, social, and economic history of the South from 1865–77 as well as the political. Had Rhodes written after and not before the publication of Fleming's source work, had he possessed as well the admirable monographs on ·Reconstruction which William A. Dunning's students were soon pouring out at Columbia University, his fifth and sixth volumes might have been very different in content. Critics must distinguish between deficiencies which were his fault, and those which a general historian, unable to wait on the slow wheels of time or to halt long enough for monographic delving, could not avoid.

The reception given the first two volumes, by both scholars and the general public, was highly gratifying. Such a history of the events leading to the Civil War had been eagerly desired, though few had expected it to appear in so interesting and authoritative a form, and none could have predicted that it would come from a retired businessman. "Nearly everybody had thought some writer like Dunning of Columbia or Albert Bushnell Hart of Harvard would step forward," Frederic Bancroft later recalled. "Great was the astonishment to learn that a former coal and iron merchant held the pen." Great, too, was the pleasure of most readers in finding that the ideas imbuing the work were those of laissez-faire liberals of the free-soil school.

"There was one universal acclaim of praise," wrote John T. Morse, Jr., of Boston—a statement true of the North though not of the South. Many people liked the work for its eulogistic treatment of Clay, Webster, Lincoln, and (with sharp reservations) Seward; nearly everybody admired the gusto and verve with which Rhodes recounted the battle over the Compromise of 1850, the Northern revolt against the Fugitive Slave Act, Harriet Beecher Stowe's production of *Uncle Tom's Cabin*, the woes of Bleeding Kansas, John Brown's melodramatic career, Preston

Brook's assault upon Sumner in the Senate chamber, and the other lurid events down to Fort Sumter. Rhodes's assertion that slavery was the root cause of the Civil War commanded general assent. His portraiture of the leading statesmen was always graphic; and the episodes which he brought to life were the more effective because they had been dimly remembered by millions from childhood days.

When the eminent W. E. H. Lecky, author of the penetrating history of morals and the monumental work upon eighteenth-century Britain just mentioned, praised Rhodes for his manifest desire "to do justice to all sides and to tell the exact truth," and when the British legal authority, A. V. Dicey, pronounced his work "the most just and the most comprehensive account" of the period, he could hope that they anticipated the judgment of posterity. Rhodes was especially pleased by a magisterial review in the *Nation*, which declared that the chapter on slavery was a model summary of a difficult subject; that the charitable estimate of Stephen A. Douglas was shrewd and fair; and that the volumes promised "a noteworthy and valuable addition to our solid literature." The one critique that gave Rhodes deep pain was an unsigned review in the *Atlantic Monthly*. He readily discerned that it was written by a Southerner, though he could not know that the man was Woodrow Wilson. Sales of the two volumes were so substantial, despite the depression following the Panic of 1893, that a new edition appeared in the autumn of 1895.

From this triumph Rhodes pressed on to the completion of his Civil War narrative, permitting no interruptions save those imposed by some uncertainties of health and a normally busy social life. His third volume appeared in 1895, his fourth in 1899, and his fifth in 1904. That they were the best volumes of his whole work, a distinct advance upon the first two, no discriminating reader could doubt. Carrying Rhodes into the full current of the Civil War and a little beyond its triumphant end, they exalted his spirit as the Peloponnesian War had exalted the heart of Thucydides. He received the praise and encouragement of national leaders like Theodore Roosevelt, or fellow historians like James Schouler and John Fiske, of literary critics like Barrett Wendell—who ranked him with Thucydides and Tacitus—and of such scholars in other fields as William James, who termed his books "admirable." Once more the usually reserved *Nation* praised him warmly. He possessed in remarkable degree, it said, the principal requirements of a modern historian: unflagging industry, accurate judgment, clarity, impartiality, and balance. H. Morse Stephens, who treated the French Revolution in a rigidly scientific spirit, asserted that among living and active writers of American history the first place undoubtedly belonged to Rhodes. As he pressed on, though with flagging energy and some signs of failing power, to complete his narrative down to the year 1877 in seven volumes, sales of his work showed a sustained appeal to both students and general readers.

By the year 1890 he had begun to spend much time in the East. He took a place for several summers at Hyannis Port on Cape Cod; he made friends throughout New England. In the autumn of 1891 he leased a house in Cambridge from Professor Adams Sherman Hill of Harvard, who had been an efficient war correspondent for Greeley's *Tribune*—and who let Rhodes use his manuscript correspondence with Sydney Howard Gay, the managing editor of the paper. Two Harvard historians, Albert Bushnell Hart and the librarian Justin Winsor, became fast friends. A little later, in 1895, Rhodes moved to Boston, enlarging his circle. Election to the Massachusetts Historical Society in 1893, the oldest and most famous of such American organizations, pleased him so much that the title pages of his sixth and seventh volumes, published in 1906, recorded his membership along with his honorary degrees. Charles Francis Adams, Henry Cabot Lodge, Robert Grant, and William Roscoe Thayer were enrolled among his intimates. He joined the Tavern Club, and it was at a club dinner that he made a speech of welcome to George Macaulay Trevelyan, an English historian whom he came to know as well as he knew James Bryce and John Morley.

Yet most involvements outside his history Rhodes avoided to the last. "I cannot make a speech," he wrote Frederic Bancroft. "I would be a poor presiding officer. 'Shoemaker, stick to your last.' My tastes are essentially those of the student. The best work I do is that in the library." The First World War put an end to his foreign travels, except for a brief sojourn in Nice-Cimiez in 1922. He took a keen interest in current affairs but kept quite aloof from politics—which was fortunate, for his letters reveal an excessively Republican and conservative set of judgments. He died in Brookline, Massachusetts, in 1927.

By two papers on the writing of history and the profession of historian in his *Historical Essays*, Rhodes made it clear that the models whom he most admired were Herodotus, Thucydides, and Tacitus among the ancients; Ernst Curtius, S. R. Gardiner, and J. R. Green along with Carlyle, Gibbon, and Macaulay among the moderns. His taste, in short, was for the great story-tellers, usually of rich literary gifts, who might be candidly partisan but must never be as inaccurate as Froude or as tedious as George Bancroft. He was frankly old-fashioned and spoke slightingly of the new ideas of innovators like Bernard Shaw. It seems probable that he was more influenced in his historical writing by Macaulay than anybody else. At any rate, he followed Macaulay's doctrine that history ought to emphasize the concrete, the individual, and the dramatic. Let history, wrote Macaulay, be like a novel, with the difference that it is true while novels are fictitious; let it be capable of "interesting the affections, and presenting pictures to the imagination"; let it "invest with the reality of flesh and blood beings whom we are too much inclined to consider as personified qualities." Macaulay's plan caused him to work on a minute scale, painting characters life-size, relating events with fullness, sustaining the interest with biographical anecdotes, and keeping up, as Cotter Morison says, "a vigilant liveliness of narrative which simulated the novel of adventure." Setting out to cover a century and a half, Macaulay actually traversed in five large volumes a period of about fifteen years. In the same way, Rhodes treated events copiously, gave close attention to vivid character portraiture, introduced a constant succession of lively incidents, and kept an element of suspense alive in his books. The story never halts; it sweeps steadily onward, without pause for philosophizing, social and institutional analysis, or scientific inquiry. And in his five fundamental volumes Rhodes, like Macaulay, covers just fifteen years—1850–65.

As narrative history these volumes remain a remarkable achievement. The first two, dealing with the eventful decade 1850–60, are the most rapid in pace. Their subject matter is almost exclusively political. In a thousand pages Rhodes pauses only once for a chapter static in quality and concerned with social and economic forces rather than with public affairs, his seventy-five pages on slavery; and even this contains narrative elements, for it includes an account of the publication of *Uncle Tom's Cabin*, its reception and influence, and the Southern rejoinders to it. The remainder of the first two volumes is pure story, flowing from year to year, event to event, with clear, direct, and often impetuous force. It is like a broad historical romance, with the characters and events all real. Rhodes pauses but briefly to set his scenes, and gives us none of that elaborate tableau painting which some devotees of narrative history, like Claude G. Bowers, offer. He uses newspapers with unprecedented thoroughness. These, with letters, memoirs, and public documents, are carefully studied to present the most striking characters—from Calhoun, Clay, Webster, and Zachary Taylor down to Buchanan, Sumner, Seward, Douglas, and finally Lincoln—in graphic strokes and with generally astute summarizations. The brief portraits of minor personages like Lewis Cass, Edward Everett, Pierre Soulé, W. L. Marcy, and Robert J. Walker are also done with finish and vigor.

But it is always the story of events which is most vital to Rhodes—the external and obvious story given with too little attention to the forces behind it, but told with a dash, a sweep, and a sense of its heroic quality which makes it absorbing. Errors of proportion, such as the devotion of nearly fifteen pages to an account of the yellow fever epidemic of 1853 in New Orleans, are few. Courage is shown in the forcible assertion of new and unpopular interpretations. Most of Rhodes's early readers were shocked, for example, by his defense of Webster's Seventh of March Speech in advocacy of the Compromise of 1850; by his treatment of Douglas's Kansas-Nebraska Bill of 1854 as an honest attempt to heal the sectional breach by a statesmanlike measure, not as a dishonest piece of demagogy; and by his frank exposition of Seward's numerous errors of judgment and faults of temper. More recent research has shown that he was correct in taking these positions. When Rhodes comes to a dramatic story like the campaign of 1856, warfare in Kansas, or John Brown's raid in Virginia, he relates it with a full but not hectic or exaggerated sense of its exciting quality. Each chapter ends on a note of suspense, and the reader is carried irresistibly forward until the two volumes 1850–60 close with events that show them to be but the prologue to a still greater drama. Lincoln has been elected; the South is in revolt; a fever of nationalism is seizing the free North and Northwest. The footlights are about to flash up more intensely, the orchestra to burst into "The Star Spangled Banner," and the curtain to rise on the First Inaugural, Bull Run, and Ball's Bluff.

The great conflict is equally well covered. No mere scientist can ever be a worthy historian of the bloody battles, the passionate political contests, and the anxious diplomacy of the Civil War period. The writer who essays a satisfactory treatment of its intricacies must have some of the qualities which Thomas Hardy brought to *The Dynasts*, Stephen Vincent Benét to *John Brown's Body*, and—most of all—those James Ford Rhodes brought to the first five volumes of his *History*. We may reproach Rhodes with lack of philosophic depth and scientific thoroughness; but we must concede to him a sweep, a vigor, and a sense of the soul-stirring quality of a great critical period such as few historians provide us. It is true that he was highly partisan. He wrote as a son of New England transplanted to northern Ohio, and as a child of the great Free Soil movement. His bias led him at times, as in his excessively severe treatment of the fire-eating advocates of slavery expansion, his contempt for Buchanan, and his condemnation of efforts at new compromises, into a somewhat misleading interpretation of men and events. Later he was too ready to make Lincoln the masterful hero of the war, and to overlook his deficiencies as organizer and administrator. To wartime administration, indeed, Rhodes gives singularly little attention, and he almost wholly ignores the greatest Northern organizer of the conflict, the redoubtable quartermaster general, Montgomery C. Meigs.

But let us recognize also that a certain amount of partisanship is indispensable to high narrative interest. The romancer creates a world in which hero is pitted against villain; the romantic narrative historian finds it necessary to identify himself with forces of right arrayed valiantly against men and institutions representing wrong. Rhodes saw in the free institutions, the democratic temper, and the reforming ideals of the North a set of protagonists fighting against evils that threatened the very life of the nation. In the broad view he was right. In some details he pushed this attitude too far, but a more balanced and impartial position would have robbed his history of half its narrative power—and might not have brought him much nearer the truth.

The historian tried to look at both sides of nearly every moot issue, and to show faults and virtues alike in the men he treated. The looming hero of his third and fourth volumes is Lincoln. Rhodes stands by him and his policies as against the Copperheads on one side and the Jacobins on the other; he demonstrates just how the election of 1864 vindicated the President's course. Nevertheless, he severely criticizes Lincoln for assenting to gross violations of civil liberties by permitting arbitrary arrests, the suppression of newspapers, and other extra-judicial procedures that Rhodes terms "inexpedient, unnecessary, and wrong." By well-marshaled evidence, again, Rhodes proves McClellan unfit for the chief command against Lee. McClellan's dilatory moves, exaggeration of the strength of the enemy, and timid underestimate of his own power brought about the failure of his campaign on the Peninsula. Yet the author pronounces Lincoln's removal of McClellan with no better replacement than Burnside a mistake. Rhodes never lacked opinions, and was seldom swayed by partialities.

Doubtlessly because economic topics did not lend themselves to the dramatic treatment that could be given political combats and martial campaigns, Rhodes instinctively left them out of his volumes. Because the discussion of organization and administration possesses no narrative color, he omitted it from his work. When Reconstruction began, the central concern of the United States swung to industry, transportation, and mercantile activity, so that Rhodes's indifference to these subjects fatally crippled his sixth and seventh volumes. He was hampered, too, by a lack of monographic work in these fields that only time could remedy.

Obviously, Rhodes had more taste, insight, and literary dexterity than George Bancroft; but, like Bancroft, he conceived of his narrative as a highly colored and frequently dramatic work that approached the character of a prose epic. Bancroft had written of colonial history as tending toward one titanic event, the establishment of American freedom, political, economic, and social, in the Revolution. That concept gave his work force, dignity, and climactic power, but it resulted in a deplorable warping of the materials. Although it had some literary justification, from the scientific point of view it was a highly inadequate approach. Rhodes similarly resolved to make his history a sweeping but well-unified narrative of the sectional conflict over slavery, in which the details of events and phases should be subordinated to the grand impact of the central theme. As the Revolution had seemed to Americans born in the next generation after Yorktown the most titanic and thrilling of struggles, so the Civil War seemed to Rhodes an epic whole, a tremendous tidal thrust in the development of democracy, which should be treated as fervently as Macaulay had treated the thrust of Whiggish forces and aims culminating in the Revolution of 1688, and with as much unity as Carlyle had achieved in his massive, million-word work on Frederick the Great.

Memories of boyhood days in Cleveland, when he had hung excitedly upon the news of battles and political clashes, intensified in Rhodes's mind the epic or histrionic view of American history from 1850 to 1877. "This period," he wrote in the first page of his *History*, "the brief space of a generation, was an era big with fate for our country, and for the American must remain fraught with the same interest that the war of the Peloponnesus had for the ancient Greek, or the struggle between the Cavalier and the Puritan had for their descendants." To give unity to his narrative, Rhodes naturally had to suppress many facts which were irrelevant to the central theme; to make this theme appear really epic, he had to simplify many other facts and movements. His first six volumes are essentially a history of the rise, development, and termination of the sectional conflict, and are very far from a history of the whole American people, in all their interests and activities, in that generation. This meant of course a distinct distortion of fact. From many points of view, the Civil War was merely an interrupting episode, not an overriding central movement, in the nineteenth-century history of America. From other points of view—the industrial, for example—it was an accelerating impulse, but nothing more.

In sum, we may say that Rhodes was at fault in this limited concept of his work, and was also at fault in the bias or preconception with which he approached his subject. To be sure, he labored to tell the impartial truth, and always disclaimed any prejudices. At some points he believed that he had leaned backward to do justice to the South. Yet he could not escape the ingrained ideas, the fundamental postulates, natural to a Yankee son of the Western Reserve growing into adolescence in the years of battle, victory, and reconstruction. Vigorously avowing his moral abhorrence of slavery, he made it plain that he would not bring an understanding temper to the Yancey-Toombs-Davis contention that Southerners had a right to carry their peculiar type of property into the Western territories that belonged to the whole nation. Though nowhere did he show the intolerant bias of his contemporary Hermann von Holst, he was basically subjective rather than objective.

This attitude comes out clearly in such matters as his over-emphatic condemnation of the Fugitive Slave Act ("the mere statement of the provisions of this law is its condemnation"), in his denunciation of the Southern oligarchy, in his acrid comparison of Southern cultural deficiencies with the cultural achievements of New England, and above all in his acceptance of the contemporaneous Free Soil concept of the wickedness of the Kansas-Nebraska Act. Few contrasts in our historical literature are more glaring than that between the fifth chapter in his history, dealing with the beginnings of the Pierce Administration and the struggle over the Kansas-Nebraska bill, and the third chapter of Volume II of Albert J. Beveridge's *Abraham Lincoln*, treating the same topics. The man who reads both at the present day will rub his eyes, wondering if the two writers can really be examining the same men and events; and if he studies the evidence, he will soon conclude that Rhodes's preconceptions led him astray. Bias was the product of Rhodes's principal fault, his lack of depth in studying the American nation.

The defects of such a work inevitably grow. Rhodes's first five volumes, coming down to Reconstruction, are by far his best; but even they become, year by year, more antiquated in point of view and faulty in factual detail. His style, sometimes pedestrian and seldom illumined by felicity of phrase or brilliance of imagery, lacks the preservative quality found in the style of Prescott, Parkman, and Henry Adams. For his own generation he did an extremely useful work. His research was wide and conscientious. To newspapers especially he continued to the end to give remarkable study. Not content with examining merely the most important journals, he delved into files East and West, North and

410

South, using organs of all parties and the independent presses to obtain a grasp of public opinion. At the same time, he knew literature unusually well. He had read much in the poetry, fiction, essays, and travel writings of the period, though with excessive emphasis on New England books, and had so arranged their salient contents in his mind and notebooks (for he used old-fashioned notebooks and not loose classifiable sheets) that their material was readily available to his pen. This material brightened many a page. But readers of a later day find his frame too narrow and his studies deficient in depth.

His sustained examination of slavery early in his *History* is an instance of this fact. Treating the system itself, its effects on master and family, upon the slave, and upon the community, summarizing the views of those who arraigned it and the apologies of its defenders, he gave the Americans of 1893 a far more judicial study of the institution than they could find elsewhere. Even after the books of Ulrich B. Phillips, Frank L. Owsley, and others, down to Kenneth M. Stampp, this treatise retains points of interest and significance. Yet on such complex subjects as the nature of slavery among yeoman farmers and the psychology of the slave, he is quite inadequate. The third volume has an entertaining discussion of social change in the 1850's, correct in pointing to immense activity in all kinds of reform and a generally high standard of ethics, and full of interesting facts. Yet how loose and superficial it seems after the recent dissections of rural and urban sociology by specialized students! In his fourth volume the treatment of British sentiment and diplomacy during the Civil War constitutes another long essay, which was remarkably fresh and illuminating when Rhodes wrote it. It was he, for example, who first proved that Great Britain did not yield to threats in preventing the armored rams from leaving Liverpool in 1863; the Ministry had acted to stop them before Charles Francis Adams's famous warning, "My lord, this is war." Yet the volumes of Ephraim D. Adams on *Great Britain and the American Civil War* inaugurated

411

a series of studies which have given us a surer understanding of the diplomacy of the war period. We now know just where Austria, Spain, and Russia, as well as Britain and France, stood.

It should be pointed out that Rhodes's grasp of character and motive was usually excellent, and that his portraits of many of the personages of the time remain valid. Indeed, his handling of the personal element in history is far surer and more vigorous than that of von Holst, Schouler, or McMaster. His picture of Douglas, which was more sympathetic and admiring than that previously drawn by Northern writers, is striking; he shows that Douglas grew with the demands of his times, and that the Little Giant of the Lecompton battle was a much stronger man in every way than the Little Giant of 1854. His presentation of Lincoln, illustrating his sagacity, patience, magnanimity, foresight, and spiritual power with apt incident and quotation, is discerning and convincing. His analysis of Southern fire-eaters has never been surpassed. He was perhaps too severe upon Seward, upon the "mingled folly and rashness" of the secessionist leaders, and upon the Congressional Radicals; in dealing with Andrew Johnson he erred painfully. Yet, on the whole, he has given us the best portrait gallery, the closest approach to the studies of leadership in crisis written by Lord Clarendon and George Otto Trevelyan, to be found in any American work.

In short, Rhodes was a great historian, limited to some extent by stylistic shortcomings, and to a greater degree by inherited restrictions of understanding and outlook, but most of all by the fact that he wrote before an array of new weapons had been supplied by the nascent social studies and the rising generation of monograph writers. With the opportunities and means available to him, he executed a magnificent piece of narrative history that offers a larger combination of enjoyment and profit than any but a few historians provide. All citizens interested in our national past should read it.

Index

INDEX

Popular historians, 6, 7–8, 22–32, 33–35
Prescott, William Hickling, 14, 71, 324
Press. *See* Journalism
Press in Authoritarian Countries, The, 83
Psychology, 145
Pulitzer, Joseph, 28, 39, 91

Quick, Herbert, 242–43

Railroad Builders, The (Moody), 113
Raymond, Henry J., 38
Reading, 43–51
Rebating, 76
Reference books, 294–301
Rhodes, Dan, 394
Rhodes, James Ford, 6, 182, 185–86, 264, 265–67, 393–412
Rise of the Dutch Republic, The (Motley), 335–37
Rivers of America Series (Skinner), 126
Roberts, Issachar J., 297
Robinson, James Harvey, 170, 176
Rockefeller, John D., 75–76, 212–13, 228, 233
Roosevelt, Franklin D., 98
Roosevelt, Theodore, 31, 45, 212, 229, 284
Rose, J. Holland, 197
Russell, Sophia Lord, 394
Russell, W. H., 230

Sammons, Wheeler, 301
Sandburg, Carl, 174
Sansom, George, 50, 187
Saveth, Edward, 194
Scholars, 36–42
Schouler, James, 17
Science history, 171–72
Scientific historian, 104

Scientists, 15–16
and historians, 133–50
Schlesinger, Arthur M., 120, 194
Schlesinger, Arthur M., Jr., 191
Scott, Walter, 338
Seitz, Don C., 91, 115
Shaw, Archer, 92
Sherman, Stuart P., 40–41
Sherrington, Charles, 135, 136
Skinner, Constance Lindsay, 126
Slavery, 61–62, 154–55
Smith, J. Eugene, 94
Smith, Justin H., 355
Social anthropology, 50
Social history, 103–22
Social History of the United States (McMaster), 363–64
Social science, 192–95
advances in, 151–57
Social welfare state, 212
Standard of Indiana, 79
Standard of New Jersey, 79
Standard Oil Company, 75–76
Statistics, 156
Steffens, Lincoln, 41, 211
Stevens, Thaddeus, 62
Still, Bayrd, 127
Strachey, Lytton, 195, 233
Strunsky, Simeon, 39
Study of History (Toynbee), 137–38
Style, 200–201
Sullivan, Mark, 109–10, 264
Sumner, Charles, 231–33

Tarbell, Ida M., 112
35,000 Days in Texas (Acheson), 92
Thomas, Keith, 192, 193
Thomas, Norman, 291
Thucydides, 162, 163
Times (London), 87–88, 96–97
Toynbee, Arnold, 132, 138, 170
Trent, W. P., 110

419